MW01002199

TULLAHOMA

The Forgotten Campaign that Changed
the Course of the Civil War,
June 23 – July 4, 1863

David A. Powell

and

Eric J. Wittenberg

SB

Savas Beatie

California

Library of Congress Cataloging-in-Publication Data
Names: Powell, David A. (David Alan), 1961- author. | Wittenberg, Eric J., 1961- author.
Title: Tullahoma: The Forgotten Campaign that Changed the Civil War, June 23 - July 4, 1863
    by David A. Powell, Eric J. Wittenberg.
Other titles: Forgotten Campaign that Changed the Civil War, June 23 - July 4, 1863
Description: California: Savas Beatie, [2020] | Includes bibliographical references and index. |
Summary: "Tullahoma: The Forgotten Campaign that Changed the Civil War, June 23 - July 4, 1863
is the first detailed tactical examination of Union General William S. Rosecrans's masterful effort to
outflank the Confederate Army out of their strong defensive positions in Middle Tennessee. Largely
eclipsed by the bloodier and more dramatic Vicksburg and Gettysburg campaigns, Tullahoma has
long been overlooked, until now. This work examines the preconditions, execution, and outcome
of the campaign."— Provided by publisher.
Identifiers: LCCN 2020007895 | ISBN 9781611215045 (hardcover) | ISBN 9781611215052 (ebook)
Subjects: LCSH: Tullahoma Campaign, 1863. | Rosecrans, William S. (William Starke), 1819-1898
            —Military leadership. | Tennessee, Middle—History, Military—
            19th century. | United States—History—Civil War, 1861-1865—Campaigns. | Tactics.
Classification: LCC E475.16 .P69 2020 | DDC 973.7/34—dc23
LC record available at https://lccn.loc.gov/2020007895

First edition, first printing

SB

Savas Beatie LLC
989 Governor Drive, Suite 102
El Dorado Hills, CA 95762
Phone: 916-941-6896 / (E-mail) sales@savasbeatie.com
www.savasbeatie.com

Savas Beatie titles are available at special discounts for bulk purchases in the United States. Contact us for more details.

Proudly published, printed, and warehoused in the United States of America.

Eric Wittenberg dedication:

To my wife and best friend, Susan Skilken Wittenberg,
without whose unflinching support, none of what I do would be possible.

Dave Powell dedication:

To my wife, Anne Powell, who has been such a tremendous help in all my endeavors,
and to my father, William
D. Powell, who first instilled in me my love of history.

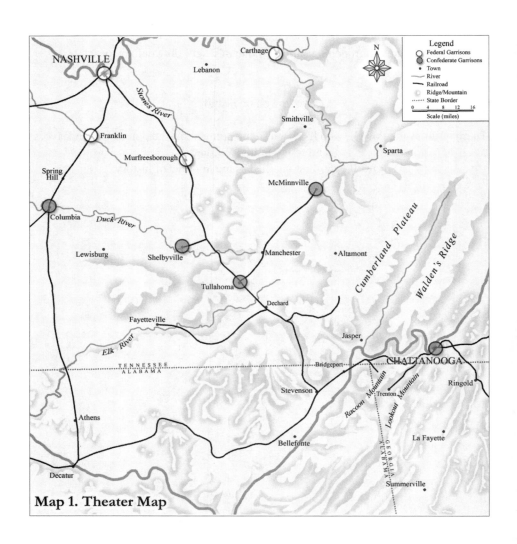

Map 1. Theater Map

Table of Contents

Table of Contents (continued)

List of Maps

Maps have been placed throughout the book for the convenience of the reader.

TULLAHOMA

Acknowledgments

Eric is grateful to Greg Biggs for his invaluable assistance with this project, including his bugging Eric for years to tackle the Battle of Shelbyville, for generously sharing his years of research, and his time in visiting sites associated with the campaign. He is also grateful to Phil Spaugy for providing his Battle Wagon for a visit to the many sites associated with the Tullahoma Campaign. Chris Kolakowski reviewed our manuscript for accuracy and readability, and we appreciate that a great deal. Eric also appreciates the fact that Dave was willing to work with him on a large project which is not within his normal area of expertise. Eric appreciates the good work done by Theodore P. Savas, managing director of Savas Beatie, LLC, our publisher, and his talented staff who do such a good job of producing and marketing handsome books. Finally, and as always, Eric is grateful to his much loved and long suffering wife, Susan Skilken Wittenberg, without whose support none of this would be possible.

Dave is, as ever, thankful for the legion of supporters who stand behind every book. Tullahoma is no exception. He would like to thank Greg Biggs, a longtime student of the Civil War in Tennessee. Greg generously shared the many resources and materials he has collected on Tullahoma, as well as helping lay out the driving tour that supplements this work. In a similar vein, Dave wishes to thank Dr. Michael Bradley, who's own work on Tullahoma (in his back yard, so to speak) was important to helping us understand the campaign. Phil Spaugy proved to be an excellent driver, and wonderful road companion. Dr. Chris Kolakowski's comments on a draft of this work provided important insights, as did Sam Davis Elliott, who also reviewed this manuscript. Sam saved us from a couple of particularly embarrassing errors concerning the Bishop Polk, for which we are indebted.

The staff at Stones River National Battlefield were also helpful, especially Ranger Jim Lewis. Tullahoma lacks any of the significant protections other fields enjoy, meaning that Stones River, in Murfreesboro, has become the Tullahoma Campaign's park by default. The park has collected significant holdings of material related to the campaign, to which Jim provided easy access as needed.

Thank you, Eric, for proposing the project and joining forces. This long-awaited partnership has been extremely rewarding.

My friend David A. Friedrichs produced the wonderful maps, as he has for several of my books. He knows how much I appreciate his help.

Finally, thanks must go to Theodore P. Savas for extending the opportunity to write this book, all the staff at Savas Beatie for all they do, and Joel Manuel for giving it a final proof. Tullahoma has long needed a full- length study, and Dave is eternally grateful Savas Beatie continues to welcome and support his work.

Sandwiched into Obscurity

The first week of July 1863 saw a cascade of triumphant news delivered to a war-weary Northern populace. Thus far the American Civil War, now more than two years old, had seemed to produce nothing but stalemate and endless casualty lists. On July 4, however, dramatic headlines splashed across the nation trumpeted the Union success at Gettysburg, Pennsylvania, where Maj. Gen. George Gordon Meade's Army of the Potomac had beaten and turned back Confederate Gen. Robert E. Lee's hitherto unstoppable Army of Northern Virginia. More details flooded forth during the next few days making it clear that the defeated Rebels were indeed retreating.

By July 6, while the full details of the fight at Gettysburg were still consuming column-inches of newsprint, yet another major triumph crowded onto the pages: Union Maj. Gen. Ulysses S. Grant had accepted the surrender of an entire Confederate army at Vicksburg, Mississippi, just two days previously in a fitting celebration of Independence Day.

The events struck many Northerners as portents that the war was—at long last—turning a corner. The national appetite for news of these victories seemed insatiable, and details of both campaigns filled papers for weeks to come. Thousands of the nation's smaller journals, unable to afford their own paid correspondents, reprinted stories ripped straight from the editions of their larger brethren, or filled in the gaps with letters from soldiers in the ranks of the victorious armies. Gettysburg and Vicksburg became true media events in an era long before broadcast journalism and the 24-hour news cycle.

But the war was not confined to Pennsylvania and Mississippi. At Helena, Arkansas, nearly 8,000 Confederates attacked a Union garrison of 4,000 in a failed effort to help relieve the besieged Confederates at Vicksburg. Unaware that Vicksburg already had fallen, the commander of the Confederate Trans-Mississippi Department, Lt. Gen. Theophilus F. Holmes, attempted to overwhelm the defenders with repeated assaults. Helena held, Holmes retreated, and yet another Union victory joined the list of triumphs on that "most glorious Fourth."

Nor was that all. At eight in the morning on July 4, Union Secretary of War Edwin M. Stanton sent a telegram announcing the details of General Meade's combat at Gettysburg to the headquarters of Maj. Gen. William S. Rosecrans, the commander of the Army of the Cumberland in Tennessee. "A three days' battle has been going on near Gettysburg," wired Stanton, ". . . thus far successful on our side, with promise of a brilliant victory over Lee." That afternoon Rosecrans proudly replied with good news of his own. After a nine-day campaign begun on June 24, Rosecrans reported that his army had driven its opponent—Confederate Gen. Braxton Bragg's Army of Tennessee—entirely out of Middle Tennessee, with the Rebels retreating "toward Bridgeport [Alabama] and Chattanooga."[1]

This news was significant. Nashville and the western third of the state had been in Union hands since the spring of 1862, but progress in restoring the rest of Tennessee to the Union had stalled. In the summer and fall of 1862, the Rebels launched an offensive of their own into Kentucky that, while not ultimately successful in transferring the seat of war to the Ohio River, managed to retain Middle and East Tennessee for the rebellion. Middle Tennessee, with its fertile farmlands, was rich in livestock and foodstuffs, making it an especially important part of the Confederate war effort. Moreover, tens of thousands of Tennesseans served in the Rebel ranks, and the loss of their homes to Federal occupation had damaged their morale. Many deserted Bragg's army, draining a command already weakened by the need to send to troops west to Mississippi in an unsuccessful bid to help save Vicksburg.

To Rosecrans, Bragg's retreat seemed a victory fully equal to Meade's repulse of Lee's invasion and nearly on a par with Grant's triumph at Vicksburg, his success made all the more impressive because of the difficult circumstances surrounding his campaign. Logistics were much more complicated in Middle Tennessee than they were in Pennsylvania or even in Mississippi, thanks to long distances, inadequate railroads, and the lack of navigable rivers. Even worse, the unceasing rains that had begun on June 24—coinciding with the Union forward movement—

---

1 U. S. War Department, *The War of the Rebellion: A Compilation of the Official Records of the Union and Confederate Armies* (hereafter *OR*), 128 vols. (Washington, DC: 1880-1901), ser. 1, vol. 23, pt. 1, 403; pt. 2, 512.

churned the dirt roads into bottomless quagmires. Despite these complications, Bragg's army was outmaneuvered and forced into precipitate flight. "The loss of the enemy," reported Rosecrans, "may be safely put at 1,000 killed and wounded, 1,000 prisoners, 7 pieces of artillery, 500 or 600 tents." And the cost? "Our losses in killed and wounded will not exceed 500."[2]

Stanton did not share Rosecrans's enthusiasm. Bragg's losses paled in comparison to those suffered by Lee, which by all reports were at least 20,000 and might run as high as 30,000, and to Grant's haul of prisoners (when that information would arrive), which tallied 29,000. President Abraham Lincoln agreed with Stanton. To him, Rosecrans's operation was more of an opportunity lost than a victory gained. In Washington, D.C., the salient fact of the campaign seemed to be that Bragg's army escaped without a general engagement, and not that Middle Tennessee was restored to Union control nearly without cost. Capturing territory was all well and good, but the rebellion would continue only so long as Rebel armies remained in the field.

As a result, the Middle Tennessee Campaign, or Tullahoma Campaign (as it came to be called, named for the capture of Bragg's main defensive position and supply depot in Tullahoma), quickly became a mere addendum to other Union successes that summer rather than being celebrated in its own right. That lack of recognition grated on Rosecrans, who felt that the Federal government downplayed his victory because it did not culminate in the bloody climax of a major battle. Relations between Rosecrans and his superiors in Washington, which had been declining throughout the spring of 1863, deteriorated further. History has followed suit by studying the campaign only in passing, or as a preliminary to the much more dramatic campaign for Chattanooga that unfolded that fall.

2 Ibid., pt. 1, 403.

GENERAL ROSECRANS

GENERAL BRAGG

Chapter One

Rebirth of an Army, Winter 1863

The relationship between William S. Rosecrans and his superiors in Washington, DC, was not always so strained. Six months earlier, in January 1863, that relationship was much more convivial. At the turn of the year, spanning from December 31, 1862, to January 2, 1863, Rosecrans's Federal army met Braxton Bragg's Rebels in deadly combat just outside Murfreesboro, Tennessee—a battle the Federals called Stones River. The two armies, equally matched, fought to a bloodily inconclusive result, but at the end of the slugging, Bragg's Army of Tennessee retreated, leaving Rosecrans and the Army of the Cumberland in possession of the field.[1]

Rosecrans claimed a victory, which was welcome news indeed to the Federal government in Washington, still dealing with the aftermath of a sanguinary and humiliating defeat at Fredericksburg, Virginia, on December 13. The praise directed at Rosecrans was effusive. A fulsome Edwin M. Stanton wired Rosecrans on January 7, five days after Bragg's retreat: "There is nothing you can ask within my power to grant to yourself or your heroic command that will not be cheerfully given."[2]

Stanton's telegram was all the more surprising given the fact that a year earlier, Stanton and Rosecrans found themselves very much at loggerheads. In 1861,

---

1 A deeper discussion of the Battle of Stones River strays far from the scope of this book. For a detailed study, see Larry J. Daniel, *Battle of Stones River: The Forgotten Conflict between the Confederate Army of Tennessee and the Union Army of the Cumberland* (Baton Rouge, LA: 2012).

2 OR 20, pt. 2, 306.

Rosecrans served in western Virginia, fighting under Major General George B. McClellan. When McClellan rose to command of all Union forces after the disaster at Bull Run, Rosecrans assumed command of what was initially called the Department of the Ohio but was soon renamed as the Department of West Virginia on July 23, 1861. Rosecrans held that command for roughly eight months until he was transferred on March 11, 1862. During his tenure, Rosecrans continually peppered the war department with demands and suggestions. He forcefully pushed Stanton, newly appointed to the job of secretary of war on January 20, 1862, on the idea of uniting various Union commands in western Virginia and the lower Shenandoah Valley to overwhelm and outflank the main Rebel army then at Manassas, Virginia. Rosecrans's suggestions had merit and eventually bore fruit, just not with Rosecrans in command. It didn't help that President Lincoln's and Stanton's efforts to coordinate those same commands from afar resulted in a succession of Union disasters, boosting the reputation of Confederate Major General Thomas J. "Stonewall" Jackson. In the meantime, a combination of politics and personal friction saw Rosecrans replaced, left for a time without orders or new duties, and eventually shipped west to serve under Maj. Gen. Henry W. Halleck. By April one of Rosecrans's confidantes informed him that "Stanton has taken a strong dislike to you." That ill-feeling became all too apparent on May 14, 1862, when, during a stormy personal encounter with Rosecrans at the war department, Stanton reputedly bellowed, "You mind your business and I'll mind mine!"[3]

Despite that history, Stanton's recent assurance was not mere rhetoric. Indeed, the secretary was already responding to a specific set of requests made by Rosecrans, who desired both to promote worthy officers and to undertake a sweeping reorganization of the army he now led. Rosecrans assumed command of what was then called the Army of the Ohio on Monday, October 27, 1862, a mere nine weeks before the fight at Stones River. He replaced Major General Don Carlos Buell, who fought the Battle of Perryville to an unsatisfying result a scant three weeks before and who had since lost the confidence of the president. At Perryville Buell repulsed the Confederate invasion of Kentucky, when the Rebel troops escaped into Tennessee without further damage, the Lincoln Administration decided Buell had to go.

3 William M. Lamers, *The Edge of Glory: A Biography of General William S. Rosecrans, U.S.A.* (Baton Rouge, LA: 1999), 75, 79.

Maj. Gen. Don Carlos Buell,
commander of the Army of the Ohio.

Generals in Blue

William Starke Rosecrans was an innovator, a modernizer, and a bit of a perfectionist. He saw plenty of problems he wanted to address, but he had little time to implement any real changes before initiating the offensive movement that would culminate in the large-scale battle outside Murfreesboro (Dec. 31, 1862 – Jan. 2, 1863). With that important victory under his belt and something of a blank check from Secretary of War Stanton in his pocket, however, the time for real change was now at hand.

Shortly before Rosecrans's arrival in the fall of 1862, Buell's Army of the Ohio had already expanded dramatically. Thousands of men in dozens of new regiments joined its ranks, all recently enrolled via Lincoln's call for 300,000 more men that summer. In September, Buell marched to Louisville, Kentucky, having chased Braxton Bragg across the width of Tennessee and through most of the Bluegrass State. The pressure to defeat this sudden Rebel incursion almost to the banks of the Ohio River soon became overwhelming. Near-panic gripped not only the Union citizens of Kentucky, but also the citizenry and governments of nearby Indiana and Ohio. Buell barely had time to sort these new formations into his existing brigades and divisions before taking the field. Prior to this expansion, the Army of the Ohio lacked any corps structure, with Buell exercising direct command over the various divisions assigned to him. At Louisville Buell implemented an ad-hoc wing organization (Right, Left, and Center Wings, each an army corps in all but official name) with officers thrust into expanded duties all along the chain of command.

This interim situation lasted until October 24, 1862, when the Federal government created the Department of the Cumberland, carving it out of the existing Department of the Ohio. The order assigned a new commander to this department (Rosecrans) and created the XIV Corps. While the departmental reorganization pared down Rosecrans's scope of geographic responsibilities to a more manageable size, the new corps designation was merely an act of administrative paper-shuffling. Instead of creating three wings of the three corps, the order simply changed the name of the Army of the Ohio to the XIV Corps. This mattered primarily in terms of rank and authority. An officially designated corps was authorized to be led by a major general, supported by aides and staff officers. Wings, by contrast, were ad-hoc organizations with no official rank requirements. Though Rosecrans had enough major generals to lead his three wings, those put in command fell short in official authority because they were not leading actual corps.[4]

Of course, Rosecrans was not sent to replace Buell merely to draw up new organizational charts. Even though Kentucky was once again free of Rebels by the time of Rosecrans's arrival, Lincoln and Stanton pushed for immediate action, aimed at defeating Bragg and restoring East Tennessee to the Union, resulting in Rosecrans's late-December advance on Murfreesboro. On the heels of that dearly won victory at Stones River, however, the new commander finally had time to turn his attention to the condition of his army, where he saw much room for improvement.

The new man brought with him an interesting and varied resume. Rosecrans graduated from the US Military Academy in 1842. His class was destined to be famous, for it produced a combined total of 29 future generals, North and South. One of his roommates while at the academy was James Longstreet, now serving in the Confederate Army of Northern Virginia. Other classmates included Union general John Pope and Confederates Daniel Harvey Hill, Alexander P. Stewart, and Earl Van Dorn. William T. Sherman was two years ahead, while Ulysses S. Grant was a class behind. Despite only a single year of formal schooling in his formative years, Rosecrans's intelligence bordered on brilliance; his class rank upon graduation was 5th out of 51.[5]

Rosecrans was born in Sunbury, Ohio, on September 6, 1819. His father, Crandall Rosecrans, was a recently returned veteran of the War of 1812 who served as an aide to General William Henry Harrison. Despite the Teutonic-sounding surname, the Rosecrans clan was of Dutch rather than German extraction, having come to the New World in the 17th century, settling in New Amsterdam, now the southern tip of Manhattan. The original Rosencranz was eventually Americanized. Upon return from the army, Crandall continued his connection with the military,

4 OR 16, pt. 2, 641-2.

5 Lamers, *The Edge of Glory*, 11, 14-15. Rosecrans attended what amounted to two semesters of formal schooling, one when he was 8 and another when he was 10.

Maj. Gen. William S. Rosecrans, commander of the Army of the Cumberland.

commanding the local militia company, which in turn exposed young William to martial affairs at an early age. However, William applied to the academy as much out of necessity as out of any desire for soldiering. The academy offered him a free college education, since his father was unlikely to pay for such an extravagance. His father had allowed him to attend what amounted to only two semesters of formal schooling while growing up; instead William worked the family farm and helped run his father's small country store.

Upon graduation, William Rosecrans entered the army's prestigious engineer branch. His duties did not carry him far afield. He married Anna Elizabeth Hageman that August and then returned to the academy to teach engineering, a post he held until 1847, despite the outbreak of the Mexican War. His next posting took him no nearer combat: Newport, Rhode Island, where he supervised the construction of fortifications. He performed more than ably for the next five years, winning praise for his design innovations in everything from building construction to underwater dredging. From there he was loaned out to the nation's other military service, spending a year at the Washington Navy Yard, doing brilliant work in building construction.[6]

Despite these plaudits, missing the war with Mexico also meant missing out on wider recognition and, most importantly for a soldier in the old army, greatly reduced his chances for advancement. Other soldiers came home with two or three brevet promotions, which, though such honors came with no extra pay or actual rank, registered favorably with promotion boards. Rosecrans had none. Frustrated with likely stagnation in rank and the slow pace of army life, Rosecrans resigned his commission in 1853 to pursue engineering and business interests. He cofounded a kerosene refinery in Cincinnati. In 1857, he suffered an industrial accident while experimenting to develop a better product, getting badly burned when a lamp exploded. He spent eighteen months recuperating, and the resultant "distorting, livid scars gave a permanent 'smirk' to his face." He resumed a full work schedule in 1859, but by then the secession crisis loomed. By 1861, he was back in uniform, initially accepting a commission from the state of Ohio, and then from the Federal government.[7]

He was also, to the dismay of some, a zealous convert to Catholicism, an anomaly in largely Protestant 19th-century America. Raised as a Methodist and exposed to Episcopalianism at the military academy (the institution's quasi-official

6 Ibid., 16.

7 Ibid., 18.

religion), Rosecrans underwent a period of deep study and thought and embraced the religion of Rome. Moreover, he waxed so enthusiastically about his newfound faith that he sometimes made a pest of himself. Brigadier General Milo S. Hascall, who served with Rosecrans in the old army, regarded him as "most emphatically a crank on that subject" and predicted that the fortunes of Catholic officers would rise with Rosecrans's arrival simply because the new man was such "a narrow-minded bigot. . . ." In fact, though he was ever willing to proselytize, Rosecrans showed no overt favoritism.[8]

The new commander of the Army of the Cumberland was Buell's opposite in many ways. He was boisterous and outspoken where Buell was "cold and formally polite," for one. But the two men shared at least one characteristic: both were "unflagging in energy." Despite a lack of ante-bellum combat experience, Rosecrans had done well so far in the war. He had been instrumental in winning the early successes in western Virginia that so quickly propelled fellow West Pointer George B. McClellan to such heights in Virginia in 1862, and since then he led semi-independent commands at Iuka and Corinth, Mississippi. His successful defense of Corinth, coming just a week before the orders to replace Buell, led to his getting tasked for the new command.[9]

Another of Rosecrans's critics focused, curiously enough, on his abundant energy. Newspaper correspondent William F. G. Shanks held strong opinions about many Federal officers, and Rosecrans was no exception. Shanks, a radical Republican who embraced emancipation, was already dubious of Democrats like Rosecrans. While this prejudice doubtless colored Shanks's view of the new man, Shanks saw Rosecrans's constant activity as "nervousness." Rosecrans became so agitated at times, recalled Shanks, as to become "incoherent. . . . I have known him, when merely directing an orderly to carry a dispatch from one point to another, [to] grow so excited, vehement, and incoherent as to utterly confound the messenger." Major General David Sloane Stanley, who served with Rosecrans over the course of several campaigns and regarded him highly, admitted that the new commander became overwrought. "Rosecrans," recalled Stanley, "habitually used himself badly

8 Milo S. Hascall, "Personal Recollections and Experiences Concerning the Battle of Stone River," *Military Order of the Loyal Legion of the United States, Illinois*, 8 vols. (Wilmington, NC: 1991), 152-4.

9 Larry J. Daniel, *Days of Glory: The Army of the Cumberland, 1861-1865* (Baton Rouge, LA: 2004), 182. Again, a detailed discussion of the Battle of Corinth strays far beyond the scope of this book. For a detailed study, see Timothy B. Smith, *Corinth 1862: Siege, Battle, Occupation* (Lawrence, KS: 2012).

in time of excitement. He never slept, he overworked himself, he smoked incessantly. At Iuka, at Corinth and Stone River, the stress of excitement did not exceed a week. His strong constitution could stand that." Longer operations, however, were more debilitating.[10]

Rosecrans's arrival met with general approval in the ranks as the men compared him favorably to the stodgy Buell. Even Shanks was forced to admit "the army threw up its hat in delight." Colonel Benjamin F. Scribner, a brigade commander in Lovell H. Rousseau's XIV Corps Division, thought Rosecrans impressed the troops "by his open and genial manner, contrasting agreeably with the taciturn exclusiveness of . . . Buell." Major General Philip Sheridan, who maintained a more favorable impression of Buell than most in that army did, noted that "the army as a whole did not manifest much regret at the change of commanders, for the campaign from Louisville on looked upon generally as a lamentable failure. . . ."[11]

Corporal George Cram got his first look at the new commander when Rosecrans reviewed his regiment, the 105th Illinois, on November 6, 1862. "The Gen'l stopped in front of us," wrote Cram, "and made the following speech, 'Soldiers, fire deliberately, aim well and shoot to kill.' The soldiers all think everything of him and are all elated that Buell is superseded."[12]

Despite being at best a tactical draw, the fight at Stones River was widely hailed as a Northern victory, coming as it did on the heels of the disaster at Fredericksburg. Effusive congratulatory telegrams from Northern politicians soon flooded army headquarters. Newspapers trumpeted the triumph across the country. Rosecrans's stock in Washington soared, as evidenced by Stanton's wire of January 7. This endorsement seemed to give Rosecrans carte blanche to now pursue a much more ambitious agenda: remaking his army into a more effective and efficient command.[13]

10 William F. G. Shanks, *Personal Recollections of Distinguished Generals* (New York: 1866), 258; David S. Stanley, "William Starke Rosecrans," *Twenty-Eighth Annual Reunion of the Association of Graduates of the United States Military Academy, at West Point, New York, June 10th, 1897* (Saginaw, MI: 1897), 70.

11 Shanks, *Personal Recollections*, 258; Benjamin F. Scribner, *How Soldiers Were Made* (New Albany, IN: 1887), 64; Philip H. Sheridan, *Personal Memoirs of P. H. Sheridan, General United States Army*, 2 vols. (New York: 1888), 1:203.

12 Jennifer Cain Bohrnstedt, ed. *Soldiering with Sherman: The Civil War Letters of George F. Cram* (Dekalb, IL: 2000), 14.

13 Lamers, *The Edge of Glory*, 246.

Going forward, Rosecrans would command the Army of the Cumberland. Thus was created one of three great commands of the War of the Rebellion, alongside the Armies of the Potomac and of the Tennessee. Cumberland veterans would proudly identify with the brand for the rest of their years. In addition, the clumsily designated Center, Right, and Left Wings would hereafter be known as the XIV, XX, and XXI Corps, respectively. This latter change was more than just symbolic: Corps commanders were authorized to have additional staff and aides-de-camp to establish a headquarters sufficient for the size of the job. Divisions and brigades were also renumbered. All told, Rosecrans created a more logical and coherent command structure, a much-needed improvement.

Beyond tending to these administrative details, and before he could contemplate any new offensive, Rosecrans saw three critical areas greatly in need of improvement: leadership, logistics, and (as previously mentioned) his cavalry.

Leadership: An Infusion of New Blood

Rosecrans looked to new men to revitalize the army. But it was not just a question of finding martial talent; army politics was also involved. Rosecrans assumed command of the Army of the Cumberland only after Buell's second in command, Maj. Gen. George H. Thomas, turned down the appointment back in September in a bid to convince the administration to retain Buell. That reprieve proved temporary, and when the Lincoln administration decided that Buell's pursuit of Bragg's army out of Kentucky was inordinately slow, Lincoln merely found someone else to take the job: Rosecrans. Thomas, initially angry that an officer junior in rank would now be promoted over him, was mollified by the fact that he was personally friendly with Rosecrans, and by a reshuffling of dates of rank so that Rosecrans was made senior. This administrative sleight-of-hand placated Thomas, and what could have been a troubling relationship between Rosecrans and his senior subordinate became instead a solid and cordial working partnership.[14]

Rosecrans immediately began cleaning house. Two other men were soon brought into the army at Rosecrans's request. One was Brigadier General Stanley, who had served under Rosecrans at Corinth. Stanley commanded an infantry division in that battle, but Rosecrans had different duties in mind for him:

---

14 Daniel, *Days of Glory*, 191-192.

Maj. Gen. George H. Thomas, commander of the XIV Corps,
Army of the Cumberland.

Library of Congress

commanding the Army of the Cumberland's cavalry, which desperately needed a
firm guiding hand.

Stanley bade farewell to his old command on November 12, 1862, reporting to
Rosecrans at Nashville on the 24th. He immediately sized up the problem. "The
cavalry had been badly neglected," he recalled. "It was weak, undisciplined and
scattered around, a regiment to a division of infantry." Exercising his new authority

(greatly helped by the weight of Rosecrans's endorsement), Stanley soon formed "three pretty substantial brigades," but could accomplish little more before joining battle at Murfreesboro. While the new commands fought well in that action, clearly there were teething pains. Going forward, Stanley would be charged with completely revitalizing the army's mounted arm.[15]

Another new man was Lt. Col. Julius Garesche. Born in Cuba, Garesche was first schooled at Georgetown University in Washington, DC, earned an appointment to the US Military Academy in 1837, and graduated with the class of 1841 (which included Buell). Garesche served with distinction in Mexico, and when the Civil War broke out, he was serving on the adjutant general's staff in Washington. A regular to the core, he declined a brigadier's commission of volunteers in 1861, preferring to accept the rank only after "he won it on the field." When Rosecrans asked for him in the fall of 1862, the war department acquiesced and Garesche journeyed west. Rosecrans and Garesche were friends, doubtless having bonded over their mutual Catholicism. More than that, Garesche was a superb organizer. "He was a very accomplished and able officer with a wonderful working capacity that knew no limit," Stanley opined. "Under his skillful organizing power and Rosecrans's energy this army soon took shape."[16]

It must have been especially traumatic for Rosecrans when an artillery round decapitated Garesche at Stones River, the shell "leaving only the lower jaw. His blood and brains splattered on the army commander's chest, and the headless body grisly rode on for another twenty paces before sliding off the horse." At the time, Rosecrans's only response was matter-of-fact: "I am very sorry. We cannot help it, brave men die in battle. This battle must be won." Later, Rosecrans came to view Garesche's death as a necessary sacrifice, demanded as the price of that victory; but

---

15 David S. Stanley, *Personal Memoirs of Major General D. S. Stanley, U.S.A.* (Cambridge, MA: 1917), 120. Interestingly, this is the same way that Maj. Gen. George B. McClellan had misused the Army of the Potomac's cavalry during the Peninsula Campaign and during the Seven Days battles in Virginia in the spring of 1862. It was a product of the belief that volunteer cavalry regiments would take longer than the anticipated duration of the war to train. Consequently, these troopers were misused as messengers and orderlies, and did not serve the basic function usually prescribed for cavalry: scouting, screening, and reconnaissance. For further reading on this subject, see Stephen Z. Starr, *The Union Cavalry in the Civil War, Vol. 1: From Fort Sumter to Gettysburg* (Baton Rouge, LA: 1979).

16 John Fitch, *Annals of the Army of the Cumberland: Comprising Biographies, Descriptions of Departments, Accounts of Expeditions, Skirmishes, and Battles* (Philadelphia, PA: 1864), 248; Stanley, *Personal Memoirs*, 119.

Garesche would be greatly missed, and Rosecrans carefully considered who might replace him.[17]

Several senior officers left the army before Stones River, creating new vacancies. The most significant departure was that of Maj. Gen. Charles C. Gilbert, a regular army martinet who proved to have no feel for how to lead volunteers and who did not distinguish himself at Perryville. Rosecrans astutely shifted George Thomas into active corps command, a vastly improved use of Thomas's considerable talents. (Buell had placed Thomas in the awkward and relatively unimportant job of second in command of the army, where he had no real troop-leading responsibilities and where he was decidedly unhappy.). There were also several divisional vacancies after Perryville; one commander had been killed in action, one taken sick, and three transferred. The situation was even more dire at the brigade level. On November 8, Rosecrans wired the war department that "he had only twenty-one brigadiers for fifty-two openings." The commands of many brigades, having fallen to senior colonels during the midwinter fight at Murfreesboro, now needed to be filled on a more permanent basis, either by promotion or transfer.[18]

Within days of his victory, Rosecrans took sick, diagnosed with "lung fever" on January 6, and spent a week or so prostrate. During this period, his military reputation probably reached its apogee. Not only did the congratulations over Stones River continue to pour in, but at one point, prior to Maj. Gen. Joseph Hooker's appointment to command the Army of the Potomac on January 26, Rosecrans's name was circulated as a candidate for the job. This idea was shot down perhaps only because after the experiment with Maj. Gen. John Pope, Washington's decision-makers were leery of importing another "'western' general [to command] the 'eastern-dominated' army."[19]

---

17 Daniel, *Battle of Stones River,* 167.

18 Gilbert was never confirmed as a general officer. His was appointed an "acting major general" and was nominated to be a brigadier general, but neither appointment was ever confirmed, probably due to his poor performance at the Battle of Perryville. His commission as brigadier general expired on March 4, 1863, and he was not reappointed. See Ezra J. Warner, *Generals in Blue: Lives of the Union Commanders* (Baton Rouge, LA: 1964), 174. For the best study of the Battle of Perryville, see Kenneth W. Noe, *Perryville: This Grand Havoc of Battle* (Lexington, KY: 2001); Daniel, *Days of Glory,* 191.

19 David G. Moore, *William S. Rosecrans and the Union Victory: A Civil War Biography* (Jefferson, NC: 2014), 72; Lamers, *The Edge of Glory,* 251. Major General John Pope was brought east in the summer of 1862 after a successful campaign to capture Island No. 10 on the Mississippi River, which surrendered on April 8, 1862. Pope was a West Pointer from the class of 1842, the same

In any case, Rosecrans's illness also slowed his rate of making demands on the war department. Still, in January he got much of what he wanted: promotions for several deserving officers, including those who distinguished themselves in battle, an expanded staff, and more of the new men he requested. On January 29, Rosecrans was delighted to receive Brig. Gen. George Crook, transferred with his brigade from the Department of the Ohio. Another West Pointer (class of 1852), Crook had seen earlier service under Rosecrans in western Virginia, where he obviously made a good impression: "Am very glad you sent General Crook," wrote Rosecrans. "No man could be more acceptable."[20]

Yet another was Brig. Gen. John M. Brannan, who was also a member of Garesche's West Point class of 1841. Brannan spent the first two years of the war on the Gulf Coast, commanding first the Department of Key West and, subsequently, the Department of the South (which embraced the coasts of Florida, Georgia, and South Carolina) until he was relieved in January and ordered to report to Rosecrans.[21]

Rosecrans's thorniest problem involved another of his corps commanders, Maj. Gen. Alexander McDowell McCook, now heading up the Union XX Corps. McCook was a son of Maj. Daniel McCook, scion of the famous Ohio "Fighting McCooks." Ultimately, 17 McCooks served in Union blue. They were also a politically powerful and remarkably well-connected family. One of Alexander's brothers was Edwin Stanton McCook, named for the current secretary of war, who

---

as Rosecrans, but he met with a chilly reception in Virginia. He was brought in to organize a new army out of the disparate elements left defending Washington, DC, while Union Maj. Gen. George B. McClellan and the Army of the Potomac waged their Peninsula Campaign against Richmond. Full of bombast, Pope compared his new command unfavorably to the troops he led out West and at one point declared that his "headquarters would be in the saddle," which led to many snide comments about Pope "having his headquarters where his hindquarters ought to be." In August, Robert E. Lee turned his attention to Pope's newly formed Army of Virginia, roundly defeating the newcomer at the Second Battle of Bull Run August 28-30, 1862. Pope was then sent packing, shipped off to Minnesota to deal with an Indian uprising. Though he remained in the army until 1886, he never again held an important Civil War field command. For the best treatment of the Second Bull Run Campaign, see John J. Hennessey, *Return to Bull Run: The Campaign and Battle of Second Manassas* (New York: 1993).

20 *OR* 23, pt. 2, 21.

21 John H. and David J. Eicher, *Civil War High Commands* (Stanford, CA: 2001), 142. Brannan would be a long time in reporting, not arriving until April. Difficult personal circumstances required him to devote some attention to his family. His wife went missing and was initially presumed to have drowned. She turned out to have run off with another officer to Paris just before the war. Her abandonment forced Brannan to find alternative living arrangements for his children.

was a family friend and the former law partner of Alexander's older brother George. Alexander McCook was another West Pointer, class of 1852, giving him both political and professional influence. He was also very young, 31 years of age, a decade younger than his contemporaries in rank.[22]

McCook led a regiment at First Bull Run and then was sent west to serve under Buell. He commanded a division at Shiloh, Tennessee, and a corps at Perryville. He led that same corps at Stones River. He proved capable at those lower echelons, but his tenure as a corps commander was troubled. His command was nearly driven off the field at both Perryville and Stones River, and though his problems were due at least in part to the neglect and inattention of senior officers—Buell at Perryville and Rosecrans himself at Stones River— the near disaster on December 31 worried Rosecrans. Publicly the army commander showed every confidence in McCook's abilities. Privately, he thought differently.

Accordingly, on January 24, Rosecrans asked Halleck for yet another officer, Brig. Gen. William Wallace Burns, whom Rosecrans knew from their mutual service in Virginia. Burns, initially a supply officer on McClellan's staff, was well-regarded and was soon given a brigade command in John Sedgwick's division of Edwin Sumner's II Corps, Army of the Potomac. He saw combat during the 1862 Peninsula Campaign outside Richmond, where he was wounded in the face. After recuperating, Burns assumed a divisional command in the IX Corps.[23]

Officially, Rosecrans did not specify what position he intended for Burns; unofficially, Burns claimed that he was offered McCook's job. In a postwar notation, Burns claimed that "it was well-known that Rosecrans had lost confidence in McCook after Stones River." In 1880, writing to another Federal general and fellow II Corps alumnus, Winfield S. Hancock, Burns elaborated that "Genl Rosecrans wishing to relieve Genl McCook after Stone [sic] River telegraphed to the president asking him that [I] . . . be sent to him for that purpose."[24]

Replacing McCook required that Burns be promoted, something that was supposedly already in the works. Burns was told that his name was on the list of

---

22 For a more detailed summary of McCook's background, see David A. Powell, *The Chickamauga Campaign, A Mad Irregular Battle: From the Crossing of the Tennessee River through the Second Day, August 22-September 19, 1863* (El Dorado Hills, CA: 2014), 18-21.

23 Telegram, Rosecrans to W. W. Burns, January 24, 1863, W. W. Burns Papers, Cushing Library, Texas A&M University.

24 Burns to W. S. Hancock, undated, ca. 1880, Burns Papers, Cushing Library.

officers to be promoted effective November 29, 1862, which was sent for Senate confirmation in early March. It would also require that Burns's current army commander—Ambrose Burnside—be willing to let him go.

All of this came at a difficult time for the Army of the Potomac, which was in the throes of its own political turmoil. Burnside was himself on the way out, replaced by Joseph Hooker on January 26. The army was already split into pro- and anti-McClellan factions, and Hooker's appointment only further hardened the pro-McClellanites' animosity into a hatred for Edwin Stanton and what they saw as dangerous political meddling by the Radical Republicans. Burns, a McClellan loyalist to his core, was destined to get caught up in this mayhem.

Burnside refused to release Burns and, initially, so did Hooker. Then, when Hooker learned that the IX Corps was being transferred out of Virginia anyway, he relented. Halleck also agreed, albeit grudgingly—thanks to incessant demands, Rosecrans's credit with the war department was already on the wane. On January 28, Halleck warned Rosecrans, "I cannot take good generals away from armies in the field, and bad ones you do not want. If General Hooker will consent, you shall have General Burns." However, cautioned Halleck, "you already have your full share of the best officers."[25]

Burns made his way to Washington, where he stopped to ensure that his name was indeed on the promotion list. He received a rude shock, for his name was nowhere to be found. He called on Stanton, who assured him it would be added, and even visited Lincoln, who told him all would be well. He also spoke to Senator Henry Wilson of Massachusetts, chairman of the military affairs committee, who "assured Burns that the confirmation should be made at once, out of the regular order."[26]

Then things fell apart. Burns proceeded on to Cincinnati, where he was told that news of his promotion would catch up with him. In early March, however, when the new list was made public, he was not on it. On March 6, angered and humiliated, Burns penned a dramatic letter of resignation, described by one historian as "florid and near- hysterical even by the standards of the day," and sent it on to Lincoln. Instead of intervening as Burns intended, the commander in chief simply accepted his resignation of his volunteer commission without comment. Both "Lincoln and Stanton had dealt with too many other touchy, paranoid

25 OR 23, pt. 2, 19.

26 Notes made on copy of resignation letter, March 6, 1863, Burns Papers, Cushing Library.

generals to placate yet another, less important one. . . . [Burns] overplayed his hand and paid for it with his career."[27]

Burns was convinced that Stanton sabotaged him because of his Democratic and pro-McClellan leanings, but there is no real evidence that this was the case. Historian David Earl Ward concluded that Burns was simply a victim of numbers; there were many more deserving officers in 1863 than there were slots for major generals of volunteers. Burns's ill-timed resignation was a costly blunder. He reverted to his regular army rank of major and returned to commissary duties in Milwaukee, assigned to the Department of the Northwest, where he served out the war under command of another military exile, John Pope.[28]

The loss of Burns frustrated Rosecrans. On March 10, having already caught wind of trouble, Rosecrans wired Halleck: "Has General Burns resigned, and will his resignation be accepted?" It was. Now he would have to find another qualified officer to replace him.[29]

Interestingly, Rosecrans also sought the return of Buell, the man he had just replaced. On February 10, 1863, Rosecrans asked Halleck "if you could give me General Buell, and he would be willing to serve in my army, it would be good for the service." The request, while surprising, showed how many officers still regarded Buell highly. Rosecrans certainly did, informing Buell that "I have often felt indignant at the petty attacks on you . . . and . . . you had my high respect for ability as a soldier, for your firm adherence to truth and justice in the government and discipline of your command."[30]

If Buell were to return, it could only be as a corps commander, probably to replace Maj. Gen. Thomas L. Crittenden. Buell, overly prideful, would have none of it. When Union General Ulysses S. Grant made Buell the same offer a year later, Buell's stiff-necked refusal disgusted Grant. "The worst excuse a soldier can make for declining service," Grant correctly opined, "is that he once ranked the commander he is ordered to report to."[31] With neither Buell nor Burns headed his

27 David Earl Ward, *The Wrong Kind of General: The Resignation of Union Brigadier General William W. Burns* (master's thesis, Texas A&M University, 2005), 84.

28 Ward, *The Wrong Kind of General*, 84; OR 22, pt. 2, 217.

29 *OR* 23, pt. 2, 127.

30 Ibid., 53 and 652.

31 Ulysses S. Grant, with John F. Marszalek, ed. *The Personal Memoirs of Ulysses S. Grant: The Complete Annotated Edition* (Cambridge, MA: 2017), 473.

way, Rosecrans retained Crittenden and McCook, and by all outward appearances retained confidence in them as long has he commanded the army.

Another officer Rosecrans requested by name was Brig. Gen. Gustave Paul Cluseret. Cluseret, a French adventurer and self-declared revolutionary, was a graduate of the French military academy at St. Cyr and a veteran of both the Crimean War and Italian general Giuseppe Garibaldi's campaign in Italy. Smelling opportunity, the Gallic soldier of fortune rushed to America in January 1862, obtained a commission in the Union army, and earned a brevet to brigadier general at the Virginia Battle of Cross Keys (fought on June 8, 1862), where he commanded a small brigade. He then served with Pope in the ill-fated Second Bull Run Campaign. Somehow Rosecrans caught wind of Cluseret's performance (perhaps from old comrades still serving in the Department of West Virginia) and inquired after him.

Since then, however, Cluseret's career had spiraled downward. Halleck informed Rosecrans that the Frenchman was currently in arrest for an unspecified misdeed, adding, "if you knew him better, you would not ask for him. You shall regret the application as long as you live . . . but if you say so, you shall have him." Given this highly dubious endorsement, the new departmental commander wisely said no more about obtaining the services of the unfortunate Brigadier General Cluseret.[32]

Another key officer who joined the army at this time was James A. Garfield. Garfield, simultaneously a newly elected Ohio Republican congressman and a brigadier general of volunteers, was eager to further his combat experience, which in turn could only help fuel his political ambitions. He was not completely green, however: he had served as a regimental and brigade commander, seeing action at the small battle at Middle Creek in eastern Kentucky and at Shiloh.

Garfield reported to Rosecrans's headquarters at Murfreesboro at 5 in the afternoon of January 25, 1863. The mode of his arrival epitomized one of the most serious problems Rosecrans faced: "I had a cavalry escort of 20 men," Garfield informed his wife, "and narrowly escaped a fight with a large body of rebel cavalry which came down the Nashville Pike from Franklin and destroyed a few cars and

---

32 OR 23, pt. 2, 11-12. Cluseret had been serving as a brigade commander in Maj. Gen. Robert H. Milroy's command, which was garrisoned in Winchester, Virginia. In January 1863, he was arrested on unspecified charges, which prompted Halleck's comment to Rosecrans. Cluseret resigned his commission in March 1863, his undistinguished military career over. See Warner, *Generals in Blue*, 85-86.

captured 25 of our men only two or three miles from us as we were on the route here."[33]

Garfield believed that he had a good shot at commanding a division, but he spent three weeks with Rosecrans while awaiting a posting. The two got along well. Rosecrans was so impressed that he offered Garfield the job of chief of staff—replacing the lamented Garesche—instead of a line command. After some soul-searching, Garfield accepted. He had a significant impact on the army's future operations.

Logistics: Securing the Lifeline

As 1863 dawned, the Army of the Cumberland depended on a vast river of supplies of all kinds, which flowed 212 miles down the rails from Louisville to Nashville on the eponymously named Louisville & Nashville Railroad and then another 30 miles from Nashville to Murfreesboro via the Nashville & Chattanooga Line. The N&C also became Rosecrans's principal lifeline southward as he advanced towards Chattanooga and into East Tennessee. Rebel cavalry had repeatedly demonstrated the vulnerability of that lifeline in 1862, and Rosecrans needed to improve virtually all aspects of his logistical framework before commencing a forward movement.

Nashville was also intermittently connected with the North by steamboat via the Cumberland River (from which Rosecrans's new army took its name), at least when the water was high. In the winter of 1862-63, it was not: even shallow-draft boats had trouble navigating up the Cumberland much past Dover, Tennessee, site of Fort Donelson. From there, supplies had to be hauled overland. Looking ahead, Rosecrans could also not count on sustaining his army via the Tennessee River, should he get that far. Muscle Shoals in northern Alabama prevented steamboats from passing all the way from the Ohio River to Chattanooga. As a result, any Union advance through Middle Tennessee and into Georgia to Atlanta would be entirely dependent on traffic over an ever-lengthening and increasingly vulnerable rail line—more than 400 miles of track by the time the Federals reached their destination.

This geography meant that the Army of the Cumberland's strategic circumstances differed considerably from either the Army of the Potomac's, in

---

33 Frederick D. Williams, *The Wild Life of the Army: Civil War Letters of James A. Garfield* (East Lansing, MI: 1964), 224.

Virginia, or the Army of the Tennessee's in Mississippi. In Virginia, supply lines were relatively short. Only 100 overland miles separated Washington and Richmond, while the eastern seaboard presented the Union navy with unlimited access to supply ports along the way. In Mississippi, where General Grant discovered how vulnerable rails could be after a raid on his depot at Holly Springs, the Mississippi River provided a similar waterborne alternative. Broader and deeper than the Cumberland or the Tennessee, even during low water the Mississippi was navigable, and it could not be blown up or burned down. Union operations in both the eastern theater and in Mississippi relied heavily on waterborne supplies and troop movements throughout the war.

Rosecrans had no such alternative. Though he intended to use the Cumberland and Tennessee Rivers wherever possible, he had to depend on rails for the bulk of his logistics, which required constant vigilance and attention. In August 1862, as the Rebels entered Kentucky, Confederate cavalry under Brig. Gen. John Hunt Morgan descended upon the Union post at Gallatin, Tennessee, capturing the entire garrison. More importantly, Morgan also destroyed the "Big South" railroad tunnel on the L&N line by running a burning train into the tunnel, where it slammed into a barrier of wood and stone piled across the tracks for that purpose. The resultant explosion set the tunnel timbers alight and ignited a coal seam, causing a massive cave-in. Morgan also burned two trestle bridges, but by far the most serious damage was to the tunnel. The railroad was shut down for months, leaving only insufficient river traffic as the primary supply source to Nashville.[34]

When Rosecrans assumed command, his priority was repairing that tunnel, which became even more urgent as falling water levels rendered the Cumberland increasingly un-navigable, further crimping the flow of supplies. Two full brigades of infantry were detailed to Gallatin, while Rosecrans ordered "all . . . available railroad force to work on bridges from Nashville to [the] tunnel." "Big South" did not reopen for 98 days, leaving the Federal army to make do with limited supplies until late November. Then, to ensure that the trains kept running, Rosecrans dispersed more than 10,000 troops to guard the rails between Nashville and Louisville, with nearly 7,000 of those troops in Tennessee.[35]

The efforts of those 10,000 men were only partially successful. In December, in two separate affairs, John Hunt Morgan once again demonstrated the

34 James A. Ramage, *Rebel Raider: The Life of General John Hunt Morgan* (Lexington, KY: 1986), 112.

35 OR 20, pt. 2, 29; Ramage, *Rebel Raider,* 136.

vulnerability of the Federal rear area in dramatic fashion. First came a December 7 raid on Hartsville, Tennessee, where, in a daring dawn attack, Morgan led 1,300 Rebel cavalrymen against a complacent and inattentive Union garrison of 2,300 troops. Hartsville, on the Cumberland River a few miles east of Gallatin, was garrisoned specifically to prevent Confederate raiders from crossing the Cumberland and moving against the railroad. Surprised in their camps, and after a fight lasting no more than "an hour and a quarter," the Federals capitulated. Rosecrans was stunned when he learned of it: "Do I understand they have captured an entire brigade of our troops without our knowing about it, or a good fight?" Morgan killed or wounded about 250 opponents and captured over 1,800 prisoners—virtually the entire brigade. It was a complete disaster.[36]

As if the Hartsville catastrophe wasn't bad enough, Morgan reprised his efforts against the L&N a couple of weeks later. Slipping across the Cumberland and into Kentucky in late December, Morgan struck the L&N around Elizabethtown, intending to destroy two large trestle bridges at Muldraugh's Hill, but he wreaked havoc all along the line. Despite Federal advance warning and accurate assessments of the Rebel strength, Morgan's attack was nevertheless a major success. This time, the raider "captured and paroled over 1,800 prisoners, inflicted 150 casualties, burned a total of 2,290 feet of railroad bridgework, wrecked thirty-five miles of track and telegraph line, and destroyed three depots, three water stations, several culverts and cattle guards, and large quantities of Federal stores. . . . The railroad was closed from December 26 until February 1, five weeks."[37]

Given that both the rails and (to a lesser extent) the rivers were subject to interdiction by Rebel raids, Rosecrans's initial efforts were directed towards securing those lines of supply and communications. Rosecrans demanded more troops to patrol and garrison strategic points, asked that Forts Henry and Donelson be made part of his command, and even requested direct control over the naval gunboats tasked with securing the Cumberland River. In this last request, he appealed directly to President Lincoln, who wisely passed the buck back down the chain of command, understanding that meddling from the top would only confuse things further. Rosecrans did not get control of the navy's gunboats, but he convinced the navy to step up their patrols.

The need for those efforts continued to be demonstrably real. In early January, amidst brutal cold, Brig. Gen. Joseph Wheeler's cavalry appeared along the east

36 *OR* 20, pt. 1, 43.

37 Ramage, *Rebel Raider*, 137.

bank of the Cumberland between Clarksville and Ashland, Tennessee, intent on disrupting river traffic to Nashville. Between January 12 and 14, Wheeler's men captured and plundered several river transports, burning them to the waterline, paroled many prisoners, and capped off the raid with the destruction of the Union supply depot at Ashland.[38]

Three weeks later, flushed with the success of his Ashland venture, Joe Wheeler tried again. This time the addition of 800 troopers under Brig. Gen. Nathan Bedford Forrest bolstered his numbers. Their combined force struck at Dover, Tennessee, on February 3. Wheeler, who had overall command of the raid, aimed to capture or destroy any Union riverboats he found there. The Federals had enough advance warning of his approach to halt river traffic, forcing Wheeler to attempt to take Fort Donelson by storm. This time the Union garrison was not caught napping and easily repulsed the Confederate assault with heavy losses. Though the Rebels were foiled at Dover, the fact that large enemy forces could wander in and out of Rosecrans's rear areas with impunity was obviously alarming.[39]

Rosecrans intended to reduce his reliance on vulnerable supply routes by creating a series of forward bases. He reasoned that if he stockpiled rations and ammunition close to the front, then his army could survive temporary disruptions in the supply flow from either Louisville or up the Cumberland without having to retreat or even cease active operations. Nashville had served that purpose for the movement towards Murfreesboro, though Rosecrans had only a month in which sufficient supplies reached the city to accumulate a surplus. For his next move forward, Rosecrans intended to scale up the concept.

On January 12, 1863, the 26th Ohio, along with the 1st Brigade, 1st Division, XXI Corps, was detailed to help Union pioneer troops construct a massive earthwork that would soon be christened Fortress Rosecrans. The pioneers consisted of four battalions of men detailed from their regular units to provide skilled labor for the army. The army's chief engineer, Brig. Gen. James St. Clair Morton, West Point class of 1851, commanded them. The pioneers were chosen for their special skills in construction and practical engineering; they were carpenters, artificers, surveyors, and the like. They numbered around 3,000 men and included a train of up to 50 wagons laden with tools. The Buckeyes of the 26th

---

38 Edward G. Longacre, *Cavalry of the Heartland, The Mounted Forces of the Army of Tennessee* (Yardley, PA: 2009), 189-190.

39 Ibid., 190-191.

Ohio and their brigade comrades were to provide additional brute force labor as needed.[40]

As envisioned, Fortress Rosecrans was enormous. The bastion "included eight lunettes, four redoubts, a steam sawmill, a magazine, and several warehouses," and could hold three months of supplies for an army of 50,000 men. The fort was located northwest of the town of Murfreesboro and was bisected by the Nashville & Chattanooga Railroad. While the fort required a sizeable permanent garrison— which was yet another drain on the department's overall manpower—once fully stocked it provided Rosecrans's answer to the vulnerability of the L&N and offered him the opportunity to operate semi-independently for several weeks at a time, if need be.[41]

In order to further un-tether his army from the logistical tyranny imposed by the vulnerable rails, however, Rosecrans needed an unprecedented number of wagons and the draft animals to haul them. On March 23, 1863, Rosecrans reported he had more than 19,000 horses with his army, but "only one third [of them] were serviceable." One week later on March 31 he reported that he had "3,747 draft horses and 23,859 mules in the army and in depots." He requested another 10,000 horses at this time because, in addition to the needs of his wagon trains, he also needed riding horses for his cavalry and the infantry he intended to mount. Union Quartermaster General Montgomery Meigs objected, pointing out that the more animals Rosecrans added to the army, the more forage he would need, and the more strain he would place on the overburdened rails—certainly true enough for a static army that had eaten up all the easily available forage in its immediate area. But Rosecrans understood this dilemma as well, arguing in return that he needed those animals "to compete with the enemy for scarce forage" farther afield. Doing so would not only ease his requirements of forage from Northern depots, but also deny that same forage to the equally strained Confederate logistical system.

Ultimately, Rosecrans prevailed. By the end of June the army commander had increased his transportation to "an extraordinary standard that may have exceeded sixty-nine or seventy wagons per 1,000 men." When he advanced, observed one writer, he "moved with 45,000 animals, the highest proportion of animals to men in

---

40 Jeffery A. Hill, *The 26th Ohio Veteran Volunteer Infantry, The Groundhog Regiment, Second Edition* (Bloomington, IN: 2010), 184; Fitch, *Annals of the Army of the Cumberland*, 186-191.

41 Edwin C. Bearss, *The History of Fortress Rosecrans* (Washington, DC: 1960), 2.

any campaign of the war." This increased transportation standard translated into an unprecedented tactical mobility beyond the Union railhead.[42]

Cavalry: "You Can't Have All the Best Arms"

Beyond the leadership and logistical issues, Rosecrans's most pressing problem lay with his cavalry—or the lack thereof. On January 31, 1863, his army showed only 4,549 officers and men present for duty in Brigadier General Stanley's cavalry division. Perhaps another 700 troopers served as escorts or on detached garrison duty.[43]

Given an overall field strength of 70,000 men, this was a smaller percentage of mounted force than that found in virtually any other Union department. To compound the problem, their counterparts in gray vastly outnumbered them. By way of comparison, on February 20 Braxton Bragg's Army of Tennessee reported 12,224 mounted men present for duty, of which no less than 11,610 served in Major General Wheeler's newly unified cavalry command—soon to be designated a corps. Bragg might be badly outmatched in infantry and artillery, but he possessed nearly a three-to-one advantage in cavalry.[44]

As if things weren't already bad enough for the Union, that ratio was about to get much worse. On February 12, Rosecrans received alarming new intelligence, which he quickly passed on to Halleck: "They have an enormous cavalry force. Van Dorn is coming to swell it, by 6,000 or 7,000 more, at least. They are [also] preparing to mount 4,000 of their infantry." If accurate, by March Rosecrans might face as many as 20,000 Rebel horsemen—enough to overwhelm his own small force of troopers and devastate his supply line.[45]

Major General Earl Van Dorn was Rosecrans's opposite number at the Battle of Corinth. He proved to be out of his depth as an army commander. Defeated there, he was then assigned to command the Confederate cavalry in Mississippi, a role much better suited to his talents. He quickly achieved a noted success when he attacked and destroyed the Federal supply depot at Holly Springs in December 1862. That raid crippled Major General Grant's first attempt to take Vicksburg and

---

42 Edward Hagerman, *The American Civil War and the Origins of Modern Warfare: Ideas, Organization, and Field Command* (Bloomington, IN: 1988), 209-212.

43 *OR* 23, pt. 2, 29.

44 Ibid., 643.

45 Ibid., 59. As will be seen, Van Dorn brought about 3,500 men to Tennessee.

stalemated the war in Mississippi for what proved to be many months. Just as Morgan's assaults on the L&N highlighted the vulnerability of the Federals in Nashville, Holly Springs made it clear that Union troops could not rely on the exposed Mississippi Central Railroad as their main supply line. Coupled with a similar raid by Nathan Bedford Forrest in West Tennessee, Van Dorn's attack left Grant's army all but paralyzed, pinned down in dozens of garrisons. Now this Rebel force was coming to augment Bragg's already impressive cavalry numbers.

While infantry and artillery did the bulk of the fighting and dying on a Civil War battlefield, effective cavalry was an essential component of any field army. It was vital in two arenas: the semi-partisan raiding war so successfully executed by the likes of Van Dorn, Forrest, and Morgan, and also in conducting successful operational movements by scouting, screening, and reconnoitering. In the partisan arena, the war had so far demonstrated that relatively small numbers of quickly moving mounted troops operating in sympathetic territory held great advantages. For example, in November 1862 Grant's whole force numbered 61,000 troops, but less than 5,000 of those were cavalry. Worse, something like half of his total strength was dispersed in regional garrisons, trying to secure the countryside. As a result, with a combined force of less than 5,000, Van Dorn and Forrest rode through Grant's area of responsibility with impunity, wreaking destruction. Federal combined arms columns simply couldn't react or assemble quickly enough to pin the Rebels down or bring them to bay against superior numbers. Thus, much of Grant's manpower advantage over the Confederate army in Mississippi was illusory. Any field army he could assemble would be far smaller than his overall strength suggested because so many troops had to be assigned to defend static positions in the rear. Rosecrans, tied to the L&N, had similar problems with Morgan and Wheeler. Every step south required additional garrisons in his wake, draining his numerical advantage as he went.[46]

Moreover, however much it remains a cliché, cavalrymen were the "eyes and ears" of an army on the march. Friendly cavalry simultaneously screened an army's movements from the enemy, deceiving one's opponent as to strength, movements, and intentions while at the same time, penetrating the enemy's cavalry screen to uncover those details about the opposition. For reasons of speed and logistics, large armies most effectively advanced along multiple routes, causing a degree of separation that created opportunities for an alert defender. A smaller force, if well informed, could concentrate to defeat parts of a larger force in detail, with

46 Ibid., 17, pt. 2, 338-40.

sometimes startling results. Numbers alone did not guarantee victory, and in that sense, cavalry could be a force multiplier. Rosecrans understood this math all too well. "One Rebel cavalryman," he informed Stanton, "takes on an average 3 of our infantry to watch our communications, while our progress is made slow and cautious. We command the forage of the country only by sending out large train guards. It is of prime necessity in every point of view to master their cavalry." The Army of the Cumberland was effectively besieged, safe enough behind its fortifications in Nashville and Murfreesboro, but unable to control the surrounding countryside. Augmenting his mounted arm became Rosecrans's overarching priority.[47]

But where was all this additional mounted strength to come from? Rosecrans's cavalry shortage was not just a problem specific to his department. Thanks to a shortsighted policy in Washington, the Union armies were almost all chronically short of cavalry throughout 1862. Early in the war the Federal government discouraged the raising of volunteer cavalry, since it took many more months to equip and train a cavalry regiment than one of foot, and it also cost the government a great deal more money. Parsimony and the equally misguided belief that the war would be over before most of that cavalry was ready to take the field led to a chronic shortage of Federal horse soldiers in all departments.

Rosecrans realized this problem. He asked for more cavalry units, as many as he could get, but he also grasped that there simply weren't sufficient Federal numbers to match Rebel recruiting at least in the short term. His engineering mind, however, was already grappling with other solutions.

First, Rosecrans needed weapons, and wanted only the best available. Within weeks of assuming command back in the fall of 1862, he began asking for arms. On November 16, he telegraphed an idea "to mount some infantry regiments, arm them with revolving rifles, and make sharpshooters of them." The next day, repeating his request, he added, "Let me entreat you to give us cavalry arms." On November 17 General Halleck responded by noting that "two thousand five hundred cavalry arms" had already been shipped and that "all revolving rifles that can be spared will also be sent." However, Halleck added a warning: "Each army receives its proportion of each kind of arms as fast as they can be procured. This rule must be followed, for we 'cannot rob Peter to pay Paul.'" On the 18th, Secretary of War Stanton also responded, noting that 1,600 Colt rifles, "all that are

47 OR 23, pt. 2, 34.

Sgt. Gilbert Armstrong, Co. E., 58th Indiana Infantry, posing with the Henry Rifle awarded to him by his comrades as a member of Rosecrans's proposed Elite Battalions.

History of the Fifty-Eighth Indiana

now manufactured in the United States" were being sent. "No effort shall be spared to supply what you ask for, but something is expected from you."[48]

These early caveats appeared not to alert Rosecrans to the fact that he might be pushing his luck. Two months later, on January 30, he telegraphed Halleck that "three regiments of Tennessee Cavalry and the exchanged prisoners of the Second Indiana are now without arms. . . ." Then adopting a lecturing tone, he continued: "revolving arms duplicate our strength. What is the use of raising and supporting a force and losing half its strength, for want of as many dollars' expense for arms as would be lost by a day's delay?"

He also continued to press the idea of mounting infantry, and not just on a small scale. Instead, he conceived a much more grandiose scheme. After Stones River, Rosecrans ordered each regiment to publish a "Roll of Honor," singling out men who performed exceptionally well in the recent action. These troops served as an example to others, inspiring every soldier to strive for similar honors. In addition to the recognition, Rosecrans decided that they would also become the basis for an elite force within the army.

Rosecrans detailed his intentions to Halleck on February 1. From this roll, each regiment would supply all the named privates, one officer, and five sergeants or corporals to form an elite battalion for each brigade. Additionally, and rashly, he "promise[d] them the best of arms when I can get them, and will mount them for rapid field movement, like flying artillery. . . . We must create military ardor." When organized, this concept would add another 30 or so mounted battalions, or roughly 6,000 men, to his mobile arm.[49]

48 Ibid., 20, pt. 2, 58-9, 60-61.

49 Ibid., pt. 2, 51.

In Rosecrans's mind, the "best arms" meant either breech-loading or multi-shot weapons. Colt revolving rifles were acceptable, but ideally he wanted repeating arms like Spencer or Henry rifles, if they could be had. Rosecrans correctly viewed these as a force multiplier, doubling or even tripling effectiveness compared to the often poorly equipped Rebel troopers. Characteristically, he wanted them as soon as he could get them.[50]

It was not to be. Rosecrans's elite battalions trespassed on legal boundaries that the war department was unwilling to cross. Only Congress could authorize the creation of a host of new army units. State governors still controlled appointments of regimental officers, which was, among other things, a source of local patronage and political power, and Rosecrans's proposal also stepped on their toes. The Confederacy solved this problem by passing a specific law granting commanders the right to form sharpshooter battalions from picked men in April 1862, and the South used it to great effect. The Federal government never followed suit. Moreover, in Halleck's view, mounted infantry was largely a waste of time. In trying to be both infantry and cavalry, it never performed as well as either, Halleck believed, reflecting a good deal of the old army's prejudice against volunteer soldiers. But he was the man in charge, and he quashed Rosecrans's idea for elite battalions as soon as he heard of it.[51]

The weapons question, however, became the single thorniest point of contention between the war department and Rosecrans that spring. On February 1, replying to the January 30 missive, Halleck exhibited increasing levels of testiness: "You already have more than your share of the best arms," he snapped.

50 The Spencer rifle was the first mass-produced repeating rifle. It fired rimfire bullets with brass casings, using interchangeable tube magazines of seven bullets per tube. Thus, a soldier firing a Spencer rifle could fire seven shots before having to reload. By contrast, a soldier proficient with conventional muzzle-loading rifles could get off three shots per minute. The Henry rifle was the first true semiautomatic weapon. It had a lever-action, breech-loading tubular 16-shot magazine and could lay down a tremendous amount of firepower without the need to reload frequently. Both the Spencer and the Henry used up ammunition much more quickly than a single-round rifled musket, which was one of the reasons why the Union's ordnance department resisted their being adopted on a widespread basis. For a good history of repeating rifles in the Civil War, see Joseph G. Bilby, *A Revolution in Arms: A History of the First Repeating Rifles* (Yardley, PA: 2005).

51 There is evidence that within some units, elites were picked and some arms were distributed. As late as the Battle of Chickamauga, in the fall of 1863, one can find fleeting references to handpicked men in a few Federal regiments carrying repeating arms, mostly privately purchased Henrys.

"Everything has been done, and is now being done, for you that is possible by the government. . . . You cannot expect to have all the best arms."[52]

This rebuke might have alerted a more perceptive commander that he was overstepping his authority. Not so Rosecrans, who often turned a deaf ear to signs of annoyance from above. The very next day, he sent Halleck another lecturing, hectoring dispatch: "I am surprised you mistake my meaning. I do not complain. I point out the way to victory." Rosecrans continued for several more sentences, pedantically explaining to Halleck how much the war was costing, in both lives and money (as if Halleck were unaware of both), and reiterating his need for "superior arms." This missive was bad enough, but then, just an hour after he telegraphed Halleck, Rosecrans went over Halleck's head, sending a wire directly to Stanton to, as Rosecrans put it, "prevent misunderstanding." Again, Rosecrans itemized his need for arms, demanded 2,000, and reprised his cost-saving argument. Finally, he concluded, "this matter is so clearly . . . of paramount public interest that I blush to think it necessary to seem to apologize for it."[53]

Both Stanton and Halleck were fast becoming fed up with this deluge of demands. Their reply came on February 3. In a lengthy dispatch, Halleck explained the realities to Rosecrans: Everyone wanted "the best arms," but the government had to think of all departments, not just Middle Tennessee. Rosecrans's forces were as well equipped as any other army in the field, Halleck pointed out: "Certainly you cannot expect that you can have all the best arms [while] other troops receive those of a lower grade." The rebuke was clear and explicit. Rosecrans had crossed a line. The question was whether he realized it.[54]

The increasingly acrimonious debate over weapons marked a turning point in the relationship between Rosecrans and Washington. For Stanton, Halleck, and Lincoln, Rosecrans's demands, delivered in such a high-handed tone, reminded them of other generals they had grown weary of—McClellan, perhaps—who demanded much and delivered little. Affairs between Rosecrans and his superiors only grew increasingly strained from this point forward. Rosecrans, ever politically tone-deaf, failed to notice, and failed to understand, why his relationship with the government seemed to be deteriorating. Still, some weapons were forthcoming. To the credit of Halleck and Stanton, they tried hard not to slight Rosecrans's army.

52 *OR* 23, pt. 2, 51.

53 Ibid., 34.

54 Ibid., 38.

Cavalry arms, and equipment, were on the way, just not as fast as the army commander desired or demanded.

In addition, some cavalry was spared from the Department of the Ohio, headquartered in Cincinnati, and all told, Rosecrans's mounted numbers increased slowly but surely that spring. By March, the cavalry division's strength grew to 6,389 effectives. The numbers declined a bit in April and May, dropping to about 5,000 as some troopers were detached to take up local garrison duties. However, and significantly for future operations, Stanley's command was retitled the Cavalry Corps, Army of the Cumberland, in May. By the end of June, army reports revealed impressive gains. The newly designated corps reported nearly 11,000 men present for duty, plus an additional 500 troopers serving at army headquarters. Moreover, although Halleck was not happy with the idea, Washington ultimately offered up no legal restriction on creating regiments of mounted infantry. Rosecrans could pursue the concept if he wished.[55]

Most famous among these efforts was the command of Col. John T. Wilder. Wilder was born on January 31, 1830, in Greene County, New York. His grandfather and great-grandfather were both veterans of the Revolutionary War (when his great-grandfather lost a leg at the Battle of Bunker Hill, his 16-year-old son took his place in the line of battle), and his father was a veteran of the War of 1812. With that sort of pedigree, Wilder was destined to become a soldier. He attended the local schools in Hunter, New York, and did well there. He "was a handsome young man, of fine physique, mentally alert, fond of research [and possessed a] genial and hospitable nature."[56]

In 1849, at the young age of 19, Wilder left the family home in the Catskill Mountains and traveled to Columbus, Ohio, where he found employment in a foundry as a draftsman, patternmaker, and millwright. In 1857, he moved to Greensburg, Indiana, and established his own foundry there. By 1861, he owned half of the largest operation of its type in the Midwest, with mills in six different states, and business was booming. The 31-year-old had become an authority in the field of hydraulics (he held patents on a number of inventions, including a unique water wheel) and had grown quite wealthy. He was married to the former Mary Jane Stewart and was the father of two little girls.[57]

---

55 Ibid., 197, 574.

56 Richard A. Baumgartner, *Blue Lightning: Wilder's Mounted Infantry Brigade in the Battle of Chickamauga* (Huntington, WV: 2007), 20.

57 Ibid.

With the outbreak of war in 1861, Wilder enlisted as a private in an artillery company, which he equipped with two cannons cast in one of his mills. The unit was not mustered as artillery, but was instead designated Co. A of the 17th Indiana Volunteer Infantry. Wilder was unanimously elected the new company's captain. In June 1861, after refusing a commission for colonel because he did not believe he was qualified for the position, he accepted a promotion to lieutenant colonel. The green regiment fought in western Virginia at Cheat Mountain and in the Greenbrier Valley. In November the 17th Indiana was assigned to the Army of the Ohio and was sent to the Western Theater of operations.

In early April 1862, Wilder was promoted to colonel of the 17th Indiana. Neither he nor his regiment made it to the front in time to participate in the Battle of Shiloh. The unit joined the advance on Corinth and then took part in defending against General Bragg's invasion of Kentucky in the fall of 1862. In mid-September, Wilder and his men were sent to Munfordville, Kentucky, tasked with defending a vital rail bridge. They were soon besieged by nearly all of Bragg's army. Outnumbered six-to-one, Wilder, now in command of a brigade, was left with no alternative but to surrender to Bragg at Fort Craig on September 17, 1862. Wilder and his men were paroled and marched to Louisville.[58]

Exchanged two months later, Wilder assumed command of a brigade in the Fifth Division of the XIV Corps in the Army of the Cumberland. The brigade included his old command, the 17th Indiana (now commanded by Lt. Col. Henry Jordan of Corydon, Indiana), and three green regiments—the 72nd Indiana, the 75th Indiana, and the 98th Illinois. Indiana physician Col. Abram O. Miller commanded the 72nd Indiana. Like Wilder, he had begun the war as a captain and had made his way up the ranks to colonel. He was an Ohio-born farmer and had been reluctant to take command of the regiment. Col. John J. Funkhouser of Effingham, Illinois, commanded the 98th Illinois. This unit, from south-central Illinois, had seen no action at all when it joined Wilder's new brigade. The 75th Indiana, commanded by Col. Milton S. Robinson, had seen limited service during the invasion of Kentucky, but was also relatively inexperienced. Colonel Wilder, one comrade remembered, "was not a starched, prim, polished commander—not a MADE commander, but a born one, and all through his career with his Brigade, he showed the grain, tenacity, the elasticity, the supreme handiwork of unspoiled Nature. He won the entire confidence of his Brigade without an effort and the men knew they could do whatever Wilder ordered. And his modesty equaled his merit.

58 Ibid., 23-24.

He never boasted; he was willing to be judged 'by his chips.' He was active; he hated the monotony of the camp and his Brigade was early imbued with the same idea."[59]

In late January, Wilder approached Rosecrans with a suggestion to mount his entire command. During the Stones River action, Wilder's men, along with the rest of Brig. Gen. Joseph Reynolds's division, spent their time not in combat but instead chasing John Hunt Morgan's raiders across Tennessee and Kentucky. They never caught him, leaving Wilder to conclude that chasing enemy cavalry with infantry was a waste of time. Instead, he proposed to confiscate suitable local livestock and mount his entire 3,000-man brigade. By using locally seized animals, the government's expenses would be reduced, always a strong argument with the war department. The idea dovetailed nicely with Rosecrans's own plans.

On February 16, Rosecrans approved. In uniquely American military fashion, the entire brigade was allowed a vote, and all regiments but the 75th Indiana chose to ride rather than walk. The 123rd Illinois took the place of the 75th , which was reassigned. The 123rd was from central Illinois, mustered in at Mattoon under the command of Col. James Monroe, a veteran of the early battles under Grant at Belmont, Missouri, and at Fort Donelson and Shiloh. The regiment was sworn in on September 6, 1862, and assigned to the Army of the Ohio. A month later, with almost no training and no combat experience, the 123rd Illinois was thrust into action at Perryville, on October 8. The regiment's brigade and division commanders were killed in the savage fighting, and the green Illinois soldiers lost 36 men killed and 180 wounded that long day. These veterans were a good addition to a largely inexperienced brigade.[60]

Once the final makeup of the brigade was set, it took about a month for Wilder to mount his entire command and Capt. Eli Lilly's 18th Indiana Battery. Lilly was a pharmacist from Greencastle, Indiana, who went on to found one of the largest and most successful drug companies in the world. His battery was armed with six Rodman guns, also known as 3-inch ordnance rifles. The 3-inch ordnance rifle was particularly well-suited to mounted operations, as it was light but durable and could be moved quickly and easily. Additionally, Wilder had found four mountain howitzers, or "bull pups," as they were sometimes called, that he organized into

---

59 *Dedication of the Wilder Brigade Monument on Chickamauga Battlefield on the Thirty-Sixth Anniversary of the Battle, September 20, 1899* (Marshall, IL: 1900), 14.

60 Glenn W. Sunderland, *Lightning at Hoover's Gap: Wilder's Brigade in the Civil War* (New York: 1969), 18.

two sections of two guns each and added to Lilly's battery, meaning that he had the only 10-gun battery in the Union service. Teams of mules pulled the bull pups.

The association of battery and brigade was a happy one. "Lilly's gunners, when they knew the distance and elevation, could hit the mark the first shot two miles away," one of Wilder's men recalled. These artillerists became famous for the accuracy of their fire.[61] "Many expeditions were made, sometimes by the whole Brigade and again by parts of it, and soon nearly the entire number of horses necessary for the mount were brought in, together with a sufficient number of mules for the Brigade wagon train and some to spare for other commands," one officer of Wilder's brigade remembered. "Whenever animals were taken, the owners, if loyal to the government, were given vouchers for the same that enabled them to get compensation from the government." Of course, families that supported the Confederacy received no such vouchers.[62]

Sergeant George S. Wilson of the 17th Indiana left a detailed account of the brigade's foraging in Tennessee for horses, the scope of which was previously unheard of during the first half of the Civil War. "Our operations in this enterprise extended east to the base of the Cumberland range of mountains, from McMinnville north to the Cumberland River, and back to Lebanon and the Hermitage. Besides overrunning this country, we made two or three excursions to the southwest. All this extensive and rich section we stripped of horses and mules, and by the middle of April the entire brigade was mounted on fairly good animals. Up to this period of the war our forces had, as a rule, respected the property rights of citizens. Now a new policy had come into operation, and we were its pioneers—the first of all the Army of the Cumberland to commence a system to forcing the disloyal inhabitants of the South to contribute to the support of the army."[63]

Consequently, the command rode a hodgepodge of mounts that ran the gamut: thoroughbred racers, plow horses, nags, brood mares, stallions, ponies, and

61 *Dedication of the Wilder Brigade Monument*, 25; For a good history of Lilly's battery, see John W. Rowell, *Yankee Artillerymen: Through the Civil War with Eli Lilly's Indiana Battery* (Knoxville, TN: 1975).

62 Richard A. Baumgartner, *Blue Lightning: Wilder's Mounted Infantry Brigade in the Battle of Chickamauga* (Huntington, WV: 2007). 37-39; *Dedication of the Wilder Brigade Monument*, 37. Baumgartner provides a detailed look at the mounting and equipping of the new brigade.

63 George S. Wilson, "Wilder's Brigade of Mounted Infantry in the Tullahoma-Chickamauga Campaigns," *War Talks in Kansas*, Kansas Commandery, Loyal Legion of the United States (Kansas City: 1906), 47.

mules. Functionality mattered, not appearance. So long as it had a saddle, it was fair game and probably good enough. Of course, this practice did little to endear Wilder's soldiers to local citizenry.

By April Wilder's brigade had added another 2,500 men to the Army of the Cumberland's mounted arm.[64] Like nearly all other Union infantry commands, Wilder's troops were originally equipped with Springfield and Enfield muzzle-loaders. The inefficiency of these weapons bothered the innovative colonel, so he armed his entire brigade with Spencers, and with hatchets instead of sabers (although the hatchets disappeared before the mounted brigade's first campaign).

Developed by Christopher Spencer, the Spencer rifle was a long-barreled breech-loading weapon that could fire seven shots before having to be reloaded. The Spencer used a rimfire bullet that was loaded into a tube. When the seven shots were fired, the soldier operating the Spencer could then either reload the tube or, more commonly, replace the tube from a ready supply of already-loaded tubes. This weapon enabled Wilder's men to lay down a tremendous amount of firepower at a high speed.

Wilder expressed his opinion clearly: "The Spencer magazine rifle . . . was a most formidable weapon. I believe them to be the best arm for army use that I have seen. No line of men, who came within fifty yards of another force armed with the Spencer Repeating Rifles, can either get away alive, or reach them with a charge, as in either case they are certain to be destroyed by the terrible fire poured into their ranks by cool men thus armed. If the government would expend the large sums now used to induce men to enlist, in arming the men now in the field with this kind of weapon, the rebellion would be, in my opinion, speedily crushed."[65]

Wilder was unable to get the army to commit to purchasing Spencer rifles for his brigade, so he went to his hometown bank to borrow the funds to purchase them himself. After being persuaded of the efficacy of the new rifles, the men of Wilder's brigade voted to reimburse their commander for the weapons if that was what it took to keep them. The cost of the guns was to be deducted from their pay, but by the time the first payments were supposed to be made, the men had proven the guns' worth. The government then reimbursed Wilder and the men.[66]

64 OR 23, pt. 2, 48-9.

65 John T. Wilder to the Spencer Repeating Rifle Co., November 28, 1863, John T. Wilder Papers, Indiana State Library, Indianapolis, Indiana.

66 Stephen Z. Starr, *The Union Cavalry in the Civil War*, 3 vols. (Baton Rouge, LA: 1985), 3:212; *Dedication of the Wilder Brigade Monument*, 36.

The problem was that the brigade was unique. As one of Wilder's officers put it, "this was the original and only Brigade of mounted infantry." New weapons required new combat methods, and since no manuals existed for this kind of force, Wilder and his men were forced to improvise. Years later, Wilder left behind a detailed description of the unique tactics he developed for his brigade:

> My brigade, composed of the 17th and 72d Indiana Infantry and the 92d, 98th and 123rd Illinois Infantry and the 18th Indiana Battery, were mounted in February 1863. They were all pretty well drilled under Hardee's tactics, and as we nearly always fought dismounted, we simply kept that manner of movement, except that we made a single line with the men at intervals of six feet, as we had Spencer rifles, a magazine gun with seven rounds in the magazine, and could use a single round without drawing on the magazine, which was kept full for fighting at short range. The caliber was 52 and carried an ounce bullet, and had a range of one mile. We always tried to get close to our opponents, as we then got the benefit of rapid fire, which was very effective then. I trained my command to hold their rapid fire until our opponents were within 300 yards, when our rapid fire with aim never failed to break their charge, and if it was desirable to advance, we did so at once, and in that way lost less men than we otherwise might have done.
>
> Magazine guns are most effective at close range. I do not believe in long range fighting, as my most effective work was done at short ranges.
>
> My command had little time for drill, as we were kept close to the enemy and our movements were mostly in firing range of our opponents, and that I found to be the most useful drill we could have. My lines were never broken [emphasis in original], as we had so many shots at close quarter no troops, however capable, could withstand the fire we could give, and I always tried to compel our opponents to charge us and then our plan of action was most effective.
>
> I tried to keep our men down under cover or lying down until attacked, and then orders were to fire and load at will, always taking aim.
>
> Volley fire was mostly a waste of ammunition, and I hardly ever practiced it.
>
> My usual artillery ammunition was 80% canister and 20% percussion shells and we always exhausted the canister first.[67]

The contributions of this untrained soldier cannot be overstated.

Rosecrans, of course, did not originally intend for Wilder's command to be unique. He intended elite battalions to play a very similar role across the entire army, either at the brigade level or, when massed, at the division level, giving each

---

67 Undated letter by John T. Wilder, quoted in George H. Morgan, "Cavalry in the Eastern Theatre, 1862," thesis, US Army War College 1913-1914.

infantry division a force similar to Wilder's. When that plan miscarried, Wilder was left to devise his tactics independently. The innovations foreshadowed the Union cavalry fighting a year later, when thousands of new Spencer carbines (a shorter cavalry version of the rifle) were available to start equipping the Union cavalry forces *en masse*.

But well-equipped armies were useless if they didn't do anything, or so reasoned Washington. The spring of 1863 was something of a low point for the Federals in terms of carrying the war forward. In Virginia, the Army of the Potomac seemed checkmated by Lee's Rebels, inactive since the disaster at Fredericksburg and an equally dismal—if less bloody—attempted campaign in January. In Mississippi, Grant's troops seemed to be similarly stalemated around Vicksburg. Months passed with little action. Something had to be done to break those stalemates. Accordingly, on March 1, Halleck dispatched a wire to all the Union departmental commanders, tersely announcing that "there is a vacant major-generalcy in the Regular Army, and I am authorized to say that it will be given to the general in the field who first wins an important and decisive victory."[68]

This was clearly an effort to goad Hooker, Grant, and Rosecrans, commanding the three largest armies of the Republic, into some sort of offensive. If so, it failed. Nor did it produce immediate action in Virginia, Mississippi, or Middle Tennessee. Hooker and Grant had simply (and wisely) ignored the offer, not rising to the bait; Rosecrans did not do the same.

Rosecrans saw this ploy as nothing more than blatant bribery: an "auctioneering of honors" as he put it and he responded angrily. Another war of wired words ensued. Halleck tartly pointed out that the government had already been rewarding officers for success for the past two years of war, adding sarcastically that Rosecrans had not objected when his own name was put forward for promotion in the wake of his twin successes at Corinth and Stones River. The matter soon died away, but it marked yet another downward step in the decaying relationship between Rosecrans and his superiors.

68 OR 23, pt. 2, 95.

Gen. Braxton Bragg, commander, Army of Tennessee

Chapter Two

The Army of Tennessee's
Winter of Discontent

There is something of an enduring mythology in the lore of the American Civil War regarding Braxton Bragg. As the tale goes, Bragg retained his position at the head of the Army of Tennessee—the Confederacy's second largest field army—because of his long-term friendship with President Jefferson Davis. Another version claims that Davis wasn't especially friendly with Bragg, but he hated to have his decisions questioned and retained the obedient Bragg much longer than wise, and for much longer than any other commander of that army (June 1862 to December 1863). Neither is accurate. Not only did Davis not harbor any special affinity for Bragg; he came within a hair's-breadth of replacing him in the spring of 1863.

Braxton Bragg looked much older than his 46 years. Born on March 22, 1817, at Warrenton, North Carolina, he entered the US Military Academy in 1833. He finished fifth of the 50 graduates in his 1837 class and was commissioned a second lieutenant of artillery on July 1. He served as the 3rd Artillery's regimental adjutant from November 19, 1837, to March 8, 1838 and was promoted to first lieutenant on July 7. He served in the wars against the Seminoles in Florida during the 1830s before being transferred to Maj. Gen. Zachary Taylor's army in Texas in 1845.

He earned a brevet to captain for his gallant conduct in the defense of Fort Brown, Texas, on May 9, 1846, and was promoted to captain on June 18. His performance in several actions around Monterey, Mexico, earned him another brevet, to major, in September. He managed his guns so well at the February 23, 1847, Battle of Buena Vista that he filled gaping holes in the American line and repulsed the numerically superior Mexican forces. In so doing, he helped make

Taylor and Mississippi colonel Jefferson Davis national figures and was breveted to lieutenant colonel for his heroism.

A decade later, angered by not getting his way regarding the use of horse artillery in the army, and after not getting his choice of duty stations, Bragg resigned his commission, on January 3, 1856. He had married a wealthy woman from Louisiana, Eliza Brooks Ellis, in 1849, and after leaving the army, moved to Thibodeaux, Louisiana, to become a sugar planter. He also served on the Louisiana Board of Public Works, which involved him in the design of the state's critical levee and drainage systems. The lack of trained engineers prompted Bragg to help found the Louisiana State Seminary of Learning and Military Academy—now Louisiana State University—in 1860.

In December, after the election of Abraham Lincoln, Louisiana Governor Thomas O. Moore appointed Bragg to the state military board to organize a 5,000-man army. On January 11, 1861, Bragg's troops captured the Baton Rouge Arsenal. Once Louisiana seceded, Bragg was appointed major general and commander of the state's military forces. On March 7, he was commissioned brigadier general in the Confederate army and was assigned to command the portion of the Gulf Coast that included Mobile, Alabama, and Pensacola, Florida. On September 12, he was promoted to major general and suggested that his forces be moved north. This suggestion was ignored until the spring of 1862, when the loss of Forts Henry and Donelson triggered a crisis in the Western Theater. Then Bragg's men journeyed to Corinth, Mississippi, where they joined Gen. Albert Sidney Johnston's gathering forces—the nucleus of what became the Army of Tennessee. Much of the Confederate success at Shiloh on April 6, 1862, resulted from Bragg's supervision of the right flank. On April 12, Bragg was promoted to full general and on June 27 replaced Gen. P. G. T. Beauregard as commander of the Army of Mississippi. He retained command of that force, soon to be rechristened the Army of Tennessee, until his resignation in November 1863, leading that ill-fated command longer than any other officer.[1]

On the face of things, Bragg seemed an excellent choice for the job. The army he inherited needed training and structure, and Bragg excelled at both. He also proved to be both a competent logistician and competent strategist. He demonstrated these latter attributes in the summer and fall of 1862, when he led his

---

1 Lawrence L. Hewitt, "Braxton Bragg," included in *The Confederate Generals*, 6 vols., eds. William C. Davis and Julie Hoffman (New York: 1991), 1:112-115. For the best full-length biography of Braxton Bragg, see Earl J. Hess, *Braxton Bragg: The Most Hated Man of the Confederacy* (Chapel Hill, NC: 2016).

army from Mississippi to Kentucky in what appeared to be a resurgence of Confederate strength. But while Bragg possessed considerable martial talents, he also possessed significant flaws. He was not a great tactician, he was often overly rigid on the battlefield, and he had difficulty getting along with anyone. "There was no man in either of the contending armies who was General Bragg's superior as an organizer and a disciplinarian, but when he was in the presence of an enemy he lost his head," recalled Maj. Gen. Henry Heth of Virginia.[2]

Bragg was, "in appearance, the least prepossessing of the Confederate officers," wrote Lt. Col. Sir Arthur Fremantle, a British officer who toured the Confederacy in the spring of 1863. "He is very thin, he stoops, and has a sickly, cadaverous, haggard appearance, rather plain features, bushy black eyebrows, which unite in a tuft at the top of his nose, and a stubby, iron gray beard; but his eyes are bright and piercing. He has the reputation of being a rigid disciplinarian and of shooting freely for insubordination. I understand he is rather unpopular on this account, and also by reason of the acerbity of his manner."[3]

Major General Daniel Harvey Hill, another North Carolinian who was notorious for inability to get along with peers, became one of Bragg's corps commanders just after the conclusion of the Tullahoma Campaign in June and July 1863. Hill had ample opportunities to observe Bragg. "He was silent and reserved and seemed gloomy and despondent," wrote Hill. "He had grown prematurely old since I saw him last, and showed much nervousness. His relations with his next in command (General [Leonidas] Polk) and with some of the others of his subordinates were known not to be pleasant. His many retreats, too, had alienated the rank and file from him, or had at least taken away that enthusiasm which soldiers feel for the successful general, and which makes them obey his orders without question, and thus wins for him other successes."[4]

Against such a backdrop, the Army of Tennessee faced numerous challenges including a commanding general who was in poor health and who could not get along with his subordinates, rancor among those subordinates, and poor morale in the ranks.

2 James L. Morrison, ed. *The Memoirs of Henry Heth* (Westport, CT: 1974), 168.

3 Lt. Col. Sir Arthur Fremantle, *Three Months in the Southern States: April-June 1863* (New York: 1864), 145-146.

4 Daniel Harvey Hill, "Chickamauga—The Great Battle of the West," included in *Battles and Leaders of the Civil War*, 4 vols., eds. Robert U. Johnson and Clarence C. Buel (New York: 1884-1887), 3:639.

When Bragg's battered army sullenly abandoned Murfreesboro after the hard-fought winter of 1862-63 action at Stones River, it retreated 50 miles to a position south of the Elk River, demoralizing both the army and Southern civilians by abandoning most of Middle Tennessee to the Yankees. When the Federals did not immediately pursue, Bragg reversed course, returning to Tullahoma, about 25 miles south of Murfreesboro, on the Nashville & Chattanooga Railroad. He stationed each of his infantry corps (under Lieutenant Generals Polk and William J. Hardee) at the towns of Shelbyville and Tullahoma, respectively. From these villages, his infantry could defend a series of gaps through a long curving ridgeline, the Highland Rim, one of the key features of Tennessee's geography.

The city of Nashville sits in a large elliptical depression known as the Central Basin, surrounded by high ground in all directions. The edges of this basin form the Highland Rim. Bragg intended to fight his next battle along the southern edge of that rim. Any Union advance would have to be channeled through a series of gaps or crowded through one in a single, slow column. In either case, Bragg would be presented with a classic opportunity of military strategy: to defeat his opponent in detail. Either he could concentrate the bulk of his own army against one of those multiple columns or—should the Federals opt for a single line of advance—bring his whole force to bear against the head of a road-bound enemy column emerging through any of those narrow gaps. If there was any flaw in Bragg's new position, it was that the Duck River ran some 10 miles to the rear of his intended line, while his main depot at Tullahoma was 10 miles farther south. Should Bragg suffer another reverse, the river would become a major obstacle to any new retreat.

But Bragg had had enough of retreat. So had his men. As his army settled into late winter quarters, internal dissent beset it. In October 1862, he had abandoned Kentucky in the wake of the Battle of Perryville, a fight his men thought they won, and without the follow-up engagement they expected. This move raised many questions, both within the army and in the halls of the Confederate capital. The Kentucky Campaign's stresses highlighted differences between Bragg and his fellow departmental commander, General E. Kirby Smith (with whom Bragg was supposed to be cooperating in Kentucky in a murky relationship that never really worked), while deepening a pre-existing split between Bragg and his senior corps commander, Polk; and creating a new rift between Bragg and his other corps commander, Hardee.[5]

---

5 Bragg and Kirby Smith were supposed to cooperate in Kentucky up to the point when the two armies met, at which time Bragg—as the senior man—took command. For a variety of

Once the army returned to Tennessee, Bragg, Smith, and Polk all took turns traveling to Richmond to air grievances. Bragg pushed for the consolidation of Smith's department with his own, while Smith and Polk advocated that Bragg be replaced with Joseph E. Johnston. Hardee did not make the journey in person, but made his dissatisfaction known via courier.[6]

Those trips resolved little. Bragg won his point about Kirby Smith's Department of East Tennessee, which was subordinated to his authority in December. Smith was transferred to the Trans-Mississippi shortly thereafter. Polk and Hardee remained as corps commanders, perpetuating a situation that only deteriorated over time as relations between Bragg and his two principal subordinates worsened.

Polk's decisions were not always the best. It was Polk who, acting on another's suggestion, unilaterally occupied Columbus, Kentucky, in 1861, thereby upsetting that state's tenuous political balance and driving her into the Union camp. He maintained a regular correspondence with Jefferson Davis through the war, often to the detriment of whomever was his immediate superior at the time. Davis sustained Polk far too often, and discipline suffered as a result. Nevertheless, Polk was greatly admired in the ranks. Brigadier General St. John Liddell later noted, "he was truly a good man, lofty in sentiment, gallant and enthusiastic in the cause. He possessed all the requisites of a great soldier, except strategy and tactical combination."[7]

---

reasons, that did not happen until Bragg met Smith at Frankfort, late in the campaign, a situation that created a confusing and disjointed strategy.

6 Thomas L. Connelly, *Autumn of Glory: The Army of Tennessee, 1862-1865* (Baton Rouge, LA: 1971), 29-33.

7 Nathaniel Cheairs Hughes, Jr., ed. *Liddell's Record: St. John Richardson Liddell, Brigadier General, CSA Staff Officer and Brigade Commander, Army of Tennessee* (Baton Rouge, LA: 1985), 100-101. Leonidas Polk was born in Raleigh, North Carolina, on April 10, 1806. He was the son of a prosperous planter. He attended the University of North Carolina and then enrolled at West Point in 1823, graduating eighth in his class. Having converted to Christianity while a cadet, he resigned his commission shortly after graduation, and enrolled in the Virginia Theological Seminary and was eventually ordained an Episcopal minister. In 1830, he married Frances Ann Devereaux. After serving as rector of a church in Richmond, Virginia, Polk spent three years in Europe and then returned to the United States. He purchased a plantation in West Tennessee and pursued farming and the ministry simultaneously. In 1838, he was appointed missionary bishop of the Southwest. In 1841, he was appointed the first bishop of the Episcopal Diocese of Louisiana. He eventually settled in New Orleans. He was an ardent secessionist and led the secession of the Louisiana diocese from the Protestant Episcopal Church of the United States. With the coming of war, he offered his services to his old friend Jefferson Davis. Davis appointed him major general on June 15, 1861, and assigned him to command the valleys of the

By contrast, Hardee was a military professional in both training and service. A West Pointer of the class of 1838, he had extensive Mexican-American War experience and was best known to both armies as the author of *Rifle and Light Infantry Tactics*, the basic drill manual for most troops in the war, North or South. Though initially he was less hostile to Bragg, he criticized him sharply after Perryville. Hardee was generally respected in the army, but as historian Thomas Connelly has observed, he had two flaws that were increasingly problematic: "his dislike of final responsibility and his love of army intrigue." Hardee eventually became Bragg's decided enemy, undermining his authority at almost every turn and turning the opinions of others as well.[8]

Mississippi and lower Tennessee Rivers. In September 1861, he violated Kentucky's neutrality by occupying the important river town of Columbus, an affair that drove many Kentuckians into the service of the Union. That fall, he commanded the Confederate troops at the Battle of Belmont and quarreled with other Confederate generals, including his old West Point roommate, Gen. Albert Sidney Johnston. Davis talked Polk out of resigning his commission. Polk became a corps commander at Shiloh and remained in that position for the rest of his life. He was promoted to lieutenant general on October 11, 1862, making him the second ranking subordinate in the Confederate service after only James Longstreet. A Union artillery shell eviscerated him on Pine Mountain in Georgia during Sherman's 1864 advance on Atlanta. Bragg summed him up perfectly. "Genl. Polk by education and habit is unfitted for executing the plans of others," he wrote. "He will convince himself his own are better and follow them without reflecting on the consequences." See Steven E. Woodworth, "Leonidas Polk," included in Davis and Hoffman, *The Confederate Generals*, 5:44-47. For the most recent full-length biography of Polk, see Huston Horn, *Leonidas Polk: Warrior Bishop of the Confederacy* (Lawrence, KS: 2019).

8 William J. Hardee was born into a locally prominent Camden County, Georgia, family on October 12, 1815. After being educated by private tutors, he entered the US Military Academy in 1834 and graduated 26th out of 45 in the class of 1838. He served in the US Army continuously for the next 23 years, rising through the ranks on merit. In 1855, he was appointed major of the newly formed 2nd US Cavalry. In June 1860, he was commissioned lieutenant colonel of the 1st US Cavalry but resigned his commission on January 31, 1861, to follow Georgia into the Confederacy. In 1855, he published the army's standard manual, *Rifle and Light Infantry Tactics*, which was intended to update the drill and tactics of the army. His new manual emphasized speed and flexibility of drill and maneuver. He spent the years 1856-1860 as the commandant of cadets at West Point. On June 17, 1861, Jefferson Davis, who appreciated Hardee's abilities, appointed him brigadier general. After spending the next couple of months recruiting and training troops, he was sent to Bowling Green, Kentucky, in September 1861, where his recruits joined what became the Army of Tennessee. On October 7, 1861, he was promoted to major general, and he soon joined Polk as the chief subordinates of the Army of Tennessee. On October 11, 1862, Hardee was promoted to lieutenant general. He was one of the leaders of the cabal against Bragg, which eventually caused him to be transferred to Mississippi in July 1863. He returned to the Army of Tennessee three months later and resumed command of a corps. The men in the ranks greatly admired him and called him "Old Reliable." He was a competent professional soldier in an army that desperately needed professionalism, even though his squabbles with Bragg damaged the army's efficiency and morale. See Richard

Gen. Joseph E. Johnston, though sent to supersede Braxton Bragg, did not do so.

Valentine Museum

Perhaps the most surprising of Davis's decisions had been to assign Gen. Joseph Johnston to a sort of overall quasi-command, the Department of the West, on November 24, 1862. It was an appointment Johnston did not want. Secretly, he coveted the return of his old command, the Army of Northern Virginia, but after he was wounded at Seven Pines on May 31, 1862, Davis replaced him with Robert E. Lee—and Lee's subsequent record of success that summer made Johnston's return to that command unthinkable, especially given the difficult, feud-prone nature of the relationship between Johnston and Davis prior to Johnston's wounding.[9]

Davis's decision to appoint an overall theater commander made sense, assuming that officer had his trust and the authority to act as he saw fit. But Johnston and Davis differed on almost everything from strategy to Johnston's relative ranking in the Confederate army. Johnston believed that the best way to defend the Mississippi Valley was to unite the Departments of Mississippi (under Lt. Gen. John C. Pemberton) and the Trans-Mississippi (under Lt. Gen. Theophilus T. Holmes) and so meet the Union commander, Ulysses S. Grant, with superior numbers in order to defend Vicksburg. Davis, on the other hand, believed that troops should be shuttled between Pemberton and Bragg as needed to meet each Union threat as it developed—a strategy based on the concept of interior lines and on the hope that Grant and Rosecrans would be obliging enough to act sequentially instead of simultaneously.

M. McMurry, "William Joseph Hardee," included Davis and Hoffman, *The Confederate Generals*, 3:58-61. For an excellent full-length biography of Hardee, see Nathaniel Cheairs Hughes, Jr., *William J. Hardee: Old Reliable* (Baton Rouge, LA: 1965); Connelly, *Autumn of Glory*, 89.

9 Craig L. Symonds, *Joseph E. Johnston, a Civil War Biography* (New York: 1992), 182.

Johnston found Davis's reasoning badly flawed. He understood that a major river—the Tennessee—separated Bragg and Pemberton, and farther south, in Alabama, there was no direct rail connection between the two departments. Troops going from Mississippi to Tennessee would have to travel southeast all the way to Mobile, Alabama, on the Gulf Coast, and then head northeast through Montgomery, Atlanta, and Chattanooga before finally heading northwest to reach Bragg at Tullahoma. The only real alternative was to take trains east to Selma, Alabama, and then march overland to Montgomery (50 miles) or to Rome, Georgia (170 miles), to pick up the rails again. Even small troop transfers took weeks to accomplish.[10]

To Johnston it seemed obvious that the Confederate armies in Virginia and Tennessee were much more geographically suited to exploit any interior lines: There was a direct rail connection from Richmond, via Knoxville, to Chattanooga. Troops shuttling between Virginia and Tennessee could do so in days, not weeks, at least if the Confederacy controlled Knoxville and East Tennessee.

In Johnston's view, both sides of the Mississippi should cooperate in the defense of that region, with Virginia and Tennessee doing the same as a sort of central front. Johnston, as it turned out, had a far better grasp of the strategic realities of the Confederate position in the West than did Davis. No matter. Johnston's "suggestion," as he stated in his memoirs, "was not adopted, nor noticed." That failure ultimately helped doom the Confederacy.[11]

In mid-December, less than two weeks after Johnston reached Chattanooga to take up his new duties, a practical example of the flaw in Davis's strategic thinking played out. Grant threatened Vicksburg via a two-pronged advance. The first thrust descended the Mississippi River under his trusted subordinate William T. Sherman, while Grant directed the main army overland along the railroad from Memphis, Tennessee. In response, and over Johnston's objections, on December 15 Davis ordered Bragg to detach Maj. Gen. Carter L. Stevenson's 10,000-man infantry division to reinforce Pemberton.

---

10 The Alabama & Tennessee Railroad ran northeast from Selma for 135 miles to terminate at Blue Mountain but was still short of Rome by 50 miles. Nearly bankrupt before the war, the railroad lacked capacity. A wartime effort to extend the line all the way to Rome failed due to lack of iron. The only direct connection, the Mobile & Ohio, which ran across the length of northern Alabama, had been severed by Federal activity in the summer of 1862 and was never restored to effective Confederate service.

11 Joseph E. Johnston, *Narrative of Military Operations, Directed, During the Late War Between the States* (New York: 1874), 150.

It took two weeks for Stevenson's command to reach Vicksburg. By then, Grant's advance down the spine of the railroad through central Mississippi had been foiled by the destruction of his depot at Holly Springs, while Sherman's direct assault against the bluffs overlooking Chickasaw Bayou (just north of Vicksburg) devolved into a bloody failure. After two days of assaults on December 28 and 29, Sherman's 37,000-man force suffered 1,770 casualties, while Pemberton's much smaller garrison lost only 200. Stevenson's men began arriving on the 29th while Sherman's last attacks were in progress (Stevenson reached Vicksburg that evening), but they saw no action. The arriving trains were clearly audible to the Federals, and probably helped convince Sherman to retreat, but it is far from certain whether Sherman would have been able to capture the bastion even if Stevenson had not arrived to swell the defending garrison.[12]

Even worse, the Federals did indeed conduct simultaneous offensives. On December 26, while Stevenson's men were headed to Mississippi, Rosecrans left Nashville to attack Bragg's army at Murfreesboro. Stripped of Stevenson's large command, Rosecrans's army now outnumbered Bragg's forces by some 41,000 to roughly 37,000. On December 31, despite being outnumbered, Bragg's army nearly defeated the Federals, routing Rosecrans's right wing. Unfortunately for the Rebels' fortunes, Bragg ran out of fresh troops before victory could be clinched. Stevenson's command was sorely missed.

Thus, within days of taking up his new duties in Chattanooga, Johnston's well-founded fears were realized. It took far too long to transfer a sizeable force from Tennessee to Vicksburg—two weeks—and the Federals armies failed to obligingly wait their turn while the Rebels rushed troops hither and yon. The absence of Stevenson's 10,000 men may well have cost Bragg his battle and failed to contribute to Pemberton's success. Davis, however, remained unswayed. The disparate theaters of Mississippi and Tennessee continued under Johnston's command, while just across the Mississippi River in Arkansas, Holmes's large department remained independent.

The various disagreements within the Army of Tennessee arising out of Perryville never received a full airing in the waning days of 1862. After all, a battle loomed. But the fight at Murfreesboro seemed to be a replay of Perryville: a tactical draw followed by a precipitous retreat. This unhappy result only worsened the army's numerous problems. The Confederates achieved a notable success on December 31, seemingly coming within inches of routing Rosecrans's entire army.

---

12 David J. Eicher, *The Longest Night: A Military History of the Civil War* (New York: 2001), 391.

Then came an exhausted pause on New Year's Day, followed by a display of Confederate tactical ineptitude on January 2, when Maj. Gen. John C. Breckinridge's lone Confederate division attacked the Union left only to be bloodily repulsed. Finally, there was only another retreat. To the rank and file, the withdrawal seemed inexplicable. To the army's assembled commanders, it seemed inevitable.

On January 4, 1863, both Polk and Hardee agreed with Bragg that since Rosecrans was being heavily reinforced, the Confederates had no choice but to retire. As noted, Bragg's initial decision took the army beyond the Elk River—a decision soon reversed, but the damage was done.

Over the next few days Southern newspapers excoriated Bragg for this move. Having triumphantly broadcast Bragg's glowing early dispatches from the battlefield, drafted in the wake of the December 31 fighting, subsequent reports informing the South of Bragg's precipitous withdrawal were met with stunned disbelief and explosions of outrage. "General Bragg has certainly retreated . . . from his victory at Murfreesboro, as he did last fall from his victory at Perryville," sneered the editor of the Richmond *Examiner*.[13]

On January 9, the Chattanooga *Daily Rebel* published a lengthy and accurate critique, hitting upon the key points of contention. "Gen. Bragg, it must be owned, is not popular. He is unfortunate in having alienated, through some cause unknown to us, many of his subordinates, whilst the rank and file of his army entertain neither confidence or affection for him." As for the retreat, "his earlier telegrams were hasty and inconsiderate. . . . He was too eager to let the country know that he had gained a smashing victory. Thus the Richmond papers . . . [were] full of an imaginary triumph. The reaction will be great when these papers and their readers learn that we have been obliged ourselves to retire." And even though the *Rebel* admitted that Bragg "deserves much credit" for "his energy and admirable talent for organization, . . . His great misfortune lies in two deficiencies—the affection of his troops and his sagacity as a field marshal. . . . His is not a Napoleonic genius."[14]

For Bragg, perhaps the worst blow came when the formerly sympathetic *Mobile Register* published a critical account penned by correspondent Samuel C. Reid. Reid drew upon officers serving on the staffs of John C. Breckinridge and William Hardee as his sources. Reid's principal conspirator was Col. Theodore O'Hara, a Kentuckian serving with Breckinridge. O'Hara, outraged over Bragg's disparaging

---

13 Grady McWhiney, *Braxton Bragg and Confederate Defeat, Volume I* (Tuscaloosa, AL: 1991), 374.

14 "The Situation," *Chattanooga Daily Rebel*, January 9, 1863.

remarks concerning Kentucky's lack of martial ardor during the Perryville campaign, hated Bragg unremittingly. "B.B. [Braxton Bragg]" O'Hara once wrote, "reminds me of the poetic simile of the 'scorpion begirt by fire.' If he bites himself he is sure to die of his own loathsome venom."[15]

Prior to Murfreesboro, there had been little enough time to resolve the army's deepening command crisis. Now, in the wake of another retreat, resentments blossomed while pointed questions were asked. Was Bragg fit to command? The public outcry cut the beleaguered commander to the quick. On January 10, Bragg assembled his staff at his new headquarters in Tullahoma to read to them one particularly damning indictment. According to Col. George Brent, the Chattanooga *Daily Rebel* "charged that 'he had lost the confidence of his Army—that a change was necessary & that the retrograde movement from Murfreesboro was against the advice of his general officers.'"[16]

Bragg was furious, especially at the suggestion that his decision to retreat was made in opposition to his subordinates. Bragg knew full well that his officers had counseled retreat after both Perryville and Murfreesboro. He viewed as a betrayal the fact that apparently some of those men now went behind his back to say otherwise.

Another enduring myth is the idea that Bragg was an unmitigated failure as a general. As has been observed, he in fact achieved considerable success logistically, operationally, and administratively. The Chattanooga *Daily Rebel* was not wrong in praising him for those things. Despite the quixotic outcome of the Kentucky campaign, it demonstrated that Bragg had real abilities. He not only orchestrated one of the largest strategic movements of the war, shifting his army from Tupelo, Mississippi, nearly to the banks of the Ohio River, but also outmaneuvered his Federal opponents and left them scrambling to catch up. Even though he abandoned Kentucky in the wake of Perryville, the campaign still reversed a spring of Union successes, restored a sense of balance to the Western Theater and bought the Confederacy at least a half year of life. Moreover, the Army of Tennessee became a well-honed force under his tutelage: effective, resilient, and potent.

However, Bragg's many flaws as a leader offset these positives. He was short-tempered, quick to find blame, quick to take credit for success, but slow to recognize others' achievements. He was often in ill-health, which, in turn, made

15 Nathaniel Cheairs Hughes, Jr., and Thomas Clayton Ware, *Theodore O'Hara, Poet-Soldier of the Old South* (Knoxville, TN: 1998), 128.

16 McWhiney, *Braxton Bragg*, 375.

him more irascible. Biographer Grady McWhiney summarized him as "courageous, and at times imaginative, resourceful, and bold. But he was never patient, either with his men or with the enemy, and he lacked that imperturbability and resolution so necessary in field commanders. Handicapped by poor health, he had no real taste for combat. And he was not lucky. Nor did he . . . inspire confidence in his subordinates. Notoriously inept at getting along with people he disliked, he simply could not win the loyalty of his chief lieutenants." As St. John Richardson Liddell, a brigade commander in Hardee's Corps, explained, "Bragg's manner made him malignant enemies and callous, indifferent friends."[17]

By the spring of 1863, his failing physical condition had grown especially bad, exacerbating these problems. Colonel John H. Savage of the 16th Tennessee described Bragg at this time as "mentally and physically, an old, worn out man, unfit to actively manage an army in the field." Even Bragg himself "admitted to a siege of boils which culminated in 'a general breakdown.'"[18]

Following that January meeting, Bragg charted what proved to be a disastrous course. Seeking justification for his decisions in Kentucky and at Murfreesboro, he sent out a written questionnaire to each of his corps and divisional commanders. Ostensibly, that document was an effort to get his generals on record as having approved the abandonment of Kentucky, thereby refuting the more scurrilous newspaper claims. He also stated that if he had lost the confidence of his officers and men, he would resign. Of course, he fully expected to be sustained. His staff, which had already been charged with obtaining informal answers to these questions, knew better. They begged him not to send out the circular. Unlike their boss, they knew what the answers would show. Bragg insisted, exposing the undercurrent of resentment among his subordinates.[19]

Hardee and his generals were the first to answer. Hardee's command included Breckinridge's division, which had become something of a hotbed of anti-Bragg sentiment, containing as it did the Kentucky Brigade and many Kentuckian officers. Hardee, Breckinridge, and Patrick Cleburne equivocated somewhat over the question of retreat, but did not materially dispute Bragg's recollections. They

---

17 McWhiney, *Braxton Bragg*, 390; Hughes, *Liddell's Record*, 116. One might take exception to McWhiney's observation that Bragg "had no real taste for combat." Bragg repeatedly proved to be an aggressive fighter.

18 John H. Savage, *The Life of John H. Savage* (Nashville, TN: 1903). 137; McWhiney, *Braxton Bragg*, 389.

19 Connelly, *Autumn of Glory*, 74-5. Connelly has an extensive discussion of the problems between Bragg and his subordinates. See 69-92 for a full accounting of the situation.

did all agree, however, that the general officers of the corps "whose judgement you have invoked, are unanimous in the opinion that a change of command of this army is necessary."[20]

Leonidas Polk was on leave in North Carolina at the time and hence did not immediately provide an answer. His divisional commanders—Benjamin F. "Frank" Cheatham and Jones Withers—split on the issue of a resignation (Cheatham very much for and Withers against) but declined to make a formal reply to that question. When Polk returned to the army in late January, he also equivocated, much to Hardee's annoyance. But on February 4, Polk sent a private correspondence directly to President Davis, explaining that had he and his generals given an honest answer, they would have joined the general chorus for resignation.[21]

On January 17, Bragg also sent a private letter directly to Davis via "a confidential Staff Officer as the bearer of a note in which reference will be made to matters that would not properly come within the scope of an official report," largely to discredit Hardee and especially Breckinridge. The officer, Lt. Col. David Urquhart, was a fellow Louisianan and family friend who had served with Bragg since Shiloh, and more than once, he conveyed sensitive documents from Bragg for Davis's personal perusal. Now Urquhart's "note," coupled with Urquhart's own observations, alarmed Davis, who finally understood the extent of the burgeoning mutiny rending the ranks of the army.[22]

On January 22, Davis ordered Joseph E. Johnston to "proceed promptly to the headquarters of Bragg's army . . . [where] you will, I trust, be able, by conversation with General Bragg and others of his command, to decide what the best interests of the service require. . . . Though my confidence in General Bragg is unshaken, it cannot be doubted that he is distrusted by his officers and troops." In short, Johnston was to determine whether Bragg needed to be replaced.[23]

Johnston reached Tullahoma on January 27. Even though he was nominally already Bragg's commander, Johnston proved a singularly poor choice for the job at hand. Many influential Confederates, both within and without the Army of Tennessee, wanted Johnston to supplant Bragg and take direct command of the

20 OR 20, pt. 1, 683.

21 Samuel J. Martin, *General Braxton Bragg, C.S.A.* (Jefferson, NC: 2011), 250.

22 Crist, *The Papers of Jefferson Davis,* 9:28-33.

23 OR 23, pt. 2, 614.

army. Johnston, who possessed a strong (some would say overly developed) sense of personal honor and whose own relationship with President Davis poisoned by recent quarrels, recoiled from the duty. Instead, Johnston cast Bragg in a positive light, noting the improvements in discipline and the health of the army. Finally, Johnston explicitly recommended that if Bragg were removed, he should not be the one to take the helm.

In truth, Joe Johnston had considerable positives to report back to the War Department. In addition to the 10,000 men lost to Mississippi in December, Murfreesboro cost Bragg 10,000 casualties. In early January, the Army of Tennessee numbered perhaps 25,000 men, and the Confederate conscription bureau was doing almost nothing to fill those gaps in the ranks. On January 16, based on a new authorization from the war department, Bragg created the Volunteer and Conscript Bureau of the Army of Tennessee. Controversial Brig. Gen. Gideon J. Pillow, whose combat record so far in this war was far from stellar, headed the new office.

This new job was a perfect fit. Pillow, a well-known Tennessee politician and Mexican War veteran with a checkered combat history, zealously pitched into his new duties. He ruthlessly rounded up stragglers, deserters, and men avoiding conscription. Supported by four companies of cavalry and details of officers from various regiments, he scoured county after county in Tennessee and Alabama, returning to the army thousands of men who were away without leave. Though his new mission brought him into repeated conflicts with the existing conscription bureau, he would not be swayed. Additionally, his efforts also brought in badly needed foodstuffs and even slaves to serve as teamsters, freeing up 2,000 detailed white men for combat.[24]

The ranks swelled so quickly that General Bragg soon complained that he lacked sufficient arms to equip them all. On January 20, the Army of Tennessee reported an "effective total" of 40,627 and an "aggregate present" of 49,002. By February 20 there were 42,088 effectives and 55,128 aggregate. By April 10, there were 49,401 effectives, with 65,077 total men present. Though the April numbers included the roughly 3,500 reinforcements of Maj. Gen. Earl Van Dorn's Cavalry

---

24 Nathaniel Cheairs Hughes, Jr., and Roy P. Stonesifer, Jr., *The Life & Wars of Gideon J. Pillow* (Chapel Hill, NC: 1993), 260-263. By March 1863, the conscription bureau managed to curtail much of Pillow's effort, so much so that on April 10, Bragg's headquarters noted that "since the enforcement of the conscript law by officers of this command has been suspended, this army has ceased to increase."

Corps, the Tennessee army's recovery was astounding and remarkably fast by any measure.[25]

"On [February] 13th," noted Bragg staffer J. Stoddard Johnston, "General Joe Johnston," having witnessed the beginning of this numerical renaissance, "left for Chattanooga, highly pleased with the condition of the army." Despite Joseph Johnston's rosy reports to the contrary, however, neither the army's command nor its morale problems were so easily resolved.

Sustained by Davis and Johnston, Bragg continued his efforts to root out the most disloyal subordinates. Frank Cheatham, who was reportedly so drunk at Murfreesboro that he fell off his horse, came in for some discredit, though no charges were filed. Bragg contented himself with ignoring Cheatham's role in his official report, which Cheatham rightly took as a snub. But he eschewed any official action against Cheatham, who retained command of his division (and eventually, a corps) for the rest of the war.[26]

Another implacable Bragg foe, Maj. Gen. John P. McCown, fared worse. McCown also commanded a division under Hardee, troops formally transferred to the Army of Tennessee after Perryville. They led the dawn attack at Murfreesboro. McCown performed poorly on December 31, but it was only when he ran afoul of the Confederacy's commissary and procurement rules (in a dispute over the purchase of hogs) on February 27 that Bragg had him "arrested, charged with disobeying orders, and sent back to Chattanooga to await trial." This was simply a convenient pretext. Bragg informed General Johnston that he would be delighted if McCown were gone for good, since "his influence is most pernicious."[27]

Bragg's main efforts were nonetheless directed elsewhere. Breckinridge, who led the unsuccessful assault on January 2, and whose staff Bragg suspected of leaking damaging innuendo to the newspapers, now faced Bragg's full fury. Bragg published his official report on the Battle of Murfreesboro in late February. It detailed numerous blunders committed by Breckinridge, as Bragg saw them.

---

25 *OR* 20, pt. 2, 503; and *OR* 23, pt. 2, 619, 643,749. "Effectives," noted a circular issued by Bragg's headquarters, "must include only the field fighting force—those who are carried onto the field of battle with fire-arms in their hands." It excluded even officers and color-bearers. The Federal armies used a category called "Present for Duty," which did included officers, making direct manpower comparisons a little problematic. "Aggregate," used by both armies, simply represented all men then with the army, including the sick and detailed men.

26 Christopher Losson, *Tennessee's Forgotten Warriors: Frank Cheatham and His Confederate Division* (Knoxville, TN: 1989), 90; Hughes, *Liddell's Record*, 119.

27 Martin, *Braxton Bragg*, 255.

Breckinridge and others took exception, especially to those parts of the report in which Bragg seemingly exceeded the truth in his haste to tarnish Breckinridge's reputation.

Officially, John Breckinridge declined to make any overt response. Breckinridge, the vice president of the United States from 1857-1861 during the ineffectual administration of James Buchanan, believed in remaining above the fray. When others urged him to challenge Bragg on the field of honor—a rumor that journeyed all the way to Richmond—Breckinridge demurred. "It is a great mistake," he falsely informed Confederate Congressman and former staff officer George B. Hodge of Kentucky, "to suppose that there is a 'controversy' between Gen. Bragg and myself. In a word, [I] have done nothing in conflict with strict military propriety."[28]

Breckinridge could personally afford to remain above the fray only because so many others were willing to fight on his behalf. A huge fight erupted in the Confederate Congress between pro- and anti-Bragg factions, nominally over a resolution of thanks extended to Bragg for Murfreesboro. Excerpts of rival battle reports were read in the halls and into the record. On March 7, the head of the Confederate bureau of war, Capt. Robert Garlick Hill Kean, reported the brouhaha. "Bragg's report of the battle of Murfreesboro . . . bears very hardly on Breckinridge, attributing the failure on the right to his blundering," he wrote. "It is

28 Davis, *Breckinridge*, 354. Major General John C. Breckinridge was born in Lexington, Kentucky, on January 16, 1821. He came from an old-line, prominent Kentucky family that included President Thomas Jefferson's attorney general. He attended Centre College and the College of New Jersey (now Princeton University), but he ultimately graduated from Transylvania University with a law degree. Breckinridge set up a law office in Kentucky and eventually became active in the Democratic Party. He served as a major in a Kentucky volunteer regiment during the Mexican War, but he saw no combat. He was elected to the state legislature in 1848 and then to Henry Clay's old Congressional district in 1851. He served two terms in Congress before accepting the Democratic Party's vice-presidential nomination in 1856 and, at 35 years old, was elected the youngest vice president in American history to date. He served one term as vice president and then ran for president in 1860, finishing second to Lincoln in the electoral vote. Learning he was to be arrested for treason, he fled Washington, DC, and accepted a commission as a brigadier general in the Confederate service in November 1861. In May 1862, he was promoted to major general and continuously headed a division in various commands until Davis nominated him to become secretary of war in January 1865. Breckinridge was appointed in February 1865 and helped improve Confederate supply and logistics. The Breckinridge family has a long and honorable history of public service; the general's grandson became a lieutenant general in the US Army and his great-great-grandson was killed in action during the Korean War. William C. Davis, "John Cabell Breckinridge," included in *The Confederate General*, 1:126-127. For a full-length biographical treatment, see Davis, *Breckinridge*.

quite manifest that there are deep quarrels in that army, and that Bragg is cordially hated by a large number of his officers."[29]

Davis acted. On March 9, wrote Kean, "General Bragg was relieved by telegram to General Johnston, directing the latter to take command of the army in Tennessee." Davis's wording brooked no argument. "Order General Bragg to report to the War Department here for conference," he wrote. "Assume yourself direct charge of the army in Middle Tennessee." On the face of it, the issue was resolved. Bragg was out, and Johnston was in. Had that order been followed, it is interesting to speculate how the course of the war might have changed. But for various reasons, it was never implemented.[30]

That telegram caught up to Johnston at Mobile on March 12. Johnston was on his way to visit Lt. Gen. John C. Pemberton, commanding the Army of Mississippi, who was then dealing with a threatened Union advance from Corinth. Johnston reversed course and headed for Tullahoma but did not reach that place until March 19. Along the way, he argued (via telegraph) with Richmond about reinforcements, explaining that he had no troops with which to bolster Pemberton, and pressed for 20,000 men to be sent from Virginia—an impossible request, as Johnston probably knew, but in making it, he reiterated his point about mutually supporting (or non-supporting) departments.[31]

Joe Johnston reached Tullahoma to find Bragg facing an active enemy of his own, as well as a personal crisis. March 1863 saw frequent skirmishes and minor engagements between the Army of Tennessee and Rosecrans's Army of the Cumberland. In addition, Bragg's wife Eliza was dangerously ill with typhoid fever. "On account of Mrs. Bragg's critical condition," Johnston wrote in a wire to James Seddon, the Confederate secretary of war, "I shall not now give the order for which I came. The country is becoming practicable. Should the enemy advance, General Bragg will be indispensable here."[32]

This curious missive contained an inherent contradiction. If Bragg's wife was too ill to travel and her condition too grave for Bragg to leave her, wasn't he also

---

29 Edward Younger, ed. *Inside the Confederate Government, The Diary of Robert Garlick Hill Kean* (Baton Rouge, LA: 1957), 42.

30 Younger, *Inside the Confederate Government*, 43; OR 23, pt. 2, 674.

31 Symonds, *Joseph E. Johnston*, 200; OR 23, pt. 2, 684-685.

32 OR 23, pt. 2, 708. Typhoid fever is a bacterial infection that comes from drinking contaminated water. Its symptoms usually last about a month, and without proper treatment with antibiotics, patients often die after the third week. It is a dangerous disease and was often fatal during the days before antibiotics were generally available.

too distracted to command the army in case of a battle? While the Braggs might not be up for the ordered trip to Richmond, certainly Eliza's illness provided another strong reason for Johnston to take command.

And yet Johnston never did so. Perhaps he felt that relieving Bragg during his wife's illness was adding insult to injury. Or perhaps it was an excuse to avoid taking command of the obviously dysfunctional Army of Tennessee. Johnston remained at Tullahoma for several weeks, but issued no orders replacing Bragg, announcing his own assumption of command, naming his staff, or any of the other necessary communications for a transfer of authority. Bragg's existing staff remained in place. Even the war department continued to issue communications addressed to "General Bragg, commanding Department No. 2, Tullahoma." In short, while Johnston supervised things in Bragg's stead, Bragg retained official command.[33]

In response, Davis sent yet another envoy to Tullahoma, 32-year-old Col. William Preston Johnston, the son of the late Gen. Albert Sidney Johnston. Colonel Johnston was one of Davis's most trusted aides, but he also proved to be the wrong man for the job. The younger Johnston arrived on March 23. One of the first things he did was visit Leonidas Polk, who had been close with his father, and Brig. Gen. William Preston of Breckinridge's division, for whom he was named and who had often acted as a surrogate father at various times in his life when Albert Sidney was absent. Given these ties, William Johnston was probably sympathetic to the Kentucky faction's desire to see Bragg gone. If so, he punted on the important question. When he met with Joe Johnston, the general pointedly stated only that "he had temporary command . . . during General Bragg's absence." General Johnston also used those conversations to reiterate again his favored strategic combinations. The young colonel next met with Braxton Bragg and explored in detail the condition of the army. His final report, which he turned in on April 15, echoed General Johnston's findings in many respects by commending the state of the army's logistics, subsistence, training, armaments, and discipline. In short, the Army of Tennessee appeared to be in pretty good shape. Significantly, the colonel made no mention of any trouble amongst the commanders, nor of Bragg being relieved.[34]

33 Symonds, *Johnston,* 200.

34 *OR* 23, pt. 2, 747. Albert Sidney Johnston, a close friend of Jefferson Davis, was mortally wounded on the first day of the Battle of Shiloh and bled to death on the battlefield.

By then, Jefferson Davis already knew full well that Joseph Johnston was not about to execute his March 9 order. Though Elise's health had improved, Johnston's was deteriorating. On April 10, Johnston wired Davis that he was "not now able to serve in the field. General Bragg is therefore necessary here." The subtext was clear: if Davis wanted to replace Bragg as commander of the Army of Tennessee, someone else would have to do it.[35]

Why did Johnston adamantly refuse to replace Bragg, even defying a direct order to do so? Johnston's most recent biographer has stated that "Johnston wanted command of the Army of Tennessee, and he wanted it badly, but would not say so officially or publicly. He would have to be ordered to take it over his own objections; in his view, there was no other way he could assume the assignment honorably." True enough on the face of it, but even when Johnston was so ordered, he still found a way to duck the responsibility. In doing so, he further exasperated both Jefferson Davis and Secretary of War Seddon. "I do not think your personal honor is involved," snapped a frustrated Davis. More gently, Seddon "urg[ed] him to disregard 'considerations of scrupulous delicacy.'" Such prodding had no effect. For whatever reason, Joe Johnston was not the man for the job.[36]

Johnston's evasiveness only further damaged his standing in Richmond. "He treats the Department as an enemy with whom he holds no communications which he can avoid, and against which he only complains and finds fault," complained the perceptive Captain Kean on April 15. "He is a very little man, has achieved nothing, full of himself; [and] above all other things, eaten up with morbid jealousy of Lee and of all his superiors in position, rank, or glory. I apprehend the gravest disasters from his command in the western department. Time will show."[37]

The divisive internal dissent roiling the ranks of the Army of Tennessee's high command was never resolved. It remained widespread, ran deep, and continued to fester through the spring of 1863. Johnston tried to pretend otherwise, and Davis hoped against hope that things would improve. But Bragg certainly knew the truth. On May 22, he gloomily informed Davis, "it will not be possible for the cordial official confidence to exist again."[38]

35 Ibid., pt. 2, 745.

36 Symonds, *Johnston*, 198.

37 Younger, *Inside the Confederate Government*, 50.

38 Braxton Bragg to Jefferson Davis, May 22, 1863, Braxton Bragg Papers, Perkins Library, Duke University.

Strategic decisions

All this internal discord seemingly obscured a more basic strategic question: how best to defend the trans-Appalachian South? Here, too, while affairs appeared to have stabilized, the core issue was never resolved.

During the first half of 1862, the nascent Confederacy very nearly came to complete ruin as its widely dispersed, badly outnumbered forces proved unable to stop the Union advance. When Gen. Albert Sidney Johnston's initial defensive line was shattered, first at Mill Springs, Kentucky, in January and then at Forts Henry and Donelson in Tennessee a month later, the Confederate strategic situation collapsed in spectacular fashion. Johnston tried and failed to redress the balance at Shiloh, which cost him his life. By June, with Johnston dead, Confederate forces retreated deep into Mississippi and Alabama. The geographic losses were near-catastrophic. Large swaths of the Confederacy, including three of the South's largest cities—New Orleans, Memphis, and Nashville—were all in Union hands.

Bragg's invasion of Kentucky helped stem that tide. For a time, and in conjunction with Robert E. Lee's invasion of Maryland, it seemed as though the South might redeem much of that conquered territory. That it did not was one reason why Bragg's retreat provoked such anger. By the beginning of 1863, Joe Johnston's strategic conundrum seemed no different than that of his predecessor: too few troops to defend too much space. He felt he could only wait for the next blow. In the first days of January, with news of Bragg's most recent defeat and retreat at Murfreesboro, it seemed like that next blow had landed.

Equally important to the mission of stopping that Union flood tide, however, was the Rebel cavalry. In conjunction with the movements of the South's field armies, a series of successful Confederate cavalry raids crippled Union logistics. In August, John Hunt Morgan's destruction of the Big South railroad tunnel at Gallatin, Tennessee, had proved more significant than the fighting at Perryville. Sherman's descent on Vicksburg might have been blunted at Chickasaw Bluffs, but it took Van Dorn's destructive December strike against Grant's supply line at Holly Springs to halt the Federal advance in its tracks and even forced Grant to retreat. Other, less spectacular raids also played their roles: Frank Armstrong and Nathan Bedford Forrest in West Tennessee, Morgan's return to Kentucky at Christmastime 1862, and even Joseph Wheeler's savaging of Rosecrans's wagon trains during Stones River all had an impact.

It was always clear that in terms of infantry and artillery, the South could never muster numerical superiority over its opponent. Those arms fought valiantly, even sometimes superbly, on the battlefield. But so too did their blue-clad enemy. In most of the battles of the war, the North brought greater numbers of those two arms to the field, and, in general, achieved parity of quality. But as noted above, Confederate cavalry had an outsize effect on the course of the war in 1862. Almost by default, then, Confederate commanders sought to exploit that advantage.

Thus, the Southern cavalry arm was an exception to the usual harsh arithmetic facing Confederate armies, which were nearly always outnumbered and outgunned. Thanks to active Confederate recruitment coupled with short-sighted Union planning that discouraged Federal cavalry enlistments in 1862, the Rebel mounted arm possessed a clear numerical advantage over its opponents. On December 31, 1862, Pemberton reported 4,883 cavalry present for duty, of which 3,882 were incorporated into a single corps capable of concerted action. Bragg's mounted arm reported 10,470, almost all organized into a single large division commanded by Brigadier General Wheeler.[39]

In addition to these 15,000 horsemen assigned to the two main Rebel armies, several thousand additional troopers were stationed in Northern Alabama or East Tennessee. Thus, by the end of 1862, Confederate cavalry strength in the West ran close to 20,000. By contrast, Grant's army contained 5,500 cavalrymen in November, with Rosecrans reporting only 4,549 in his February return. While there was some additional blue cavalry in theater, those units were broken into small escorts assigned to infantry commands or were parceled out to guard rear areas—a problem the Confederates did not have because they were operating mainly in friendly territory. Effectively, Rebel cavalry enjoyed nearly a two-one numeric superiority over its opponents.[40]

When Joseph Johnston learned of Bragg's retirement to the Duck River, he was in Jackson, Mississippi, conferring with Pemberton. Bragg needed help, but Johnston was loath to send Carter Stevenson's division back to Tennessee. The moment he did so, Grant and Sherman might unite and renew their advance on Vicksburg. The endless shuttling of 10,000 Rebel infantrymen back and forth was Johnston's worst strategic nightmare.

Instead, he decided to send Maj. Gen. Earl Van Dorn. Van Dorn now commanded four cavalry brigades, stationed at Grenada, Mississippi, where they found it difficult to subsist in that picked-over country. Moving them to Tennessee would be the most efficient means of reinforcing Bragg quickly, while

---

39 *OR* 17, pt. 2, 814; *OR* 20, pt. 2, 446. At Bragg's behest, Wheeler was promoted to major general on January 20, 1863.

40 Ibid., 17, pt. 2, 337-338.

simultaneously providing these troopers with better forage for man and beast. General Pemberton was leery of losing the bulk of his mounted arm, but Johnston prevailed. He saw the cavalry as his only effective means of quickly reinforcing the Tennessee front. To Bragg, Johnston explained that "one of Van Dorn's great objects will be to cover your left by preventing Federal troops from going from West to Middle Tennessee. . . . This is the only pressure possible by the troops in Mississippi."[41]

Earl Van Dorn was one of the Confederacy's more colorful characters. Diminutive, flashy, and confident, he looked like the epitome of a cavalryman. A West Pointer (class of 1842, the same as James Longstreet and William S. Rosecrans), he was also a Mexican-American War hero and friend of Jefferson Davis. He first saw service in Virginia, but soon was transferred to Arkansas. His record was controversial. He led an ambitious—some said reckless—offensive that culminated in defeat at the Battle of Pea Ridge in March 1862. Transferred east of the Mississippi River, he suffered another defeat at the hands of his old classmate Rosecrans at Corinth in October. Having twice failed at the head of an army, Pemberton decided that Van Dorn was better suited to cavalry operations than to full-fledged field command. Holly Springs proved the merit of that decision.[42]

Initially, Van Dorn's command consisted of nothing more than a motley assortment of various regiments and battalions. On January 20, 1863, prior to departing for Tennessee, Van Dorn issued General Order No. 3, creating four brigades, three of which formed a division under Brig. Gen. William H. "Red" Jackson. The fourth, under Colonel Philip T. Roddey, was not yet ready to undertake field operations. Roddey had only been made a colonel in December of 1862 and was still in the process of recruiting and forming his own regiment, the 4th Alabama Cavalry. So far, his brigade consisted only of the 4th Alabama and "other troops not designated."[43]

Because many of his regiments were only recently remounted after serving as infantry through much of the fall of 1862, Van Dorn instituted top-to-bottom reforms. Cavalry procedures had to be relearned. Here, recalled Private A. W. Sparks of the 9th Texas Cavalry, "Van Dorn issued his celebrated 'Order No. 5,' in which he prescribed the minutest rules for the government of his corps, whether in

---

41 Ibid., 833.

42 Ezra J. Warner, *Generals in Gray: Lives of the Confederate Commanders* (Baton Rouge, LA: 1959), 314-315.

43 *OR* 24, pt. 3, 592; *OR* 23, pt. 1, 733.

camp or on the march. Proper distances were prescribed to be observed on the march between companies, regiments, brigades and divisions; a regular system of bugle calls was formulated: challenges and replies of videttes, etc., etc. —the whole concluding with the impetuous declaration: 'Cavalry knows no danger—knows no failure; what it is ordered to do, it must do!'"

Two weeks later on February 2, having shifted his command 70 miles east from Grenada to Okolona, Van Dorn shuffled the deck again. He swapped some regiments between brigades to balance numbers, but his primary purpose was to create a second division within his corps to be led by newly arrived Brig. Gen. William T. Martin, fresh from Virginia. Though born in Kentucky Martin was a lawyer and district attorney in prewar Natchez. He spent the first two years of the war in the East as major and lieutenant colonel of the Jeff Davis Legion Cavalry, serving under Maj. Gen. Jeb Stuart. With more troops being raised in the West, Martin was promoted two grades and sent to take command of a brigade of fellow Mississippians, first under Wheeler and now under Van Dorn. With this latest reorganization, he stepped up to lead his old brigade, now under newly promoted Brig. Gen. George B. Crosby, and Colonel Roddey's nascent command.[44]

The trip to Tennessee proved arduous. Heavy rain flooded the creeks and rivers, slowing the move. On February 16, Van Dorn and three of his brigades crossed the Tennessee River at Florence, Alabama. Roddey was left in northern Alabama to complete his organization and to guard that part of the state from Northern incursion. He remained there for most of the rest of the war. On February 21, the remainder of Van Dorn's command reached Columbia, Tennessee, where Van Dorn, ambitiously, reported to Johnston that his men were ready for action "on the north bank of the Cumberland [River] and on the banks of the Ohio, unless General Bragg is threatened by Rosecrans very soon." With his arrival at Columbia, Van Dorn added 3,443 officers and men to Bragg's mounted strength.[45]

At virtually the same moment, on February 20, Bragg's other mounted units reached a new high, reporting 12,222 officers and men present for duty. Of those, 11,610 were theoretically concentrated in that single cavalry "division" led by Joseph Wheeler, recently promoted to major general. With the addition of Van

44 Ibid., 24, pt. 3, 614; Stuart W. Sanders, "Maj. Gen. William Thompson Martin," in *Kentuckians In Gray, Confederate Generals and Field Officers from the Bluegrass State,* eds. Bruce Allardice and Lawrence Lee Hewitt (Lexington, KY: 2008), 194-195.

45 Douglas Hale, *The Third Texas Cavalry in the Civil War* (Norman, OK: 1993), 160-61; OR 52, pt. 2, 425.

Dorn's troopers, Bragg now had 15,000 cavalrymen at his disposal, about one-third as many men as his entire army.[46]

Just 26 years old in 1863, Wheeler was young, but he was a West Pointer of the class of 1859 with prewar cavalry service. Although he began the war as colonel of the 19th Alabama Infantry, Bragg transferred him to the mounted arm after Shiloh.

On paper Wheeler was perfect for the job. Even though he had graduated last in his class in cavalry tactics, he spent nearly a year at the cavalry school at the army's Carlisle Barracks in Pennsylvania and another year or so out West on active duty. His experience was just what Bragg needed to turn raw recruits into effective horsemen. Wheeler proved adept at training but had significant problems enforcing discipline. Moreover, even though he escaped most of the recriminations that came out of the Kentucky Campaign, he failed to divine Federal movements and intentions during that period. It isn't surprising, then, that many of the decisions Bragg, Kirby Smith, and other senior commanders reached proved to be flawed. Bragg either overlooked or was not fully aware of these issues and regarded Wheeler highly. One reason might have been Wheeler's loyalty; in stark contrast to the dissent and discontent emanating from many of Bragg's senior infantry commanders, Wheeler remained steadfastly committed to Bragg. Still, unifying the various mounted brigades into a single command was a sound decision.

The horsemen at Bragg's disposal could be divided into two categories: conventional cavalry intended for scouting, screening, and other traditional mounted missions; and large numbers of irregular partisans who proved more adept at raiding. The force was loosely grouped into four brigades of unequal size, each reporting to the army commander independently. Wheeler's own brigade and that of Brig. Gen. John Wharton were both large, each numbering between 2,500 and 3,000 men. The brigades of Brigadiers Abraham Buford and John S. Pegram were much smaller, consisting of only two or three regiments apiece. Wheeler's and Wharton's commands were too big to be managed by a single brigadier, while Buford's and Pegram's commands were too small to be particularly effective.

Two partisan brigades rounded out the picture, those of Nathan Bedford Forrest and John Hunt Morgan. Both men had already achieved a certain degree of fame (notoriety, in the North) for successful raids in the fall and winter of 1862.

---

46 OR 23, pt. 2, 645. The rest of the Army of Tennessee's cavalry was serving as company-size escorts at various headquarters. Wheeler's division was more an administrative designation than a tactical one.

Forrest's exploits in West Tennessee from December 15 to 29 captured troops and supplies and badly disrupted Federal communications in the region.[47]

Morgan had been even more daring. The destruction of the rail tunnel at Gallatin was a tremendous coup, with a significant practical effect, fully equal to Van Dorn's success at Holly Springs. Then came the raid on Hartsville and the late December raid deep into Kentucky. Christened the "Christmas Raid' for obvious reasons, the affair was clearly a brilliant success, especially since it shut down the just-reopened railroad for another five weeks.

Each brigade was large, comprising 2,000 to 2,500 men. Forrest's force was mainly Tennesseans, while Morgan's men were virtually all Kentuckians. Both generals came to view their commands with a proprietary eye, having built them up over the previous months. On January 22, Bragg promoted Wheeler to major general and placed him "in command of all cavalry in Middle Tennessee." As if to mirror the Army of Tennessee's command problems, Wheeler faced considerable opposition from two of his subordinates: Wharton and Forrest.

John Wharton was a Texas lawyer, the colonel of the 8th Texas Cavalry until promoted to brigadier on November 10, 1862, just 10 days after Wheeler achieved the same grade. Wharton and his large brigade performed well at the battle of Murfreesboro, helping to turn Rosecrans's right flank and taking many prisoners. But with Bragg's promoting Joe Wheeler and making him chief of his cavalry, Wharton, sensitive to slights and prone to argument, was resentful.

Forrest was resentful, too, stemming from the engagement at Dover, Tennessee, on February 3, 1863. Bragg's first mission for his newly promoted cavalry commander was to again try to interdict the Cumberland River downstream from Nashville near the site of the former Confederate stronghold of Fort Donelson, now a Union post. In early January, Wheeler had led a raid near Clarksville that destroyed several transports. Now Bragg and Wheeler hoped to again seize and sink any Union riverboats they could find; with the L&N Railroad out of action thanks to Morgan, the Cumberland was Rosecrans's only remaining viable supply route. Wheeler set off with Wharton's brigade, and Bragg ordered Forrest to join him with 800 more troops.

Wheeler found and destroyed no riverboats because the alert Federals had halted river traffic. Frustrated, Wheeler decided that his combined force— about 2,800 men, once Forrest arrived—should be able to overpower Fort Donelson's

---

47 For a full accounting of Forrest's West Tennessee Raid, see Jordon and Pryor, *Campaigns of Forrest*, 193-222.

800 defenders. Forrest strenuously objected, but Wheeler persevered. The result was a bloody failure, compounded by a lack of coordination between Wheeler's main force and Forrest's command. Losses were heavy, at least 350 Confederates, with Forrest's smaller detachment suffering the greater share. Enraged at the outcome, Forrest acidly informed Wheeler that evening, "I will be in my coffin before I again fight under your command."[48]

In addition to this undercurrent of tension from within, Van Dorn's arrival only complicated Wheeler's position. Van Dorn outranked Wheeler and by rank would automatically command "all cavalry in Middle Tennessee." But Van Dorn was also subject to Johnston's orders and possible recall to Mississippi should the need arise. After some reshuffling and reorganization, Bragg settled on two cavalry corps, one stationed on each flank: Van Dorn would screen the Confederate left at Columbia, while Wheeler would guard the right, east of Wartrace.

Van Dorn's corps now consisted of two divisions. William H. "Red" Jackson continued in command of the one from Mississippi. William T. Martin initially led the other, but on March 14, after the engagement at Thompson's Station, Martin was transferred back to Wheeler's command. Forrest ranked Martin and so could not be placed under him. This led to an awkward period where Martin's division included only a single brigade, with Forrest reporting directly to Van Dorn as an independent force. The solution was to send Martin back to Wheeler, moving Forrest up to divisional command of Brig. Gen. Frank Armstrong's brigade along with Forrest's own brigade, now under Col. George Dibrell. Significantly, this was Forrest's largest command to date and expanded his duties to include more traditional cavalry scouting and screening missions as well.[49]

Will Martin did not take a demotion in the transfer. Wheeler's corps now consisted of three divisions, each of two brigades, led by John Wharton, John H. Morgan, and now Martin. Morgan's large Kentucky command swelled in the wake of the recent campaign and again after his Christmas Raid, and now needed to be divided into two brigades. Bragg had his doubts about the wisdom of Morgan's elevation and informed Joe Johnston on March 2, "I fear Morgan is overcome by too large a command; with a regiment or small brigade he did more and better service than with a division." But, Bragg added, "Wheeler will correct this."[50]

48 John Allen Wyeth, *That Devil Forrest: The Life of Nathan Bedford Forrest* (Baton Rouge, LA: 1989), 132.

49 OR 23, pt. 2, 695.

50 Ibid., pt. 2, 656.

As with Bragg's infantry, his cavalry numbers were on the increase. Wheeler commanded 11,000 men in January. On February 28, Bragg's cavalry numbered about 13,500 sabers, and on March 31, despite the departure to East Tennessee of a full brigade of cavalry (1,600 men) under Brig. Gen. John Pegram, the Army of Tennessee still reported no less than 16,247 troopers present for duty, marking a peak for Bragg's mounted strength. By June 1, the force stabilized at just over 15,000 men, not counting those companies serving as headquarters escorts, with another 3,000 men available relatively nearby: Roddey's brigade in northern Alabama and Pegram in East Tennessee.[51]

Bragg's main cavalry force was deployed across a front nearly 80 miles wide. Forrest (and subsequently Van Dorn) on Bragg's left flank occupied Columbia and Spring Hill, Tennessee; Wharton's line centered on Unionville, screening Polk's front. Martin's men extended that line eastward towards Bell Buckle, screening Hardee's Corps while Morgan's division guarded Bragg's deep right flank, stretching from Manchester to McMinnville.[52]

Thus stood affairs in the Army of Tennessee that spring of 1863. Despite intractable problems of command and personality that roiled the army's high command, Bragg's army showed definite gains. Numbers, modern arms, training, and discipline all improved. Most importantly, Bragg's significant advantage in cavalry translated into immediate success and overall intimidation of his Federal opponents. As March arrived and active operations resumed, the war in Tennessee was characterized by a series of small clashes and minor affairs which, taken as a whole, kept the Federals under Rosecrans wary and off base. Nothing drove home Confederate mounted superiority like the small but significant engagement between Van Dorn's newly arrived veterans and a Federal infantry brigade at Thompson's Station in early March.

51 Ibid., pt. 2, 654, 733, 846.

52 Longacre, *Cavalry of the Heartland*, 192-193.

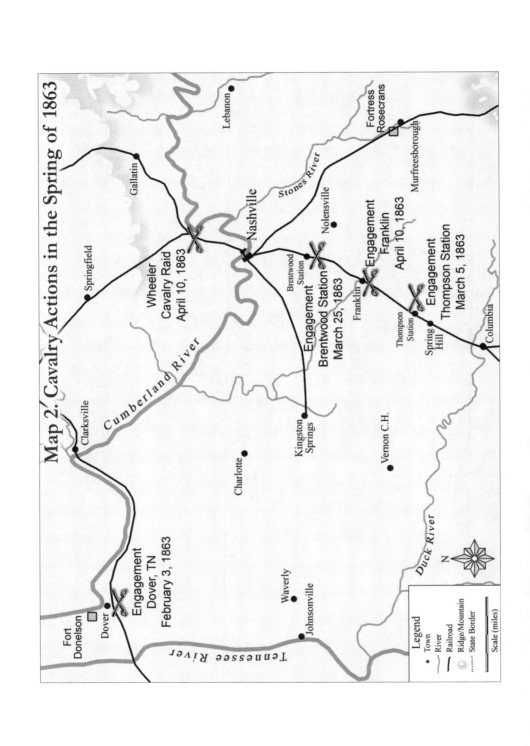

Map 2. Cavalry Actions in the Spring of 1863

Chapter Three

Besieged

Franklin, Tenn., March 3, 1863

Brig. Gen. C. C. Gilbert:

The general commanding directs you to send a brigade and a sufficient cavalry force to-morrow on the Columbia pike as far as Spring Hill. Send out a party from there towards Columbia, and one through to Raleigh Springs, on the Lewisburg pike. A cavalry force from here [Murfreesboro] will communicate with your party at that place some time during the day after tomorrow. We desire to know what is in our front. Take a forage train along. Have you any news?

J. A. Garfield, Brigadier-General and Chief of Staff[1]

The news sought by Garfield, and by extension General Rosecrans, pertained to Earl Van Dorn, who was expected to arrive any day. Intelligence concerning his movements had been reaching Union headquarters since early February. Rosecrans was already plagued by logistical shortages thanks to Rebel cavalry harassing his supply lines. The Louisville & Nashville had only recently reopened after Morgan's December raid, and while Wheeler's strike at Dover came to naught, it halted river traffic on the Cumberland for several days. Had Wheeler and Forrest met with more luck, they might have damaged or destroyed any number of river transports.

---

1 OR 23, pt. 1, 77.

Smaller pinpricks bedeviled other Union outposts. The arrival of Van Dorn and his (rumor-inflated) strength of up to 8,000 hardened troopers was cause for worry.

The Spring Hill expedition was not intended to be a solo venture. It was meant to support a larger reconnaissance across much of Rosecrans's front. Two other columns were also ordered south: Brig. Gen. John B. Steedman's command at Nolensville (halfway between Franklin and Murfreesboro) was ordered to move toward the hamlets of Eagleville and Unionville, while Brig. Gen. Philip Sheridan was ordered to take his division southwestward from Murfreesboro toward those same villages. A Federal cavalry brigade under Col. Robert H. C. Minty supported Sheridan. All three expeditions were to set out on March 4. Given how disastrously Gilbert's portion of the reconnaissance turned out for Union arms, and how much it revealed of Union martial shortcomings, this engagement deserves a closer look.

Brigadier General Charles C. Gilbert led a small division of 2,500 men at Franklin, 20 miles south of Nashville on the south bank of the Harpeth River. His immediate superior, Maj. Gen. Gordon Granger, was tasked with securing Rosecrans's flanks and rear. In March, Granger's force of nearly 11,000 men organized into three divisions would later be designated as the Army of the Cumberland's Reserve Corps. When Rosecrans began advancing toward Chattanooga, he would have to leave large detachments behind to guard the all-important Nashville & Chattanooga railroad. Granger's corps drew the job. Unlike the army's three main corps—the XIV, XX, and XXI—Granger's command lacked veteran officers and troops. Most regiments were new, recruited into service in the fall of 1862, or had troops experienced mostly in occupation duty.

Gilbert's wartime career is a case in point. He was a West Pointer, class of 1846, who, unlike many of his fellow officers, remained in the army. He was a regular army captain when he was wounded at Wilson's Creek, Missouri, in 1861. He then served as a staff officer under Buell. During the crisis of the Kentucky Campaign, he was appointed a provisional brigadier and then major general, leading one of Buell's three corps at Perryville, but he saw little action there. Many of his troops hated him. He never shed his regular army ways or developed the lighter leadership touch needed to handle volunteers. His insistence on harsh discipline and his demands for unyielding obedience, coupled with an obvious contempt for amateurs, made him a difficult man to like. Though he did not yet know it, his career as a general was about to end. The US Congress was scheduled to vote on his promotion on March 4. The nomination would fail to pass.[2]

---

2 Warner, *Generals in Blue*, 173-4.

Brig. Gen. Charles C. Gilbert commanded a
division in the Army of the Cumberland
in the spring of 1863.

Library of Congress

Gilbert's command was small, but fortunately he had another brigade nearby. Colonel John Coburn's men belonged to another of Granger's divisions commanded by Brig. Gen. Absalom Baird, and had been sent to Brentwood (about halfway between Nashville and Franklin) to support Gilbert's garrison. Gilbert, believing that his own forces "were scattered through the town or engaged in work . . . of importance," selected Coburn for the mission at hand. Coburn's men had another very different explanation for their selection. Captain Charles P. Lincoln of the 19th Michigan later sneered, "Gen. Gilbert's division was comfortably quartered in Franklin and he evidently believed it to be . . . good generalship to . . . send [Coburn's Brigade] on this expedition."[3]

Coburn, an Indiana lawyer and politician, commanded four infantry regiments: the 33rd and 85th Indiana, the 19th Michigan, and the 22nd Wisconsin, numbering about 1,845 effectives. The 400-strong 124th Ohio Infantry was also attached, charged with safeguarding and escorting an 80-wagon forage train. The 18th Ohio Battery and a composite force of about 600 cavalrymen drawn from the 4th Kentucky, 2nd Michigan, and 9th Pennsylvania cavalry regiments further accompanied Coburn. All told, the force numbering some 3,000 men departed Franklin on the morning of the 4th. Its objective, Spring Hill, was just 13 miles distant.[4]

As the Federals had worried, Van Dorn was indeed present, having joined with Nathan Bedford Forrest's brigade at Columbia on February 22. Van Dorn's and

3 Richard R. Groves, *Blooding the Regiment, an Account of the 22d Wisconsin's Long and Difficult Apprenticeship* (Lanham, MD: 2005), 87.

4 *OR* 23, pt. 1, 75, 83-4; Groves, *Blooding the Regiment*, 84-85.

Forrest's junction combined the forces of two of the most aggressive cavalrymen in Confederate service. And both were itching to attack Franklin. On February 19, Forrest proposed just such a move, supported by a strike toward Brentwood by Wharton's division of Wheeler's corps. [5]

The day of his arrival, Van Dorn wired Joseph E. Johnston to reiterate Forrest's request, but that just raised the curtain on a much bolder plan. Van Dorn further proposed striking north of Nashville, and even driving on into southern Kentucky. The more cautious Johnston replied that if Rosecrans was not about to attack, then Van Dorn might "move into Kentucky or farther," but went on to add, "There should be no attack on Franklin until full information is obtained of the enemy's strength." In order to accomplish that reconnaissance, Van Dorn contented himself with sending William Jackson's division to occupy Spring Hill on February 28.[6]

Van Dorn had reason to be confident. With Forrest, his force now numbered 5,800 troopers. Moreover, virtually all of his cavalrymen were proven fighters. Many of the regiments in William Jackson's division were veterans of multiple battles, including Pea Ridge and Corinth. The Texas cavalry regiments comprising Col. John W. Whitfield's brigade had seen combat as both cavalry and infantry. They fought dismounted at Corinth, where they gave as good a fight as any infantry unit on the field. While the Texans were delighted to be finally remounted, they could still deliver versatile service from horseback or on foot. Forrest's command had already proven itself equally tough in fights such as Parker's Crossroads and Dover in Tennessee.

Corporal Harvey Reid of the 22nd Wisconsin found himself in the middle of Coburn's moving column. Reid noted that, though the march began at 8 a.m., "when we reached the [Harpeth] river some delay was occasioned by some imperfection in the pontoon bridge, and we stood waiting nearly an hour. It was freezingly cold and it made the boys very impatient to . . . stand so long." Once across, the column continued for another 4 miles, before colliding with Rebels somewhere south of Winstead Hill.[7]

---

5 OR 23, pt. 2, 641.

6 Ibid., 646; Homer L. Kerr, ed. *Fighting with Ross' Texas Cavalry Brigade, C.S.A.: The Diary of George L. Griscom, Adjutant, 9th Texas Cavalry Regiment* (Hillsboro, TX: 1976), 59.

7 Frank L. Byrne, ed. *The View from Headquarters: Civil War Letters of Harvey Reid* (Madison, WI: 1965), 29.

Maj. Gen. Earl Van Dorn, commander,
Cavalry Corps, Dept. of Mississippi and East Louisiana.

National Archives

Van Dorn had planned his own reconnaissance to Franklin on March 4. He dispatched the 9th Texas Cavalry westward to cover the Carter Creek Pike (which approached Franklin from the southwest) while he sent the rest of Jackson's division due north along the Franklin-Spring-Hill Pike. Jackson's Confederates rode into the scattering of buildings denoting Thompson's Station at about the same time Coburn's men finished crossing the Harpeth. With little pause, Jackson continued northward. The two forces collided about halfway between Franklin and Thompson's Station.[8]

Both sides halted. Jackson deployed Captain Houston King's Missouri battery of horse artillery and opened fire on Coburn's Yankees. Coburn responded by ordering his own cavalry forward and deploying his four leading infantry regiments into line astride the pike. Combat was so new to Corporal Reid and his comrades that "at first we supposed [the shot] to be a blank cartridge from our battery. . . ." More artillery fire from King's Missourians and the 18th Ohio quickly disabused them of that notion.[9]

Colonel Thomas J. Jordan, commanding the 9th Pennsylvania Cavalry, reported that Capt. Charles C. Aleshire's 18th Ohio Battery opened the action with its first round at 10:40 a.m., firing at "the lines of the enemy's cavalry [which] were drawn up in full view on the face of the hills, within half-mile range. . . ." Initially, neither side ventured a serious attack. "A few rounds from our guns caused the enemy to withdraw behind the hills," continued Jordan.[10]

This artillery duel continued for anywhere from one and a half to two hours, with little effect. Early in the afternoon, Van Dorn ordered Jackson's men to fall back to Thompson's Station, toward the rest of his still-approaching command. Neither Martin's division nor Forrest's brigade were yet up, and though Van Dorn fully intended to fight, he wanted to do so with all his numbers. The day's skirmishing was nearly bloodless. Colonel Jordan later recalled that the Rebels left behind 15 dead men, as well as some horses—quite possibly an exaggeration, since the Confederates made no mention of such a loss—while the Federals suffered 2 or 3 men wounded. Captain Aleshire also lost one of his 18th Ohio guns, which snapped an axle and had to be sent to the rear.

Coburn seemed paralyzed with uncertainty, halting to send a series of dispatches back to General Gilbert's headquarters. In the first, he plaintively noted that the Rebel artillery had been an unpleasant surprise, one that made it "unsafe, for the teams at least" to proceed. The forage train, he fretted, "is so long and requires so much force to watch it." In a second, Coburn estimated the enemy cavalry at "2,000 to 3,000," adding that while they had disappeared from his front,

8 Kerr, *Fighting with Ross' Texas Cavalry Brigade*, 59; Hale, *The Third Texas Cavalry*, 165.

9 Byrne, *The View from Headquarters*, 30.

10 OR 23, pt. 1, 80.

other reports soon placed the Confederates slipping around his flank via the Lewisburg Pike. "What shall we do?" he queried. "I think we can advance, but there will at once be a force in our rear."[11]

Coburn spent the rest of the day waiting for additional instructions. He occupied the ground vacated by the Rebel cavalry, but advanced no farther. In response, Gilbert dispatched Captain Thomas Johnston of the 2nd Michigan Cavalry to investigate the reason for Coburn's inaction, but Johnston found no real cause for alarm. Based on the terrain, Johnston estimated the Rebel cavalry at no more than "1,000 men, all cavalry, and three pieces of artillery." He further concluded that Coburn was "in a good deal of doubt as to the intentions of the enemy, and not over-confident." Coburn camped for the night and, with Gilbert's approval, sent the cumbersome forage train back to Franklin, even though only 39 of the wagons were full.[12]

As night fell, noted Corporal Reid, "Colonel Coburn anticipated . . . that we should be attacked by morning," but no such blow landed. March 5 dawned clear and cold. Captain Charles Day of Company C, 33rd Indiana, was the officer of the day. He questioned "two negro boys, about twelve years of age" who brought alarming news. "They had come from Van Dorn's army, that it was out this side of Spring Hill, and was coming on to take Franklin." Upon hearing this, Coburn sent the boys to Gilbert under escort. Lieutenant Hamlet Adams, of Coburn's staff, asked Coburn what they were going to do. "I am going ahead," was the response Adams recalled. "I have no option in the matter." Lieutenant Edwin Bachman of the 33rd, who had charge of the baggage train, remembered an even franker reply: "My orders are imperative, and I must go on or show cowardice."[13]

The Federal column marched out at 8 a.m. Coburn took no chances, deploying a heavy screen of dismounted cavalry skirmishers at the outset. According to Reid, the 2nd Michigan and 9th Pennsylvania led the column mounted, followed by Coburn, the brigade staff, the artillery, and then the infantry, with the 22nd Wisconsin in front. First contact came a mile out, with a scattering of enemy pickets, soon dispersed. At the 4-mile mark, just north of the few buildings that

11 Ibid., 78.

12 Ibid., 79.

13 Byrne, *The View from Headquarters*, 32; John R. McBride, *History of the Thirty-Third Indiana Veteran Volunteer Infantry during the Four Years of Civil War from Sept. 16, 1861, to July 21, 1865 and Incidentally of Col. John Colburn's Second Brigade Third Division, Twentieth Army Corps, including Incidents of the Great Rebellion* (Indianapolis, IN: 1900), 75; OR 23, pt. 1, 94, 98.

comprised Thompson's Station, they encountered more-significant resistance. "The skirmishers on the left became quite actively engaged," Reid noted, "the firing becoming hotter and hotter until their cheers indicated that they [the Federals] had gained an advantage."[14]

Van Dorn, who had been well informed of Coburn's approach, was ready. Private A. W. Sparks of the 9th Texas Cavalry found himself near Brig. Gen. William H. Jackson's headquarters that morning and watched as a series of couriers brought word of the Federal advance. Unruffled, Jackson "proceeded with his toilet . . . [and] his breakfast" until at last, near 8 a.m., he ordered the Texas brigade to deploy in a dismounted line of battle "behind a stone wall" about a half-mile in advance of the station.[15]

The fight that followed proved far more significant than the minor dustup the day before. Both sides soon opened with artillery, and Coburn quickly deployed his infantry to back up the Michigan cavalry skirmishers. The 22nd Wisconsin and 19th Michigan deployed to the left, onto a hill east of the railroad and the Franklin Pike (which ran alongside each other through a defile at this point), while the 33rd and 85th Indiana swung onto a summit on the right, overlooking the station. The battery was divided, with two guns sent to support the Indianans, and three more accompanying the Michigan and Wisconsin troops.

Private Carlos Baker of the 19th Michigan was detailed to serve one of the 18th Ohio fieldpieces supporting the Hoosier infantry. Baker remembered that initially, "the rebels . . . opened on us with one big gun, straight ahead" and then, as Aleshire's crews deployed, "opened on us with six or eight guns besides the big one. . . ." After a considerable artillery duel, during which Coburn completed his own deployments while Van Dorn's troopers watched with interest, Coburn ordered the 33rd and 85th "to take a battery about a mile south west . . . in the woods south of the depot."[16]

"They immediately formed in line of battle and marched down the hill and across some corn field under cover of the depot buildings when the rebels opened fire on them from behind a stone wall," wrote Baker; "their line seemed to extend a half mile." The Federals had stumbled into the four Texas dismounted cavalry regiments of Whitfield's brigade. The Texans immediately followed that volley

14 Byrne, *The View from Headquarters,* 32.

15 A. W. Sparks, *The War between the States as I Saw It: Reminiscent, Historical and Personal* (Tyler, TX: 1901), 76.

16 *Allegan Journal,* April 13, 1863.

with a charge of their own. "[We] soon drove them back across the open field to their starting point," recalled newly promoted Lt. S. B. Barron of the 3rd Texas Cavalry. "Here they rallied, and being reinforced, they drove our forces back to the station and stone fence."[17]

The Indianans' counterattack was short lived. Brigadier General Frank Armstrong's brigade reinforced the Texans, and both Rebel brigades hurled the two blueclad regiments back to their hilltop. The 33rd and 85th rallied and broke the Confederate momentum, but wisely eschewed another charge of their own. The Rebels reorganized for a third assault.

Both sides suffered heavy losses in the intense fighting. The action also induced one of those improbably romantic tales that often punctuate stories of the war. Seventeen-year-old Alice Thompson was sheltering in the basement of a substantial manor house along the Columbia Pike when the 3rd Arkansas Cavalry swept by, charging into action on foot. Young Alice watched the 3rd's color-bearer go down, dropping the flag. She impetuously rushed out to raise the banner and rally the regiment, which was by then under an intense fire and becoming disordered. "Boys," bellowed Col. Samuel G. Earle, commanding the Arkansans, "A woman has your flag!" Sufficiently abashed, the 3rd "raised a yell and drove the Yankees back." Earle himself was killed a short while later.[18]

Despite their rawness, the pair of Indiana regiments fought ably on the west side of the pike. Things were not as well in hand on the east side of the pike, where the 19th Michigan and 22nd Wisconsin were engaged. Coburn initially intended to hold both commands in reserve, but they soon found themselves opposed by elements of Nathan Bedford Forrest's command—Capt. Samuel L. Freeman's Tennessee Battery of four guns, supported by the 4th and 11th Tennessee Cavalries, commanded by Col. James W. Starnes as a demi-brigade. Freeman and Forrest got along well, perhaps because they both relished their fights up close and personal. "[Freeman's] favorite guns were his twelve-pounder howitzers, his preferred ammunition two thirds canister, and his distance as close as his general would let him go," recalled one of Forrest's staff officers.[19]

---

17 Ibid.; S. B. Barron, *The Lone Star Defenders: A Chronicle of the Third Texas Cavalry, Ross' Brigade* (New York: 1908), 149.

18 Fannie May Laws, "In Connection with Thompson's Station," *Confederate Veteran*, vol. 8, no. 6 (June, 1900), 263.

19 Thomas Jordan and J. P. Pryor, *The Campaigns of General Nathan Bedford Forrest and of Forrest's Cavalry, with Portraits, Maps, and Illustrations* (New York: 1868), 247.

Taking fire from Freeman's guns, Col. Henry Gilbert pulled his 19th Michiganders back from the left flank to a more sheltered position behind the three eastward facing left-hand guns of the 18th Ohio Battery. Their retreat allowed Starnes's Tennesseans to occupy a hill to the 22nd's left, bring up a section of Freeman's guns, and enfilade the Badgers' left flank.[20]

Forrest now led the rest of his brigade around and behind Starnes directly into the Union rear, seizing the Columbia Pike. Heavily outnumbered, Colonel Jordan's cavalry offered little resistance to this movement. In fact, Forrest's appearance triggered the beginning of a wholesale retreat on the part of the Federal cavalry and Aleshire's artillery. "Acting on the homely maxim that 'prudence was the better part of valor,'" admitted Baker, "our teamsters put spurs to the horses and down the hill they went; and we (the gunners) took the gun[s] and gun carriages down by hand." Baker's portion of the battery opposed the Texans, but when the three guns east of the road departed, the rest of the battery followed suit, acting on orders of Captain Aleshire, who in turn obeyed Colonel Jordan's instructions.[21]

The day ended in Union disaster. The cavalry, the artillery, and half of the 22nd Wisconsin escaped, but virtually all the rest of Coburn's force fell into Rebel hands, including Coburn himself, personally captured by Forrest. Van Dorn won a smashing victory. Confederate losses were 357 killed, wounded, and missing. Two hundred ninety-three Federals fell in the combat, and another 1,200 were made prisoner, effectively eliminating Coburn's command in a little over four hours' time.[22]

There were recriminations aplenty, of course. Army Chief of Staff Garfield derided Coburn as "a fool" and fellow Union Col. Emerson Opdycke thought that Coburn "desired a victory for the sake of the 'stars.'" Blame also fell on General Gilbert, who had paid scant attention to Coburn's worries and made no effort to support him on March 5. In any case, Gilbert was soon gone, relegated to duty as a major and as a mustering officer for most of the rest of the war. Coburn's infantry blamed Jordan and Aleshire for abandoning them in the heat of battle, but Jordan offered up as a defense the fact that he was acting on Coburn's own order for the cavalry to cover the brigade's retreat. There also developed an ugly rift in the 22nd

20 Jordan and Pryor, *Campaigns of General Nathan Bedford Forrest*, 233-236; William M. Anderson, *They Died to Make Men Free, A History of the 19th Michigan Infantry in the Civil War* (Dayton, OH: 1994), 166; Groves, *Blooding the Regiment*, 94-97.

21 *Allegan Journal,* April 13, 1863.

22 OR 23, pt. 2, 84, 91, 119.

Wisconsin between Col. William L. Utley and Lt. Col. Edward Bloodgood, whom Utley accused of abandoning the field. In a personal letter, penned on March 5, Bloodgood described that moment:

> In the confusion we could get no orders; each regiment had to look out for themselves. I was at the right of our regiment; the Colonel was in the center. I was notified . . . that a large body of the enemy was moving . . . to cut us off completely. I sent word down the line to the Colonel to move the regiment in that direction, and as he left me with the management of the right of the regiment, I gave the order, as there was no time to hesitate. . . . I supposed the whole regiment was moving, but when I crossed the pike, I found they had not done so. The next moment the rebels came over the hill by thousands.

Bloodgood left the field with about 150 men. Utley and the remainder of the regiment fell into Rebel hands. Bad blood festered between the two officers for the rest of their mutual time in service.[23]

The disaster at Thompson's Station, though a small affair when compared to many other actions, confirmed Rosecrans's worst fears about the puissance of Rebel cavalry and the inadequacy of his own troopers. It was the second time a full brigade of infantry had been eliminated from the Union order of battle in the space of four months, the first being John Hunt Morgan's success at Hartsville on December 7. Worse yet, this time the Federals were not surprised in their camps, caught flatfooted and defeated piecemeal, as bad as that incident was. Instead, they marched wittingly into harm's way, conducting a reconnaissance in force barely 10 miles beyond their lines.

Newspaper accounts exaggerated Van Dorn's numbers, positing him with anywhere from 12,000 to 18,000 men, including a division of infantry. It was a gross overestimation, close to the size of Van Dorn's whole army at Corinth the previous October. Rosecrans's intelligence sources provided figures that were a bit lower, but still greatly exaggerated: on March 10, Rosecrans's headquarters attributed 8,000 to Van Dorn, 12,000 to Wheeler, and 6,000 men to Morgan—26,000 troopers in all. On April 10, however, Bragg's own returns showed that all

---

23 Anderson, *They Died to Make Men Free*, 179; "Lieutenant Colonel Bloodgood's Letter," included in Frank Moore, *The Rebellion Record, A Diary of American Events,* 12 vols. (New York: 1863), 6:442-443; Groves, *Blooding the Regiment,* 105-106. Colonel Utley ultimately resigned his commission in July 1864, citing disability. Lieutenant Colonel Bloodgood led the regiment for the rest of the war.

the cavalry in his army amounted to only 15,338 officers and men present for duty.[24]

Even if the Rebel cavalry did not actually possess the overwhelming numbers attributed to it, there could be no question that it was well mounted and aggressively led. Even when outnumbered, such as at Hartsville, it had demonstrated its superiority. Now, newly reinforced, Rosecrans could expect it to become more dangerous than ever.

The other two elements of the March 4-5 reconnaissance were uneventful. Colonel Robert H. G. Minty of the 4th Michigan Cavalry had the most success. Leading a mixed force of "863 men," Minty led Sheridan's infantry column to the hamlet of Rover, where he met the 4th Alabama Cavalry, 400 strong. His objective was "to drive the rebel detachments, who had reoccupied Rover and Unionville, from those positions." The Alabamians fell back before they could be outflanked. Then the 7th Pennsylvania Cavalry charged, sabers drawn, overrunning the Alabamians' camp, taking wagons, prisoners, and stores. "Being thrown into confusion by the fugitives from Rover," recalled the 7th's historian, William Sipes, the Rebels "broke and fled until they found refuge behind [Confederate General] Polk's [infantry] corps, within five miles of Shelbyville." Lt. Joseph Vale, who served on Minty's staff, "and four or five men of the Seventh, actually rode into the line of one of Polk's Divisions and received a heavy volley from a full brigade. Every man and horse in this squad was struck by the enemy's bullets, but none of the men injured."[25]

Minty was rightfully proud of his brigade's performance. "The fruits of this charge—in which not one shot was fired by my brigade, the entire work being done with sabers—were 28 killed, 58 wounded (who fell into our hands), 151 un-wounded prisoners, 17 wagons, 94 horses, 12 mules, 31 tents, two portable forges, and several wagon-loads of commissary stores; all of which I sent into Murfreesboro," he wrote.[26]

Minty then fell back to Eagleville, 6 miles north of Rover, where he and Sheridan awaited Steedman's column coming from Nolensville. On March 5, men

---

24 Entry for Cavalry Force, March 10, 1863, "Summary of Daily Intelligence Received," Army of the Cumberland, Record Group 94, National Archives. Hereafter, "Intelligence Summary," RG 94, NARA; *OR* 23, part 2, 749.

25 William B. Sipes, *The Seventh Pennsylvania Veteran Volunteer Cavalry Its Record, Reminiscences and Roster, with an Appendix* (Pottsville, PA: 1906), 54; *Vale*, Minty and His Cavalry, 134-135.

26 Robert H. G. Minty, "The Saber Brigade: An Expedition with the Gallant 'Little Phil' Sheridan," *The National Tribune*, December 15, 1892.

of both columns reported hearing the heavy firing from the west, where Coburn met his doom at Thompson's Station, 18 miles distant. Over the next few days, Federal and Rebel cavalry clashed repeatedly, losing a man here, two men there, but with no significant outcome—except, of course, to the handful of men killed, wounded, or captured on each side. To the historians of Forrest's cavalry, these incidents provided "some profit as a species of sharp battle-drill, and of moral effect among the men."[27]

There were other reverses, as well. Few of these Federal losses were as sizeable as the defeat of Coburn's force, but they added up. On March 8, an entire Union forage train was captured near Carthage, Tennessee, east of Hartsville. Morgan's cavalry surrounded 18 wagons and their escort, two companies of the 18th Ohio Infantry. Brig. Gen. George Crook noted that the train had only gone "1 ½ miles farther" than usual, just far enough to allow Morgan's men to snatch it up. Crook then echoed a familiar lament, noting his "utter failure to accomplish any result here without cavalry."[28]

The main area of contention for both armies remained that irregular rectangle of no-man's land that lay between the Union garrisons at Murfreesboro and Franklin and the Confederate-held towns of Spring Hill and Shelbyville. There were almost daily skirmishes at Triune, Thompson's Station, Eagleville, Salem, and other soon-to-be well-known locations. Rosecrans's objective in these affairs was to try to aggressively patrol the crossings over the Harpeth River, which separated the two armies, or at least to provide early warning of any Rebel approach. However, those patrols were not always sufficient, nor the warnings always timely: disaster struck again just three weeks later at Brentwood Station on March 25.

Sometime in mid-March, Forrest put out a call for "a well mounted man who knew the country between Spring Hill and Nashville, for special duty." That "man" turned out to be 16-year-old Corporal Newton Cannon of the 11th Tennessee Cavalry, who lived within 5 miles of Spring Hill. As Cannon recalled it, "The General said he wanted me to pass to the left of Franklin . . . and to go up around Brentwood, see the position and number of the force there, take notes of all roads and creeks of any size that I crossed, and where I saw any bodies of the enemy. . . ." Dubious, Forrest asked if "I thought I could do it. I told him I could if anybody could: he seemed to think I was rather young and small."

---

27 Jordan and Pryor, *Campaigns of General Forrest*, 241.

28 *OR* 23, pt. 1, 140.

Nevertheless, off Cannon went, returning within 24 hours. Upon his return, he was able to draw a detailed sketch map of the intervening terrain, which proved more than satisfactory. "Forrest told me to report to my company," wrote Cannon, "and said to Major [John] Strange that he had sent several of the best men he had and that damned little boy made him the only sensible report."[29]

On the night of March 24, with Cannon's information in hand, Forrest divided his division, sending Colonel Starnes and two regiments to cross the Harpeth east of Franklin to approach Brentwood from the rear, while Forrest, with the rest of Starnes's (formerly his own) brigade and all of Frank Armstrong's brigade completed the pincer movement, following Cannon's route.

The remnant of Coburn's Union brigade, which was now led by the unfortunate Lt. Col. Bloodgood of the 22nd Wisconsin, the senior surviving officer of the brigade, garrisoned Brentwood. Bloodgood and the four companies of the 22nd that had escaped capture at Thompson's Station were camped near Brentwood Station along with the brigade's surviving wounded and convalescents. The remnant of the 19th Michigan occupied a stockade guarding the railroad bridge over the Little Harpeth River, some 2 miles south. Bloodgood's force numbered about 550, of which no more than 300 were effectives. The Michiganders added perhaps 250 more.

Forrest intended to surround Bloodgood's detachment at dawn on March 25, hoping to converge Starnes's column and his own on Brentwood simultaneously. That plan proved overly optimistic. Starnes arriving first and, not finding Forrest, stealthily withdrew out of sight to wait. Forrest arrived shortly thereafter, but with only part of his column. Armstrong and the Confederate artillery lagged behind. Lacking Starnes's manpower, a more cautious commander might have waited. Not Forrest. He attempted an immediate bluff, deploying his escort and one other mounted company to fool Bloodgood into thinking he was surrounded.[30]

Meanwhile, a courier reached Bloodgood that morning with the mistaken report that the 19th Michigan was under attack at the railroad bridge. The Union commander quickly organized a relief column and set out, only to stumble into Forrest's cavalry. Under a flag of truce, Forrest demanded that the Federals surrender or "be cut to pieces." Bloodgood initially hesitated, but Armstrong

29 Campbell H. Brown, ed. *The Reminiscences of Newton Cannon, First Sergeant, 11th Tennessee Cavalry, C.S.A.,* from holograph material provided by his grandson Samuel M. Fleming Jr. (late Lieutenant Commander, U.S.N.) (Franklin, TN: 1963), 27.

30 Jordan and Pryor, *Campaigns of General Forrest,* 242.

appeared, along with supporting artillery, and backed up Forrest's bluff, deciding the matter.

The affair was almost entirely bloodless, with the Federals admitting to only three men wounded during the skirmishing preceding the capitulation. In trying to excuse Bloodgood's conduct, Wisconsin Chaplain C. D. Pillsbury opined, "some men might have fought longer . . . but to have done so, in my judgement, would have been a reckless sacrificing of life." Shortly thereafter, the 19th Michigan followed suit. In all, Forrest bagged 759 prisoners in the day's work.[31]

Again, Union reports overestimated Forrest's strength at 5,000, but those odds did not deter Maj. Gen. Gordon Granger from dispatching Union cavalry from Franklin to intercept the Rebel raider before he could slip back across the Harpeth. Brigadier General Green Clay Smith led that force, a mere 545 men drawn from four Federal regiments. Smith was a pro-Union Kentucky lawyer and politician who was a brother-in-law of Brig. Gen. John Buford, who was soon to become one of the heroes of the Battle of Gettysburg. While Smith was not a professional soldier, he did not lack for aggressiveness. He offset some of the day's disasters when he stumbled into Forrest's column, inflicting losses and recapturing some wagons. A glowing account of Smith's exploits in the Cincinnati *Commercial* suggested that Forrest's column "broke in confusion, appearing to be panic-stricken," abandoning "Federal clothing, sutler's goods, etc., which they had stolen at Brentwood" and pursuing the Rebels for "six miles." Forrest's biographers dismissed this as "a characteristic example" of "gross exaggerations," insisting that there was no such pursuit at all. Certainly, the *Commercial* sought to play up any Union success, but even Corporal Cannon recalled that "they pressed our rear-guard pretty hard."[32]

---

31 Moore, *Rebellion Record*, 6:482.

32 Moore, *Rebellion Record*, 6:481; Jordon and Pryor, *Campaigns of General Forrest*, 244-245; Brown, *Reminiscences*, 28. Marcus Bainbridge Buford, *A Genealogy of the Buford Family in America* (San Francisco, CA: 1904), 129-130. John Buford and Green Clay Smith were married to two sisters, Martha McDowell Duke Buford and Caroline Duke. Their father, James Keith Duke, was the uncle of Basil W. Duke, who became a brigadier general of Confederate cavalry. When Basil's parents perished in the cholera epidemic that swept Kentucky in 1832 and 1833, James Keith took in his nephew and raised him as his own son. John Buford's first cousin, Abraham Buford, named for Caroline Smith's paternal grandfather, Revolutionary War veteran Col. Abraham Buford, became a brigadier general of cavalry under Nathan Bedford Forrest in 1864. Against that backdrop, Smith was destined to become a cavalry officer. Green Clay Smith, a nephew of the famous abolitionist Cassius Clay, might have garnered a larger reputation as a Federal cavalryman, but he was elected to the US House of Representatives in the fall of 1862.

Rosecrans was disgusted by the Brentwood affair and, more importantly, a bit cowed by all these Rebel successes. In Washington, the war department worried that Rosecrans's army was too inactive, enabling the Confederates to siphon troops away from Bragg's command to reinforce either Virginia or Mississippi. That afternoon, General Halleck wired Rosecrans, insisting, "It is exceedingly important at the present time that you give the enemy in your front plenty of occupation." In response, the harassed army commander sarcastically retorted, "Rebels appear to me just now engaged in giving me occupation. Regret to learn from Granger, at Franklin, that 300 of his men were captured to-day at Brentwood, 9 miles in his rear, by cavalry. . . . I do not think it prudent or practical to advance from this position until I am better or differently informed."[33]

Rosecrans himself was almost a target of raiding Confederates, for plots were a-hatching. Late on March 14, Lt. Col. James C. Malone Jr., commanding the 14th Alabama Cavalry Battalion, rode into Shelbyville. He gained an audience with Leonidas Polk, outlining a scheme to boldly kidnap Rosecrans from his headquarters in Murfreesboro. Malone's commander, John Wharton, had already signed off on the idea. The plan seems to have been spawned at least in part because "a prisoner . . . who claims to be Rosecrans' orderly" had been captured by Col. James Hagen's cavalry brigade while picketing the Murfreesboro pike some days before. Malone went to interrogate the prisoner personally. On the 17th, Polk gave his tentative approval. "[He] thought the idea had much to recommend it and urged that, along with Rosecrans, the abductors grab all the papers in his adjutant-general's office."[34]

Polk went to pains to insist, however, that Rosecrans not be harmed, since that would violate the norms of civilized warfare. "We owe it to ourselves to be true to our own good word. . . . From the work of assassination we would recoil with just abhorrence." Polk also dispatched his aide, Lt. William B. Richmond, to deliver these instructions and, apparently, to accompany the expedition. At this point, according to Polk's most recent biographer, "the adventure then petered out and came to naught." Perhaps the overall impracticability of the scheme finally dawned

---

He resigned his military commission in early December 1863 to take his seat in the new Congress, alongside fellow general James A. Garfield.

33 *OR* 23, pt. 2, 171. It is not clear whether Granger underestimated the losses sustained at Brentwood or Rosecrans understated them in his dispatch to Washington.

34 Huston Horn, *Leonidas Polk, Warrior Bishop of the Confederacy* (Lawrence, KS: 2019), 302; *OR* 23, pt. 2, 694. The 14th Alabama Cavalry Battalion was merged into the 9th Alabama Cavalry in May.

on everyone involved, especially since no one could risk injury to the Union commander, who was after all surrounded by the bulk of the Army of the Cumberland at Murfreesboro.[35]

As March transitioned to April, there appeared to be little letup in the Rebel activity, either locally or farther afield. Of the latter, the most worrisome was Confederate Brig. Gen. John Pegram's expedition into Kentucky. Pegram, who had previously served as an infantry colonel in Virginia before joining Wheeler's command in time for the battle of Stones River, now commanded a cavalry brigade in East Tennessee. On March 22, Pegram led 1,600 men across the Cumberland River "at Stigall's Ferry, near Somerset Kentucky." Two days later he attacked an unsuspecting Union garrison at Danville, capturing the town after an extended street battle that, according to Louisiana Lt. Howell Carter, "might have riddled us had their soldiers been better marksmen."[36]

Danville was 35 miles southwest of Lexington, not far from the old battleground at Perryville, and uncomfortably close to the L&N tracks that ran through central Kentucky. Fortunately for Rosecrans's logistics, a vigorous Union response halted Pegram's raid short of those tracks, and by March 30, Pegram had fallen back to Somerset, hotly pursued. He was defeated there and driven back into Tennessee by April 1, but for a short time the news appeared alarming indeed. On March 25, the governor of Kentucky worried that he might have to evacuate the state archives in Frankfort, and the next day, Union Brig. Gen. Jeremiah T. Boyle, at Louisville, informed Rosecrans that the "Rebels [are] estimated at from 7,000 to

---

35 Horn, *Leonidas Polk,* 303.

36 Walter S. Griggs, Jr. *General John Pegram, C.S.A.* (Lynchburg, VA: 1993), 69. Brig. Gen. John Pegram, born on January 24, 1832, in Petersburg, Virginia, was a member of the West Point class of 1854 (he graduated 10th of 46). Following graduation, he was commissioned into the Second Dragoons and served with his company until he was ordered to report to West Point to serve as an instructor of cavalry in January 1857. In September, he was ordered to report back to his regiment, and he served in the Utah Expedition of 1857-58. He was given a leave of absence to go to Europe to observe the Papal War of 1859 and returned to active duty after doing so. He resigned his commission on May 10, 1861, earning the distinction of being the first former US officer to offer his services to Virginia. He was commissioned lieutenant colonel of the 10th Virginia Infantry and was captured at the Battle of Rich Mountain on July 11, 1861. He was exchanged and returned to duty on the staff of Gen. P. G. T. Beauregard, and then served as chief of staff to Maj. Gen. Edmund Kirby-Smith. He was promoted to brigadier general on November 10, 1862, and assumed command of a brigade of cavalry in the Army of Tennessee. He was promoted to division command in Forrest's Corps just before the Battle of Chickamauga. He was the older brother of Col. William "Willie" Pegram, the supremely gifted young Confederate artillerist who was killed during the Battle of Five Forks, Virginia, on April 1, 1865. Davis and Hoffman, *The Confederate General,* 5:5-6.

15,000" and reputedly commanded by Gen. John C. Breckinridge. Worse yet, according to Boyle, "it is reported, and believed to be, the advance of a much larger force."[37]

Was Bragg about to reprise his campaign of last fall? Speculation quickly spread through the ranks. Writing home on the 25th, Lt. Orville Chamberlain of the 74th Indiana reported, "There are camp rumors in circulation that we are soon to go again to Kentucky, probably to remain there." Fortunately, Rosecrans's own intelligence reported no movement by either Breckinridge or Bragg, who were both still ensconced in Middle Tennessee, and with Pegram's defeat at Somerset the threat of a new invasion of Kentucky abated.[38]

Lieutenant Chamberlain thought that a move to Kentucky "would please our boys very much." The reason for that desire was simple: Middle Tennessee was hostile country. On March 24 General Granger reported from Franklin, "I would say that my portion of the country is swarming with the meanest, bitterest kind of enemies. I know of no other way to report the names and numbers of active enemies than to say that everything in this neighborhood would come under that head, and that the use of a fine-tooth comb of immense size moving southward would have more effect that any other mode I can propose to get rid of their presence." Chamberlain was stationed at Lavergne, about halfway between Murfreesboro and Nashville. He recorded a sentiment similar to Granger's: "Guerrillas are about as thick as blackberries about here. This morning [March 22] they fired upon the train from Nashville." Chamberlain's black mess servant, "Tom," also disappeared. While "out after provisions . . . , he was probably captured."[39]

Joseph Wheeler intended something more than mere harassment. Wheeler's last headline-grabbing exploit had been at Dover at the beginning of February, and that affair had not ended well. More recently, Van Dorn and Forrest had drawn all the attention, which grated on Wheeler. The Army of Tennessee's various troopers —even the no-nonsense Forrest—thrived on publicity. In the first week of April, Wheeler went to Braxton Bragg to outline his scheme: strike simultaneously at the L&N line north of Nashville and the N&C southeast of the Tennessee capitol. This would be the most daring Confederate raid yet, conducted in the very midst of the Union army. To accomplish this feat, Wheeler wanted to take 1,900 picked men

37 *OR* 23, pt. 2, 173-175.

38 "Dear Friends," March 24, 1863, Orville Chamberlain Papers, Indiana Historical Society.

39 *OR* 23, pt. 2, 168; "My Dear Brother," March 22, 1863, Chamberlain Papers.

from Wharton's division, augmented by another 600 troopers drawn from Morgan's command. Bragg approved the audacious plan.[40]

After concentrating his force at the small hamlet of Alexandria, Tennessee, on April 8, Wheeler led his combined command of 2,500 to the Hermitage (President Andrew Jackson's former home), where they camped undetected on the 9th. The next morning Wheeler "detach[ed] 500 picked men under Lieutenant Colonel [Stephen C.] Ferrill [of the 8th Texas Cavalry] with orders to cross Stone's River, attack the railroad trains, and do any other good in his power." Meanwhile, leaving Morgan's detachment under Col. Basil W. Duke to secure the Hermitage and protect his line of retreat, Wheeler and the remainder of Wharton's force moved northwest toward the Cumberland River.[41]

Wheeler also brought along White's Tennessee Battery, light 6-pounders under command of Lt. Arthur Pice. The cavalryman headed for Neeley's Bend, a place where the Cumberland River curved and where the L&N tracks ran alongside the north bank within 300 yards of the channel. Unfortunately for Wheeler's plan, a pair of Union blockhouses covered the only useable ford, preventing the Rebels from crossing the river, but by stealthily planting Pice's cannon and supporting dismounted cavalry along the south bank, they could engage any passing trains. At 4 p.m., a target hove into view.[42]

Wheeler's men opened fire and, as Wharton reported, secured a damaging hit to the locomotive with the second shot: "the steam-pipe was cut, the steam escaped, and the train was slowly stopped." The cargo included horses intended for the Union cavalry, some cattle, and Company B of the 23rd Michigan, riding a platform car in the middle of the train. Losses of both animals and men mounted as Pice's 6-pounders worked over their stationary target, although ultimately only two Michiganders were reported wounded, one mortally. Pleased with this success, by 4:45 p.m. Wheeler ordered a withdrawal.[43]

Meanwhile, Lieutenant Colonel Ferrill struck the N&C rail line just south of Antioch Station, about halfway between Lavergne and Nashville. Upon reaching

40 Longacre, *Cavalry of the Heartland*, 198. At first blush Forrest seems unlikely to be labeled a publicity hound, but men on his staff often authored favorable articles for newspapers, which at times led to conflict between him and other Confederate commanders.

41 OR 23, pt. 1, 219.

42 Robert L. Willett, "We Rushed with a Yell," *Civil War Times Illustrated*, vol. 8, no. 10 (February 1970), 18-19.

43 Willett, "We Rushed with a Yell," 19; OR 23, pt. 1, 220.

the tracks, the Rebels removed "two rails from a curve in the track in order to derail any train approaching." There was a Union stockade protecting a bridge over nearby Mill Creek, out of sight behind a clump of dense cedars. Deploying 200 men to watch the stockade, Ferrell and the rest of his men waited for some traffic.[44]

At 4:30 p.m., a heavily laden train approached, and was unable to stop before the break. With the cars derailed, the passengers inside—Federal soldiers, civilians, and even 40 Confederate prisoners—were all helpless against repeated Confederate volleys delivered at between "10 to 50 yards." The train guard, 46 officers and men drawn from the 10th Michigan Infantry, suffered heavily from the initial Rebel fire. George Turner of the 8th Texas Cavalry was one of those lying in wait. "[J]ust as the Engineer saw the broken track and whistled on the breaks, we fired, some at the guard on top and the rest at the windows and platforms," he wrote; "they returned the fire in an instant and jumping out and rallying behind the Cars were about to make us a stubborn fight, when the old Col ordered a charge."[45]

The outnumbered Yanks made a brief fight of it from behind the cars but fled toward a nearby tree line when several hundred yelling Texans came rushing at them. The whole affair took 20 minutes, and the booty was rich. Ferrill estimated that his men killed "75 or 80" of the enemy (the Michiganders reported 6 killed and 12 wounded), took 11 officers prisoner, including three members of Rosecrans's staff, paroled perhaps another 150 prisoners on the scene, and captured $30,000 in Union greenbacks. Then Ferrill departed before any Federal response could appear.[46]

Taken by themselves, the two attacks hardly amounted to more than a pinprick—more serious, perhaps, than a few passing shots from guerrillas, but hardly amounting to any significant interdiction of Rosecrans's supply line. However, they demonstrated that large bodies of Confederate could ride into and out of Union lines with impunity and that almost no place that was not fortified and heavily garrisoned was safe from attack, a fact every Federal was well aware of. Two days later Indiana Lieutenant Chamberlain recorded the incident in his weekly letter home. "Last Friday," he wrote, "some guerrillas (estimated to number 400 or

---

44 Willett, "We Rushed with a Yell," 19; OR 23, pt. 1, 216.

45 H. J. H. Rugeley, ed. *Batchelor-Turner Letters, 1861-1864, Written by Two of Terry's Texas Rangers* (Austin, TX: 1961), 48. At the time of this fight, George Turner was technically still a civilian. He enlisted as a private in the 8th in 1861 but was discharged due to Illness in 1862. Once well, he returned to his regiment, but was not formally reenrolled until July.

46 OR 23, pt. 1, 216-217, 220-221.

500) threw the passenger train . . . off the track, within three miles of here, and completely sacked it." Several officers of the 10th Kentucky Infantry, in Chamberlain's brigade, were present, but "gave their 'leg bail'" and escaped. The 74th Indiana's regimental sutler was not so lucky. He was captured, losing considerable stock, but the Rebels did overlook $3,000 hidden in his boot.[47]

April 10 was a busy day on the Franklin front as well. That Friday, Generals Van Dorn and Forrest made yet another effort to sting the Yankees. The Confederate camps were equally awash in speculation that spring, with the common gossip suggesting a Federal retreat. Lieutenant James Bates of the 9th Texas Cavalry noted, "we have rumours here daily of the evacuation of Nashville and Murfreesboro, but I think they are without foundation. It is true the yanks are fortifying Boling green [Bowling Green, Kentucky] and other points in their rear, but I think these are only precautionary measures. . . ." Accordingly, when Brig. Gen. William Jackson passed word to Van Dorn on April 9 that the Union garrison at Franklin might be pulling out, Van Dorn decided to investigate. This investigation turned into a full-scale expedition involving both Jackson's and Forrest's divisions, numbering 6,516 officers and men.[48]

Despite the size of the force, it is likely that Van Dorn did not expect to find Franklin vulnerable. The Rebels knew full well that the Union garrison there had been strongly reinforced since March's disasters, and despite the losses suffered at Thompson's Station and Brentwood, Maj. Gen. Gordon Granger reported his strength as just short of 8,000 men: "5,194 infantry, 2,728 cavalry, eighteen pieces of artillery, and two siege guns." Van Dorn later averred that "his purpose was to create a diversion in favor of Bragg's troops at Tullahoma." Given the lack of surviving records in the Confederate cavalry commands, it cannot be known whether Van Dorn specifically intended to create a distraction in support of Wheeler's raid, but the timing suggests it.[49]

If there was a real shot at capturing Franklin, Van Dorn intended to seize it. Colonel Lawrence Sullivan "Sul" Ross currently commanded the Texas Brigade in Jackson's Division as a result of the frequent absence of the regular commander,

47 "Near Lavergne Tenn. April 12th 1863," Chamberlain Papers. The sutler was among those captured and paroled, even though he was technically a civilian, not a soldier.

48 Richard Lowe, ed. *A Texas Cavalry Officer's Civil War: The Diary and Letters of James C. Bates* (Baton Rouge, LA: 1999), 242; Jordan and Pryor, *Campaigns of Forrest's Cavalry*, 245; OR 23, pt. 2, 749.

49 Arthur B. Carter, *The Tarnished Cavalier Major General Earl Van Dorn, C.S.A.* (Knoxville, TN: 1999), 174; OR 23, pt. 1, 222.

Col. John W. Whitfield. "Whitfield," Ross grumbled, "has been frolicking around seeing his friends & Enjoying himself and scheming to get the appointment of Brgd. Genl, leaving me all the work to do." On April 12, Ross wrote that "Day before yesterday Genl Van Dorn moved . . . up to Franklin. . . . [H]e was under the impression the Enemy had withdrawn . . . and he might be able to take it by storm."[50]

Jackson's division marched north from Spring Hill along the Columbia Pike, while Forrest did the same along the Lewisburg Pike. Just after noon, Jackson's leading brigade encountered Union pickets, seven companies of the 40th Ohio Infantry. They numbered "less than three hundred men," reported Ohio Capt. Charles G. Matchett, who commanded the Ohioans that day, deployed in an arc across both roads. Shortly thereafter, Brig. Gen. Frank Armstrong's brigade, of Forrest's command, ran into more of Matchett's men deployed on the Lewisburg Pike.[51]

Over the next two hours, Van Dorn cautiously skirmished with the Federal picket line. Even when Armstrong's brigade joined the fray on Van Dorn's right, the short-statured Mississippian chose not to press. When no Union reinforcements appeared to bolster his own line, Matchett ordered a careful withdrawal back to the outskirts of town, where his Buckeyes could resist from existing rifle pits and more substantial fortifications. During this movement, noted Matchett, "a formidable line of cavalry . . . composed of from one thousand five hundred to two thousand five hundred men . . . were just beyond the range of our guns to [our] front." These were probably Ross's Texans, now visible across an open field. Van Dorn's troopers easily could have overrun the 40th had they pursued the fight more aggressively, but for some reason, they chose not to do so. The 40th's losses for the entire day amounted to three killed, four wounded, and 10 missing.[52]

The Rebels were made cautious since Ross could now see the "huge Forts & fortifications with their Bristling siege guns" and, more importantly, so could Van Dorn. "By this time," wrote Ross, Van Dorn "had seen all their Infantry & knew he could not take the place." Instead, Van Dorn ordered his artillery to toss a few shells into the town, prompting the Federal cannon to respond in kind. By 5:00

---

50 Perry Wayne Shelton, ed.*Personal Civil War Letters of General Lawrence Sullivan Ross with Other Letters*, (Austin, TX: 1994), 49.

51 Moore, *Rebellion Record*, 6: 519.

52 Ibid., 519-520.

p.m., the Rebels departed, and Matchett's Ohioans cautiously resumed their original positions.[53]

Despite enlivening Captain Matchett's otherwise dull afternoon, Van Dorn's action at Franklin amounted to little more than a skirmish. Quickly asserting victory, Gordon Granger bombastically proclaimed that "our siege-guns and light batteries . . . literally strew[ed] the ground with [dead] men and horses." Van Dorn made no official report of his loss, but Ross admitted to losing "many horses" and about 69 of his men wounded and killed. Granger subsequently concluded, "Since this attack I have been informed that it was made with the belief that my infantry had been removed to Nashville." He further sneered, "Since Van Dorn's repulse, he facetiously calls his attack an armed reconnaissance in force." No one was going to cheapen General Granger's triumph if he could help it.[54]

Forrest and his men had a more difficult day, culminating in an incident that reverberated through the ranks of both sides and proved more important than another day's outpost squabbling. As noted, Forrest's lead brigade under Armstrong joined in the fighting against the Ohioans mid-afternoon. Forrest's other brigade, now under Colonel Starnes, trailed Armstrong on the Lewisburg Pike by about 2 miles. The 9th Tennessee Cavalry led Starnes's column, and behind it came Capt. Samuel L. Freeman's artillery battery.[55]

The Lewisburg Pike ran along the south bank of the Harpeth for several miles southeast of Franklin. That morning, Union Maj. Gen. David S. Stanley and 1,600 troopers were camped just east of town, north of the Harpeth. As Van Dorn probed Franklin's defenses, Stanley took his own force four miles to the southeast, crossed the river at a ford near Hughes's Mill and moved to take Forrest's column in flank. The Rebels were careless. Colonel Starnes "supposed there was no risk, and omitted to throw out flankers on his right." Upon crossing the river, the 4th U.S. Cavalry spotted Starnes's column leisurely moving up the road and immediately charged.[56]

"The Fourth cavalry dashed upon the center of Starnes' line, broke it, driving it demoralized from the field; then charged upon [Freeman's] battery," recorded Lt. Joseph Vale, who later became the brigade historian for Robert Minty's cavalry.

53 Shelton, *Personal Civil War Letters*, 49.

54 Ibid., 49; OR 23, pt. 2, 220-221, 227.

55 Jordan and Pryor, *Campaigns of General Forrest*, 247.

56 OR 23, pt. 1, p. 230; Jordan and Pryor, *Campaigns of General Forrest*, 246.

What Vale described as "a short but desperate encounter" occurred as the Federals overran the guns and captured several prisoners—a view of the action generally agreed upon by both sides. From there, however, Northern and Southern accounts diverged.[57]

The Confederates claimed that Freeman was among those captured when the regulars seized his guns. "The gunners and drivers not captured quit their pieces," admitted Forrest's historians, "and some of the caissons . . . were driven into the first [Rebel] regiment to the rear, causing at first a good deal of disorder." Dismounting Col. Jacob Biffle's 9th Tennessee Cavalry, Starnes organized a counterattack, which drove off the regulars but failed to rescue "that gallant and most valuable officer," Freeman, along with 30 other members of the battery. The retreating Federals ordered Freeman to run, and when he couldn't keep up, "an officer rode up and shot him through the head, to prevent his recapture." Starnes had his horse shot out from under him in this charge, and the Federals captured the gold-mounted saber that Forrest had given him, which was strapped to his saddle. Starnes never recovered that saber.[58]

Freeman's murder—had it occurred as described—would have been an atrocity and an outrage. Naturally, the Federal side of the story is much different. Vale, in his postwar history, recounted that Freeman was indeed shot at close range by Sgt. Maj. Sherlock E. Strickland, but only after Freeman refused to surrender and fired three shots at Lt. Joseph Rendlebock of the 4th, missing each time. The Confederates, wrote Vale, "invented a cock and bull story . . . that Captain Freeman was murdered . . . after he had surrendered" to obscure Starnes's blunder. Vale also accused Forrest's men of trying "to give a color of excuse for atrocities committed by themselves," though he listed no specific incidents.[59]

The attack certainly embarrassed Forrest. According to Vale, the Rebel losses in this fight were "fifty-seven killed and over one hundred and fifty wounded or

---

57 Vale, *Minty and the Cavalry*, 145-146.

58 Jordan and Pryor, *Campaigns of General Forrest*, 247; H. Gerald Starnes, *Forrest's Forgotten Horse Brigadier* (Bowie, MD: 1995), 64.

59 Vale, *Minty and the Cavalry*, 146. One very famous incident was the murder of Col. Robert L. McCook by Rebel cavalry in August 1862. McCook was ill and being transported when he was overtaken by bushwackers near Huntsville, Alabama (less than 100 miles from Franklin), and shot while prostrate in an ambulance. The news of his murder spread quickly through the Army of the Cumberland, and a Rebel officer was even arrested for the deed. It is interesting to speculate about whether General Polk would have been so solicitous of Rosecrans's own welfare in the course of Malone's kidnapping scheme had it come after the news of Freeman's death had spread through the army.

captured," set against "five killed and eighteen wounded" among the 4th. Vale probably exaggerated the Rebel numbers, since Forrest reported only 70 total casualties, including 31 taken prisoner, but Col. Ross's informal estimate of the Confederate losses did more closely mirror Vale's: "near 150 men killed & wounded & many horses." Freeman's battery was also badly damaged. The guns were spiked and several caissons were chopped up during the short time they were in Federal possession.[60]

Whatever the truth of the matter, the rumor of murder-most-foul spread quickly through the Rebel ranks. Cavalry Lt. James Bates of the 9th Texas, in Jackson's division, described the incident a week later. "[T]hey deliberately shot the Capt. of the battery & thus made their escape. I should not be surprised if the prisoners captured by us should be made to suffer for the very cowardly acts of their men. This is the Second Man who has been murdered by the Scoundrels since we have been in Tenn. It looks hard that men who may be innocent should be made to suffer for the crime of others, but in such instances . . . I think the law of retaliation should be carried to its full extent." Vale acknowledged that Freeman's death and the ensuing rumors created "a bitter, blood-thirsty feeling on the part of their soldiers against efficient cavalry regiments in general and the Fourth Regulars in particular." Here again, an outwardly inconsequential affair proved to have larger repercussions.[61]

Of course, the Confederates did not initiate every raid. Rosecrans, in his struggle to gain ascendency over his opponent, pushed his own forces to take the war to the enemy wherever they could and, besides, he constantly needed to requisition forage and livestock from the surrounding farms. As spring approached, those efforts began to bear fruit, especially over on the Confederate right, east of Murfreesboro. The first harbinger of a growing Union assertiveness on the Confederate right came on March 1, at the hamlet of Bradyville, about 16 miles east and a little south of Murfreesboro. Major General Stanley led the expedition in person, consisting of "a foraging train of 400 wagons" escorted by three brigades of cavalry and one of infantry— perhaps 6,000 men in all. They met Brig. Gen. Basil Duke's brigade of Morgan's Kentucky division just outside Bradyville and, in keeping with Rosecrans's desires, immediately attacked.[62]

---

60 Vale, *Minty and the Cavalry*, 146; OR 23, pt. 2, 239; Shelton, *Personal Civil War Letters*, 50.

61 Lowe, *A Texas Cavalry Officer's Civil War*, 242; Vale, *Minty and the Cavalry*, 146.

62 OR 23, pt. 1, 65.

The Union 1st Middle Tennessee Cavalry opened the fight, soon supported by elements of the 3rd and 4th Ohio Infantry. Colonel Eli Long of the 4th reported that his regiment charged, driving the enemy back some three and a half miles, through and beyond Bradyville. The Confederates were more embarrassed than bloodied, for while they suffered somewhere between 50 and 100 casualties, the next day General Rosecrans was able to inform Halleck, "we took 70 prisoners, including 8 officers, their camp equipage, tents, saddles, and some 70 horses, and Basil [W.] Duke's regimental papers. . . . We lost 1 man killed and 1 captain and 7 men wounded." However, in one respect the expedition was a washout: Union Col. John F. Miller, commanding the infantry brigade, reported that "there was no forage on or near the Bradyville Road."[63]

On March 18 Union Col. Albert S. Hall of the 105th Ohio led a brigade of 1,300 men on an expedition to toward Liberty, Tennessee, where one of John Hunt Morgan's brigades was headquartered. On the 19th, Morgan attempted to attack Hall's column. With only 1,000 men and two pieces of artillery, and absent the services of his ablest brigadier, Basil Duke, Morgan hoped to ambush Hall's force (estimated at 2,000 to 4,000 infantry) "while they were moving and vulnerable." Alerted, Hall's men took up a strong position. "Morgan dispatched detachments to the right and left to flank [the Federals] . . . Then he brought up his artillery, and on the first volley, ordered a frontal assault. . . . Men charged up the rough and broken ground and were cut to pieces by grape and canister from the Union artillery." The result was a bloody repulse. Morgan lost at least 150 men, including a number of officers, while Hall reported a loss of 6 dead, 42 wounded, and 8 prisoners. Rosecrans later crowed that Hall "whipped and drove" Morgan from the field.[64]

Other probes soon followed. From April 2 to 6 (just before fighting at Franklin), Colonel Minty's brigade reconnoitered to Auburn, Tennessee, skirmishing with Wheeler's cavalry on April 3. From April 1 to April 8, Col. John T. Wilder took his brigade of 2,500 mounted infantrymen to Carthage, Tennessee, on a foraging mission, returning via the hamlets of Snow Hill and Liberty. Wilder reported, "the fruits of the expedition are about 400 horses and mules, 194 negroes, and 88 prisoners of war," besides "destroy[ing] 5,000 bushels of wheat and a large quantity of bacon."[65]

63 Ibid., 65, 69.

64 *OR* 23, pt. 1, 156-159; Ramage, *Rebel Raider,* 152.

65 *OR* 23, pt. 1, 200-202, 207-214.

Late in April, Rosecrans ordered out a larger expedition to McMinnville, Tennessee, 40 miles east of Murfreesboro. He sent a combined force of 6,600 troops under command of Maj. Gen. Joseph J. Reynolds to destroy the rail spur from Manchester to McMinnville, carry off as much provender as he could, and destroy whatever he could not bring back to Union lines. McMinnville was deep in enemy territory, a source of supply for the Army of Tennessee, and the location of General Morgan's headquarters.

Departing on April 20, Reynolds's leading elements thundered into McMinnville the next day, achieving complete surprise. Two companies of the 7th Pennsylvania Cavalry ran into Rebel pickets about a mile and a half away and drove them back into town. There, the rest of the 7th came up and the whole force charged the Confederate defenders, "numbering about seven hundred infantry and cavalry. The charge was entirely successful—the rebel cavalry scattered and fled, and the infantry, numbering over a hundred, was captured." General Morgan was also almost made prisoner. He had sent his recent bride, Mattie, away in an ambulance when the first reports of Union troops reached him, but he himself was still in town when the Pennsylvanians arrived. The quick thinking of two subordinates saved him from capture. Colonel Robert M. Martin of the Confederate 10th Kentucky Cavalry shouted "run for it" and then "spurred his horse directly toward the charging enemy, his bridle rein held between his teeth and both pistols blazing." Martin's escapade bought time for Morgan to escape, though at the cost of a chest wound. Major Dick McCann, a guerilla leader and one of Morgan's most accomplished scouts, "provided a second diversion," identifying himself as Morgan to the approaching Yankees, who seized him and imprisoned him in a stable. McCann escaped that night, much to the Federals' chagrin.[66]

These Rebel heroics could do little to mask what was clearly a significant reversal, and Reynolds's expedition returned successfully a week later with minimal casualties. Reynolds found large numbers of loyal citizens along the way, however, some of whom returned to Union lines as refugees, and many others who worried about their futures. "We were everywhere met with the questions," Reynolds reported, "'will the Federal army remain in Middle Tennessee?' 'Will it go forward and leave us, or will it go back and leave us?'"[67]

McMinnville's occupation, however brief, triggered a significant Confederate response. Brig. Gen. William T. Martin reported Reynolds's movement to Bragg at

66 Sipes, *The Saber Regiment*, 59; Ramage, *Rebel Raider*, 154-156.

67 *OR* 23, pt. 1, 269-270.

Tullahoma on April 21, including in that report additional details of Federals moving against Manchester via Hoover's Gap and toward Beech Grove, just north of Wartrace. That same day, Bragg ordered General Hardee to move his entire corps from Tullahoma to Wartrace and to reinforce Manchester. "Fairfield and Bell Buckle will be picketed," Bragg further instructed. Hardee's move began on April 22, and though it did not result in any encounter with Reynolds's expedition, it did have the effect of shifting Bragg's army to positions well north of Tullahoma.[68]

Smaller actions continued to punctuate daily affairs, clashes of a couple of hundred men here, a couple of hundred there. Rosecrans encouraged these efforts all he could, hoping to instill that spirit of aggression in as many of his cavalry officers as possible, but it was slow going and he was impatient by nature. On April 6, Brig. Gen. Robert B. Mitchell, commander of the Nashville garrison, took a patrol of 400 men "for the purpose of cleaning out the Stones River country." Upon Mitchell's successful return, Rosecrans wired congratulations. "Only one complaint," he added. "Some of your cavalry officers ought to have snap enough to do such things without troubling you to command in person."[69]

If Rosecrans wanted "snap," he found it in Col. Abel D. Streight of the 51st Indiana Infantry, who proposed a raid to match any ever conducted by Forrest or Morgan. Streight's intended target was the Western & Atlantic Railroad in northern Georgia, which ran from Atlanta to Chattanooga. Since the beginning of the war, Atlanta had developed into a budding industrial and transportation hub. A spur line, the eponymous Rome Railroad, ran west to the city of Rome, another place bustling with the commerce of war.

This was not the first time the Federals attempted a strike at this Confederate lifeline. In 1862, a party of 22 Union volunteers led by civilian scout James J. Andrews slipped into Georgia on that same mission in support of a simultaneous advance on Chattanooga by Maj. Gen. Ormsby Mitchel. Andrews and his band (men drawn from the 2nd, 21st, and 33rd Ohio) rendezvoused at Marietta, Georgia, in April 1862, intending to seize a locomotive and then run north toward Chattanooga, damaging the rails as much as they could along the way. Though Andrews's men successfully stole a train, the Rebels immediately pursued, and the raiders inflicted minimal damage before being caught near Ringgold. Though this colorful episode was afterwards dubbed the Andrews Raid or the Great

68 Ibid., pt. 2, 279-80.

69 Ibid., 215.

Locomotive Chase, it was really more of a commando mission. Andrews and seven other raiders were hung as spies. The rest eventually escaped and returned to Union lines.

Andrews failed, but now Streight, with an entire brigade, believed he could succeed. A businessman from Indianapolis, Streight helped raise the 51st Indiana Infantry and was appointed its colonel by Indiana Governor Oliver P. Morton in December 1861. Since then, the regiment had seen little action, much to Streight's dismay. Its closest brush with combat came at Shiloh, where the men participated in the counterattack on April 7, 1862, but were relegated to a supporting role. The regiment saw no action at Perryville, and though it did see fighting at Stones River, Streight hungered for more prominent duty. An independent raid deep into enemy territory seemed just the thing. It didn't hurt the mission's chances of securing approval that Abel Streight was a friend of James Garfield. On March 5, 1863, he pitched his idea to Garfield, asking him to bring it to Rosecrans's attention.[70]

Here was "snap" indeed. Rosecrans enthusiastically endorsed the idea. Streight hurried to Nashville to handpick four regiments—the 51st and 73rd Indiana, the 80th Illinois, and the 3rd Ohio—along with companies of the locally raised 1st Alabama (US) Cavalry to act as guides and scouts. He had a total of 1,700 men. The first snag came when the Federal army couldn't find enough horses to mount Streight's whole force. In early April, it was decided to use mules instead, but that was no solution—there weren't enough mules either. When Streight departed Nashville on April 10, he had only 800 animals, many of them unbroken colts. The rest of the command was "ordered to supply their own mounts on the way to Georgia."[71]

To deceive the Rebels, Streight's men boarded boats at Fort Henry and steamed south up the Tennessee River to Eastport. Mississippi, where the Tennessee turned east. Debarking there, Streight intended to finish collecting his needed livestock and then set out across northern Alabama toward Rome and the W&A. Union Brig. Gen. Grenville M. Dodge was to launch a supporting mission in northern Mississippi, rendezvousing with Streight at Eastport on April 16. When Streight arrived, two days late, Dodge dubiously noted that Streight still had only 1,000 mules, and of those "at least 400 of them were unserviceable." Worse, during the unloading, "200 strayed away." Streight's assumption that animals would be

70 Robert L. Willett, *The Lightning Mule Brigade: Abel Streight's 1863 Raid into Alabama* (Carmel, IN: 1999), 11.

71 Ibid., 30.

plentiful in the Tuscumbia River Valley also proved false. Eventually, Dodge loaned the ill-fated expedition 600 of his own animals. Both forces moved together as far as the town of Tuscumbia, where they separated on April 26. Streight was on his way.[72]

Confederate Col. Phillip D. Roddey's cavalry brigade defended northern Alabama. As Dodge and Streight moved into Alabama, Roddy sent word to Bragg, who in turn ordered Forrest to move south. Bragg's order was well timed, because relations between Van Dorn and Forrest were deteriorating. In the week following the most recent Franklin fight, Van Dorn took issue with Forrest and called him to account in a confrontation that nearly escalated into violence. Various reasons were given for the blowup. Van Dorn was "irritated by newspaper reports that tended to magnify Forrest's role in . . . recent . . . victories," but also, "the generals quarreled over the distribution of captured military supplies." By one account, Forrest demanded satisfaction, and by another, Van Dorn drew his saber. The tension of the moment dissolved when, according to Col. Edward Dillon of the 2nd Mississippi Cavalry, Forrest spoke up, "the truth is you and I have enough Yankees to fight without fighting each other." Major J. Minnick Williams, of Van Dorn's staff, recalled something very similar. "Forrest passed his hand slowly across his forehead and then spoke. 'I have been hasty, General, and I am sorry for it. I do not fear that anyone will misunderstand me, but the truth is that you and I have enough Yankees to fight without fighting each other, and I hope this will be forgotten.'"[73]

Forrest departed for Alabama with his old brigade, leaving Armstrong's men with Van Dorn. Over the next 11 days, he pursued Streight's Federals across the width of Alabama with his and Roddy's commands in what became one of the most storied exploits of Forrest's colorful career. After a series of running engagements, Forrest ran Streight's expedition (which never really had much of a shot at success) to ground on May 3 near Gaylesville, Alabama, 20 miles west of Rome. Streight's exhausted men, stuck with unmanageable animals, were forced to abandon many of their wounded along the way. Morale was shot. Streight

---

72 OR 23, pt. 1, 246-248. Dodge was part of Grant's Army of the Tennessee, where coincidentally, Ulysses S. Grant was organizing his own cavalry raid. On April 17, Brig. Gen. Benjamin H. Grierson and 1,700 cavalrymen departed La Grange, Tennessee, headed to Baton Rouge, Louisiana, their mission to divert attention from Grant's operations around Vicksburg.

73 Brian Steel Wills, *A Battle from the Start: The Life of Nathan Bedford Forrest* (New York: 1992), 107; Edward Dillon, "General Van Dorn's Operations between Columbia and Nashville in 1863," *Southern Historical Society Papers,* 52 vols. (Richmond, VA: 1876-1959), 7:144-146; Carter, *The Tarnished Cavalier,* 178.

surrendered 1,400 men to Forrest and 600 Rebels in another humiliating Federal defeat.[74]

Streight and his men did eventually reach Rome. Forrest marched them there after the surrender, where the enlisted men were paroled while the officers were sent to Richmond's Libby Prison. The town, which had been bracing for the arrival of disaster, greeted the arrival of Forrest and his men as triumphant heroes. They gave Forrest "a beautiful horse named 'King Philip'" and planned a celebration for May 6. The Federals fared less well. Though no one was physically harmed, many Yanks reported that citizens stole their haversacks and other personal possessions, which Forrest had allowed them to keep.[75]

The loss of Streight's brigade, while a more predictable defeat than the disasters at Hartsville, Thompson's Station, and Brentwood, provided yet more proof that Rosecrans had every reason to be cautious in the face of such an aggressive enemy. Effectively, the Confederate cavalry had eliminated what amounted to an entire division of Union troops—three brigades, nearly 6,000 men—in the space of a few months, at minimal cost to themselves and without fighting a major battle. "Snap" was all well and good. Losing whole brigades at a crack was another thing entirely.

There was an interesting pattern to this season of skirmishing, one Rosecrans could not help but notice. As historians Dennis W. Belcher and Michael R. Bradley have noted, throughout these clashes, "Rosecrans was far more successful . . . [against] Wheeler and Morgan [to the east], and . . . was roughly handled by Van Dorn and Forrest on the west."

74 Willett, *The Lightening Mule Brigade*, 165. Although there does not appear to be any evidence that Rosecrans and Maj. Gen. Ulysses S. Grant coordinated their actions, the simultaneous launch of Col. Benjamin Grierson's extended cavalry raid through Mississippi and Louisiana distracted sufficient Confederate attention, and drew off sufficient resources, to give Grant the opportunity to get his entire Army of the Tennessee across the Mississippi River undetected so it could march on Vicksburg. Streight and 107 other Union officers being held at Libby Prison dug a tunnel and escaped. Streight made his way back to Union lines and eventually returned to duty. For a good recent treatment of the escape by Streight and the other Union officers, see Joseph A. Wheelan, *Libby Prison Breakout: The Daring Escape from the Notorious Civil War Prison* (New York: 2010).

75 Willett, *The Lightening Mule Brigade*, 170-71. Nathan Forrest and his troopers never got that celebration. On May 5, General Bragg ordered them to rejoin the Army of Tennessee near Columbia.

For example:

Actions on the Western Flank:

March 3, Thompson's Station: Confederate Victory
March 24, Brentwood: Confederate Victory
April 10, Franklin: Confederates achieved goals
April 29-May 3, Streight's Raid: Confederate Victory

Actions on the Eastern Flank:

March 1, Bradyville: Union Victory
March 19-20, Liberty: Union Victory
April 3, Snow Hill: Union Victory
April 21, McMinnville: Union Victory[76]

By the beginning of May, it looked as though the Army of Tennessee's eastern flank was vulnerable.

---

76 Dennis W. Belcher, *The Cavalry of the Army of the Cumberland* (Jefferson, NC: 2016), 86; Michael Bradley, "Varying Results of Cavalry Fighting: Western Flank vs. Eastern Flank," *Blue and Gray*, vol. XXVII, no. 1 (2010), 21.

Chapter Four

Numbers Gained, Numbers Lost

With May's arrival, the Confederate Army of Tennessee peaked in strength, efficiency, and morale. Bragg's April 30 return to the field came with 52,069 "effectives" (defined by army headquarters as "only . . . those who are carried onto the field of battle with firearms in their hands," a category that excluded officers), 56,999 "present for duty" (officers and enlisted, excepting those sick, detached, or otherwise not ready for combat), and 67,838 "aggregate present" (including all the men excluded from "present for duty"). Of those, 15,125 were cavalry, principally in Joe Wheeler's and Earl Van Dorn's two corps. Bragg's growing strength allowed him to issue a very popular order. "All [consolidated] Regts. numbering over 400 men were to again to return to themselves & under their old officers," noted Pvt. Robert M. Holmes of the 24th Mississippi Infantry. "The men were very glad to hear this for they had become tired of the officers that are now in comd. of them."[1]

With the Confederate cavalry handling most of the day-to-day cut and thrust between the two armies, the infantry found more time to enhance its train. Captain Arthur T. Fielder of the 12th Tennessee chronicled daily drills, morning and afternoon, all through the month of April. First came drills by company and

---

1 OR 23, pt. 2, 619, 806; Frank Allen Dennis, ed. , *Kemper County Rebel: The Civil War Diary of Robert Masten Holmes, C.S.A.,* (Jackson, MS: 1973), 89. Over the past year, attrition and desertion forced many regiments to combine, consolidating companies and in some cases forcing men to serve under officers from other commands. Fiercely individualistic, Civil War soldiers usually elected their own officers and resented it when that franchise was overridden, as often happened with consolidation.

battalion, working up to brigade level toward the end of the period, all interspersed with frequent reviews by senior officers. In addition, there was instruction of another sort, so far quite rare within Civil War armies to this point in the war: rudimentary marksmanship.[2]

Probably the most famous tactical innovation to occur during this period had to do with the creation of Confederate Whitworth Sharpshooter units, a distinctly different animal than the existing sharpshooter battalions already serving in many Confederate infantry brigades. The sharpshooter battalions had been organized in 1862 and were aimed at producing more skillful and effective skirmishers. They were a de facto American version of European light infantry. Until the Union war department shot down General Rosecrans's "elite battalions," his idea was intended to accomplish the same mission for the Army of the Cumberland. The Whitworth Sharpshooters, by contrast, were small numbers of expert marksmen detailed for long range work—snipers, in modern parlance, though that term had yet to come into common use.[3]

In the spring of 1863, a handful of very expensive British-manufactured Whitworth rifles were shipped to the Army of Tennessee. The Whitworth was a precision long-range weapon capable of hitting targets at up to 1,500 yards. While popular lore generally credits Confederate Maj. Gen. Patrick R. Cleburne for coming up with the idea, the concept actually originated at Bragg's headquarters. And the entire army embraced it. Each division received an allotment of the new guns, to be distributed based on proven skill. To determine the level of that skill, brigades and regiments held shooting competitions. The best shots received the weapons and were then detailed away from their regiments directly to divisional headquarters.

Since effective long-range fire with low-muzzle-velocity weapons also required a great deal of skill in the arcane art of range estimation, the new sharpshooters next received intensive training in that area. Captain Irving Buck of Cleburne's division recalled that "Major [Calhoun] Benham, of the division staff instructed . . . them to judge distance by the eye (no range finders were in use) by marching them to ground of different topographical features. An object pointed out, and distance to

---

2 M. Todd Cathey, ed., *Captain A. T. Fielder's Civil War Diary, Company B, 12th Tennessee Infantry, C.S.A., July 1861-June 1865,* (Nashville, TN: 2012), 209-216.

3 Infrequent use of the term "sniper" dates to the 18th century, but it did not become common in British military usage until the Boer War. The US military picked it up in World War One.

it estimated, after which the actual distance would be measured. By constant practice the men became quite expert in doing this."[4]

The Whitworth men received the most attention, but almost everyone in the army received at least some training in ranged fire. On April 24, 1863, Mississippian Robert Holmes recorded that at evening parade, "an ordor [from General Polk] was read . . . that every man should [shoot] four times a piece at a tarket & the ones that made the best shots should be made known to hd.qt." Six days later, Captain Fielder's company of the 12th Tennessee, in Frank Cheatham's division, "was marched out this morning to shoot at a Target in Compliance with an order from Gen. Polk to his corps," with more target

Maj. Gen. Patrick R. Cleburne, commander, Cleburne's Division, Hardee's Corps, Army of Tennessee.

Generals in Gray

practice the next day, May 1. Private E. H. Rennolds of the 4th Tennessee Infantry, also in Cheatham's division, noted that his company made "one shot at two hundred yards, 2 at 400 and one at 600 with their Springfield rifles." Accuracy was not stressed. Rennolds "had the misfortune to miss every shot."[5]

Cleburne, who had prewar British army experience, expanded the instruction in rudimentary range estimation and target shooting to his entire command, as did at least some other Confederate divisions. The practice caught Bragg's eye. Later that summer Bragg arranged for Maj. Calhoun Benham to write a manual based on Cleburne's training methods—derived in turn from the methods used at the British

4 Howell and Elizabeth Pardue, *Pat Cleburne, Confederate General: A Definitive Biography* (Hillsboro, TX: 1973), 185-187; Irving A. Buck, *Cleburne and his Command* (New York: 1908), 128. Some Kerr rifles, similar to Whitworth rifles, also found their way to Tennessee and were issued at this time.

5 Dennis, *Kemper County Rebel*, 91; Cathey, *Fielder's Civil War Diary*, 216; E. H. Rennolds Diary, Tennessee State Library and Archives, Nashville, TN.

School of Musketry at Hythe—and have it printed for distribution through the army. Though Benham's work was not finished until September, it quantified the type of training experienced by at least some of the men in the Army of Tennessee while stationed around Shelbyville and Wartrace.[6]

Far more attention was paid to drill. As the weather improved, morning and afternoon drills became a daily staple. Historian Andrew Haughton has estimated that during this period "an average unit would have spent from 18 to 24 hours each week" drilling. Haughton thought that all that effort had a "diminishing benefit" due to a lack of overall innovation within the army, but there was a definite battlefield payoff to such work. Tactical maneuver became reflexive in well-drilled units, increasing reaction speed and unit coherence under fire. Officers also gained greater proficiency in the complicated evolutions of changing formation and maneuver. This was the sort of skill set that armies on the move rarely had time to hone, and the Army of Tennessee had been moving a great deal since the fall of Forts Henry and Donelson back in February 1862. The results were obvious to Davis's envoy, Col. William Preston Johnston. In between trying to resolve the command crisis gripping the army, Johnston spent time observing various exercises and parades. After witnessing one such exhibition put on by the Kentucky "Orphan" Brigade, he wrote: "These troops . . . went through battalion drill, by regiments, and in the afternoon had a brigade drill. Their performance was rapid, yet precise, their appearance tough and active, and they will compare for efficiency with any brigade in the Confederate army. . . . There is vast improvement in this army since I inspected it last June at Tupelo."[7]

Another British officer who had come to witness the American struggle was Lt. Col. James Arthur Lyons Fremantle of the Coldstream Guards. That spring he landed in Mexico and journeyed across the South, spending a week with Bragg's

---

6 Purdue and Purdue, *Pat Cleburne, Confederate General*, 185-187; Calhoun Benham, *A System for Conducting Musketry Instruction, Prepared and Printed by Order of General Bragg for the Army of Tennessee* (Richmond, VA: 1863). The debate over range training, weapons training, and combat effectiveness during the Civil War is ongoing. English historian Paddy Griffith challenged the conventional wisdom of Civil War combat with his controversial *Battle Tactics of the Civil War* in 1987. More recent works include Brent Nosworthy, *The Bloody Crucible of Courage* (New York: 2003); and Earl J. Hess, *The Rifle Musket in Civil War Combat: Reality and Myth* (Lawrence, KS: 2008).

7 Andrew Haughton, *Training, Tactics, and Leadership in the Confederate Army of Tennessee* (London: 2000), 118; *OR* 23, pt. 2, 757-758. Houghton feels that the army's tactics stagnated during its stay at Tullahoma, leaving the force unprepared to face the changing nature of war in 1864-65. Given that much more professional and experienced armies would still be unprepared a half century later, in 1914, this seems an overly harsh judgement.

army at the beginning of June, visiting both Polk's and Hardee's headquarters. On June 1, Fremantle watched a review of Brig. Gen. St. John Liddell's Arkansas brigade. "They drilled tolerably well," Fremantle conceded, "and an advance in line was remarkably good; but General Liddell had invented several dodges of his own, for which he was reproved by General Hardee." The mix of civilian and military attire that most troops wore struck Fremantle as worthy of note. He was also a bit put off that so many of the troops lacked bayonets. Hoping to watch a brigade or regiment deploy into squares, he was further disappointed to discover that the Rebel infantry never used that formation. "The country did not admit of cavalry charges, even if the Yankee cavalry had stomach to attempt it," explained one of his hosts.[8]

Perhaps the greatest exhibition mounted by the Army of Tennessee during this interlude occurred at Tullahoma on April 11. Lieutenant James P. Baltzell of Bragg's staff witnessed the spectacle. "There has been a grand review of the army today—beyond all doubt the grandest of the war. The troops were reviewed by General J. E. Johnston. Sixty thousand infantry marched in the grandest order," he enthused. "I think I can safely say that we have here one of the grandest armies that ever walked upon earth, and General Bragg has made it what it is." Though Baltzell exaggerated the Rebel numbers, the assembled men obviously made for an impressive sight. Lieutenant Joshua Callaway of the 28th Alabama—comprising "Withers's, Cheatham's and McCown's divisions"—described the same pageant to his wife. He also took stock of his commander. "The review gave me a nearer view of General Bragg than I have ever had before," he wrote. The general's face "looks sad and careworn. I could not avoid a feeling of reverence when he took off his Cap to acknowledge the salute of [our] Colors . . . although, as you are aware, I am not

---

8 Fremantle, *Three Months in the Southern States*, 155-156. The tactic known as "forming square" is a classic Napoleonic technique for infantry to defend against mounted cavalry attacks. Each side of a square was four or six ranks deep, with the front rank kneeling while holding their muskets out, their bayonets thereby forming an intimidating wall of sharp points. These squares themselves were relatively small, with considerable gaps between them, which in turn forced charging cavalry to veer away in order to avoid crashing into them. Their ability to repel enemy cavalry relied upon presenting a solid, impenetrable front rather than overwhelming firepower. The soldiers manning them had to demonstrate tremendous discipline while holding their position—and while holding their fire—awaiting the oncoming horse soldiers thundering toward them. If they held their formation, squares were nearly invincible against the mounted charges. This task, while it sounds relatively easy, was infinitely harder to pull of in practice. Rory Muir, *Tactics and the Experience of Battle in the Age of Napoleon* (New Haven, CT: 1998), 130-132.

Maj. Gen. John C. Breckinridge, commander, Breckinridge's division, Hardee's Corps, Army of Tennessee.

Library of Congress

an admirer of his, by any means." Baltzell, for his part, added, "we are not expecting a fight soon. General Rosecrans is badly frightened."[9]

Reviews and parades were often conducted to build morale, as evidenced by one such event held by Maj. Gen. John C. Breckinridge's division in March. Breckinridge's wife Mary donated two silk dresses—one red, one white—to make "a very handsome regimental flag, which she requested her husband to present to the most gallant regiment in his division." The unit chosen was the 20th Tennessee Infantry. After a divisional review, the entire command formed a hollow square with the 20th in the center. Col. Theodore O'Hara put his rhetorical gifts to work in presenting the color. "Soldiers, to you I commit the gift," he said; "in its folds rest your honor. Let it never be contaminated by a foeman's hand."[10]

Though there were clear benefits to a stationary army in terms of morale-building, training, and discipline, there were also logistical challenges. Armies on the move could usually find sufficient food and forage from a countryside that had not been depleted and then move on to new pastures. Stationary forces, by contrast, soon ate up all the locally available resources, forcing them to depend on a steady flow from more remote areas or, alternatively, to send out their wagons farther each week.

As has been seen, supply was an ever-present concern for General Rosecrans and the Federal army, especially given the large numbers of Rebel cavalry that

---

9 OR 23, pt. 2, 750-751; Judith Lee Hallock, ed., *The Civil War Letters of Joshua K. Callaway*, (Athens, GA: 1997), 83.

10 W. J. McMurray, *History of the Twentieth Tennessee Regiment Volunteer Infantry, C.S.A.* (Nashville, TN: 1904), 252.

constantly swarmed. But it was also a major, if sometimes overlooked, problem for Braxton Bragg. At first glance, Bragg's supply line appeared to be considerably more secure than Rosecrans's. Not only was Bragg's army deployed across a wider arc of Middle Tennessee than were the Federals, but in theory Bragg could use both the Nashville & Chattanooga and Nashville & Decatur Railroads to maintain his force. Even better, it was only 100 miles to Chattanooga, a major staging area for Confederate supply, and it was about the same distance along the N & D to Decatur, Alabama, from where Bragg could draw rations out of the northern part of that state.

In reality, Bragg's logistics were far from secure. The primary reason for this insecurity was simple: logistical needs in Virginia. By 1863, Gen. Robert E. Lee's Army of Northern Virginia could no longer subsist on its own where it fought, drawing foodstuffs from the Carolinas, Georgia, and even East Tennessee. Beyond supporting local garrisons, those regions were reserved for Lee's use. Bragg's army was expected to live off the resources found in the rest of Tennessee. In 1862 that had been possible, for despite the reverses suffered that year, Tennessee still produced "twelve million pounds of meat" for the Confederate war effort. Now, however, many of the most productive parts of the state were in Union hands. Even worse, when Lee's army faced crippling food shortages during the early months of 1863, Confederate "commissary agents denuded the Duck and Elk river valleys," in Bragg's immediate rear, "of corn, hogs, and beeves, which were placed in the central depot in Atlanta for the use of Lee's . . . army." The Nashville & Chattanooga line, far from being a lifeline for Bragg's command, was hauling large quantities of materiel to Atlanta, where it was hoarded for use in Virginia.[11]

The situation bordered on the absurd. At one point that spring, in a moment of severe shortage, "the deputy commissary officer at Atlanta, Major J. F. Cumming, grudgingly allowed [Bragg's] army only 60,000 pounds of meat . . . scarcely three days' supply. Meanwhile during March, the Atlanta depot, which had eight million pounds of salt meat and several thousand head of cattle on hand, was shipping Lee a half million pounds of meat per week." Ironically, had Union Col. Abel Streight's mule raid succeeded in wrecking the rail line between Atlanta and Chattanooga beyond all expectations, Lee's men might have felt the pinch more than Bragg's troops.[12]

---

11 Richard D. Goff, *Confederate Supply* (Durham, NC: 1969), 153; Thomas Lawrence Connelly, *Autumn of Glory: The Army of Tennessee, 1862-1865* (Baton Rouge, LA: 1971), 114.

12 Connelly, *Autumn of Glory*, 114.

Then there was the Nashville & Decatur line, which ran south from Nashville through Franklin, Columbia, and Pulaski, Tennessee, and then to Athens and Decatur, Alabama. Had it been functional, the line might have provided considerable relief. Unfortunately for Bragg, after the evacuation of Nashville in February 1862, more than 30 miles of its track was torn up. Retreating Rebels and Federal cavalry took turns destroying many of the trestle bridges to deny their use to the other side. By the beginning of 1863, this line was thoroughly wrecked and unusable. There were plans to restore it, since that part of Tennessee and northern Alabama could provide abundant sustenance, but for a variety of reasons, that project was badly managed. Initially, it was estimated that the effort would take two months and cost $10,000.

In Richmond, bureaucratic delays hindered the project at the outset. On Bragg's end, keeping the Nashville & Chattanooga line running became a priority, since it had also suffered damage in earlier campaigns and needed constant attention. In March, Bragg finally ordered Maj. John W. Goodwin, the Army of Tennessee's chief of military transportation, to begin repairs. Actual work didn't begin until late that month, by which time the spring floods made each trestle replacement an arduous undertaking. Private contractors failing to meet delivery dates for timbers due to labor shortages also slowed Goodwin's work. Not until June 19 was the line open from Decatur to Pulaski, with the final leg, to Columbia, still unfinished. The actual cost amounted to $60,000. In the interim, any supplies coming from that part of Middle Tennessee or Alabama's Tennessee River Valley had to come by wagon, if they came at all.[13]

These shortages, in addition to dispersing Bragg's men across too wide a front, significantly degraded the army's tactical mobility. Bragg's wagons suffered as they were pressed into service in an ever-widening foraging circuit, wearing out vehicles and draft animals. Bragg's military center of gravity was also kept farther to the west than he desired, a situation that only worsened as forage became depleted east of the N&C. In March, there were 2,276 wagons with the army, supporting an aggregate strength of 65,582 men (as of April 1), which worked out to approximately 35 wagons per thousand troops. Many of those wagons were "old and in many cases unserviceable," worn out by overwork and rough roads. Some were impressed civilian vehicles of varying sizes, inferior in both construction and

---

13 OR 23, pt. 2, 732; Jeffrey L. Nash, *Destroyer of the Iron Horse: General Joseph E. Johnston and Confederate Rail Transport, 1861-1865* (Kent, OH: 1991), 57-66. There is an extensive discussion of the Nashville & Decatur project's many delays and miscues.

capacity to the standard 2.5-ton army wagon. The simple fact is that the Army of Tennessee never had sufficient military-grade transport to meet its needs, a problem that only worsened over time.[14]

Transportation shortages plagued every Southern army in 1863. That spring, Lee reduced his wagon allowance to 35 vehicles per thousand men, and in early fall, both Bragg and Lee reduced the standard to 28 per thousand. In the Army of Tennessee, tactical mobility was increasingly impaired. In May, "[General] Hardee estimated . . . that if the army retreated, there were not even enough wagons to carry off the baggage." Despite regular rumors of a renewed Kentucky offensive circulating among the men, Bragg and Joseph Johnston both understood that their only tactical option was to wait for Rosecrans to advance and then hopefully find an opportunity to counterattack.[15]

May brought with it another campaign season, and the initiative lay with the Federals in both the east and the west. In Virginia, Joseph Hooker's Army of the Potomac—at 150,000 strong, the largest of all Federal forces—readied for another drive on Richmond. In northern Mississippi, Ulysses S. Grant was beginning to move as well, presumably against the Confederate citadel at Vicksburg, defended by Lt. Gen. John C. Pemberton's Army of Mississippi. Bragg and Rosecrans faced off in Middle Tennessee.

Believing that the decisive theater would be Middle Tennessee, Joe Johnston spent a great deal of time with Bragg that spring, trying to resolve the army's command problems. Even though he declined to replace Bragg outright, he was the Confederacy's senior man in the Western Theater, and he had firm ideas about what the Yankees were likely to do. On April 5, he informed Adj. Gen. Samuel Cooper in Richmond that "a spy reports that in Nashville large reinforcements are expected for Rosecrans." Another informant, "just in from Louisville," added, "the Federals are sending all boats to bring [Ulysses S.] Grant's troops to Tennessee." Similar information from Pemberton in Mississippi apparently confirmed the news concerning Grant, leaving Johnston to assert, "it seems . . . unlikely that General Grant's troops can be intended for any other field than [Middle Tennessee.]" Johnston was so convinced that on April 11, he ordered Maj. Gen. Simon B. Buckner, then commanding the post at Mobile, to "send [his] infantry to [Tullahoma] as expeditiously as possible," as soon as Pemberton sent word that Grant's men were on the move. On April 15, in what turned out to be a serious

14 OR 23, pt. 2, 733, 764-765.

15 Connolly, *Army of the Heartland*, 115-116; Hallock, *Joshua K. Callaway,* 81, 84.

misreading of Union intentions, Pemberton even informed Buckner, "I am sending troops to General Johnston, being satisfied that a large portion of Grant's army is reinforcing Rosecrans."[16]

Grant was moving, but not to Tennessee. His objective remained the Confederate fortress at Vicksburg, Mississippi. All through the winter and early spring, the persistent Federal commander explored ways to get at or bypass Vicksburg via Yazoo Pass, Steele's Bayou, or numerous hand-dug canals. Nothing succeeded. He finally decided that the only way to take the Confederate fortress was to cross the Mississippi River below Vicksburg, then move inland and isolate the Rebels from the rear. It was a risky plan, exposing Grant's army to isolation and destruction, but its very risk bolstered the element of surprise. On April 16, Acting Rear Admiral David D. Porter's fleet of gunboats and transports steamed downstream past the river batteries at Vicksburg. On April 17, Union Col. Benjamin Grierson commenced his famous cavalry raid through Mississippi and Louisiana (made in conjunction with Streight) as a diversion. On May 1, the lead elements of Grant's army, 17,000 strong, crossed the river at Bruinsburg, Mississippi. Moving inland, Grant fought a small battle at Port Gibson and then marched toward Jackson, the state capital and the junction of the only railroad supplying the river stronghold.[17]

These developments caught Joseph E. Johnston flat-footed. Expecting a move by a reinforced Rosecrans, Johnston was at Tullahoma with Bragg and still unwell when he received an alarming wire from the Confederate war department on May 9. "Proceed at once to Mississippi and take chief command of the forces, giving to those in the field . . . the encouragement and benefit of your personal direction," read the wire. "Arrange to take for temporary service with you . . . 3,000 good troops who will be substituted in Bragg's army by a large number of prisoners recently returned." At 6:40 that evening Johnston replied, "I shall go immediately, although unfit for field service." Bragg was not sorry to see him go, grumping to

16 OR 23, pt. 2, 739, 741, and 750 and OR 24, pt. 3, 745. Only one large brigade of 4,000 men began the move to Tennessee. By the very next day, April 16, Pemberton was having second thoughts, and by the 17th, he told Johnston that "a large attack" was expected; he could spare no more men.

17 Eicher, *The Longest Night,* 443-459. Grierson's raid, which served as the basis for the famous John Wayne movie *The Horse Soldiers,* lasted from April 17 to May 2, 1863. For the best study of the Grierson Raid, see Timothy B. Smith, *The Real Horse Soldiers: Benjamin Grierson's Epic 1863 Civil War Raid through Mississippi* (El Dorado Hills, CA: 2018), which sets the raid and its command decisions and outcome in context with the wider Vicksburg theater-based operation.

Lt. Gen. John C. Pemberton, commander,
Dept. of Mississippi and East Louisiana.

Library of Congress

Dr. Charles Quintard, a chaplain and medical officer on the army's staff, that Johnston "was kept here to watch me too long."[18]

With him went Matthew D. Ector's and Evander McNair's brigades of Confederate infantry, the first of many troops destined to depart Tennessee over the next month. May 1 turned out to be the apogee of the Army of Tennessee's combat power that summer. Johnston reached Jackson, Mississippi, on the evening of May 13, to find the city defended by only 6,000 men, the survivors of a fight at Raymond, Mississippi, the day before. Confusion followed. Johnston abandoned Jackson after another sharp fight on May 14. On May 16, Pemberton, with 23,000 men, fought a battle at Champion Hill against Grant and 32,000 Yankees. Defeated, most of Pemberton's command retreated toward the trenches of Vicksburg. They were completely invested by the 19th.[19]

Grant did not try to hold Jackson. He merely burned part of city and wrecked the rail yard. Johnston reoccupied the town, and over the next month, it became the focal point for a growing "Army of Relief." By May 20, he assembled 15,000 men, including the troops from Bragg; survivors of the Raymond fight; one division of Pemberton's command that had escaped the Union trap after Champion Hill; and troops sent from Charleston, South Carolina. But Grant had also been reinforced to a strength of at least 75,000, giving him enough manpower both to fully besiege Pemberton and to hold Johnston at bay. If the Army of Relief were to live up to its name, still more Rebels would be needed.

18 OR 23, pt. 2, 825-826; Arthur Howard Noll, ed. , *Doctor Quintard, Chaplain C.S.A. and Second Bishop of Tennessee, Being His Story of the War (1861-1865)*, (Suwanee, TN: 1905), 70.

19 Symonds, *Joseph E. Johnston*, 205-210.

One of Pemberton's great deficiencies was in cavalry, particularly true after Van Dorn's men were transferred to Tennessee. In March, when Pemberton asked for the return of those men, Johnston refused, expecting to need them against a reinforced Rosecrans. In addition to capturing incautious brigades of Yankees, Van Dorn's presence in Columbia was vital to keeping supplies from that region flowing to Bragg's main body. Now, the crisis in Mississippi could not be ignored. More cavalry was needed. Forrest, fresh from his victory over Streight, was one possibility, but his brigade was too worn out to be immediately useful. On May 16, Bragg ordered Brig. Gen. William H. Jackson's division of Van Dorn's corps to head for Mississippi. They did so without Earl Van Dorn, who by this time was dead at an assassin's hand.[20]

At about 9:00 p.m. on the evening of May 7, Dr. George Peters, a resident of Spring Hill, visited Van Dorn to ask for a pass through Confederate lines. It appeared to be a routine request, since Peters had General Joseph Johnston's leave to come and go freely. Instead, when the chance offered, Peters shot Van Dorn in the back of the head. Van Dorn had made his headquarters in a cabin on the grounds of the Peters's plantation, six miles from Spring Hill. Van Dorn had a reputation as a womanizer; one newspaper reported that he was "the terror of ugly husbands and serious papas." Dr. Peters's wife was younger, attractive, fond of parties (the doctor was not), independently wealthy (the money and the plantation were hers, not his), and flirtatious. Van Dorn was clearly interested. When their mutual interest became public knowledge, Dr. Peters acted, assassinating the general as he turned away after filling out the requested pass. Peters then immediately departed for Nashville and the security of Union lines.[21]

---

20 OR 52, pt. 2, 472.

21 Carter, *Tarnished Cavalier,* 185-87. There is another version of Van Dorn's murder, recounted as oral tradition among local families and historians. According to this rendition of the tale, Dr. Peters killed the general not because he was keeping company with his wife, Jesse, but with his 16-year-old daughter Clara from his first marriage, who was now pregnant. While Dr. Peters's second marriage was one of convenience, mainly arranged for the money, the doctor could not ignore the insult to his daughter. There is some circumstantial evidence to support the idea. Clara entered a St. Louis convent later in 1863 and is listed as residing there in January 1864. She joined the convent formally in 1868. The only written account of this theory appears in a work of fiction—or, at best, fictionalized history—by Bridget Smith, *Where Elephants Fought: The Murder of Confederate General Earl Van Dorn* (Mechanicsburg, PA: 2015). The late Civil War historian Dr. Nathaniel Cheairs Hughes Jr. grew up in Spring Hill and later attested that this was the same story he had heard about the incident. Dave Powell interview with James H. Ogden III, park historian at Chickamauga-Chattanooga National Military Park, May 24, 2019.

Whatever Van Dorns's failings, his demise robbed the Confederates of an effective cavalry leader—probably the most effective cavalry commander in the Army of Tennessee—at a critical time. While Van Dorn had been found wanting as an army commander in Arkansas and at Corinth, he subsequently excelled in this more limited role, at least when he was not paying court to other men's wives.

His loss triggered mixed reactions through the army. His interest in Mrs. Peters was an open secret. Lieutenant James Bates of the 9th Texas Cavalry noted, "Maj Genl Van Dorn was killed at this place [Spring Hill] about ten days since by one Dr Peters—cause Van Dorn's intimacy with his wife." On May 9 Lieutenant Callaway informed his wife of "the infamous death. . . . We are all sorry to lose his valuable services, but we are not sorry to hear of his death under the circumstances. Infamy & shame have blackened his fame . . . , namely that of a vile seducer." A month after the killing, Arthur Fremantle noted that among many of Bragg's officers, "his loss does not seem to be much regretted, as it appears he was always ready to neglect his military duties for an assignation."[22]

After reporting to Bragg at Shelbyville on May 13, Nathan Bedford Forrest assumed command of Van Dorn's corps at Spring Hill on May 16, the same day Bragg issued the order returning Jackson's division to Mississippi. Within a few days Jackson departed, with Forrest reverting to command of his division. The hard-bitten raider exercised corps command for barely half a week.[23]

The next drain on the army's strength came on May 22. That day, Jefferson Davis informed Bragg that "the vital issue of holding . . . Vicksburg is dependent on the success of General Johnston. . . . The intelligence there is discouraging. Can you aid him?" Bragg was dismayed to lose more troops, but he was nothing if not a Confederate patriot. The next day, Bragg replied that although he had already "sent 3,500 with the general [Johnston], three batteries of artillery, and 2,000 cavalry, [he] will dispatch 6,000 more immediately. Have no orders." However, he warned, Johnston "did not consider it safe to weaken this point." Bragg directed Hardee to send John C. Breckinridge's division to Mississippi, except for the Tennessee regiments. He probably was not sorry to see Breckinridge exit his command, since Breckinridge and his staff had caused much of the army's internal turmoil.[24]

---

22 Lowe, *A Texas Cavalry Officer's Civil War*, 247; Hallock, *Joshua K. Callaway*, 88; Fremantle, *Three Months*, 146.

23 Jordan and Pryor, *Campaigns of General Nathan Bedford Forrest*, 284.

24 OR 23, pt. 2, 847-848.

By June 10, the Army of Tennessee reported an effective strength of 44,636, with 49,032 officers and men present for duty and 57,436 aggregate present—a decline of 8,000 effectives, and more than 10,000 aggregate, since April 30. In total, Bragg shipped more than 12,000 men to Mississippi: 1,357 with Ector, 1,533 with McNair, 6,713 under Breckinridge, and Jackson's 3,019 horsemen. Additional returns via Pillow's recruiting efforts and the improving health of the army made up some of the difference. Still, the loss of 9,500 veteran infantry reduced Bragg's main combat power by 25 percent.[25]

One final departure was wholly unauthorized. Brig. Gen. John Hunt Morgan had a campaigning season in the spring of 1863 that fell short of his storied exploits of the previous year, and it grated on him. There was considerable talk around the army that commanding a division was too much for him, a fact noted even by Bragg, especially regarding the handling of regular cavalry duties. Others speculated that his recent marriage to Martha "Mattie" Ready in December 1862 had somehow sapped his martial prowess. George St. Leger Grenfell, an English soldier of fortune who traipsed all over the globe joining wars and served under Morgan for eight months, snorted that the Kentuckian "was enervated by matrimony, and he would never be the same man he was."[26]

Morgan certainly seemed infatuated with his new wife. That winter, he had spent a great deal of time away from the front. The couple established itself in McMinnville, indulging in parties and other social outings while supplies ran short among his troops. "Consciously, [Morgan] put gambling and high risks behind him, and depended on Mattie for security," wrote biographer James A. Ramage. "The close of 1862 marked the beginning of Morgan's deterioration as a leader."[27]

Morgan also had problems more prosaic than matrimonial enervation. Certainly, General Hardee thought so. In an echo of Bragg's fears about Morgan back in March, Hardee wrote to Johnston on May 8, urging that officer to give Morgan a talking-to. "I learn that Morgan's command is in bad condition and growing worse. . . . I hear that he is greatly dissatisfied with being under Wheeler. His conduct, if this be true, cannot be justified, and he has suffered, and will continue to suffer, in public estimation. . . . [Morgan] likes you and will receive kindly any suggestions you may make to him." That conversation never occurred.

25 *OR* 23, pt. 2, 873; *OR* 24, pt. 2, 925, 945, 947. The numbers for men sent to Mississippi are aggregate figures, not just effectives.

26 Fremantle, *Three Months*, 150.

27 Ramage, *Rebel Raider*, 147.

Johnston was ordered to Mississippi the next day. Had the two met, things might have gone differently.[28]

While supplies were often tight in the Army of Tennessee, most troops were satisfied with their daily rations. This was not true among Morgan's men, who were now stationed in the rough terrain north of McMinnville and east of Nashville, country less productive than the bottomlands of Middle Tennessee and more heavily foraged in past campaigns. There were often shortages of oats and fodder for the animals. Pay was all but non-existent. Rations were poor, and other supplies were equally wanting. "It is hard to maintain discipline when men are required to perform the most arduous and hazardous duties without being clothed, shod, paid or fed," admitted Col. Basil Duke, Morgan's brother-in-law and trusted second-in-command. Though Duke excused Morgan's quartermaster and commissary officers as doing the best they could, based on letters and diaries from other commands, it is apparent that Morgan's men suffered an unusual degree of shortage—all while Morgan was enjoying his honeymoon in McMinnville. At one point, the men of the 2nd Kentucky Cavalry staged a sort of mutiny, "refusing to carry their weapons. They remained in camp and answered bugle calls, but simply fell in sans rifles." The rebellion was quelled when the men were ordered to drill with fence rails instead. The missing rifles rapidly reappeared.[29]

Morgan nursed a great ambition: to launch not just another raid into his native Kentucky, but an even more spectacular incursion north of the Ohio River, bringing the war to Indiana, Ohio, or Illinois. When Morgan pitched the idea, however, Bragg "refused him permission to make the raid . . . and ordered him to confine himself to Kentucky." Undaunted, on June 13, Morgan proposed an attack on Louisville, where "the enemy . . . were but 300 strong." Bragg and Wheeler agreed to this more limited effort, provided Morgan took no more than 1,500 troopers with him. A final appeal upped the authorized limit to 2,000 men, with the understanding that Morgan was to "as far as practicable, break up and destroy the Louisville and Nashville Railroad." John Pegram's earlier raid had done no damage to Rosecrans's lifeline. Now, Bragg hoped that Morgan's old magic could be rekindled.[30]

---

28 *OR* 23, pt. 2, 824.

29 Basil W. Duke, *A History of Morgan's Cavalry* (Cincinnati, OH: 1867), 411-412; Ramage, *Rebel Raider*, 151.

30 Duke, *Morgan's Cavalry*, 451; *OR* 23, pt. 1, 817.

Morgan never had any intention of confining his activities to Kentucky, nor was he going to leave any fit man or mount behind. After a short diversion to chase a Union raid out of East Tennessee, Morgan crossed the Cumberland River with his whole division (2,500 men, less those with horses too weak for the trip) in early July and crossed the Ohio River into Indiana on the 8th. Federals hotly pursued him across Indiana and Ohio. They severely defeated him at Buffington Island in Meigs County, Ohio, on July 19 while he was trying to recross the Ohio into West Virginia. He lost many prisoners, and his command was badly fragmented. Morgan himself was captured on July 26 near the village of West Point, Ohio. The raid accomplished little of note, neither diverting large forces from Rosecrans nor damaging the Louisville & Nashville line. It did wreck a large body of Confederate cavalry, increasing the Army of Tennessee's total loss of strength during this period to 9,500 infantry and 5,500 mounted men and shrinking Bragg's cavalry force from five divisions to three.[31]

As Bragg's strength declined, so did his military options. If his dearth of field transport ruled out a major offensive, his declining combat power also limited his likely counterattack options. Instead of meeting Rosecrans with something like equal odds, Bragg would probably be outnumbered by at least three to two when the Federals finally opened the ball in Middle Tennessee. Accordingly, the Confederates increasingly turned to prepared defenses to augment their combat power.

In March, Bragg and Johnston envisioned a line of entrenchments at Tullahoma strong enough to be held by all or part of Hardee's corps while Polk's corps and the numerous Confederate cavalry struck at any exposed Union flanks. By early June, Bragg ordered more works to be dug, primarily at Shelbyville and Wartrace. Those dug by Polk's men at Shelbyville were especially extensive, covering a front of several miles, "a large semicircular line . . . that stretched from Duck River on the west, across the north side of Shelbyville, to the Highland Rim on the east." Once begun, the work proceeded at a rapid clip.

On June 12, for example, Capt. Edward B. Sayers, Polk's chief engineer, requested "a detail of 1,050 men to report to . . . the fortifications on the east side of the Fairfield turnpike," where they would work in shifts: "350 to report at 6 a.m., 350 at 9 a.m., and 350 at 2 p.m." for the better part of a week. Hardee's entrenchments at Wartrace, while not as extensive, were pushed similarly hard.

---

31 For the best recent study of Morgan's Raid, see David L. Mowery, *Morgan's Great Raid: The Remarkable Expedition from Kentucky to Ohio* (Charleston, SC: 2013).

Bragg's plans still called for some sort of vague counterattack against the Federal right flank once active operations commenced, but the heavy fortifications, especially in front of Leonidas Polk's command, essentially shoved Bragg's intentions aside.[32]

Beyond entrenchments, Bragg took steps to try to convince Rosecrans that the Army of Tennessee was growing stronger rather than weaker—or at least that troops that had been sent away were being rapidly returned. To accomplish this, Bragg relied primarily on false accounts planted in the newspapers, especially the *Chattanooga Daily Rebel*. Owned by Francis M. Paul and edited by Henry Watterson, the *Rebel* was not generally friendly to Bragg; nor was Watterson circumspect about reporting troop movements and strengths. However, Paul and Watterson published so much news about the Army of Tennessee that they soon sold up to 10,000 copies a day within its ranks, shipped up the rails from Chattanooga.

Of course, the Army of the Cumberland also avidly digested this news, especially Rosecrans's headquarters. Bragg lacked the authority to shut down the *Rebel*, but he could ban its sale within the Army of Tennessee if he chose. Those economics worked wonders, and soon Bragg's chief of intelligence, Col. Alexander McKinstry, struck a deal whereby the army would pre-approve articles before they were published, and further, he could plant fake news in the *Rebel* when it suited Bragg. As Confederate troop departures peaked, McKinstry exercised the latter option. On June 3 he wired Paul, "please publish an article conveying this idea. . . . 'We are at a loss to comprehend why General Johnston should have sent Breckinridge's corps back to Middle Tennessee. He must be in a secure condition, either from his position or from an abundance of troops.'" Bragg could only hope Rosecrans took that bait.[33]

The men in the ranks of the Army of Tennessee now widely expected a battle. In a letter home on June 7, Lt. James B. Mitchell of Company B, the 34th Alabama Infantry, informed his father that he would not be granted a furlough any time soon. "I would be exceedingly delighted to witness the commencement exercises of the female college," he teased,

and indeed I should be there were it not for the grand commencement which Madame Bragg assures us is about to take place up here in a few days, and at which I feel myself

32 Connelly, *Autumn of Glory*, 116-117; OR 23, pt. 2, 874.

33 Roy Morris, Jr., "The Improbable, Praiseworthy Paper: The *Chattanooga Daily Rebel*," *Civil War Times Illustrated*, vol. 23, no. 7 (November, 1984), 21; OR 23, pt. 2, 860.

constrained to be present. Messers Bragg and Rosecrans, presiding, sermon by Bishop L. Polk and addresses by these three celebrated gentlemen— Breckinridge, Cheatham, and Withers. Music lively and solemn, mostly instrumental but frequently vocal. I hope it will be a glorious affair and the southern actors will acquitt themselves with extraordinary credit.[34]

34 "Dear Father," June 7, 1863, James B. Mitchell Letters, 34th Alabama file, Stones River National Battlefield.

Chapter Five

The Changing Balance:
Army of the Cumberland,
May to June 1863

Despite the Army of the Cumberland's lack of success at either thwarting the aggressive Confederate cavalry or launching deep cavalry raids of its own, Rosecrans's army was in fine fettle by June. His efforts to increase his mounted force had succeeded.

At the end of April Rosecrans reported 4,786 officers and 77,938 men present for duty in his department; of those, only 332 officers and 4,629 men were cavalry. The May 31 return was similar: 4,876 officers and 75,110 men, its Cavalry Corps numbers unchanged. In early June, however, Rosecrans began to concentrate his forces in anticipation of a forward move. On June 20 the department reported 5,112 officers and 79,258 men—a small increase in overall numbers—but the mounted arm doubled in strength to 608 officers and 9,952 men. Additionally, with Wilder's brigade and the 39th Indiana now acting as mounted infantry, Rosecrans's total mounted strength rose to more than 13,000 troops.[1]

Of course, not all of Rosecrans's soldiers could take the field. Of the 84,000 men listed as present for duty, roughly 20,000 were needed as garrison troops. This left approximately 51,000 infantry and artillery plus those 13,000 mounted troops for offensive uses. And, at long last, Rosecrans was thinking offensively.[2]

---

1 OR 23, pt. 2, 298, 37-39; pt. 1, 410-411.

2 Chief of Staff Garfield calculated Rosecrans's available field force at "65,137 bayonets and sabers," not counting officers—close to 69,000 all told. See OR 23, pt. 2, 423.

Rosecrans was not about to move before he was ready, however, which proved to be a source of renewed conflict between him and Washington. The Union defeat at Chancellorsville, Virginia, at the beginning of May caused intense distress in the halls of government. President Lincoln "turned as pale as a corpse" when he read the details of that disaster. "With tears streaming down his ashen face, [he] paced the room exclaiming: 'My God! My God! What will the country say!'"[3]

To make matters worse, many Union soldiers' two-year enlistments expired after Chancellorsville, significantly reducing Hooker's numbers. Robert E. Lee, buoyed by his recent victory and the waning strength of his opponent, felt sufficiently emboldened to launch his own offensive, just has he had the previous year. In early June, he started moving troops toward Culpeper, Virginia. On June 9, Union and Confederate cavalry clashed in the largest mounted battle of the war at Brandy Station, and by June 13, elements of the Confederate Second Corps were approaching Winchester, 50 miles north of Culpeper and well on the way into Maryland via the Confederates' favored invasion corridor: the Shenandoah Valley. This time Lee was headed deep into Pennsylvania. Each Rebel step northward left Lincoln and Stanton more agitated.

As previously noted, Grant also was on the move. Rosecrans reported as much on May 17, when he forwarded a report gleaned from a Confederate newspaper, substantiating that "Grant has Jackson [Mississippi]. Took it after a hard fight." While this was timely news (more so because Grant was out of direct communication with Washington at the time), it offered no insight into what was happening on Rosecrans's own front. From Halleck's perspective, the news filtering out of Tennessee was alarming: In response to Grant's success, Rebels appeared to be flooding into Mississippi in large numbers. On May 18, Halleck, seeking confirmation of that news, informed Rosecrans that "dispatches just received say that General Joe Johnston, with a considerable force, has left Tennessee to reinforce Vicksburg." If so, lectured Halleck, "the best way to counteract this is to concentrate your forces and advance."[4]

Rosecrans refused to believe Halleck's information could be accurate. "No considerable force of any arm, and none of infantry, have left our front. How reliable is the information you telegraph?" Rosecrans insisted that the troops going to Johnston "were from Charleston and Savannah," not from Bragg. While he correctly noted that Confederates were indeed coming from those places, he

3 Michael Burlingame, *Abraham Lincoln: A Life,* 2 vols. (Baltimore, MD: 2009), 2: 499.

4 *OR* 23, pt. 2, 337.

missed the very real detachments being made by Bragg. On June 3, only a few days after John C. Breckinridge's division entrained for Mississippi, Halleck telegraphed again, with a stark warning. "Accounts received here indicate that Johnston is being heavily reinforced from Bragg's army," he wrote. "If you cannot hurt the enemy now, he will soon hurt you."[5]

Rosecrans never accepted the fact that Bragg had been detaching men, even long after the war. In 1887, he reiterated that point while describing a conversation between himself and Maj. Gen. George L. Hartsuff, deputy to Maj. Gen. Ambrose Burnside, commander of the Department of the Ohio. Hartsuff had been sent to coordinate strategy. As far as Bragg was concerned, explained Rosecrans, "we must not drive [him] out of Middle Tennessee until it shall be too late for his command to reinforce Johnston's." He elaborated:

> Bragg is now, apparently, holding this army [Army of the Cumberland] in check. It is the most important service he can render to his cause. The Confederate authorities know it. They will not order, nor will Bragg venture to send away any substantial detachments. In fact, he is now holding us here by his nose, which he has inserted between our teeth for that purpose. We shall keep our teeth on his nose . . . until we are assured that Vicksburg is within three weeks of its fall.[6]

General Hartsuff, recently recovered from a hip wound incurred at Antietam, took command of the newly created XXIII Corps at the end of April. Burnside's department now included both the IX and XXIII Corps, some 37,000 men, enough both to defend Rosecrans's supply line in Kentucky and to undertake offensive operations. One of Burnside's objectives was Lincoln's long cherished goal of liberating East Tennessee, a stronghold of Union sentiment deep in the Confederacy. In late May, via Hartsuff, Burnside and Rosecrans worked out a plan whereby the XXIII Corps would advance on McMinnville when Rosecrans began his own offensive. Seizing McMinnville would protect Rosecrans's left flank while providing an excellent forward base for Burnside's projected move to Knoxville.[7]

Meanwhile, Rosecrans's own intelligence sources provided more of a mixed bag concerning Bragg's strength, which was not unusual for a Civil War army in the

---

5 Ibid., 337, 383.

6 William S. Rosecrans, "The Campaign for Chattanooga," *The Century Illustrated Monthly Magazine*, vol. 34 (May to October, 1887), 130.

7 William Marvel, *Burnside* (Chapel Hill, NC: 1991), 243-244.

field. For example, on June 5, Col. William Truesdail, the Army of the Cumberland's chief of army police and the head of Rosecrans's scout and spy network, reported that, far from sending troops away, "Bragg has been reinforced by an entire new brigade, which is at Shelbyville & came from Charleston [South Carolina] & that there is no doubt of the truth of this report." That same day, news gleaned from the Chattanooga *Rebel* of May 31 claimed that "Genl Breckinridge's division has been broken up & the parts scattered, & that he and his staff with one fragment have been sent to another field of labor."[8]

A contradictory, yet ultimately accurate, report insisted that "Genl Breckinridge has left & taken with him all of his old division except [Brig. Gen. John C.] Brown's Brigade." Additionally, on "June 6th—Scout ——— who left Nashville May 29th learned from a citizen who had been at Bragg's Headqrs on the 30th that nearly half of their army had gone to Vicksburg, [but] that as soon as he could Johnston would return & with all the reinforcements that could be found attack Nashville." On June 12 word came that "two brigades of Van Dorn's old division Jackson's and Whitfields' have gone to Mississippi." That same day, five deserters from the 3rd Kentucky Infantry (C.S.) entered the Union lines at Clarksville, Tennessee, where post commander Col. S. D. Bruce questioned them. "They said [Breckinridge] had 10,000 men, and was on his way to Vicksburg."[9]

No commander is ever blessed with a complete, clear, and fully accurate intelligence picture. Intelligence is instead a puzzle that must be pieced together from bits of incomplete and often contradictory data. Such was the case in Middle Tennessee in June 1863, and, in this instance, Rosecrans guessed wrong. He concluded that Bragg was not shipping men to Mississippi. It was a rare but significant lapse on Rosecrans's part, one that bolstered his reluctance to advance before he was completely prepared to do so. That failure further soured his status in Washington. Lincoln and Stanton knew that the Confederate army at Jackson was gaining strength daily, and that strength had to come from somewhere.

If Rosecrans could not prevent Rebel detachments from being sent to Mississippi (or even accept that those detachments were occurring), then the Federal government had to bolster Grant in other ways. On June 3, Halleck ordered Burnside to "immediately dispatch 8,000 men to General Grant, at

---

8 Army of the Cumberland, "Summaries of Intelligence Received, June 5 1863," NARA. As noted in the previous chapter, Col. McKinstry was using the *Rebel* to plant false intelligence, which bore fruit in this instance.

9 Ibid., June 11-12, 1863; *OR* 23, pt. 2, 427.

Vicksburg." Burnside informed Rosecrans of the order right away, since it would affect the Army of the Cumberland's long-awaited advance. "My plans are all deranged," lamented Burnside; the same was now true for Rosecrans.[10]

Halleck's abrupt intervention derailed the very thing he hoped to accomplish: a forward movement by the Army of the Cumberland. The day before, June 2, Rosecrans had wired Burnside, "our movement has begun, and we want you to come up as near and as quickly as possible. It will not interfere with your East Tennessee movement, but will strengthen it." Initially, Rosecrans wanted Hartsuff's XXIII Corps to occupy Carthage, Tennessee, nestled on the north bank of the Cumberland River about 50 miles east of Nashville and another 50 miles north of McMinnville. With the loss of two divisions of the IX Corps to Mississippi, however, Burnside retained Hartsuff's corps in Kentucky.[11]

On June 2, James A. Garfield, Rosecrans's chief of staff, informed his wife that "the movement has begun and I confidently expect to be in the saddle by Saturday [June 6]." But on June 6, he explained, "we should have gone out with the whole army but for some delay occasioned by Burnside's change of plan in sending an army corps away to Grant." Optimistically, Garfield felt the delay would be short, writing that "nothing in particular preventing I think the army will move" on Monday, June 8. He was about to be deeply disappointed.[12]

With the loss of Burnside's support, the collective mood of the army's senior officers darkened. On June 8, Rosecrans, stung by Halleck's criticisms and Burnside's abrupt redirection, issued a confidential questionnaire to his corps and divisional commanders, 17 officers in all, asking of them three questions:

From the fullest information in your possession, do you think the enemy in front of us has been so materially weakened by detachments to Johnston or elsewhere that this army could advance on him at this time, with strong reasonable chances of fighting a great and successful battle?

Do you think an advance of our army at present likely to prevent additional reinforcements being sent against General Grant by the enemy in our front?

---

10 *OR* 23, pt. 2, 384.

11 Ibid., 381-382.

12 Williams, *The Wild Life of the Army*, 273, 275.

Do you think an immediate or early advance of our army advisable?[13]

Garfield subsequently refined these three inquiries into five discrete questions, tallied the answers, and reported the results to Rosecrans on June 12:

Has the enemy in our front been materially weakened by detachments to Johnston or elsewhere? [6 yes, 11 no.]

Can this army advance on him at this time with strong reasonable chances of fighting a great and successful battle? [2 yes, 11 no.]

Do you think an advance of our army at present likely to prevent additional reinforcements being sent against Grant by the enemy on our front? [4 yes, 10 no.]

Do you think an immediate advance of this army advisable? [0 yes, 15 no.]

Do you think an early advance advisable? [0 yes, 2 no.][14]

Though not every officer answered every question, and there were a few answers in the affirmative on specific points, a clear majority of Rosecrans's commanders were reluctant to begin an offensive. This lack of enthusiasm was predicated on a sense of strategic caution, articulated by Rosecrans when he informed Washington that "with Hooker's army defeated, and Grant's . . . in a yet undecided struggle, it is bad policy to risk our only reserve army to the chances of a general engagement." Instead, Rosecrans reasoned, "this army ought to advance as soon as Vicksburg falls." He thought it "better [to] wait a little to get all we can ready to insure the best results." Delay, he told Halleck, would allow the Union armies "to observe a great military maxim not to risk two great and decisive battles at the same time." Halleck might not have been the most charismatic general in the Federal service, but the old army did not call him "Old Brains" for nothing. He could wage theoretical warfare with the best of military pedants, and he wasted no time in responding. The maxim in question, rebutted Halleck, "did not apply to two armies acting independently of each other. It was in the interest of Johnston and

13 Ibid., 394-395.

14 Ibid., 420-421.

Brig. Gen. James A. Garfield, chief of staff,
Army of the Cumberland, and a
future U.S. President.

Library of Congress

Bragg to fight at different times." Besides,
scoffed Halleck, "there is another military
maxim, that 'councils of war never
fight.'"[15]

The one strident voice of dissent
within the Army of the Cumberland was
James Garfield. Perhaps because he was a
politician rather than a professional
soldier, Garfield better understood the
pressures on the administration and the
need for action. His letters home reflected a growing sense of frustration at the
army's continued inactivity. On Thursday, June 11, while tallying the responses to
Rosecrans's survey, Garfield confessed that "a sense of disappointment and
mortification almost akin to shame has kept me from answering any letters for
some time. . . I had drafted a plan of campaign, drawn the first rough draft of the
order for movement, fixed the times of departure, arrival and attack, entered
minutely into all the details, and submitted the document to General Rosecrans
who approved it, and all things seemed ready. But there have been most strange
and unexpected interferences. . . . Just on the eve of our movement there seemed to
fall down upon the leading officers of this army . . . a most determined and decided
opinion that there ought to be no immediate or early advance."[16]

The delay so upset Garfield that he appended his own detailed opinion to the
document he prepared summarizing the responses to Rosecrans's questionnaire,
though he was not among the intended respondents. It was a remarkable
document, concise and well-reasoned, demonstrating a firm grasp of strategy.
Garfield's appendix, in the words of biographer Theodore Clarke Smith, "showed
soundness of judgment . . . and courage. When it is considered that [Garfield] was

15 Ibid., 421; Lamers, *The Edge of Glory*, 272.

16 Ibid., 275-276.

setting his opinion—that of a man who had been a school teacher and preacher two years before—against that of professional soldiers, including such men as Thomas, Sheridan, and Granger, his boldness is undeniable."[17]

Garfield raised nine specific points, each aimed at rebutting a specific concern raised by the professionals. They ranged from the practical to the theological (befitting a preacher talking to so devout a Catholic as Rosecrans). Garfield insisted that Bragg's army was weaker, but that no matter the outcome of the campaign for Vicksburg, its resolution likely would free up Rebels to return to Middle Tennessee; that inflicting a defeat on Bragg now "would be disastrous to the rebellion" and would bolster the Federal government "in the polls and in the enforcement of the Conscription Act"; and that even the Union cavalry, "if not equal in numerical strength . . . is greatly superior in efficiency and morale. For all these reasons, I believe an immediate advance of all our available forces is advisable, and under the providence of God will be successful."[18]

Garfield's plea did not trigger an immediate advance. However, despite this most recent stumble, Rosecrans's plans continued to mature, ripening into a complex but carefully detailed turning movement orchestrated across a broad front, designed to leverage Bragg's army out from behind that formidable range of hills known as the Highland Rim. Even Burnside's need to send two divisions to Mississippi was at best a hiccup, not a disaster. The Army of the Cumberland was a powerful force, and ready for action.

In December 1862, Rosecrans had used a similar tactic when advancing to Murfreesboro, dispatching Crittenden's XXI Corps directly down the Murfreesboro Turnpike to threaten Bragg's front while sending the XIV and XX Corps via the Franklin and Nolensville turnpikes, respectively, to approach the town from the west and northwest. This allowed Rosecrans to concentrate his entire force in Bragg's front before the fighting commenced. The subsequent battle overshadowed that achievement, as Rosecrans's direction of the actual combat was less successful; he failed to anticipate that McCook's corps alone might not be able to hold the Union right against an expected Rebel onslaught, and made no contingency to bolster the XX Corps in case it faltered, which it did. As a result, he canceled his own flanking attack and mounted a desperate, haphazard defense

---

17 Theodore Clarke Smith, *The Life and Letters of James Abram Garfield,* 2 vols. (New Haven, CT: 1925), 1: 303.

18 *OR* 23, pt. 2, 423-424.

along the Nashville Pike. Only Bragg's retreat on January 5 left Rosecrans to claim the field and the victory.[19]

In the advance toward Murfreesboro, Rosecrans executed a turning movement with his right wing. This time, he planned to turn Bragg's right with his left. In doing so, he intended to negate Bragg's advantages of terrain—the Highland Rim—and the extensive Confederate works. "His main position in front of Shelbyville," noted Rosecrans, "was strengthened by a redan line extending from Horse Mountain, on the east, to Duck River, on the west, covered by a line of abatis," a distance of nine miles. A leftward movement also shortened the Union approach to the Nashville & Chattanooga tracks, which ran southeast. Turning Bragg's right flank would put those tracks much closer to the Federal flanking column than a similar move against the Confederate left would have. Rosecrans planned to have the XXI Corps march to the hamlet of Bradyville, and from there, quickly move on to Manchester, which sat on the south bank of the Duck River just 12 miles northeast of Bragg's main depot at Tullahoma. Bradyville was 16 miles west-southwest of Murfreesboro. Manchester lay another 21 miles almost due south from Bradyville.

Even though the roads available to carry the XXI Corps to Bradyville and Manchester were inferior to the main turnpikes in the area, if Crittenden's men could complete those 37 miles of marching within two days, Bragg's army would be seriously disadvantaged. Once at Manchester, Crittenden would be much closer to Tullahoma or the all-important railroad bridge over the Elk River at Allisonia, north of Dechard, than most of Bragg's own infantry would be.[20]

One additional factor complicated Rosecrans's planning. The Cumberland Plateau, the geographic region south and east of the Highland Rim that was also known as "the Barrens," was relatively infertile and often shallow, with bedrock lying just a few inches below the surface, prohibiting decent crop yields. Rocky gorges and steep ravines cut the plateau, making for difficult travel. In contrast to the great valleys of Tennessee, which were abundantly blessed with rich bands of topsoil, the Cumberland Plateau was settled much later; its eventual population growth was fueled largely by the construction of railroads, which made access easier for settlers. All of this meant that Rosecrans would need more wagons to haul extra food and forage once his army was operating there, especially in the XXI

19 David J. Eicher, *The Longest Night, A Military History of the Civil War* (New York: 2001), 419-428.

20 *OR* 23, pt. 1, 404.

Corps. And, as might be expected, those additional wagons and teams could prove problematic on the inferior roads of the mountain region.[21]

To keep Bragg's attention fixed elsewhere while Crittenden moved, Rosecrans intended to send other Union columns south to threaten or capture three gaps through the Highland Rim. George Thomas's XIV Corps was to advance 19 miles south to Hoover's Gap, near the crossroads village of Beech Grove, on the direct road from Murfreesboro to Manchester. McCook's XX Corps was to launch similar efforts against Liberty and Guy's gaps, through which ran roads to Wartrace and Shelbyville, respectively (both towns were 25 miles south of Murfreesboro). Most of the Union cavalry, supported by elements of Granger's Reserve Corps, would make the westernmost demonstration, a movement out of Triune toward the hamlets of Eagleville and Unionville, threatening Shelbyville from the northwest.[22]

Thomas's was the most important of these additional moves, because it was not merely a demonstration. Rosecrans needed Hoover's Gap to establish direct communications between Crittenden, at Manchester, and the rest of the army. To complete the concentration of the Federal army beyond the Confederate right flank, Thomas would have to seize Hoover's Gap quickly, and be ready to reinforce Crittenden.[23]

From Manchester, Rosecrans could move on Tullahoma, thus placing himself in Bragg's rear and astride the enemy's line of communications, preventing the Army of Tennessee from retreating instead of fighting. The last thing Rosecrans wanted was for Bragg's army to slip away to join forces with Johnston's men or some other Rebel force. In sum, Rosecrans intended to outflank Bragg, trap him in Middle Tennessee, bring him to battle on terms favorable to the Federals, and destroy the Army of Tennessee if possible.

To achieve these ambitious objectives, Rosecrans saw three vital prerequisites. The first two were oft mentioned in Rosecrans's communications with Washington. He needed a secure forward depot with sufficient accumulated rations to sustain the army for an extended period. "[That] depot was established

---

21 For more information on this region, see James M. Safford, *A Geographical Reconnaissance of the State of Tennessee: Being the Author's First Biennial Report Presented to the Thirty-First General Assembly of Tennessee, December, 1855* (Nashville, TN: 1856), 23-24. Safford viewed the soil in the Barrens as potentially productive, should lime and scientific farming methods be introduced.

22 OR 23, pt. 2, 442.

23 Ibid., 446-447.

Maj. Gen. Gordon Granger, commander of the Army of the Cumberland's Reserve Corps.

Library of Congress

and in a defensible condition by the 1st of May," Rosecrans acknowledged. He also had to have cavalry that was ready to take the field against the Confederates on an equal basis, along with adequate "long forage" (hay and grass) to maintain the livestock during hard use. In his report of the campaign, submitted at the end of July, Rosecrans wrote that his cavalry numbers and the availability of sufficient forage prevented the Army of the Cumberland from being ready to move until June 15.[24]

The third factor was transport. While Bragg (along with the other Confederate armies in the field) was forced to reduce his ratio of troops to wagons during the summer of 1863, Rosecrans built up his supply trains to an unprecedented size. At first glance this seemed counterintuitive, for more wagons meant more animals, more clogged roads, and the need for ever more forage. Union Quartermaster General Montgomery C. Meigs "doubt[ed] the wisdom of building up such masses [of animals], which crumble under their own weight." Meigs certainly had a point, but he failed to fully grasp Rosecrans's true needs. Once Rosecrans moved, he would be operating in mountainous terrain anywhere from 30 to 60 miles from his supply depot. He wanted those additional wagons in order to haul supplies over a country that had been largely stripped of sustenance over the past six months, not to carry excessive baggage or any extravagances. With a larger train, the Union army could operate farther from its base of supplies, and for a much longer time. Rosecrans succeeded in that goal, for by the time he was ready to move, the Army

24 Ibid., pt. 1, 403. It is worth noting that in this report Rosecrans makes no mention of the aborted advance begun on June 2 in conjunction with Burnside. If the cavalry and forage were not adequate until mid-June, why had he almost commenced operations two weeks earlier?

of the Cumberland's wagons numbered 69 or 70 per thousand men, with no less than 45,000 animals.[25]

By Rosecrans's own admission, all preparations were complete by the 15th of June. When would he strike?

*   *   *

Meanwhile, the *petit guerre* in Middle Tennessee continued unabated. On June 4, motivated by the shifts in Union deployments, Forrest set out from Spring Hill and launched another strike at Franklin. The Federal garrison there had been reduced to just two regiments as Rosecrans moved men farther east to Triune, anticipating the start of the long-awaited offensive. Forrest's division consisted of two brigades and two batteries: Frank Armstrong's command and Forrest's old brigade, now led by Col. James W. Starnes of the 2nd Tennessee Cavalry—3,500 men all told.[26]

After some initial skirmishing, Forrest ordered two companies of the 8th Tennessee Cavalry, Starnes's Brigade, to charge, a successful effort that forced Col. John P. Baird of the 85th Indiana to order his garrison back behind the walls of Fort Granger, the large Union earthwork on the north side of the Harpeth River overlooking the road and rail bridges. There, Forrest mistook a Union signal flag for a flag of truce, but once it was clear the Federals weren't going to give in as easily as they had at Brentwood, he sent Armstrong's brigade across the Harpeth east of town to try to attack Fort Granger from the north bank.[27]

At Triune, Major General Granger was prepared to deal with just such a crisis. Receiving word of the attack, he immediately dispatched a mounted brigade under Col. Archibald Campbell of the 2nd Michigan Cavalry to Franklin. The Union horsemen arrived late in the afternoon, just in time to attack Armstrong in the flank and rear, prompting one Wolverine to declare, "in twenty minutes the enemy were fleeing in every direction." Armstrong fell back across the Harpeth, losing (by Campbell's report) "18 prisoners, killed and wounded 15." Baird reported capturing "28 prisoners," adding, "[a]mong the trophies of this engagement was a new and beautiful Texas flag that had recently been presented to the Confederate General Armstrong." On June 6, two days after the battle, Baird vowed that, "if

---

25 OR 23, pt. 2, 302; Edward Hagerman, *The American Civil War and the Origins of Modern Warfare: Ideas, Organization, and Field Command* (Bloomington, IN: 1988), 212.

26 Jordan and Pryor, *Campaigns of Forrest*, 285.

27 Ibid., 286-287.

attacked, I will fight as long as we can fire a shot." Clearly, the harsh lessons of Thompson's Station and Brentwood had been taken to heart. Subsequent skirmishing continued around Franklin and Triune over the next couple of days.[28]

On June 8, Franklin was the scene of a more mysterious affair. Just before dark, with Forrest's attack fresh on his mind, Colonel Baird watched two Federal officers ride into Fort Granger. They presented orders identifying themselves as "Colonel Lawrence W. Auton," an "Acting Special Inspector-General," and "Major George Dunlop, Assistant Quartermaster," both fresh from the Army of the Potomac and Washington. Their mission was to "minutely inspect 'The Department of the Ohio' and 'The Department of the Cumberland.'" The orders were signed by Adjutant General Edward D. Townsend. The men also carried a letter of introduction and a special pass, both apparently signed by Chief of Staff James Garfield. "There were two unusual features about these documents. . . . One was that printed forms were [usually] used for such orders, whilst [these] were entirely in manuscript." In a second discrepancy, Garfield was misidentified as an assistant adjutant general. Nevertheless, Baird initially took the men and their papers at face value. They told him they needed to get to Nashville that night and asked for a "loan of fifty dollars." Auton said that he and Dunlap had been attacked by a party of Rebels at Eagleville, and they had lost "their orderlies, overcoats, and baggage," which explained why they carried civilian overcoats on their saddles.[29]

Baird accepted their story, gave them the money, and watched them depart. As they did so, however, they rode past Col. Louis D. Watkins of the 2nd Kentucky Cavalry, formerly a lieutenant in the 2nd U.S. Cavalry. Watkins had been appointed to his position in 1861, filling a vacancy that had opened when Lt. William Orton Williams resigned his commission in June of that year. Colonel Auton's face jogged Watkins's memory. He quickly had Auton and Dunlop arrested.[30]

A series of telegraph exchanges with army headquarters established that the two men were frauds and that Garfield had not issued them any passes or orders. Garfield told Baird to "call a drumhead court-martial to-night, and if they are found to be spies, hang them before morning." Baird, probably embarrassed by the near

---

28 Marshall P. Thatcher, *A Hundred Battles in the West: St. Louis to Atlanta, 1861-65. The Second Michigan Cavalry* (Detroit, MI: 1884), 129-130; *OR* 23, pt. 1, 361-362.

29 W. F. Prosser, "A Remarkable Episode of the Late War," *United Service* (Dec. 1889), 621.

30 Prosser, "A Remarkable Episode," 623; David A. Powell and Steven L. Wright, "Last Clash at Chickamauga," in *The Chickamauga Campaign—Barren Victory: The Retreat into Chattanooga, the Confederate Pursuit, and the Aftermath of the Battle, September 21 to October 20, 1863* (El Dorado Hills, CA: 2016), 139. See also the *Louisville Journal*, June 10, 1863.

gaffe, responded aggressively. "My bile is stirred, and some hanging would do me good."[31]

The men soon confessed to being Rebels, though not spies. Auton was in fact Confederate Col. William Orton Williams (also known as "Lawrence Williams Orton") of Bragg's staff. A cousin of Robert E. Lee, he was all but engaged to Lee's daughter, Agnes. Dunlop turned out to be Lt. Walter "Gip" Peter, Williams's cousin, and a member of Joseph Wheeler's staff.[32]

Baird convened the court. There was little doubt of the outcome, though both Rebels testified that they were "not spies in the ordinary sense." A last-minute appeal for clemency, or at least the chance to die by firing squad instead of hanging, was denied. At 4:40 a.m. on June 9, Rosecrans ordered them "to be hung at once, thus placing it beyond the possibility of Forrest's profiting by the information they have gained." By 10:30, Baird reported, "the men have been tried, found guilty, and executed, in compliance with your order."[33]

Williams's and Peter's mission remains a mystery. Baird was certainly puzzled. They "asked no questions about forces" and "wanted no information about [Fort Granger]. . . Said they were going to Canada and something about Europe; not clear." Among their papers was a list of Federal commanders and assistant adjutant generals for various Northern states, but they did not specify what purpose they served or why they needed that information. "Their conduct was very singular, indeed; I can make nothing of it," Baird concluded.[34]

On June 12, at morning parade, Baird presented Williams's horse and saber to Col. Louis D. Watkins in recognition of the latter officer's "critical role" in unmasking the duo. That part of the ceremony was well received, but the execution itself left everyone feeling subdued for several days. The pair's bravery in facing their fate impressed the Federals. Major William Broaddus of the 78th Illinois, writing home that same day, noted, "I have never saw anyone meet death with more courage than they did. . . Their [sic] was a feeling of sadness on all the troops here. Everything went off very quietly and yet—all felt as they ought to be hung."[35]

---

31 OR 23, pt. 2, 398.

32 Prosser, "A Remarkable Episode," 616.

33 OR 23, pt. 2, 416.

34 Ibid.

35 Tonia J. Smith, "Gentlemen, You Have Played This D—d Well!" *North & South,* vol. 8, no. 3 (September 2005), 82. Smith's article is the best account of this odd incident yet published.

The affair puzzled numerous Confederates as well. Word of the hangings reached the Rebel camps of Polk's Corps at Shelbyville on June 16. When Pvt. Simon Mayer of the 10th Mississippi Infantry, clerking at Brig. Gen. Patton J. Anderson's brigade headquarters, heard the news, he recorded it in his diary, attributing the event to Orton's mental incapacity. "This is a sad affair," he wrote, "and it is thought that Col. Orton had lost his mind."[36]

Intrigue of another sort was also afoot. Politically, Rosecrans aligned with the Democrats, but he was a War Democrat through and through. Nothing illustrated this more clearly than when Clement L. Vallandigham passed through Murfreesboro on his way south in late May. Vallandigham also was an Ohio Democrat, but unlike Rosecrans, he vigorously opposed the war, insisting that the Union could be restored only via peaceful means. On April 30, while running for governor of Ohio on an antiwar platform, he gave an inflammatory speech at the Ohio state capitol. Ambrose Burnside had him arrested on May 5 and tried by a military court the following day. The court-martial sentenced Vallandigham to two years at hard labor. Lincoln, realizing the folly of Burnside's ham-fisted handling of the affair, commuted the sentence to exile on May 19.[37]

On the evening of May 24, Vallandigham arrived in Murfreesboro, under guard. Near midnight, Rosecrans met with him, curious to converse and warned Vallandigham that if left unprotected, the troops "would tear [him] to pieces in an instant." Vallandigham replied that if given the chance to explain his position, "when they have heard me through, they will be more willing to tear Lincoln and yourself to pieces." He never got that chance. That very night he was sent south to Shelbyville, where a cordial but confused Braxton Bragg received him.[38]

The Confederates were no more welcoming to the Ohioan than the Federals had been, since they were fighting for independence, not peaceful reunion. But Vallandigham did make for good propaganda. They soon put him on a blockade runner, and he eventually made his way to Canada. Colonel Fremantle encountered him in mid-June at Wilmington, North Carolina. Fremantle was headed for Virginia and Vallandigham was waiting for a ship to Bermuda, "from whence," recalled Fremantle, "he should find his way to the Clifton Hotel, Canada, where he

---

36 Simon Mayer, "The Diary of Major Simon Mayer," June 16 entry, accessed at www.nps.gov/stri/learn/historyculture/upload/SimonMayerDiary.pdf on March 23, 2019.

37 Frank L. Klement, *The Limits of Dissent: Clement L. Vallandigham and the Civil War* (Lexington, KY: 1970), 177.

38 Ibid., 194-195, 202-203.

intended to publish a newspaper and agitate Ohio across the frontier. . .[He was] much elated by the news of his having been nominated for the governorship of Ohio; and he declared if he was duly elected, his state could dictate peace."[39]

At about this time, Rosecrans entertained another visitor, one who potentially posed a much bigger threat (to the Lincoln administration, anyway) than did Vallandigham. New England businessman and novelist James R. Gilmore appeared in Murfreesboro about the middle of May. Gilmore, having made his fortune in commerce, had taken up writing as a second profession. Under the pen name "Edmund Kirke," he wrote several novels that described Southern life and customs. In them, he advocated for the abolition of slavery. His nominal purpose in visiting Murfreesboro was to gather material for his next book. According to his memoir, however, Gilmore was also an undercover emissary on behalf of *New York Tribune* editor Horace Greeley, sent to sound out Rosecrans about the possibility of running for president on the Republican ticket in 1864. Greeley viewed Lincoln as weak, especially on the question of abolition, and felt the Union could only be saved and slavery destroyed with a different man at the helm of state. Rosecrans, whose political capital and public reputation were both in the ascendant in early 1863, might be that man— assuming of course that he was, in Greeley's colorful phase, "sound on the goose"; or, in other words, a firm abolitionist.[40]

Gilmore's account of his time with the Army of the Cumberland is both dramatic and a bit self-serving, but the basic outline of his interview with Rosecrans has been widely accepted. His first task was to feel out the general concerning the ever-present "Negro Question," and to do so "without asking him any direct questions." Fortunately, the loquacious Rosecrans loved late-night conversations. In one such discussion, Rosecrans said of the slave, "Give him the Bible and a spelling book, freedom, and a chance for something more than six feet of God's earth—and let him alone." With those words he passed the first hurdle, at least as far as Gilmore (and by extension, Greeley) was concerned.[41]

Sometime later, having first broached the idea of a presidential run with Garfield, Gilmore revealed his real purpose to Rosecrans. "He heard me through with evident surprise and gratification," noted Gilmore, and then said, "but, my good friend, it cannot be. My place is here. The country gave me my education, and

---

39 Fremantle, *Three Months*, 203-204.

40 James R. Gilmore, *Personal Recollections of Abraham Lincoln and the Civil War* (Boston, MA: 1898), 101.

41 Ibid., 120-121.

so has a right to my military services . . . so this, and not the presidency is my post of duty." Further, Rosecrans insisted, Gilmore and Greeley were "mistaken about Mr. Lincoln. He is in his right place."[42]

Gilmore's 1898 recollection is the only detailed account of this meeting. In an 1880 presidential campaign biography of James A. Garfield, Albert Gallatin Riddle penned a much different version of the incident. Gilmore, wrote Riddle, "a writer of some ability and shrewdness, was sent forward with letters to Garfield . . . with instructions to remain at headquarters, observe, gather up opinions, learn the views of the chief of staff, and if all concurred, Rosecrans was to be approached." Garfield "saw the futility and probable evil consequences . . . at once. He gave it such emphatic discouragement that it is believed no whisper of it ever reached Rosecrans, or any considerable number of men not in the secret."[43]

The idea that Rosecrans was never approached, and remained unaware of Gilmore's purpose, is almost certainly incorrect. In an 1885 letter to Rosecrans, Gilmore referred to the meeting in familiar terms, as part of an effort "to urge you not again to decline such a nomination as you did in 1863, when I was the medium of assessing you." This phrasing strongly suggested that the two men discussed the offer face to face. And while Garfield wrote or said very little about the incident, others certainly heard about it; rumors and gossip habitually spread through the ranks of armies like wildfire. Brigadier General William B. Hazen, a brigade commander in the Army of the Cumberland at the time, definitely caught wind of the incident. Writing in 1866, Hazen remembered that "Mr. Edmund Kirk [Gilmore's nom de plume] of the N. Y. Tribune had visited the Hd. Qrs. of our army at Murfreesboro and told Gen. R[osecrans] that the country looked to him as our next President." In retrospect, Hazen, along with an "ample staff of newspaper men," viewed Gilmore's offer as dangerous, "inflat[ing] the man until he was no longer the careful vigilant commander of the second great army of the nation."[44]

At least one other journalist visited the army at this time. German émigré Henry Villard, a staunch Republican who also worked for the *New York Tribune*, had an opinion on Rosecrans that contrasted starkly with Gilmore's. Villard eyed

42 Ibid., 145-146.

43 A. G. Riddle, *The Life, Character and Public Services of Jas. A. Garfield* (Philadelphia, PA: 1880), 69-70.

44 "My Dear General," Gilmore to Rosecrans, January 26, 1885, William S. Rosecrans Papers, University of California, Los Angeles (hereafter UCLA); "D. Sir," Hazen to Benjamin H. Lossing, August 23, 1866, William P. Palmer Collection, Western Reserve Historical Society, Cleveland, OH.

with distaste the constant presence at Rosecrans's headquarters of yet another newspaperman, William D. Bickham, who wrote for the *Cincinnati Commercial*. Bickham had been with Rosecrans for many months, filling his columns with praise for the general, in effect acting as little more than a "puffer." Villard also was struck by how contemptuously (and liberally) Rosecrans spoke of Halleck and Stanton, with "broad intimation" that both men needed "to be got out of the way, leaving me to infer that, after this was done, the next necessary step was to put [Rosecrans] in [Halleck's] place." Villard's memoir, penned in 1900, benefits from a good deal of hindsight, but his writing suggests that loose talk was quite common around the upper echelons of the Army of the Cumberland.[45]

It is likely Stanton and Lincoln knew of the scheme, at least in broad outline; Horace Greeley was hardly subtle in his efforts. If so, this only created additional impetus to get Rosecrans moving. While a major victory in Tennessee would enhance his standing in the public eye, it also would go a long way toward convincing voters the Lincoln administration was, at long last, winning the war.

Thus, the pressure mounted on Rosecrans to advance. On June 11, Halleck informed Rosecrans, "I deem it my duty to repeat to you the great dissatisfaction that is felt here at your inactivity." On June 12, however, responding to the results of Rosecrans's survey, Halleck explicitly stated, "if you say you are not prepared to fight Bragg, I shall not order you to do so." In that same communication, he again warned Rosecrans that "the prolonged inactivity of so large an army in the field is causing much complaint and dissatisfaction, not only in Washington, but throughout the country." On June 16, Halleck dropped any pretense, demanding, "Is it your intention to make an immediate movement forward? . . . A definite answer, yes or no, is required."[46]

Rosecrans still equivocated. "In reply to your inquiry, if immediate means to-night or to-morrow, no," he replied. "If it means as soon as all things are ready, say five days, yes."

Eight days later, at 2:10 a.m. on June 24, Rosecrans wired a single sentence to Washington. "The army begins to move at 3 o'clock this morning."[47]

---

45 Henry Villard, *Memoirs of Henry Villard, Journalist and Financier, 1835-1900, in Two Volumes* (Boston, MA: 1904), 2: 67. Villard good friends with Maj. Gen. Alexander McCook, who would be blamed by Rosecrans for the disaster at Chickamauga that Septemver. It is very likely that Villard's low opinion of Rosecrans was colored by the falling-out between those two men.

46 OR 23, pt. 1, 9-10.

47 Ibid.

Chapter Six

A Feint to the Right,
June 23 to 25, 1863

"At 2 o'clock in the morning of June 23, I received orders from the general commanding . . . to move at daylight with all the forces under my command," reported Maj. Gen. Gordon Granger, head of the Union Reserve Corps. Granger's command included Brig. Gen. Absalom Baird's First Division of Granger's own corps, Brig. Gen. John M. Brannan's Third Division of the XIV Corps, and Brig. Gen. Robert B. Mitchell's First Division of the Cavalry Corps—a total of about 10,000 infantry and 5,800 cavalry. Brannan's division of three brigades was detached from George Thomas's command to augment Granger's infantry since most of the Reserve Corps would remain in the lines around Nashville and Murfreesboro. Only two brigades of Baird's command— barely 3,000 men—were available to take the field. Since Granger's mission was to deceive the Rebels into thinking his was the main attack, he needed sufficient strength to be convincing.[1]

The other division of the Cavalry Corps, under Russian-born Brig. Gen. John B. Turchin, was tasked with leading the XXI Corps to Bradyville on the Union far left. This put a substantial distance between the two wings that would have kept their commander, Maj. Gen. David S. Stanley, from actually commanding both divisions effectively. For several reasons, Stanley decided to move with Mitchell and Granger.

1 OR 23, pt. 1, 535.

Maj. Gen. David S. Stanley, commander of the
Army of the Cumberland's Cavalry Corps.

Library Congress

The Cavalry Corps had reached its current organization and strength only within the past month, as regiments arrived from the north to augment it. For most of the spring, it had operated largely as detachments, with no effective field force much larger than a brigade. Now, Stanley commanded two divisions, but he was none too happy with either of their commanders. He felt that both had been imposed on him, "dictated by Garfield, and worse could not be found: Turchin, a fat, short-legged Russian, who could not ride a horse, and Robert Mitchell, a politician, always thinking of the votes he could make in Kansas." Initially Stanley chose to keep close to Mitchell, perhaps because Turchin was at least a professional

Brig. Gen. Robert B. Mitchell, commander,
First Division, Cavalry Corps,
Army of the Cumberland.

Library of Congress

soldier; he had been educated in military schools and then had served in the Russian Imperial Guard during the 1840s.

Mitchell had no such military credentials, though by 1863 he did have some practical experience, leading a regiment at Wilson's Creek and a division at the Battle of Perryville. Further, Mitchell's role in the opening stages of the current campaign was vital; if Bragg was not deceived, he could either escape or counterattack. To further complicate matters, Mitchell reported himself "very sick" on June 23, though he still took the field. All these considerations meant that Stanley needed to be on the Union right with Mitchell to start the campaign.[2]

2 Stanley, *Personal Memoirs*, 135; *OR* 23, pt. 1, 532. Robert Byington Mitchell was born in Mansfield, Ohio, on April 4, 1823. He studied law in Mt. Vernon, Ohio, and then started a practice in Mansfield. He served as a lieutenant in the 2nd Ohio Infantry during the Mexican-American War. In 1855, he was elected mayor of Mt. Gilead, Ohio. The following year, he moved to Linn County, in the Kansas Territory, where he established the Free State movement. Although a Democrat, he was elected to serve in the territorial legislature, as a delegate to the Leavenworth constitutional convention, as territory treasurer, and as a delegate to the 1860 Democratic convention in Charleston, South Carolina. With the outbreak of war, he was commissioned colonel of the 2nd Kansas Infantry and was badly wounded at the Battle of Wilson's Creek in August 1861. He was commissioned a brigadier general of volunteers, to rank from April 8, 1862, and was given command of a mixed brigade at Fort Riley, Kansas. He commanded the 9th Division of Gilbert's Corps at the October 1862 Battle of Perryville and then was stationed in Nashville, where he was given command of a division of cavalry in the Army of the Cumberland. Mitchell was a far better politician than he was a general, and he eventually was relieved of field command and sent to a backwater of the war. He briefly served as governor of New Mexico after the war, but was removed from office for malfeasance. After an unsuccessful bid for Congress in 1872, he moved to Washington, DC, where he died on January 25, 1882. He was buried in Arlington National Cemetery. Warner, *Generals in Blue*, 328-329.

Colonel Thomas J. Jordan's 9th Pennsylvania Cavalry, from Col. Archibald P. Campbell's brigade, led Mitchell's column southeast along the Shelbyville Pike from Triune on a warm morning that foreshadowed a hot day ahead. About midday, they rode into the village of Eagleville, eight miles distant, without incident. Two miles beyond the village, however, and three and a half miles short of the even smaller hamlet of Rover, Jordan's Pennsylvanians ran into Rebel cavalry. There, noted Pvt. William Thomas, the Pennsylvanians dismounted, formed line, and "a brisk skirmish ensued."[3]

This first contact was with approximately 300 Georgians of Col. Charles C. Crews's brigade of John Wharton's division, camped at Rover to

Col. John T. Morgan, commander, Morgan's Brigade, Martin's Division, Wheeler's Cavalry Corps.

Library of Congress

picket the Shelbyville Pike. Outnumbered, they fell back when pressed. After a lengthy running fight, Colonel Campbell replaced the worn-out men of the 9th with a fresh line of troopers from the 2nd Michigan, and the Federals overran the Rebel tents. By now, all of Crews's men—the 2nd, 3rd, and 4th Georgia, plus the 7th Alabama Cavalry—were engaged. Additionally, the Federals identified at least one other Confederate regiment, the 51st Alabama Partisan Rangers of Col. John T. Morgan's brigade, William Martin's division. The fight was expanding.[4]

The Rebel defense firmed south of Rover, and both sides deployed artillery. Mitchell reported that a large force of Southern infantry became involved, although he probably mistook some of the Confederate cavalry—who often used infantry

3 John W. Rowell, *Yankee Cavalrymen: Through the Civil War with the Ninth Pennsylvania Cavalry* (Knoxville, TN: 1971), 134.

4 *OR* 23, pt. 1, 543-547.

tactics when dismounted—for foot troops. As an added complication, the temperature started to rise. It was, noted the 2nd Michigan's historian, "a very hot day and men were falling out continually." By late afternoon, Campbell's entire brigade was fighting on foot, supported by "six companies of the First Wisconsin [and] part of the Fourth Indiana" cavalry regiments. "Soon a flank firing was heard, followed by a charge from the enemy. This was handsomely met by a counter charge from the First Tennessee [U.S.] and the flankers retired in confusion."[5]

Neither side lost heavily, with each incurring only a handful of casualties. One Confederate was captured in a most unusual fashion. During the countercharge, the Michiganders watched in amazement as "a single horseman was seen to leave the enemy's ranks and charge down along upon our brigade. . . .Nearly every man in [the 1st Tennessee] and not a few from the Second fired at the charging figure," but he did not falter. For a time, "hostilities ceased on both sides" as soldiers in blue and gray marveled at the man riding, unscathed, into the Union lines. Then the reason for his behavior became apparent. "A bullet had cut both reins, and the horse had refused to cease charging. . . .His clothes were riddled and the horse had many a scratch, but the man's skin was whole."[6]

In an eerie echo of that remarkable episode, Col. James P. Brownlow of the 1st Tennessee had a similarly traumatic experience. In his diary, Private Thomas of the 9th Pennsylvania wrote that Brownlow "shot his [own] horse trying to shoot a rebel that had come through our lines." Capt. Thomas S. McCahan, also of the 9th, added more detail to this rather cryptic notation. According to McCahan, a battalion of the 1st Tennessee (U.S.) "was dismounted, laying down in line holding their horses when a rebel battalion charged them. Col. Jim was there with his men mounted and charged [the] rebels who soon wheeled. The curb in Col. Brownlow's bridle broke. He was riding a large blooded horse and he could not stop him, was making for the rebel lines [so] he drew his revolver, shot him back of the ear. [The horse] fell instantly and Jim lit about 20 feet ahead of him in the road. [Brownlow] said he never went so fast as he did then, said he felt the rope around his neck. Presence of mind saved him."[7]

---

5 OR 23, pt. 1, 543, 547; Thatcher, *A Hundred Battles in the West*, 131.

6 Thatcher, *A Hundred Battles in the West*, 131-132.

7 Rowell, *Yankee Cavalrymen*, 134; "Entry for June 24, 1863," Thomas S. McCahan Journal, Historical Society of Pennsylvania (hereafter PHS), Philadelphia, P.A. James P. Brownlow was the younger son of William G. "Parson" Brownlow, a vehement pro-Unionist Methodist

Private Horatio Foote of the 1st Wisconsin also remembered a hot fight. "Our regiment was drawn in line within 60 rods of a rebel gun that was apelting Shell at us quite lively, some of them coming so close to my head that I was forced to bow in acknowledgment of their good marksmanship. One shell struck about 25 feet in front of our company but fortunately did not explode."[8]

With darkness approaching, Mitchell broke off the engagement, retreating "about 1 mile north of Rover," where the Federals camped. Both sides claimed victory. Mitchell was satisfied that "the enemy [had] been driven to the support of the main force at Unionville," leaving him in control of their camps and the Shelbyville Pike. One trooper of the 3rd Georgia Cavalry, by contrast, exulted, "This day was Brilliant & Glorious. . . .We whipped them in every attempt to drive us." Private Julius Dowda, also of the 3rd Georgia, noted simply that "we fought them at Rover and drove them down the Nashville Pike." Crews's Georgians remained in front of Shelbyville, while the 51st Alabama fell back southeast through Unionville to Liberty Gap.[9]

The participation of the 51st Alabama Partisan Rangers from Martin's division (and the probable presence of the rest of Colonel Morgan's brigade) stood out. It meant that on June 23, with Forrest still at Spring Hill, all or part of all three of Bragg's remaining cavalry divisions—Wharton's, Martin's, and Forrest's—were at or west of Shelbyville. Thus, though Bragg had reported no less than 14,223 officers and men present for duty in the combined cavalry commands on June 20, five of the six available mounted brigades of the Army of the Tennessee were massed on his left flank, leaving only Col. Thomas Harrison's Texas brigade to cover the now-exposed Confederate right. John Hunt Morgan's departure could not have come at a worse time for Bragg, while Wheeler's lopsided deployment of his corps compounded the problem.[10]

How could such neglect happen? Certainly, that is not what Bragg intended when, on June 6, he ordered Wheeler to "concentrate his whole force" and place Wharton's division in front of both Liberty Gap, north of Wartrace, and Hoover's

---

preacher and newspaper editor from Knoxville. Many Confederates viewed the Brownlows as traitors and Tories.

8 "Dear Father," July 12, 1863, Horatio Kirkland Foote Letters, Wisconsin Historical Society (hereafter WHS), Madison, WI.

9 John Randolph Poole, *Cracker Cavaliers: The 2nd Georgia Cavalry under Wheeler and Forrest* (Macon, GA: 2000), 78; Rex Miller, *Wheeler's Favorites: 51st Alabama Cavalry* (Austin, TX: 1991), 7.

10 See *OR* 23, pt. 1, 585, for the army's cavalry strength.

Maj. Gen. Joseph Wheeler, commander, Cavalry Corps, Army of Tennessee.

National Archives

Gap, covering the direct road to Manchester. On June 21, however, apparently convinced that the long-awaited Federal advance was about to commence, Wheeler proposed "to take a portion of the troops at Spring Hill, and by a dash around

Rosecrans's rear, capture his trains and create a diversion." A portion of Martin's division (either 930 men or 1,500—accounts vary) was ordered to reinforce Forrest at Spring Hill. Since it never came to pass, the details of this "dash" remain unclear. Did Wheeler intend to lead Martin's men on this raid personally, augmented by elements from Forrest? Or was Martin merely to replace Forrest while that officer conducted the strike?[11]

*   *   *

And what of Morgan? On June 21, he was just departing on his grand Ohio raid, intending to create a diversion, at least as far as Bragg knew. According to Bragg's final instructions—which Morgan completely ignored—if Rosecrans began to move, Morgan was to return at once and strike at the Union rear, exactly as Wheeler now proposed to do. From Bragg's perspective, Wheeler's raid duplicated Morgan's effort at the expense of the already greatly weakened cavalry force that was intended to screen Bragg's exposed right. Nevertheless, Bragg authorized Wheeler's "dash." Perhaps he simply didn't trust Morgan to follow orders; if so, his intuition proved correct.

The impact of Bragg's decision cannot be understated. Martin's westward shift stretched Wharton thin and, worst of all, there seemed to be no organized body of Confederate cavalry left to cover the Manchester approaches. As a result, most of the intelligence flowing to Bragg concerning Union movements over the next two days came from the Shelbyville front, not from points farther east, leaving Bragg with an incomplete picture of the situation.

June 23 proved to be merely tedious for Granger's infantry. Corporal Charles Edwin Cort of the 92nd Illinois Infantry, Baird's division, typified the universal soldier's experience when he complained in a letter home, "we left Triune on June 23 . . . got in line at 8 AM and did not get outside of the pickets until after 2 p.m. although there was troops moving out two roads all the time. We camped at a place called Salem a little after dark." The day's march, about 13 miles, was a lateral move, with Baird's troops closing on Murfreesboro. Brannan's division followed suit, though it went by a more roundabout route. Orville Chamberlain of the 74th

---

11 OR 23, pt. 2, 866; W. C. Dodson, *Campaigns of Wheeler and His Cavalry, 1862-1865, from Material Furnished by Gen. Joseph Wheeler to which is Added his Concise and Graphic Account of the Santiago Campaign of 1898* (Atlanta, GA: 1899), 86.

Brig. Gen. John Brannan, commander,
Third Division, XIV Corps,
Army of the Cumberland.

Library of Congress

Indiana estimated his day's march at 18 miles, adding only that "we suffered from the heat."[12]

At Salem, Granger received additional orders directing him to turn south toward Christiana, another dozen miles away. This route placed Granger's infantry on a converging course with Mitchell's cavalry, which Granger now ordered to Middleton "to attack that place." These moves simultaneously maintained the threat to Shelbyville and protected the right flank of the Union XX Corps, which began its own march south the next day.[13]

Though the XX Corps had yet to take to the road, its camps buzzed with preparation that Tuesday. Captain William A. Robinson, leading Company E of the 77th Pennsylvania Infantry in Richard Johnson's Second Division, penned a few brief thoughts on the forthcoming movement in his diary. "Orders to be ready with twelve days' rations and one hundred rounds," he wrote. "March light, at 3 in the morning. Rosey is tired and the North is uneasy. Halleck orders and we must go. If our General is ready, 'tis well. If not, the stake is immense, and we must work. God grant success."[14]

Wednesday, June 24, brought rain. That morning, the entire Union army stirred, and the XX Corps was up early. General McCook reported, "[Maj. Gen.

---

12 Helyn W. Tomlinson, ed., *"Dear Friends": The Civil War Letters and Diary of Charles Edwin Cort* (1962), 91; "Near Elk River," Orville Chamberlain Letters, INHS. Though the 92nd Illinois later joined Wilder's Lightning Brigade of mounted infantry, they were not a part of that command during the Tullahoma Campaign.

13 *OR* 23, pt. 1, 535, 542.

14 "Entry for June 23rd," William A. Robinson Diary, WRHS.

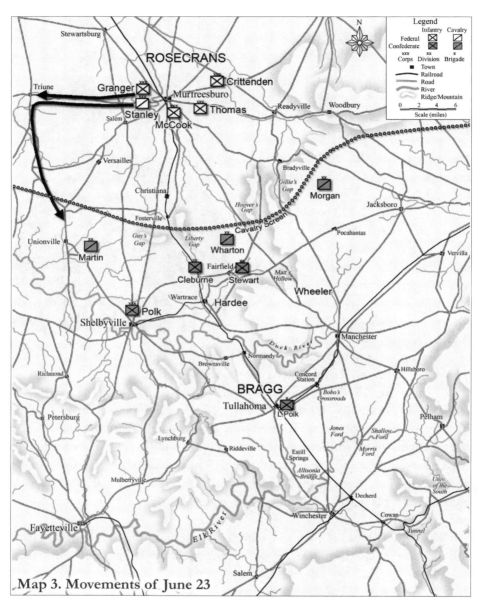

Map 3. Movements of June 23

Philip H.] Sheridan's (Third) division . . . marched at daylight . . . on the Shelbyville pike, with instructions to proceed as far as Walnut Grove Church [a half mile west of Christiana on the Shelbyville Pike], 9 miles from Murfreesborough." Sheridan was to hold that line until replaced by Brannan's men, coming via Middleton. Once Brannan arrived, Sheridan was to move east to Millersburg. "[Brig. Gen. Richard W.] Johnson's (Second) division followed Sheridan . . . for 6 miles, where it turned off to the left, marching direct to old Millersburg . . . . [Brigadier General Jefferson C.] Davis' (Third) division followed Johnson's." McCook placed himself at the head of Johnson's command, reaching "Millersburg at 12 m." From Millersburg, the road to Wartrace led through Liberty Gap.[15]

Thus, Granger and McCook simultaneously moved to threaten Shelbyville (via Guy's Gap) and Wartrace (via Liberty Gap) with powerful Union columns, each at least corps-strength. It was an intricate orchestration of multiple moving columns, made more complicated by the relative dearth of good roads. The Franklin, Nolensville, and Shelbyville pikes were the only improved toll roads in the area, and the Nolensville Pike ended barely 3 miles south of Triune; as a result, it was not much use to the Federals after June 23. The Civil War had already spawned numerous examples of armies coming to grief over similarly complicated march schedules, which could lead to unexpected delays, failures of coordination, and wrong turns. It stood as a testament to Rosecrans and his headquarters staff that the Army of the Cumberland's many moving parts usually showed up when and where they were expected over the course of the next few days' operations.

No amount of efficient staff work could overcome the vagaries of nature, however. That Wednesday, the weather turned. "It began to rain early next morning and rained hard all day," wrote Corporal Cort, slogging along with the 92nd Illinois. "[S]tarted toward Shelbyvill at 2 PM. We . . . marched on a mud road with the mud from 1 to 6 in[ches] deep." He also recorded "heavy fireing ahead all day," though none of Baird's infantry became engaged. "[A]n hour before dark haulted until 8 then moved on again marching over the worst roads I ever saw and wading two creeks still raining hard." Cort and his comrades finally stopped at midnight to snatch a scant three hours' sleep. Almost every soldier in both armies would share Cort's experience over the coming fortnight.[16]

Despite being soaked to the skin, McCook's and Granger's forces each made significant contact with the enemy. That morning, Mitchell's Federal cavalry rode to Versailles Post Office, where, near noon, Mitchell received Granger's orders to head for Middleton. "Rain had fallen steadily and heavily since 1 a.m.," Mitchell reported, "and the road was in very bad condition." Nevertheless, he set off at once. The Federals encountered a line of mounted Rebel skirmishers a mile north of Middleton, and a brisk fight developed. Colonel Edward McCook's cavalry brigade led the column, consisting of the 2nd and 4th Indiana, 2nd Tennessee, and

15 *OR* 23, pt. 1, 465.

16 Cort, *"Dear Friends,"* 91.

1st Wisconsin. The 2nd Indiana and 1st Wisconsin deployed and began driving the Confederates slowly southward.[17]

Once again, the Rebels belonged to Colonel Crews's brigade. Crews had arrayed the bulk of his troops in the town, filling Middleton's "strong log-houses" with dismounted sharpshooters. Mitchell halted here, waiting as directed for Brannan's infantry to arrive. He waited in vain. The steady rain meant that the infantry toiled far to the rear, and Brannan eventually moved to Christiana by a different route. Late that afternoon, Mitchell decided to attack.

Mitchell first ordered the two guns of Lt. Nathaniel M. Newell's section of Battery D, 1st Ohio Light Artillery, to shell the town and suppress or drive off the Rebels ensconced in the cabins. He then sent Colonel Campbell's 2nd Michigan and a battalion of the 9th Pennsylvania in on foot. "[T]hey drove a stubborn enemy from their chosen position in a ravine and log buildings of the town," reported Campbell, "and with the aid of the artillery, completely routed [them]." The 2nd Michigan's regimental history noted with evident satisfaction that their "[Colt] revolving rifles soon dislodged them, with severe punishment for the time engaged."[18]

Middleton was in Union hands, but not for long. Short of forage, Mitchell, with his supply wagons bogged down in the rear and with the local area

---

17 OR 23, pt. 1, 544, 548.

18 OR 23, pt. 1, 545, 547; Thatcher, *A Hundred Battles in the West,* 132; "June 24," McCahan Journal, PHS. The men of the 2nd Michigan Cavalry carried .56-caliber Colt revolving rifles, which were among the first repeating rifles to enter mass production. Rosecrans was a great admirer of this firearm. "These weapons were basically a larger version of Colt's world-famous handguns and were loaded in the same manner—cartridges (or loose powder and balls) were inserted one at a time into the revolving chambers and then the corresponding nipples were capped with standard pistol percussion caps," noted Civil War weapons expert Dean S. Thomas. See Thomas's *Round Ball to Rimfire: A History of Civil War Small Arms Ammunition, Part Two: Federal Breechloading Carbines & Rifles* (Gettysburg, PA: 2002), 43-44. The war department purchased less than 5,000 of these rifles during the war, in part because they required special ammunition and cartridges. They had a longer range than most cavalry carbines and were fairly accurate (they were the standard weapon carried by Berdan's Sharpshooters early in the war), but they also had several problems that rendered them largely obsolete once more Spencer and Henry rifles went into production. The Colt revolving rifle could lay down a great deal of firepower, but also took a long time to reload due to its cumbersome revolver mechanism. Joseph G. Bilby, *A Revolution in Arms: A History of the First Repeating Rifles* (Yardley, PA: 2006), 44-48. The historian of the 9th Illinois Cavalry noted a major problem with the weapon. "The Colt's revolving rifle was an excellent arm, and had served us well on many an occasion," he wrote; "but there was serious objection to them; when being discharged they would shoot splinters of lead into the wrist and hand of the man firing." Ken Bauman, *Arming the Suckers, 1861-1865: A Compilation of Illinois Civil War Weapons* (Dayton, OH: 1989), 53.

"devastated," fell back north seeking food and fodder. It was a timely decision, since he soon received an order from army headquarters directing him "to move your command back by way of Versailles . . . and join . . . Granger's column . . . en route to Christiana." As they pulled out, and despite the rain, Capt. Thomas McCahan saw flames everywhere. "When [the Confederates] left they set fire to all the Union property [in Middleton]," he wrote. "[W]hen we left it looked as though the whole town was on fire."[19]

The cavalry fights on June 23 and 24, though substantial and prolonged, were not accompanied by heavy bloodletting. Union losses amounted to a dozen men killed, wounded, or missing. Confederate casualties went unreported and, despite Union estimates that they were "severe," probably approximated those of the Federals. All this activity, however, accomplished Rosecrans's main goal: drawing both Wheeler's and Bragg's attention to the Shelbyville front. The scrap at Rover also induced David Stanley to reinforce Mitchell with a brigade taken from Turchin's division, which had a much quieter time out on the Union left, screening the XXI Corps. On the morning of June 24, Stanley ordered Col. Robert H. G. Minty's powerful cavalry brigade to march from Cripple Creek (eight miles east of Murfreesboro) to a position supporting Mitchell on the Salem Pike.[20]

On the afternoon of June 24, the leading elements of Alexander McCook's XX Corps infantry also had their first hostile encounter of the campaign. At 2 p.m., the van of Richard Johnston's division entered the northern mouth of Liberty Gap. Colonel Thomas J. Harrison and five mounted companies of the 39th Indiana Infantry led the way. Harrison was an independent-minded Hoosier lawyer from Kokomo who had recruited a company for the 6th Indiana Infantry, a three-month regiment, before returning home to raise the 39th. The 39th had seen action at Shiloh and was heavily engaged at Stones River, where it suffered terrible losses: 31 killed, 118 wounded, and a staggering 231 missing, the latter being mostly men who were captured on December 31. The following April, having grown weary of infantry service, they emulated the men of Col. John T. Wilder's brigade and converted to mounted infantry, rearmed in part with Spencer repeaters.[21]

That first contact near Liberty Gap proved to be bloodless. Harrison captured three Confederates cutting wheat in the rain. From them, he learned that a squadron of the Confederate combined 1st/3rd Kentucky Cavalry screened the

19 OR 23, pt. 2, 451; "June 24," McCahan Journal, PHS.

20 OR 23, pt. 1, 547-548, 556.

21 *Kokomo Tribune* (Kokomo, IN), October 3, 1871; OR 20, pt. 1, 315.

gap. Beyond them, two regiments, the 5th and 15th Arkansas Infantry, defended the main passage. Harrison quickly pushed forward and soon reported that he "was skirmishing with some 800 infantry." Brigadier General August Willich, commanding Johnson's First Brigade and leading the day's march, ordered Harrison to halt and wait for his own brigade to deploy.[22]

* * *

August Willich was one of the Civil War's more unusual characters. Born in 1810 to a family of recent Prussian nobility, he was christened Johann August Ernst von Willich. His father, a captain of Hussars who had fought in the Napoleonic Wars, died in 1814. Throughout August's life, rumors circulated among his father's German comrades that the boy was actually the illegitimate child of one of the crown princes of the ruling Hohenzollern family. His mother was foreign, and very attractive, but not overly motherly. Of her Willich once commented, "My mother was a beautiful Polish woman—and how I hated her." After his father's death, Willich and a brother were raised in the household of Professor Friedrich Schleiermacher, a noted theologian at the University of Berlin. At age 12, Willich began to follow his father's path. He was educated in military schools, including the Royal Military Academy in Berlin, where he studied under the direction of Karl von Clausewitz. After graduation, he was commissioned as an officer in the Prussian army. Along the way, however, he became an avowed republican (in the revolutionary sense) and a dedicated communist. When Willich tried to resign his commission in 1846, his inflammatory departure letter led to his being arrested and court-martialed. After an acquittal, he eventually left the service.[23]

Willich subsequently fought against his former comrades in the German revolutions of 1848-49, serving alongside the likes of Franz Sigel, Friedrich Hecker, and Carl Schurz. His adjutant was Friedrich Engels, Karl Marx's close companion and future collaborator. To Marx, Engels "described Willich as 'brave, cold-blooded, skillful, and of quick and sound perception in battle.'" However, "outside of battle" Engels found Willich "a somewhat boring ideologist and true socialist," contrasting sharply with Engel's (and Marx's) own more pragmatic views of communism and revolution. After they were defeated in 1849, Willich and

---

22 OR 23, pt. 1, 486. "800 Infantry" was an overestimate.

23 Loyd D. Easton, *Hegel's First American Followers: The Ohio Hegelians: John B. Stallo, Peter Kaufmann, Moncure Conway, and August Willich, with Key Writings* (Athens, OH: 1966), 160-164.

Col. August Willich, commander,
First Brigade, Second Division, XX Corps,
Army of the Cumberland.

Library of Congress

others made their way to London, where they established their revolutionary government in exile. By 1850, Marx's and Willich's differences had so deepened that Willich challenged Marx to a duel. Marx ignored the challenge, dismissing it as a "Prussian officer trick," but one of Marx's more hotheaded supporters challenged Willich in turn. Willich accepted. No one was killed, but Willich's challenger suffered a minor head wound.[24]

The failed revolutionary eventually traveled to America, working for the U.S. Coast and Geodetic Survey in Washington, DC, for a time, before finally settling in as editor of a German-language newspaper in Cincinnati. In 1861, Willich saw the nascent American Civil War as a continuation of the worldwide struggle of the working class against the landed nobility and immediately joined the Union army. After serving three months in the 9th Ohio Infantry, Willich then accepted an offer to raise the all-German 32nd Indiana Infantry. He excelled at both regimental and brigade command, seeing action at Shiloh and Perryville. He was injured and captured during the opening stages of the Battle of Stones River and had only recently returned from Libby Prison in May 1863.

Captivity had given Willich plenty of time to think. Seeking a better means of controlling his brigade during the confusion of battle, where verbal commands often proved inadequate, Willich adapted his prewar experience in the Prussian service to teach his brigade to respond to a detailed series of bugle calls. To ensure that the Confederates wouldn't be able to decipher his orders immediately, he used Prussian bugle calls. As a result, his command was soon christened "Willich's Horn Brigade," or, more simply, the "Bugle Brigade." His other ideas included a plan to

24 Ibid., 169.

mount his troops on wagons—20 men to a wagon bed—and the use of a new form of infantry formation, which he called "Advance, Firing." The wagon idea proved impractical, not least because the army was already wagon-heavy, and no wagons could be spared for use as equine-powered personnel carriers; but the brigade quickly adopted Willich's new tactical formation.[25]

Confronting Rebels at Liberty Gap, Willich now advanced with the 15th Ohio Infantry to the left and the 49th Ohio on the right as skirmishers. He next ordered Capt. Wilbur F. Goodspeed's Battery A, 1st Ohio Artillery, to fire six rounds "to draw the fire of the enemy's batteries, supposed to be secreted on the hills" to the south; "but no reply was made." Willich then moved the rest of his brigade forward, pushing the Rebel skirmishers back until they reached the main Confederate position on "the crest of the hills forming the northern entrance to Liberty Gap." There, "the enemy had a very strong, and, in front, easily defended position."[26]

Colonel Lucius Featherston of the 5th Arkansas Infantry commanded 540 men of his own along with the combined 13th/15th Arkansas Regiment, supported by one section of Capt. Charles Swett's Mississippi Battery and a handful of cavalry. Featherston was sitting down to lunch when a courier brought word of the cavalry engagement at Middleton. He had just forwarded that news to his superior, Brig. Gen. St. John Richardson Liddell, when a second courier galloped up to report the arrival of Johnson's Federals at the northern end of the gap. After sending a second rider to pass along this latest report, Featherston noted, "I immediately formed my regiment, and sent Colonel [John E.] Josey orders to turn out" the 13th/15th Arkansas.[27]

Both Willich and Featherston understood that while the Confederates held strong positions overlooking Liberty Gap, the combination of hills and side defiles made for a line far too long to be defended by a few hundred men. Besides the main route, there were at least three other secondary passages close by: one a half mile to the east sufficient for use by both infantry and cavalry, the gap through which the railroad ran, and a smaller passage near a hill called Bald Knob. Willich decided that "a mere front attack was out of the question, as we would have had to pay 10 for 1."

25 Philip J. Reyburn, *Clear the Track: A History of the Eighty-Ninth Illinois Volunteer Infantry, The Rail Road Regiment* (Bloomington, IN: 2012), 368.

26 OR 23, pt. 1, 486.

27 Ibid., 594.

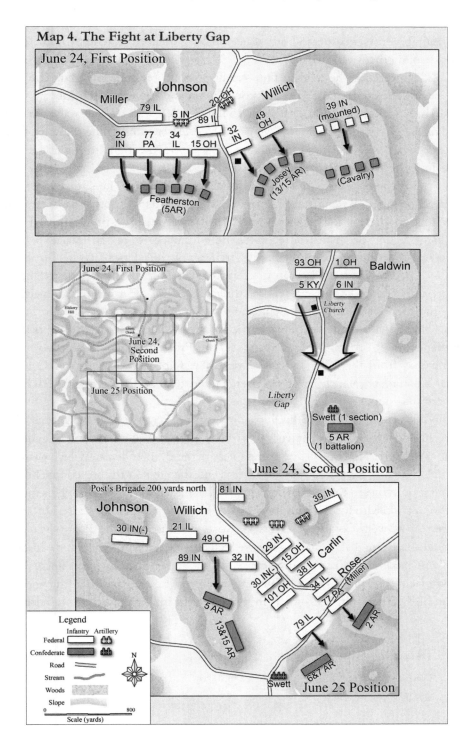

Map 4. The Fight at Liberty Gap

Instead, the Prussian ordered both of his Ohio regiments to extend their lines and work around the Rebel flanks.[28]

Liddell reached the field to find Featherston's force fully engaged. The two Rebel officers conferred at Featherston's command post near the Liberty Gap Church. Liddell instructed Featherston to hold the left with his own regiment and two or three companies from Josey's 13th/15th. After summoning the rest of his brigade from Bell Buckle, Liddell himself went to the right to supervise the remainder of Josey's force.[29]

Willich's initial effort to drive the Arkansans fell short. The 49th Ohio, with Companies A and B deployed as skirmishers, worked its way across an open field toward a wooded hillside. "Our advance was resisted by a brisk fire," reported Col. William H. Gibson. The Confederates, he continued, were "concealed behind fences, in ravines, and behind rocks and trees on the hill slopes." As his Buckeyes advanced, Willich ordered Gibson to capture another hill farther to the right. Gibson divided his command, sending three companies off toward that objective, but they found it equally well defended. Gibson reinforced this second effort with three additional companies and sent word to Willich that this new position outflanked him on the right. In response, the Prussian ordered over two more companies from the 32nd Indiana. Eventually, Gibson prevailed, and Colonel Josey's command, which had been greatly overextended to begin with, fell back toward the church.[30]

Willich supported the 15th Ohio's drive against Featherston's Arkansans with the 29th Indiana and 77th Pennsylvania of Col. John F. Miller's Second Brigade, as well as Colonel Harrison's five companies of the 39th Indiana. Willich wanted Miller's men to "find the end of the enemy's line, then to take the crest of the hill, to swing round toward the left, and advance in the direction of the gap." This move, in conjunction with Josey's withdrawal, forced Featherston's 5th Arkansas Infantry to retreat as well. Colonel Thomas E. Rose, commanding the Pennsylvanians, likened ascending that hill to "scaling the Heights of Abraham," with men climbing up from handhold to handhold. Surprised by the apparent lack of resistance, Rose soon discovered the reason. "While we scrambled up one side . . . [the enemy] scrambled down on the other in great confusion." Featherston's account

28 Ibid., 486.

29 Ibid., 588, 595.

30 Ibid., 495-496, 599-600.

contrasted with Rose's version of the Rebel retreat, insisting instead that it "was done in good order."[31]

This ended the day's fight, conducted amid a driving rain that greatly hindered Willich's movements. Once the hills were clear, he moved his reserve regiments through the gap as far as Liberty Gap Church, capturing several Confederate camps. Featherston and Josey fell back about a half mile south of the church, where they met the rest of Liddell's sodden Arkansans plodding north from Bell Buckle. Willich's command reported 11 killed and 30 wounded, while Miller's regiments added 6 more wounded. The 13th/15th Arkansas reported 4 killed and 7 wounded. While Featherston did not delineate the losses his regiment suffered on June 24 alone, he probably lost a number similar to Josey's.

One more regiment suffered a substantial loss at Liberty Gap on June 24. The 51st Alabama Partisan Rangers reported the capture of 118 men in its regimental service records. After the action of June 23, Will Martin's cavalry fell back to screen the terrain from Liberty Gap to Guy's Gap. The 51st was posted at Fosterville, just west of the northern entrance to Liberty Gap. "The pouring rain," asserted historian Rex Miller, "made it almost impossible to keep rifles in firing order and the men and horses were exhausted from days on the road." Thus, the men of the 51st "were somewhat lax in their guard duty and the Yankees were upon them . . . before they could react properly. Colonel [John] F. Miller of Illinois pushed his troops through the gap before the cavalry could mount up and escape."[32]

Curiously, no official reports, Union or Confederate, shed any additional light on this incident. Confederate cavalry records are especially sparse for this campaign, and Federal reports, usually more complete, fail to provide much more information. How could such a large capture go unnoticed and unrecorded? The existing record only hints at what occurred. Colonel Josey vented frustration in his report, noting that "west . . . [of the gap] was Brigadier General Martin's cavalry. I had been led to believe that this cavalry was vigilant and would give timely notice of the approach of an enemy. The enemy surprised this invincible cavalry, and (to use their language) rode over them; consequently the enemy was within 600 yards of Liberty Gap before Colonel Featherston or myself knew of the advance."[33]

---

31 Ibid., 486-487, 498, 595. Rose was referring to the "Heights of Abraham," more commonly known as the "Plains of Abraham," where British General James Wolfe had scaled the cliffs to capture Quebec City in 1759.

32 Miller, *Wheeler's Favorites*, 8.

33 OR 23, pt. 1, 600.

In seizing Liberty Gap, Alexander McCook's XX Corps fulfilled Rosecrans's first objective in a timely manner, while also drawing Braxton Bragg's full attention. But this was a feint, not an assault; the XX Corps would not be pressing forward the next day. McCook positioned Jefferson C. "Jef." Davis's men just north of the gap, with one of Davis's brigades detailed to escort the corps trains, while Sheridan's men closed up on the village of Millersburg, about 4 miles north.[34]

Back in Shelbyville, Bragg attempted to make sense of the various reports now reaching the headquarters of the Army of Tennessee. Sometime on the evening of June 24, he received word of Liddell's engagement, as well as the news of another fight at Hoover's Gap. Corps commander William J. Hardee, headquartered at Wartrace, was responsible for guarding both important passes. Hardee himself did not glean the details of these actions until late in the day, and it took additional time for that information to reach Shelbyville.

Once those reports were in hand, Bragg decided that the main thrust was coming via Liberty Gap, a thought that coincided with Hardee's greatest worry. On June 5, Hardee had warned that the army was too scattered. "An enterprising enemy," he had written, "could force a passage through Liberty Gap and cut my command in two, dividing the force about Hoover's Gap from, the force about Wartrace and Bell Buckle." In keeping with that idea, Hardee, at 10:15 p.m. on June 24, instructed Maj. Gen. Alexander P. Stewart, the senior officer in command at Hoover's Gap, that "if hard pressed tomorrow, you will fall back gradually towards Wartrace."[35]

---

34 General Jefferson C. Davis often signed his name "Jef." as a way of distinguishing himself from the Confederate president.

35 Connelly, *Autumn of Glory*, 127-128; *OR* 23, pt. 2, 883. St. John Richardson Liddell was born at Elmsley Plantation near Woodville, Mississippi, on September 6, 1815. He was appointed as a member of the West Point class of 1837, but did not graduate for reasons that are unclear but seem to stem from poor grades. His wealthy father bought him a plantation in Louisiana, and he farmed there. He became embroiled in a blood feud with a man named Charles Jones that would cost Liddell his life in a postwar duel. He was tried and acquitted of the murder of two of Jones's friends. Liddell knew many of the Confederate high command before the Civil War and served as a volunteer aide at First Manassas (Bull Run) on July 21, 1861. He was commissioned colonel of a Missouri regiment and served as a staff officer until May 1862, when he was given command of a two-regiment brigade at Corinth, Mississippi. Liddell was promoted to brigadier general on June 17, 1862, and led a brigade of Arkansas infantry at Perryville, earning the praise of superiors for its performance. Liddell's brigade fought especially well at Stones River, where it broke two Union lines and again earned high praise. He was promoted to division command just before Chickamauga, and his division suffered nearly 50 percent casualties in that battle. Liddell was a solid subordinate commander, but was prone to carping and did not get along with many of his superior officers. Davis and Hoffman, *The Confederate General*, 4: 74-75.

Maj. Gen. Alexander McCook, commander, XX Corps,
Army of the Cumberland.

National Archives

Bragg was not entirely focused on his left, however. Increasingly concerned about the dearth of news from the army's right, Bragg informed Leonidas Polk at 6:15 p.m. (after the June 23rd threat to Guy's Gap dissipated when Granger veered eastward) that "General Wharton has been ordered to take two regiments of cavalry from the front and move toward Manchester," directing Polk to replace them with infantry.[36]

Thursday, June 25, opened with more rain. Lieutenant Chesley Mosman of the 59th Illinois, Davis's division, noted that the "boys don't fancy reveille at 4 in a heavy rain. Rained till 10 A.M." After a sodden breakfast, "we moved one mile to the front and bivouaced on Rebs' camp ground." At noon, the weather cleared, though it was "still cloudy. Rebs one mile ahead." Now in the middle of the gap and in close support of Johnson's men, Mosman eyed the terrain dubiously. "Country rough, hillsides nearly all at an angle of 40 degrees, hard on skirmishers."[37]

St. John Liddell and his brigade spent the night on a range of hills a mile south of the gap. His only support was Brig. Gen. S. A. M. Wood's mixed Alabama and Mississippi Brigade, which division commander Patrick Cleburne had ordered to march at daylight for Bell Buckle.[38]

Cleburne himself arrived on the scene shortly after dawn to find that there was no more than the normal minor skirmishing taking place. Liddell deployed three of his five regiments—the 2nd, 5th, and combined 13th/15th Arkansas—atop a series of hills or knobs on the Sugg farm astride Wartrace Creek, facing open corn and wheat fields about 500 yards in width. He retained the combined 6th/7th Arkansas and Swett's Battery in reserve. Colonel John H. Kelly's 8th Arkansas was stationed about a mile and a half to the rear, guarding the railroad gap. Liddell was prepared to hold his position "until ordered or forced away," but desperate measures were not required. The Federals showed little interest in a fight.[39]

Private Oliver Protsman of the 1st Ohio Infantry, from Johnson's Third Brigade, attributed the morning's inaction to "the inclemency of the weather." That would change, he noted, when at "12 o clock the rain subsides and the fight commences." The skirmishing now picked up in earnest, with both sides believing that the other was seeking to attack. Willich posted his skirmishers on a series of hills north of those same open fields near the Sugg farm, and reinforced his skirmish line, currently composed of half his brigade—the 32nd Indiana on the left and the 89th Illinois to the right. The 15th and 49th Ohio provided extra support. He was soon glad he did so, because had it not been for what the Prussian called the

---

36 OR 23, pt. 2, 883-884.

37 Arnold Gates, ed., *The Rough Side of War: The Civil War Journal of Chesley A. Mosman, 1st Lieutenant, Company D, 59th Illinois Volunteer Infantry Regiment* (Garden City, NY: 1987), 60.

38 OR 23, pt. 1, 587.

39 Ibid., 587-588; Hughes, *Liddell's Record*, 127.

"multiplied feints. . . the enemy would have had his own way for selecting time and place for his attack. . . . The enemy advanced continually, on different points . . . with from 30 to 50 skirmishers, supported by cavalry." The action, though confined primarily to skirmishers in extended order, was brisk. The Federals repeatedly pushed out into the field in response to Rebel sallies, only to be driven back to cover by Confederate counter-strokes. Several times, Willich's men called for more ammunition, and by 3:30 p.m. or so, the 15th Ohio reinforced the 32nd and 89th regiments.[40]

The tenor of the fight changed about 4 p.m., when Liddell received a dispatch from Lt. Col. Paul Anderson of the 4th Tennessee Cavalry, Wharton's division. Anderson's troopers also picketed the hills west of Liberty Gap, near Fosterville, from where his scouts observed the Union concentration around Millersburg. Anderson "reported the enemy going back the way they came." Liddell's own observations supported that conclusion. From a nearby hill, Liddell "could see a large regiment . . . moving back to the gap, with numerous wagons and ambulances disappearing through the defile." Sensing an opportunity, Liddell asked Cleburne for permission to attack. Cleburne assented.[41]

The Louisiana brigadier opened his assault by sending Colonel Featherston's 5th Arkansas forward to press the Union skirmish line, catching the Federals in the middle of a transition. Though the XX Corps was not retreating, Willich was in the act of replacing his skirmish line with fresh troops. When Featherston advanced, the 15th Ohio was still passing out ammunition and moving companies up to the skirmish line as the 89th Illinois "Railroad" Regiment pulled out of line. The 89th's right flank had been anchored on "a high, wooded hill," which in turn anchored Willich's entire right flank. Featherston's Rebels seized that hill, throwing the 89th into disorder.[42]

Stepping in to relieve the 89th was the 21st Illinois. Belonging to Brig. Gen. William P. Carlin, of Davis's division, the 21st had been loaned out to support Willich. Colonel John W. S. Alexander counterattacked with six companies of the 21st, accompanied by many of the 89th's skirmishers, who were determined to retake their former position by pushing Featherston's men off the hill. "I drove him from the [hill] with skirmishers," boasted Featherston; "[but] it required his battle

40 "Entry for June 25," Oliver Protsman Civil War Diary, Wright State University, Dayton, OH; OR 23, pt. 1, 487.

41 OR 23, pt. 1, 587, 589.

42 Ibid., 479, 491.

lines to drive me." Seeing Featherston's straits, Liddell ordered Josey's 13th/15th Arkansas forward to support the 5th, while Col. Daniel C. Govan sent two companies of his 2nd Arkansas down the slope of the hill where he was posted to support Featherston's right flank.[43]

"The enemy now returned with fresh reinforcements," noted Liddell, "apparently abandoning his seeming intention to withdraw." That was an understatement. The Federals responded to this thrust with overwhelming force. Colonel John F. Miller led his brigade forward into the field against Govan's 2nd Arkansas, deploying the 79th Illinois and 77th Pennsylvania into line, with the 34th Illinois in support. Carlin contributed the 38th Illinois to Miller's advance, initially trailing the 34th, then moving up to extend the 77th Pennsylvania's right; the 38th was joined by the 101st Ohio, following the 79th Illinois. They traversed what Col. Thomas Rose of the 77th described as a "sea of mud," all the while taking fire from the 2nd Arkansans in front as well "as raking fire of artillery and musketry" from Swett's Battery and at least some of Josey's 13th/15th Arkansas off to their right.[44]

Willich now brought up his reserve regiment, the 49th Ohio, to assault Featherston. Moving up between the 32nd Indiana and the newly arrived 21st Illinois, the 49th now employed Willich's tactical innovation for the first time under fire. "Advance, Firing," recalled Adjutant Alexis Cope of the 15th Ohio, "was one of the 'leetle dings' [Willich] had promised to show us" after returning to the brigade from his sojourn as a prisoner of war in Richmond. "The movement was quite simple, being a line of battle in four ranks, each rank advancing a few paces in front and firing, then stopping to load while the other ranks advanced alternately, thus keeping up a steady advance and a steady fire all the time." It might have been a simple concept, but it proved highly effective, generating a rolling wall of continuous fire that drove all foes before it. The Arkansans, already worn out from the afternoon's work and now running low on ammunition themselves, fell back precipitously, losing several prisoners. One Federal witnessed a captured Confederate sergeant's stunned reaction to the new tactic. "Lord Almighty, who can stand against that!" he wrote home six weeks later. "[F]our lines of battle, and every d——d one of them firing!"[45]

---

43 Ibid., 593, 596.

44 Ibid., 501-502, 589-590. The 29th and 30th Indiana, both also of Miller's brigade, were still on picket and were not available to support or join the attack.

45 Alexis Cope, *The Fifteenth Ohio Volunteers and Its Campaigns, War of 1861-5* (Columbus, OH: 1916), 279; "From Tullahoma," *Columbus Daily Ohio State Journal*, August 8, 1863.

Willich observed Gibson's assault from "a hill near the [Federal] skirmish line," growing more excited by the minute. "The General turned suddenly to his bugler and said, 'Hornist! Why the devil don't you blow!'" Caught off guard, the bugler asked, "But General, what shall I blow?" Willich, now exultant, bellowed back, "'Don't you see how the fight goes on; don't you see those rebs getting away from that fence; blow fight! blow fight!' And 'Hornist' did blow fight!" [sic][46]

At this point, Featherston's and Josey's men all fell back to or behind their original positions, where they replenished their ammunition. Fortunately for Liddell's roughly handled Razorbacks, the Federals did not press their assault. The Confederate retreat, however, left Govan's line exposed. Liddell ordered up the 6th/7th Arkansas to support Govan, but events outpaced their arrival. Colonel Govan was attempting to recall his forward companies and bring them back up the slope of the hill when Miller's brigade swarmed his line. Colonel Miller went down with a nasty head wound early in the move across the field, but his fall did not stop the charge. The 77th Pennsylvania and the 38th and 79th Illinois all reached the foot of the hill and began to pour fire up-slope at Govan's scrambling Arkansans. "My ammunition was now entirely exhausted," Govan reported. "[E]xposed to a heavy fire without being able to inflict any punishment on the enemy, I requested permission to withdraw to the rear." As Govan fell back, Lt. Col. Peter Snyder's 6th/7th Arkansas arrived to cover the retreat.[47]

Private William E. Patterson, a twenty-two-year-old former schoolteacher in the ranks of Company K, 38th Illinois, also described the charge. "We went forward double-quick, passed through an orchard and into a very muddy field of young corn. . . . The rebels, with fixed bayonets, advanced to the foot of the hill and prepared to charge. Willich's men, when we met them, laid down and we passed over them and opened a sharp fire on the advancing rebs, which quickly sent them back to the top of the hill." By the time Patterson and his comrades reached the fence at the foot of the hill themselves, "not a live reb was to be seen."[48]

Snyder arrived in time to check the last Union advance, which was already disordered by its own difficult climb up the slope of Govan's hill, but the fight was

---

46 "The 49th at Liberty Gap," *Tiffin Weekly Tribune* (Tiffin, OH), August 28, 1863.

47 *OR* 23, pt. 1, 484, 590, 595. Miller's wound was initially thought to be fatal. He lived, but at the cost of an eye. He later commanded the garrison at Nashville in 1864.

48 Lowell Wayne Patterson, ed., *Jasper County Yankee: Campaigns of the 38th Regiment, Illinois Volunteer Infantry, Company K, Written by William Edward Patterson, 1861-1863* (Westminster, MD: 2011), 49.

relatively brief. "My men rushed into action, loading as they went," Snyder reported; "[We] were engaged in line fight about twenty minutes, with a loss of ten wounded." Then the 6th/7th Arkansas also fell back. Liddell's reconnaissance was over.[49]

Each side greatly exaggerated the other's casualties. Snyder felt sure the Federals had lost between 400 and 500 men in the assault against the 2nd Arkansas alone. Federal brigadier William Carlin, writing in his memoirs, gave Liddell's casualties as "100 killed and 750 wounded." The actual losses were heavy enough: 264 Federals, including 36 killed, while Liddell recorded 28 killed, 75 wounded, and 17 missing, for a total loss of 120.[50]

At the base of Govan's hill, Private Patterson and his cohorts from Company K came across an unusual sight: the "battle flag of the 2nd Arkansas . . . [with] the color sergeant laying across it on his face, dead: his hands grasping the staff of the 'Bonnie Blue Flag.'" Govan omitted any mention of the loss of a flag in his report, but Liddell reported what happened. "Two color-bearers . . . were killed, and the third, standing on the declivity of the hill, was fatally struck, and falling forward headlong, cast his colors towards the base, in close proximity to the line of the enemy," he wrote. "The colors were not missed until the regiment . . . retired. . . . This is a source of great mortification to the regiment as well as the brigade."[51]

Though most of the men involved did not know it, the fight for Liberty Gap was over. The next day, Friday, June 26, dawned quietly. Private William Stahl of the 49th Ohio wrote home, informing his father of the previous day's action. "We made [the Rebels] clime and clime a big hill where they stopped and fired purty fast, but they was on the hill and they fired over us. . . ," he reported. "[I]t is morning and I just finished my breckfast. I don't know what will turn out yet and I will keep this letter and write some more to it if the rebs don't kill me." Private Stahl survived to finish his letter.[52]

Liddell pulled his brigade back another half mile to join with Brig. Gen. S. A. M. Wood's men, and they prepared to put up another fight. But the XX Corps did

49 OR 23, pt. 1, 597.

50 Robert I. Girardi and Nathaniel Cheairs Hughes, Jr., eds., *The Memoirs of Brigadier General William Passmore Carlin, U.S.A.,* (Lincoln, NE: 1999), 90; OR 23, pt. 1, 422, 592.

51 Patterson, *Jasper County Yankee*, 49-50; OR 23, pt. 1, 590. The "Bonnie Blue Flag" Patterson mentioned was a Hardee-pattern regimental flag with a white disc on a field of blue.

52 "Dear Father," June 26, 1863, William Stahl diary and letters, U.S. Army Heritage and Education Center, Carlisle, PA.

not press, and both sides spent June 26 observing each other from a respectful distance. The Federals again deployed skirmishers, but the Rebels largely lay low. Instead, recalled Capt. Irving Buck of Cleburne's staff, "there being no ammunition to spare, no reply was made to the continual fire of the enemy, except with five Whitworth rifles," which were employed mainly against the Union artillery. "Mounted men were struck at distances ranging from 700 to 1,300 yards," Buck noted.[53]

By the 26th Bragg hadn't yet realized the full import of all this Union activity; and, unbeknownst to the Confederate commander, events at Hoover's Gap had already forced his hand.

53 Buck, *Cleburne and His Command*, 131.

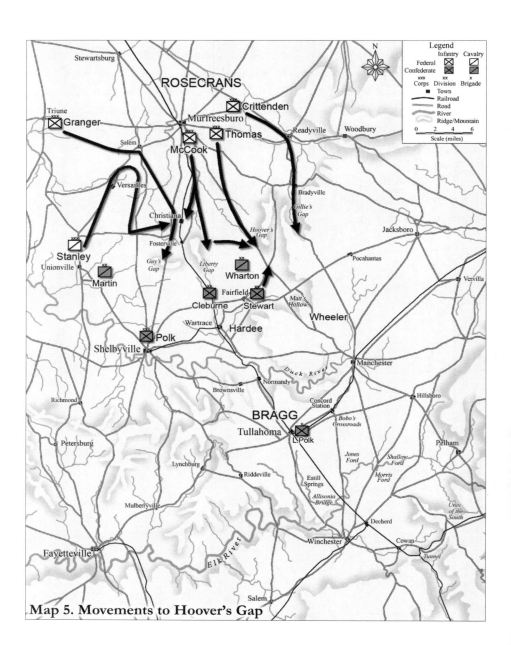

Map 5. Movements to Hoover's Gap

Chapter Seven

Wilder's Brigade Earns its Name at Hoover's Gap, June 24, 1863

While large Union forces threatened Shelbyville from the north, engage in skirmishes at Rover and Middleton, and waged a two-day affair at Liberty Gap, Rosecrans delivered his next blow. This move by his most trusted command, George Thomas's reliable XIV Corps, triggered the single sharpest engagement of the entire campaign: Hoover's Gap.

The Army of the Cumberland had the rugged Highland Rim to its front, with forces placed to defend the gaps through the rim between Murfreesboro and Chattanooga. As previously noted, only a handful of mountain gaps were passable. The four available to the Federals were Hoover's Gap, along the road connecting Murfreesboro and Manchester; Liberty Gap, near the towns of Bell Buckle and Wartrace; the Bell Buckle or Railroad Gap; and Guy's Gap. Bragg recognized this and deployed his army with his left anchored at Shelbyville and his right at Beech Grove, a hamlet close to Hoover's Gap and a few miles northeast of Wartrace. Bragg's right flank rested about four miles short of the actual gap. While Hoover's Gap was a superb defensive position, it was not well suited as a campsite for a large body of soldiers. Lieutenant General William Hardee, known as "Old Reliable," commanded the sector from Wartrace to Beech Grove, including Hoover's Gap and Liberty Gap.[1]

---

1 McMurray, *History of the Twentieth Tennessee*, 253.

Grayclad cavalry was supposed to extend Bragg's line. Joseph Wheeler's cavalry corps nominally extended the army's right flank in an arc running from Hoover's Gap to McMinnville. The easternmost portion of this arc included the most direct route to Chattanooga for Rosecrans's army. As has been discussed, the Confederate cavalry was not without its share of problems. Nathan Bedford Forrest, who was just coming to prominence, categorically refused to serve under Wheeler, which is how he came to be guarding Bragg's left flank. John Hunt Morgan's long-planned insubordination would become obvious to Bragg in just a few weeks when Morgan crossed the Ohio River into Indiana instead of striking Rosecrans's rear. Wheeler's command was never known for its discipline, and the whole corps was somewhat dysfunctional, but Wheeler was loyal to Bragg, so Bragg protected him. Thus, the command assigned the task of holding this critical arc was not entirely dependable.[2]

Key to the upcoming campaign's success was the Federal army's ability to seize and hold Hoover's Gap, so that the bulk of the Army of the Cumberland could advance on the Manchester Road, both to exploit Crittenden's expected success and to reinforce the XXI Corps if needed. Colonel John T. Wilder's brigade of mounted infantry, soon to be dubbed the "Lightning Brigade," received the most important assignment: to seize and hold Hoover's Gap so it could be used by the bulk of the XIV Corps.[3]

"Inspection of horses by Col. Wilder," wrote Pvt. James Bolens of the 17th Indiana in his diary on the eve of the campaign. "Army ready for a grand move which we make soon. Boys in good spirits for a game of ball with the rebles. . . . Orders to march tomorrow. Bully, we want to try our Spencers on the bloody Rebs." On the night of June 23, with Granger already well underway, Wilder received orders to break camp and prepare to move. The soldiers were to cook and carry 10 days' rations and 80 rounds of ammunition. Wilder's mounted infantrymen would move out at dawn on June 24.[4]

Wilder was concerned. He knew that Rosecrans's cavalry chief had reservations about his brigade. "General Stanley seemed anxious to send a cavalry brigade with General Thomas, as he said, to take care of my 'tadpole' cavalry, as he

2 Michael R. Bradley, *Tullahoma: The 1863 Campaign for the Control of Middle Tennessee* (Shippensburg, PA: 1999) 36; John Watson Morton, *The Artillery of Nathan Bedford Forrest's Cavalry* (Nashville, TN: 1909), 77.

3 *OR* 23, pt. 1, 404-405.

4 Baumgartner, *Blue Lightning*, 85.

Col. John T. Wilder,
commander of the Lightning Brigade.

Library of Congress

called us, fearing I would rush into the enemy and get captured, and Stanley would have those magazine guns to fight," Wilder later recalled. "General Thomas assured General Rosecrans that if my brigade were captured there would be no need for cavalry about." Wilder's fast-moving force was about to prove George Thomas right, and David Stanley very wrong.[5]

At 4:00 a.m. on the morning of June 24, Wilder's 2,000 men, along with Capt. Eli Lilly's battery, moved out on the macadamized road at a quick walk, headed straight for Hoover's Gap. "As we moved through the camps in Murfreesboro, the rattle of drums, sounding of bugles, and clatter of wagons, told us plainly that the whole army was to follow in our wake, and we knew full well, from the direction we were taking, that a few hours' march would bring the brigade to some of the strongholds of the enemy, so there was silence in the column as we moved along through the mud, and every ear was strained to catch the sound of the first gun of our advance guard that would tell us of the presence of the enemy," recalled Maj. James A. Connolly of the 123rd Illinois.[6]

"Wilder's Brigade had been restless all night, for it had the post of honor in the morning's move," noted another member of that unit. "It was its first trial as an organized command and every man in it felt that the honor and fame of the Brigade rested on his shoulders." Sergeant Benjamin Magee, later the historian of the 72nd Indiana, left a good description of the advance. "Up[,] feed [the horses], get breakfast and move at daylight," Magee wrote. "We reach Murfreesboro and find

5 John T. Wilder, "The Battle of Hoover's Gap," *Sketches of War History, 1861-1865*, vol. 6, Ohio Commandery, Military Order of the Loyal Legion of the United States (Cincinnati, OH: 1908), 169.

6 Paul M. Angle, ed., *Three Years in the Army of the Cumberland: The Letters and Diary of Major James A. Connolly* (Bloomington, IN: 1959), 90.

that the whole army of 50,000 men have struck tents. What a change in one short night! One can never realize it till one sees it. Everything is loaded on wagons, and the regiments, brigades and divisions are rapidly taking their places in line."[7]

Once Wilder's brigade was six miles out, the rest of the XIV Corps fell in behind the fast-moving horsemen. It began raining, the same drumming rainfall that made Granger's and Mitchell's columns so miserable. The macadamized road gave way to dirt a bit south of Murfreesboro, and the pounding of thousands of horse hooves and wagon wheels soon churned the road into a deep quagmire. "The falling rain, the muddy roads, the gloomy forests and the enveloping fog made that early morning march anything but an opening pathway to glory," noted one of Wilder's officers. "The scouts, consisting of one man from each regiment, moved in advance as soon as we cleared the picket lines of the army. In solemn quiet and darkness the column plodded on through mud knee deep to the horses. The peculiar hush of the hour before dawn enveloped the forests and the only sounds were the trampling of the horses in the mud and the pattering of rain on the ponchos." By 10 that morning, Wilder and his command were some nine miles ahead of the lead elements of Thomas's infantry.[8]

Hoover's Gap lies 11 miles southeast of Murfreesboro, dividing the waters of the Duck River and the headwaters of Stones River. The Manchester Pike passed through the gap, which extends for seven miles. The valley was barely wide enough to permit the passage of two wagons side by side, and the hills on either side commanded the valley. If properly manned, a defensive force could hold the gap almost indefinitely, and thus bottle up Rosecrans's army. One of Wilder's veterans subsequently observed that Hoover's Gap was "a natural fortress in the mountains where a few men could check an army." Fortunately, the gap was lightly defended, held only by about 200 troopers of the understrength combined Confederate 1st/3rd Kentucky Cavalry, which had to cover a front nearly six miles long. These cavalrymen believed that friendly infantry occupied breastworks behind them, at one of the pass's narrowest points, roughly midway through the seven-mile length of Hoover's Gap.[9]

7 *Dedication of the Wilder Brigade Monument*, 14; Benjamin F. Magee, *History of the 72d Indiana Volunteer Infantry of the Mounted Lightning Brigade* (LaFayette, IN: 1882), 128.

8 *Dedication of the Wilder Brigade Monument*, 14.

9 Angle, *Three Years in the Army of the Cumberland*, 90; *Dedication of the Wilder Brigade Monument*, 14; "Soldier in Gap", "The Capture of Hoover's Gap," *Memphis Appeal* (Memphis, TN), July 21, 1863.

Lieutenant Colonel Samuel C. Kirkpatrick and five companies of his 17th Indiana led the way, with approximately 25 scouts of the 17th and 72nd Indiana regiments as the "extreme advance guard" of the brigade. The scouts encountered the Confederate pickets eight miles out from Murfreesboro and a couple of miles short of the mouth of the gap, farther out than Wilder expected. The advance guard charged the picket post, which scattered to raise the alarm. The Kentuckians tried to make a stand on a heavily wooded hill, but Kirkpatrick's determined attack quickly drove them off. The rest of the 1st/3rd Kentucky came up to meet the threat, but Kirkpatrick deployed one company on each side of the road, driving the Southern horse soldiers away with a sustained heavy fire. Wilder's men also captured the small Confederate signal post that had been positioned at the mouth of the Gap in order to provide an early warning to Hardee's infantry, meaning there was no way for word of the Union advance to reach the Confederate foot soldiers quickly.[10]

After entering the gap, Wilder's men drew no enemy fire and soon realized that the Confederate breastworks were unoccupied. "Judge of my astonishment, when we reached their supposed position, to find no force there," Wilder recalled years after the war. "Looking down the valley to the village of Beech Grove, two miles to the west, down the valley of the Garrison Fork, we could see the tents of an encampment." Reacting quickly to the possible opportunity, Wilder set his command in motion, ordering his brigade to charge the entire length of the gap. "I directed the advance to push speedily forward and take possession of Hoover's Gap, and, if possible, to prevent the enemy from occupying their fortifications, which I learned were situated at a narrow point of the gap, 16 miles from Murfreesboro."[11]

Lieutenant Colonel Kirkpatrick immediately executed Wilder's orders, sweeping the few remaining Kentucky cavalrymen before him. The Union soldiers dashed down the bed of the creek, pushing the enemy out of the way by the sheer impetuosity of their attack. Kirkpatrick's troopers drove the Kentuckians so hard that the Rebel horsemen had no time to rally and occupy the all-important breastworks. Instead, they dashed right by them, scattering through the hills, running for safety. Major James Q. Chenoweth, commander of the 1st/3rd Kentucky, wisely ordered his troopers to retreat in the face of such an

10 OR 23, pt. 1, 457-458; "Soldier in Gap," "The Capture of Hoover's Gap."

11 Wilder, "The Battle of Hoover's Gap," 170; OR 23, pt. 1, 457.

overwhelming force. He lost one man killed and a few captured, as well as his regimental battle flag.[12]

Chenoweth called for a dozen volunteers to serve as a rear guard to cover the withdrawal of the rest of his regiment toward the main Confederate camp at Fairfield. These twelve brave but ill-fated troopers put up a stout fight, but by the time they reached the southern mouth of the gap, only three of them remained in the saddle. "From that time on a mad race of pursuers and pursued chases down that Tennessee road, through mud and rain until exhausted men and horses were glad to stop," wrote Major Connolly, "but not until we have raced after the enemy through the formidable Hoover's Gap and seized it as our own." Company E of the 72nd Indiana chased the fleeing Kentuckians for almost two miles beyond the mouth of the gap before being cut off by Confederate infantry responding to the crisis.[13]

"We soon came into the camp of a regiment of cavalry," Connolly continued, "which was so much surprised by our sudden appearance that they scattered through the woods and over the hills in every direction, every fellow for himself, and all making the best time they could bareback, on foot, and every other way, leaving all their tents, wagons, baggage, commissary stores and indeed everything in our hands, but we didn't stop for anything, on we pushed, our boys, with their Spencer rifles, keeping up a continual popping in front. Soon we reached the celebrated 'Gap' on the run."[14]

Learning that Hardee's foot soldiers were camped nearby, Wilder now made another bold decision. "I determined to take the entire gap, and, if possible, hold it until the arrival of the infantry column, now some 6 miles behind us, believing that it would cost us at least a thousand men to retake the ground we now held, if it was reasonably contested by the rebel force close at hand." Wilder pushed his entire brigade rapidly forward to the southern end of the gap, capturing seven enemy wagons along the way, and sent a courier to hurry up reinforcements. By the time they reached the southern exit, these Federals were 12 miles in advance of the rest of the Army of the Cumberland, a precarious position at best.[15]

---

12 W. H. H. Benefiel, *History of Wilder's Lightning Brigade During the Civil War* (Pendleton, IN: n.d.), 8; OR 23, pt. 1, 457; Sunderland, *Lightning at Hoover's Gap*, 37; Magee, *History of the 72d Indiana*, 128.

13 Sunderland, *Lightning at Hoover's Gap*, 37; *Dedication of the Wilder Brigade Monument*, 15.

14 Angle, *Three Years in the Army of the Cumberland*, 90.

15 OR 23, pt. 1, 458.

Capt. Eli Lilly,
commander, 18th Indiana Battery.

Eli H. Lilly Company Archives

Eli Lilly promptly came up and planted his cannons on the high ground just beyond the mouth of the gap, where the gunners could defend the vale's narrow entrance against Confederate counterattacks. Hearing the drums beating the long roll in the nearby camps of Maj. Gen. Alexander P. Stewart's Rebel infantry division at nearby Fairfield, the Federals dismounted and deployed on a series of hills overlooking Garrison Fork, sending their horses to the rear. There they waited for the Confederate infantry to appear.[16]

The 72nd Indiana was deployed to the right and thrown forward on a hill near a graveyard. Lilly placed two of the mountain howitzers in front of them and then positioned his 3-inch rifles on a second hill to their right. The 123rd Illinois occupied a hollow behind Lilly's pieces, while the 17th Indiana deployed a quarter mile to Lilly's right on another heavily wooded hillside. Except for two companies that took a position on the high ground on the other side of the Manchester Pike, Wilder held the 98th Illinois in reserve behind the 123rd Illinois. "Our regiment lay on the hillside in mud and water, the rain pouring down in torrents, while each shell screamed so close to us as to make it seem that the next would tear us to pieces," shuddered Major Connolly of the 123rd.[17]

Wilder's men thus occupied precisely the same position that the Confederates had intended to use to defend the southern mouth of Hoover's Gap, albeit facing south instead of north. As Sergeant Magee of the 72nd Indiana put it, "This was the key to the whole position, and two hours later could scarcely have been charged

16 Benefiel, *History of Wilder's Lightning Brigade*, 9.

17 Sunderland, *Wilder's Lightning Brigade*, 39; Angle, *Three Years with the Army of the Cumberland*, 92.

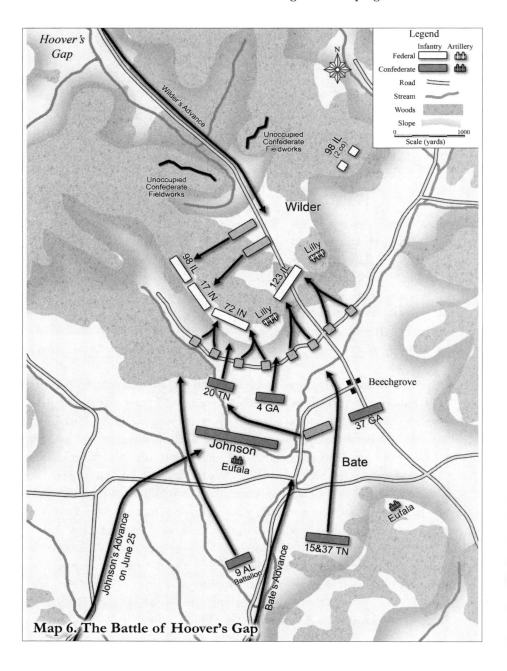

Map 6. The Battle of Hoover's Gap

and taken with 10,000 men." Against only minimal resistance, Wilder had seized the critical mountain pass. But could he hold it?[18]

Upon learning that Wilder's men had secured Hoover's Gap, Hardee ordered Stewart's division to retake it. To accomplish that, Stewart had only two of his four brigades on hand, those of Brig. Gen. Bushrod Johnson and Brig. Gen. William Bate, plus supporting artillery. Stewart had just assumed command of this division on June 17 after receiving a promotion to major general. Because of Hardee's earlier-expressed concerns, the loss of Breckinridge's command, and Stewart's own shorthandedness, Stewart had not been ordered to place troops in Hoover's Gap or to hold the earthworks that had been constructed there, which was why the Federals took possession of it so quickly and easily. However, leaving the gap undefended by anything but a small force of cavalry with no artillery support was a serious error on both Hardee's and Bragg's parts.[19]

18 This does not include the Confederate earthworks situated farther to the north in Hoover's Gap that had been left unmanned by the Southern infantry. Magee, *History of the 72d Indiana*, 129.

19 *OR* 23, pt. 1, 611. Stewart's other two brigades, those of Brig. Gen. Henry D. Clayton and Brig. Gen. John C. Brown, were detached for other duties. Clayton was near Wartrace, while Brown was stationed at Tullahoma. William B. Bate was born on October 7, 1826, in Bledsoe's Lick, Sumner County, Tennessee. He was educated in a local school before leaving to become second clerk on a riverboat. He enlisted as a private in a Louisiana regiment during the Mexican-American War, earning a promotion to first lieutenant. After receiving his discharge in 1849, he settled in Gallatin, Tennessee, where he established and edited a Democratic newspaper. Before the end of that year, he was elected to the state legislature. He served a single one-year term and then enrolled in the law school in Lebanon, Tennessee (now part of Cumberland University). He received his degree in 1852 and opened a practice in Nashville. In 1854, he was elected attorney general of a three-county district and held this post until 1860. An ardent supporter of states' rights and secession, Bate served as a presidential elector for John C. Breckinridge in 1860. He enlisted as a private in a Tennessee infantry regiment after secession and soon was elected captain of his company. He was then elected colonel of the 2nd Tennessee Infantry and commanded his regiment at Columbus, Kentucky, and at Shiloh, where he received a severe leg wound. Bate was promoted to brigadier general on October 3, 1862, commanding an administrative post until fully recovered. He returned to active duty on February 23, 1863, and was assigned to lead Brig. Gen. Gabriel J. Rains's brigade on March 12. When Stewart's division was created, he transferred to that command, serving under Stewart through the Battle of Chickamauga. He eventually received a promotion to major general and commanded a division until the end of the war. Bate was a fighting general; he was wounded in battle three times, and had six horses shot from under him. After the war, he returned to politics and served in the U.S. Senate for 19 years. Laurence L. Hewitt, "William Brimage Bate," included in William C. Davis and Julie Hoffman, eds., *The Confederate General*, 6 vols. (New York: National Historical Society, 1991), 1:70-73; "Huntsville," "Hoover's Gap," *The Daily Rebel*, July 26, 1863; "Rosecrans in Tullahoma," *The Raftsman's Journal* (Clearfield, PA), July 8, 1863.

Maj. Gen. Alexander P. Stewart, commander,
Stewart's Division, Hardee's Corps,
Army of Tennessee.

Alfred R. Waud, Library of Congress

The scene must have been dramatic. Stewart was eating lunch at Fairfield with his wife Harriet and their guests, divisional surgeon Watson M. Gentry and his wife Martha. The first inkling of trouble arrived when, Mrs. Gentry recalled, "the merry conversation during the meal [was] interrupted when a boy in a slouch hat brought Stewart some dispatches. Stewart's expression visibly changed, but he continued the conversation." Within minutes, however, any pretense at normalcy was abandoned. "[A]nother courier came in with a furrow from a bullet in his scalp. Stewart and the doctor immediately went into camp, which," Stewart biographer Sam Davis Elliott noted, "was in something of an uproar."[20]

Four days later, a member of the 20th Tennessee Infantry described that moment. "About two o'clock, a courier came galloping up, pale with fright and excitement, and announced the enemy [with]in two miles of our camp," he recalled. "The drum beat the long roll immediately, and in a very short time our regiment and the Georgia Sharpshooters were on the march to the threatened point. The other regiments were to follow as soon as ready." Another of Bate's men complained that "we were discussing a sumptuous camp dinner, when the order came." As they advanced, they encountered small groups of straggling Confederate cavalry that had escaped from the gap, including Colonel Butler of the 1st Kentucky, who advised that a large force of mounted infantry advancing along the Manchester Pike had routed his pickets. The Confederate infantry marched about one and a half miles before a stray cavalryman announced that the Yankees

---

20 Sam Davis Elliott, *Soldier of Tennessee: General Alexander P. Stewart and the Civil War in the West* (Baton Rouge, LA: 1999), 91.

Brig. Gen. William B. Bate, commander,
Bate's Brigade, Stewart's Division,
Hardee's Corps, Army of Tennessee.

Generals in Gray

were in sight. Wilder would have to make a stand against an entire division of some of Hardee's best veteran infantry.[21]

By 3:00 p.m., the Rebel infantry was bearing down on Wilder's position. "Their masses of infantry, with flags flying, moved out of the woods on our right in splendid style," recounted Major Connolly. "There were three or four times our number already in sight and still others came pouring out of the woods beyond."[22]

Soon "a cloud of skirmishers" appeared in front of Wilder's position. These men, from the 20th Tennessee and 37th Alabama of Bate's Brigade, deployed into line of battle. Bate did not realize how large a force faced him; he believed it was only a handful of cavalry scouts that could be easily driven back, and he made his dispositions accordingly. Once the 4th Georgia Sharpshooter Battalion came up, Bate decided to try to outflank Wilder's position to the left.[23]

The three Confederate units advanced in good order and in plain view of Wilder's waiting Federals. Lilly's mountain howitzers and rifled guns opened on them with volley after volley of grapeshot and canister, tearing great holes in their

21 George W. Winchester, "The Battle for Hoover's Gap," *The Daily Rebel,* July 3, 1863; "Tennessee Citizen," "Battle at Hoover's Gap," *Memphis Appeal,* July 29, 1863; James L. Cooper, "Service with the Twentieth Tennessee Regiment," *Confederate Veteran,* vol. 33, no. 3 (March 1925), 100. While Stewart was new to division command, these were veteran troops. The division had been created in the wake of the departure of Maj. Gen. John C. Breckinridge's division for Mississippi, and Stewart's formation was still a new command in terms of unit coherence.

22 Angle, *Three Years in the Army of the Cumberland,* 91-92. As is not unusual in such engagements, the Federals consistently overestimated the size of Stewart's command. Wilder's 2,000 men actually faced about 3,000 Rebels.

23 J.T.G., "A Reliable Account of the Fight at Hoover's Gap," *Georgia Journal and Messenger* (Macon, GA), July 8, 1863.

ranks. "Our position was very much exposed to their shell, and three of our men were killed at the same time," recounted Pvt. James L. Cooper of the 20th Tennessee. "To add to our discomfort, it had begun to rain and we were almost overflowed." The undeterred Southerners pressed on, heading straight for the guns and for the 72nd Indiana, which laid down a heavy fire with its repeaters. "They vigorously assaulted our line and strove hard to dislodge us from the grove of beech timber behind which we had posted ourselves," recalled a Hoosier, "but we held our position and slaughtered them as they came, until they succeeded in gaining our right so far as to be enabled to cross-fire on us, when the 98th Illinois was sent for and, with fixed bayonets, fired a volley into them and then started them out of the wood on double quick, and with a shout we rushed upon them and pursued them so closely as to capture about 40 prisoners."[24]

The determined Confederate attack drove in the skirmishers of the 72nd Indiana, but Wilder shifted the 17th Indiana to reinforce them, and the men of the 17th also opened on Bate with their Spencer rifles. "We went at it shooting and continued for some 2 hours when we got them to running, which was one of the nicest sights I have ever seen," reported Corp. Martin D. Hamilton of the 17th. According to one of Bate's Georgia infantrymen, the Rebels took heavy punishment. "For the space of fifteen minutes the firing was hot and furious. Our men were falling around me on every side."[25]

Colonel Miller threw Company C of the 17th Indiana forward to a rail fence as skirmishers, and there they engaged the sharpshooters of the 4th Georgia. Not long after the Hoosiers took position, remembered a sergeant of Company C, "there suddenly burst from a thicket a short distance to our left front, two rebel regiments, who bore down on us at a run, with their accustomed yell. About this time I developed a sudden desire to retire to the seclusion of the wood-covered hill where the regiment lay, and looked around to see if the other fellows were not of the same mind. They were. If we didn't make tracks to the rear at the same speed it was because some of the boys couldn't run as fast as the rest of us. When a few paces from the fence I heard a man to my left exclaim, 'My God, I'm killed!'" That man proved to be Lt. James T. Moreland, mortally wounded. The 17th Indiana,

24 James L. Cooper, "Service with the Twentieth Tennessee Regiment," *Confederate Veteran*, vol. 33, no. 3 (March, 1925), 101; "Harry," "Letter from the 17th Indiana Regiment," *Weekly Wabash Express*, (Terre Haute, IN), July 22, 1863.

25 Dr. Gerald S. Henig, ed., "'Soldiering is One Hard Way of Serving the Lord': The Civil War Letters of Martin D. Hamilton," *Indiana Military History Journal* (October 1977), 9; J.T.G., "A Reliable Account."

deployed in a single rank and sorely stretched, doubled back to conform to the lay of the land and the presence of the enemy until the regiment's flanks were less than 100 yards apart.[26]

The 98th Illinois also changed front to support the Hoosiers, and the combined firepower of the three Federal regiments took the starch out of Stewart's men, who finally retreated. "We were ordered up to support the 17th Ind. on the right flank," noted a soldier of the 98th. "We had a hard road over fences, gullies & up hill under cover of woods, and came up just in time to save the 17th Ind. from being flanked. Our boys drove the rebels from the start in splendid style." For a few minutes, the fighting raged at the very short range of about 20 yards before the Confederate attackers wavered and fell back in confusion. "They moved four regiments around to our right and attempted to get in our rear," remembered Major Connolly, "but they were met by two of our regiments posted in the woods, and in five minutes they were driven back in the greatest disorder, with a loss of 250 killed and wounded." The Confederate commander, Maj. Frederick Claybrooke of the 20th Tennessee, was mortally wounded during this attack.[27]

"The effect of our terrible fire was overwhelming to our opponents, who bravely tried to withstand its effects," declared a rightfully proud John Wilder. "No human being could successfully face such an avalanche of destruction as our continuous fire swept through their lines. This was the first battle where the Spencer repeating rifles had ever been used, and in my estimation they were . . . strong and not easily injured by the rough usage of army movements."[28]

Stewart brought up a battery of his own—the Eufala Light Artillery, armed with six 3-inch rifles—and had them open on the mountain howitzers. "Three shells in quick succession pass through our regiment," recalled a member of the 72nd Indiana; "one cuts one of the gunners in two; another tears off the face of Sergt. [Wesley B.] Pike, of Company D, and another passes through the neck of an artillery mule." This determined fire forced the outclassed "bull pup" cannons to limber up and get out of the way, leaving Lilly's 3-inch rifles as Wilder's sole artillery support. Gamely, Lilly's rifled guns answered, belching death in reply.[29]

---

26 Wilson, "Wilder's Brigade of Mounted Infantry," 51.

27 Edward Kitchell diary, entry for June 24, 1863, Illinois State Historical Library, Springfield, IL; Angle, *Three Years in the Army of the Cumberland*, 92; OR 23, pt. 1, 459, 612.

28 Wilder, "The Battle of Hoover's Gap," 173.

29 *OR* 23, pt. 1, 458.

Brig. Gen. Bushrod R. Johnson, commander,
Johnson's Brigade, Stewart's Division,
Hardee's Corps, Army of Tennessee.

Generals in Gray

Lilly could not see the results of his first shot due to the heavy smoke hanging over the battlefield. One of his gunners indicated that the shell had landed about 10 feet to the right of the Southern cannon that was his target. "I will try them again," responded Lilly. The next shell struck the muzzle of the Confederate gun, dismounting it. With the extremely accurate shooting of Lilly's cannoneers wreaking havoc among the Southern artillery, the grayclad gunners limbered up and changed position to escape the Hoosier artillerists' punishing fire.[30]

"The artillery occupied the heights on the north and south side of the now foaming stream, Garrison Creek, and were hurling shot and shell into the opposing columns with all the dispatch possible," observed another of Wilder's mounted soldiers. "The wind was blowing a perfect gale and the rain descending in sheets, almost blinding all who were exposed to it, while the rattle of small arms was incessant; but above all this could be heard the cries of agony of the enemy's dead and dying."[31]

Heartened by the mountain howitzers' withdrawal, the Confederates attacked again. Even though they enjoyed the advantage in manpower, the Spencers' firepower offset raw numbers. Wilder's men held their own. The 72nd Indiana opened a heavy enfilading fire on these Confederates, who went to ground "to escape the tornado of death which was being poured into their ranks," as Wilder colorfully described it. "But finding no cessation of our leaden hail, they crawled

30 Rowell, *Yankee Artillerymen*, 80.

31 "Harry," "Letter from the 17th Indiana Regiment."

back as best they could, under cover of the hills, and made no further attempt to take our left."[32]

After another brief but savage firefight, the Confederates withdrew once more. The heavy artillery fire from the Southern guns resumed, causing considerable anxiety among Wilder's troops. "The rebel battery kept belching forth a perfect shower of shot and shell," remembered one of Lilly's sergeants, "but had done us no damage, every one of their shots going above us or striking the ground in our front and glancing over our heads." However, the Confederate artillery had the advantage, maintaining a three-way crossfire that, if unchecked, would eventually tell on the blue-clad cannoneers.[33]

At just the right moment the 19th Indiana Battery, commanded by Capt. Samuel J. Harris, came thundering up. Harris's battery, armed with 10-pound Parrott rifles, took position and immediately opened on the Southern artillery. Harris's added firepower turned the tide. "As the guns belch forth fire and shot over our heads we feel great relief and anxiously watch the telling effect the shots have on the enemy, and in a short time the rebel guns are seen to limber up and move to a more respectful distance," recalled Sergeant Magee of the 72nd Indiana. Major Connolly of the 123rd Illinois agreed, writing, "We were nearly exhausted with the rapid march since before daylight in the morning, yet the prospect of assistance nerved the men to maintain the unequal conflict a little longer."[34]

About the time that Wilder repulsed these attacks, a staff officer from the lead division of Thomas's infantry arrived, bearing an order for Wilder to retire from the field. Wilder refused to obey, indicating that he could maintain his position until the XIV Corps foot soldiers could come up. The adjutant threatened to place Wilder under arrest, but the intrepid colonel told the staff officer that he would assume responsibility for the consequences, and the rebuffed aide rode back to report Wilder's intransigence.[35]

Bate made one final attempt to turn Wilder's right, attacking with all five of his regiments. Only the 700 men of 17th Indiana and 98th Illinois repulsed these Southerners, again demonstrating the firepower of the Spencer rifles. "The enemy, anticipating the move, met it with a line of battle fronting the wood which skirted

32 OR 23, pt. 1, 459.

33 Henry Campbell journal, Special Collections, Lilly Library, Wabash College, Crawfordsville, IN.

34 Magee, *History of the 72d Indiana*, 131; Angle, *Three Years in the Army of the Cumberland*, 93.

35 Sunderland, *Lightning at Hoover's Gap*, 42.

the bank of the creek," Bate glumly reported. "A bloody engagement here ensued with great odds against us, and after a futile but most persistent and gallant effort to dislodge him, Colonel Rudler properly withdrew his [37th Georgia] under cover of the bank. At this juncture every gun and piece in that portion of my command which had arrived on the field was engaged in a spirited and deadly contest."[36]

"We ran against a line of Yanks that was too strong for us, and, falling back in no confusion, but with considerable swiftness, was then the order," noted Private Cooper of the 20th Tennessee. "We fell back a quarter of a mile and reformed, but no advance was made."[37]

The frustrated Confederates had had enough. They made no effort to mount a fourth attack, leaving the infantry combat to peter out. "In this position we fought for nearly an hour, when by his excess of numbers, the enemy turned our already extended left flank, giving an enfilading fire to the Twentieth Tennessee," wrote Bate. "It recoiled from the shock, was rallied, and formed in good time on a fence running a short distance from and perpendicular to our line of battle."[38]

Thanks to the Spencers, Bate now believed that his command was badly outnumbered. He shifted his infantry and artillery to a position where they could check Wilder's men while the cannon duel continued. The Southern gunners "opened a furious cannonading upon our battery, without doing much harm or receiving harm in return, they being under cover of the hills." As darkness fell, the artillery fire also tapered off, and silence fell over the battlefield.[39]

About 4:00 p.m., Maj. Gen. Joseph Reynolds arrived with his division of the XIV Corps. He placed one brigade on either side of the road to extend Wilder's line in both directions. That night, one of Maj. Gen. Lovell Rousseau's brigades also came up to reinforce Wilder's position. "About half past seven in the evening along came a weary, jaded regiment of infantry, trying to double quick, but it was all they could do to march at all," wrote Major Connolly; "[W]e greeted them with such lusty cheers as seemed to inspire them with new vigor, and they were soon in position; then came two more regiments of infantry, weary and footsore, but hurrying the best they could to the dance of death." The mounted infantrymen had

36 *OR* 23, pt. 1, 612.

37 Cooper, "Service with the Twentieth Tennessee Regiment," 101.

38 *OR* 23, pt. 1, 612.

39 Cooper, "Service with the Twentieth Tennessee Regiment," 101; Winchester, "The Battle of Hoover's Gap"; *OR* 25, pt. 2, 459. One of Bate's men claimed that Bate faced at least two brigades of infantry at Hoover's Gap that day.

held long enough. Hoover's Gap was now solidly in the capable hands of George Thomas.[40]

The fight was not entirely over, however. As Rousseau and his staff officers reached the field, they drew the attention of Confederate artillerists, who opened fire. The Rebel gunners dropped rounds closer and closer as they perfected their range. Some shells burst so close that Rousseau told his staff, "Gentlemen, you must scatter." One of them recalled, "we rode off in different directions," though he was quick to add, "none went to the rear."[41]

Bushrod Johnson's four Tennessee regiments arrived after dark to reinforce Bate, but they did not reach the field in time to join the fighting. Johnson's men went into position to Bate's right, but the die was already cast. Hoover's Gap was firmly in the hands of the mounted infantrymen who had held off the determined Southern attacks against heavy odds. John Wilder had every reason to be proud of his men.[42]

Bate's soldiers suffered significantly that day. "I don't know the Rebel loss, but it must have been heavy, as they massed their force in an open field," recounted a member of the 72nd Indiana, "and we cross-fired on them, while the Battery poured in Canister and grape shot." Captain Eli Lilly agreed. "Their loss must have been considerable at this point from the number they were seen to drag off by the arms." The colors of the 20th Tennessee bore evidence of the battle's intensity; its flagstaff was broken in two by a Spencer bullet, and the eagle on the top of the staff shot away. Bate, himself wounded in the fighting, reported losses of 19 killed and 126 wounded, for total casualties of 145, but this number likely understates the actual losses, not to mention significant straggling. Private Cooper of the 20th Tennessee found the day trying indeed. "We marched about through the mud that night until every bone in my body had a thousand aches, but still no rest." He further noted, "numbers of our men were scattered through the country, not expecting this fight. Some of them were captured, and others did not get in for weeks."[43]

---

40 Angle, *Three Years in the Army of the Cumberland*, 93-94; Rowell, *Yankee Artillerymen*, 82.

41 Michael Hendrick Fitch, *Echoes of the Civil War as I Hear Them* (New York: 1905), 125.

42 David A. Powell and David A. Friedrichs, *The Maps of Chickamauga: An Atlas of the Chickamauga Campaign, Including the Tullahoma Operations, June 22-September 23, 1863* (El Dorado Hills, CA: 2009), 8.

43 Margaret Black Tatum, ed., "'Please Send Stamps': The Civil War Letters of William Allen Clark, Part II", *Indiana Magazine of History*, vol. 91, no. 2 (June 1995), 223-224; Report of Eli Lilly,

By sundown, Wilder's weary Illinoisans and Indianans had been lying in mud and water for hours, suffering in the heavy rains with no rations and no campfires for warmth. "We lay on the ground five hours," recounted William A. Clark of the 72nd Indiana. "The Shells were whizzing over us all that time." Lieutenant Colonel Edward Kitchell of the 98th Illinois noted in his diary, "Rained all night. Will go to bed on my blanket without supper." Later that night, Brig. Gen. George Crook's infantry brigade of Reynolds's division relieved Wilder's exhausted men. As they moved back, Wilder's regiments had every reason to be satisfied. They had met the challenge, making a bold dash to seize Hoover's Gap and then holding it against several determined assaults by veteran Confederate infantry. When George Thomas arrived on the field, he informed Wilder, "Your work today right here has saved the lives of 1,000 men. I didn't expect to have the gap for three days."[44]

When Rosecrans got to the southern end of Hoover's Gap, he took off his hat, handed it to an orderly, and pumped Colonel Wilder's hand, saying, "You took the responsibility to disobey the order, did you? Thank God for your decision. It would have cost us two thousand lives to have taken this position if you had given it up." Soon after, Maj. Gen. Joseph Reynolds rode up. "Wilder has done right," he declared to Rosecrans. "Promote him, promote him." Rosecrans, after surveying the position, agreed. "You did right, and should be promoted and not censured." The next day, Rosecrans recommended that Wilder be made a brigadier general in recognition of his feat.[45]

Wilder's men lay on the hillside in line of battle that night. Major Connolly recalled that he "slept as well there, without blankets and soaking wet, as I ever did at home. . . .At 3 o'clock in the morning two other brigades came up and took our places in line, so as to be in readiness to renew the fight in the morning, and we fell back to eat and rest."[46]

By the next morning, Thomas had elements of four divisions in place on the field. Now desperately outnumbered, the Confederates, with General Stewart

---

July 16, 1863, Eli Lilly Papers, Archives, Eli Lilly and Company, Indianapolis, IN; McMurray, *History of the Twentieth Tennessee*, 261; OR 23, pt. 1, 614; Cooper, "Service with the Twentieth Tennessee Regiment," 101.

44 Tatum, "Please Send Stamps," 223; Kitchell diary, entry for June 24, 1863; *Dedication of the Wilder Brigade Monument*, 15.

45 Wilder, "The Battle of Hoover's Gap," 172. Earlier that year, Reynolds had complained to Rosecrans about excessive foraging and a lack of discipline among Wilder's men when they were rounding up horses, suggesting that Wilder needed to be reined in.

46 Angle, *Three Years in the Army of the Cumberland*, 94.

himself in command, made no further effort to drive the Federals from their stout position at the southern end of the gap. "We lay in line of battle, supporting battery all day," noted Colonel Kitchell. "As at times the Rebs attempted to place in position their batteries, the cannonading was terrific. We could plainly see the line of the enemy's skirmishers, as well as ours. Firing continued all day along the line but with small loss to either party." On June 25, there was little in the way of infantry fighting done, with the soldiers of both sides suffering through a long day of skirmishing and artillery fire in the heavy rain.[47]

The relatively bloodless seizure of Hoover's Gap did indeed save the lives of many of McCook's and Thomas's soldiers. Wilder's cost for taking and holding Hoover's Gap was one officer killed (Chaplain John R. Eddy of the 72nd Indiana, who had just joined the regiment on June 17 and who had preached his very first sermon only the day before, was killed when Confederate artillery overshot Lilly's guns and a shell landed in the road and exploded), one officer mortally wounded (Lt. James T. Moreland of the 17th Indiana), and 12 enlisted men killed and 47 wounded, for a total of 61 casualties. "The conduct of both officers and men was all that the most sanguine could ask," Colonel Wilder proclaimed proudly. "Each officer seemed to appreciate the importance of taking and holding the very strong position of Hoover's Gap, and the men were eager to obey and sustain their officers. Their conduct was the same whether in driving in the rebel outposts or defending their position against fearful odds, or when lying in support of our battery, exposed to a terrible cross fire of shot and shell, or when advancing against the rebel columns; always earnest, cool, determined, ready, and brave, seeming best pleased when necessarily in greatest danger."[48]

On June 25, an order lauding the Hoover's Gap attack was read to every regiment in George Thomas's XIV Corps. The order declared that "the conduct of [Wilder's] brigade should be emulated by all," and went on to direct "that the command should thereafter be known as Wilder's Lightning Brigade." The force had been officially christened with a moniker that the men bore with great honor for the rest of the war and the remainder of their lives. As a member of the 17th Indiana noted, "this engagement thoroughly tested the power of the Spencer rifles and proved their great superiority to the muzzle-loader. For us it did more; it inspired us with a confidence in ourselves which of itself was worth double our

47 Kitchell diary, entry for June 25, 1863.

48 Bradley, *Tullahoma*, 54-59; OR 23, pt. 1, 459.

numbers. Ever after the brigade would cheerfully have fought ten times its own strength."[49]

Another exulted, "our Spencer Rifles work like a charm, and had we not been armed with them, nothing could have prevented our being captured." Though the Lightning Brigade had been badly outnumbered, the firepower of the Spencers evened out the odds. "One half of our boys emptied the chambers of their guns seven shots in half a minute," noted a member of the 98th Illinois. "The Rebs couldn't stand it, but supposed the woods were full of Feds." One of Lilly's artillerymen boasted, "They outnumbered us three to one, but we held our line until reinforcements came to our aid." The firepower of the Spencers made that stand possible.[50]

The rapid movement of the Lightning Brigade punched through Bragg's right center and enabled the Army of the Cumberland to threaten the Confederate flank and rear. The door to Manchester—and to Tullahoma, beyond—was now thrust wide open. "Thus," as a correspondent of the *Cincinnati Gazette* correctly observed, "the first and most critical step of the campaign was won by Wilder's soldiership."[51]

49 Wilder, "The Battle of Hoover's Gap," 172; Wilson, "Wilder's Brigade of Mounted Infantry," 53.

50 "Harry," "Letter from the 17th Indiana Regiment"; Kitchell diary, entry for June 24, 1863; Joseph A. Scott reminiscences, Archives, Indiana Historical Society, Indianapolis.

51 Wilder, "The Battle of Hoover's Gap," 172; *Cincinnati Gazette* (Cincinnati, OH), July 29, 1863.

Chapter Eight

The Union Left Hook,
June 24 to 27, 1863

On June 23, 1863, Col. Emerson Opdycke paused to pen a letter to his wife Lucy, a task he made time for whenever possible. Opdycke commanded the 125th Ohio Infantry, part of Col. Charles G. Harker's 3rd Brigade in Brig. Gen. Thomas J. Wood's 1st Division of the XXI Corps. Opdycke seemed well pleased with his circumstances. "Col. Harker is highly spoken of by all," he noted. "Genl Wood . . . seems to have almost universal confidence: They are both Regular officers." The previous day, Opdycke "called on Gen. Garfield . . ., he looks stout and well. He presented me to Gen Rosecrans, with whom I was much pleased: he appears to have more brain force than I had before thought him possessed of." After discussing a few regimental matters and passing on some army gossip, Opdycke closed his missive with important news. "We have orders to march in the morning with twelve days rations," he wrote. "I hope we shall meet the enemy, as it is better to do so near our supplies, I shall keep you well informed by letter or telegraph, in proportion to the interest of events here. Much love to all."[1]

These preliminary instructions set in motion the larger movement that Rosecrans, with all his "brain force," intended to be the main effort of his entire offensive. It also began one of the most difficult weeks in the XXI Corps's history. Reflecting on the experience many years after the war, Sgt. Ralsa C. Rice, then

---

1 Glenn V. Longacre and John E. Haas, eds., *To Battle for God and the Right: The Civil War Letterbooks of Emerson Opdycke* (Urbanna, IL: 2003), 80.

serving under Opdycke in the 125th Ohio, opined, "the Tullahoma campaign, while not marked by any severe fighting on our part, taxed our powers of endurance beyond any other during our term of service."[2]

Two of Maj. Gen. Thomas L. Crittenden's XXI Corps divisions, those of Maj. Gen. Thomas J. Wood and Maj. Gen. Horatio Van Cleve, were currently encamped around Murfreesboro. His remaining division, under Illinois politician-turned-soldier Maj. Gen. John M. Palmer, occupied camps east of Murfreesboro. Two of Palmer's brigades were stationed along the Woodbury Pike where that road crossed Cripple Creek, a tributary of the West Fork of Stones River, seven miles from town. Brigadier General William B. Hazen's brigade was positioned another five miles east of Cripple Creek in Readyville. "Readyville was a name, not a town," noted the 41st Ohio's regimental history; "the place afforded a good camping ground . . . [and] the duty on the whole was not hard." The hamlet included a dozen houses, including the now-abandoned farm of a man named Peter Talley. Hazen's brigade had been camped there since mid-January, long enough that "quarters had been made as comfortable as possible, and the time was really an enjoyable one." Hazen commandeered the Talley farm as his headquarters, probably because the Federals viewed doing so as fair game. In the words of a member of the 41st Ohio, Talley was "an old rebel" who had once hosted Nathan Bedford Forrest and his cavalry in 1862.[3]

Rosecrans's plan called for Crittenden to move first with Palmer's and Wood's commands to the settlement of Bradyville (itself little more than a post office), about a dozen miles south of Readyville, by June 24. Their next objective was Lumley's Stand, to be reached on the 25th, and then Manchester on the 26th. Van Cleve's division remained behind, initially to defend Fortress Rosecrans. Later, Van Cleve was scheduled to move east and occupy McMinnville.

For those of Palmer's men stationed at Cripple Creek, the campaign opened with a grim prelude. On the evening of June 22, Sgt. William H. Busbey, Company I, 1st Kentucky, noted, "the sentence of the man under arrest as a deserter from Co. I arrive[d] confirmed. To be shot on the morrow. The guards [were] strengthened and his quarters changed. [He] is very much agitated." The next day, Busbey wrote,

---

2 Ralsa C. Rice, *Yankee Tigers: Through the Civil War with the 125th Ohio,* eds. Richard A. Baumgartner and Larry M. Strayer (Huntington, WV: 1992), 56.

3 OR 23, pt. 1, 521; Robert L. Kimberly and Ephraim S. Holloway, *The Forty-First Ohio Veteran Volunteer Infantry in the War of the Rebellion, 1861-1865* (Cleveland, OH: 1897), 45; Edward S. Cooper, *The Brave Men of Company A: The Forty-First Ohio Volunteer Infantry* (Madison, NJ: 2015), 63.

Maj. Gen. Thomas L. Crittenden, commander,
XXI Corps, Army of the Cumberland.

Library of Congress

Brig. Gen. Thomas J. Wood,
commander, First Division, XXI Corps,
Army of the Cumberland.

Library of Congress

"John Shockman . . . [was] shot in the presence of the entire command at three oclock for desertion. The two brigades formed in two lines three sides to a square. The prisoner marched around between the 2 lines, each band playing the dead march. He was calm but dejected and the scene was most impressive." Shortly after the execution, Busbey and his comrades "receive[d] orders to move."[4]

Rosecrans's final orders were delivered to Thomas Crittenden's headquarters at 2:15 a.m. on June 24. All troops were directed to be on the march by 7:00 a.m. Fifteen minutes later, the orders reached Thomas Wood's hands. "This order required the troops to move as light as possible," Wood later reported, "taking with them twelve days' subsistence for the men and six days' forage for the animals." The men cooked and carried three days' worth of those rations in their haversacks, with the rest hauled in the lumbering wagons. Tom Wood was a hard-bitten Regular Army officer who nevertheless favored volunteer soldiers. "Volunteers can 'stick,'" was how he once put it. "You can fight them as long as you please. . . . The Regulars are too sharp, they know when they are whipped, but the volunteers don't; they will fight as long as they can pull a trigger." As was to be expected,

4 "Entries for June 22 and 23," William H. Busbey Diary, Stones River National Battlefield, Murfreesboro, TN. According to John Shockman's service file, Shockman was "shot to death by musketry" for the crimes of desertion from the 1st Kentucky in December 1861, for reenlisting in the 4th Ohio Cavalry without being properly discharged from the 1st Kentucky, and, most damningly, "offering violence to his superior officer while in the execution of his office" during the course of his arrest. "Compiled Service Records of Volunteer Union Soldiers Who Served in Organizations from the State of Kentucky," RG 94, microfilm roll M397, NARA.

Maj. Gen. John M. Palmer, commander,
Second Division, XXI Corps,
Army of the Cumberland.

Library of Congress

Wood took pride in the fact that his men were ready and stepped off "precisely at the hour fixed."[5]

John Palmer's division made a less auspicious start. Wood's headquarters was only minutes from the corps commander's, while Palmer was stationed seven miles away at Cripple Creek. Palmer reported that he did not receive the final order until 4:00 a.m., too late for him to get his troops moving by 7. The work of issuing 12 days' rations, wrote Palmer, was still taking place at 7, and "it was nearly 9 o'clock before the column was in motion." The delay convinced Palmer that there was no time to send his excess baggage back to Murfreesboro so, contrary to orders, he decided to bring it with him. That decision surprised William Hazen when he received word of it at Readyville. "Thinking there was some mistake about the amount of baggage, I at once sent a messenger to division headquarters," who soon returned and reaffirmed the directive. Hazen's men finally moved out at 10:00 a.m.[6]

---

5 OR 23, pt. 1, 523; Wilbur F. Hinman, *The Story of the Sherman Brigade: The Camp, the March, the Bivouac, the Battle, and How "the Boys" Lived and Died during Four Years of Active Field Service* (Alliance, OH: 1897) 426.

6 OR 23, pt. 1, 528, 530. John McCauley Palmer was born in Scott County, Kentucky, on September 13, 1817. At 14, his antislavery, Jacksonian Democrat father relocated the family to Illinois. He attended Shurtleff College for two years before moving to Carlinville in 1839. He read law there and was admitted to the Illinois bar. He was involved in antislavery politics and served in the state senate as a Democrat. In 1856, he was instrumental in helping found the Illinois Republican Party. He ran for Congress as a Republican in 1859 but was defeated. In 1860, Palmer served as a delegate to the Chicago convention that nominated Abraham Lincoln for president. When the Civil War began, Palmer was named colonel of the 14th Illinois Infantry. He was promoted to brigadier general of volunteers on December 20, 1861, and then to major general of volunteers on March 16, 1863, to rank from November 29, 1862. He led a division of infantry at times, and eventually became commander of the XIV Corps when

The additional wagons burdened Palmer's columns, but his division was the left flank of the entire Union army. His force had been scrapping with Morgan's cavalry, headquartered just 20 miles away at McMinnville, for months. Palmer apparently felt that either detaching a strong force to escort the baggage back to Murfreesboro or waiting until those wagons were safely away before starting his own move south would take longer than simply adding the wagons to his column. Of course, Palmer had yet to learn that Morgan's entire division was headed for Ohio and no longer posed a threat to him.

Curiously, even though Palmer's column was to lead the way for Crittenden's XXI Corps, no cavalry reported to him on June 23 or 24. Palmer also was apparently unaware that David Stanley had ordered John Turchin's 1st Division to Cripple Creek on the 24th. Though Stanley subsequently detached half of Turchin's troops (Minty's brigade—see chapter 6) that afternoon in order to reinforce Mitchell at Christiana, this still left Col. Eli Long's large command theoretically at Palmer's disposal. Long's horsemen left Murfreesboro at 6:00 a.m., moving first to Cripple Creek before turning south, and they followed Palmer's column all day long. Even if it wasn't leading the column, this cavalry should have been adequate to screen Palmer's surplus baggage.[7]

And then there was the rain. Hazen noted that it began about 8:00 a.m., two hours before his men filed out of Readyville. Sergeant Busbey of the 1st Kentucky recorded that his brigade left Cripple Creek "about 7½ o'clock" and, further, that it "rain[ed] steady all day." The 84th Indiana of Col. William Grose's brigade drew the worst assignment—rear guard, behind the entire division's trains. "We were hardly upon the road, before a heavy rain set in. . . . We marched nearly south from Cripple Creek to strike the pike . . . and in so doing followed an old woods or neighborhood road, which, after a few hours of incessant rain became almost impassable. The artillery cut it up so that the wagon trains found it impossible to pass, until new routes were selected and cut out through the woods." At the head of the column, Busbey noted that Palmer's van halted "about 4 oclock" and made "camp in Dug Hollow 1½ miles beyond (south of) Bradyville"; but the 84th's

---

George H. Thomas rose to head the Army of the Cumberland in the fall of 1863. After the war, he was elected governor of Illinois as a Republican, but soon made his way back to his roots in the Democratic Party. In 1891, he went to the U.S. Senate as a Democrat, and later ran for president as the nominee of the National Democratic Party, or "Gold Democrats," who supported the free-silver doctrine of William Jennings Bryan. He died in Springfield on September 25, 1900. Warner, *Generals in Blue*, 358-359.

7 OR 23, pt. 1, 567.

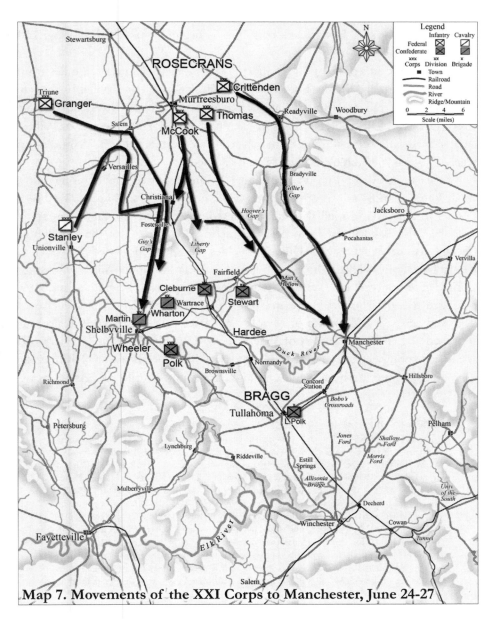

Map 7. Movements of the XXI Corps to Manchester, June 24-27

regimental historian, L. A. Simmons, recorded that his regiment and the trains didn't reach camp until six hours later, at "10 o'clock p.m., about a half mile south of Bradyville." The day also proved expensive, at least to the United States Treasury. According to Simmons, "Before night all of the teams of the division were found to be overloaded, many wagons were broken down, and considerable baggage abandoned." It was not a promising beginning to Rosecrans's grand campaign.[8]

General Wood's destination for June 24 was Donald's Church, 12 miles from his starting point at Murfreesboro and four miles short of Bradyville. In the late morning, Wood ran into Palmer's lumbering column where the road from Cripple Creek intersected his route, despite the fact, noted a disdainful Wood, of Palmer having "had only some 4 miles to march to reach the intersection." Wood's van reached Donald's Church at 2:00 p.m. and camped.[9]

At least enemy opposition was minimal. Palmer reported encountering only a small Rebel outpost a bit north of Bradyville, near Welles's Church. The 110th Illinois Infantry skirmished with these Confederates, slowly driving them some distance, until Palmer turned to his own escort, Company C of the 7th Illinois Cavalry, to hurry them along. Union casualties were limited to two: cavalry Pvt. Henry Lasman was killed and Sgt. William A. Statia "wounded slightly." Extant Confederate sources are silent on who these troops were, but they probably belonged to Col. Thomas Harrison's brigade of Wharton's division, which was deployed across a wide swath of Middle Tennessee. The 8th Texas Cavalry was stationed at Bell Buckle, south of Liberty Gap. The 4th Tennessee Cavalry had spent that spring deployed along the Caney Fork River northeast of McMinnville, more than 50 miles to the east, and remained there until after Rosecrans's forward

---

8 "Entry for June 24," Busbey Diary; L. A. Simmons, *The History of the 84th Regt. Ill. Vols.* (Macomb, IL: 1866), 57-58. Ivan Vasilovich Turchinoff, also known as John Basil Turchin, was born in the Province of the Don in Russia on January 30, 1822. He was educated at the Imperial Military Academy in St. Petersburg and subsequently rose to the rank of colonel in the Russian Imperial Guard. During the Crimean War, he served on the personal staff of Crown Prince Alexander II. He also planned and erected the coastal defenses of Finland. In 1856, he immigrated to the United States, settling in Chicago, where he worked as a railroad engineer. He was commissioned colonel of the 19th Illinois Infantry on June 17, 1861, and soon had his unit well trained. Turchin was a thorough soldier, but his European roots were evident, and his men became notorious for their disregard of personal property rights. In February 1862, he assumed command of a brigade and captured Huntsville, Alabama. A month later, his brigade sacked Athens, Alabama, and he encouraged his men to rob and pillage the town indiscriminately. He was relieved of command and was convicted by a court-martial, which recommended that he be cashiered. President Abraham Lincoln intervened, the conviction was reversed, and Turchin was promoted to brigadier general effective July 17, 1862. He became known as "The Russian Thunderbolt" and performed well throughout the rest of his service. He went on sick leave on July 15, 1864, and had to resign his commission due to ill health on October 4, 1864. Late in life, he suffered from dementia and died on June 19, 1901, in the Southern Hospital for the Insane in Anna, Illinois. Turchin was the only notable Russian contributor to the American Civil War. Warner, *Generals in Blue*, 511-512.

9 *OR* 23, pt. 1, 523.

movement had commenced. Elements of both the 1st/3rd Kentucky and 3rd Confederate cavalry regiments were variously identified as screening Liberty and Hoover's gaps (unsuccessfully, as it turned out), while no reports of the 11th Texas Cavalry's whereabouts during this time have survived. Palmer's opponents were most likely other detachments of the 1st/3rd Kentucky or 3rd Confederate, but it is also conceivable that they were some of Morgan's men, left behind because their animals weren't in condition to make the intended raid.[10]

While this fleeting Confederate presence meant that Crittenden's advance barely registered at the Army of Tennessee's headquarters, it did register. At 3:45 p.m. on June 24, A. P. Stewart notified Hardee of a possible Union move toward Manchester, though he identified it only as a cavalry force. In turn, at 6:15 that evening, Stewart's dispatch prompted Bragg to order John Wharton "to take two regiments of cavalry . . . and move towards Manchester." A few hundred cavalry reinforcements would not stop Crittenden's corps, but Wharton might be able to provide Bragg with timely intelligence if he could move quickly.[11]

Following an equally sodden night, June 25 dawned wet and cheerless. That morning, Capt. William E. Crane, who commanded company C of the 4th Ohio Cavalry and was a meticulous diarist, recorded his impressions of the campaign so far. On June 24, he noted, it "rained hard all day and was chilly as November. [We] camped near Bradyville and had a miserably disagreeable night, nothing but wet sod under . . . and hard pouring rain above."[12]

At this time, Turchin reported to General Palmer for orders, since Crittenden was not yet forward. Palmer directed the Russian to take the lead with Col. Eli Long's cavalry brigade and head for Lumley's Stand, halfway to Manchester, a march of a dozen miles. Since Turchin's brigade trains were still behind Palmer's wagons, his 2,500 horsemen were forced to leave their own baggage behind. The troopers rode out at 6:00 a.m., climbing through a place called "Hawes Gap" and

10 Ibid., 528; Ephraim S. Dodd, "The Diary of Ephraim Shelby Dodd," in J.K.P. Blackburn, L.B. Giles, and E.S. Dodd, *Terry Texas Ranger Trilogy* (Austin, TX: 1996), 205; George B. Guild, *A Brief Narrative of the Fourth Tennessee Cavalry Regiment, Wheeler's Corps, Army of Tennessee* (Nashville, TN: 1913), 19. None of the sources for Harrison's units provide any detail concerning their activities during late June, prior to the fight at Shelbyville on June 27.

11 *OR* 23, pt. 2, 883-884. Since Stewart's original dispatch does not survive, it is impossible to determine whether Stewart was referring to Crittenden's movement or merely to the Union effort at Hoover's Gap; but in any case, his intelligence was the first to suggest a Federal threat to Manchester.

12 "Entry for June 25," William E. Crane Journal, Cincinnati Historical Society, Cincinnati, OH, vol. 1, 154.

passing "the artillery and Palmer's division of infantry." It was "heavy work for the artillery climbing the mountains," observed Sgt. Thomas Crofts of the 3rd Ohio Cavalry, but it was easier for the horse soldiers, who reached their objective "early in the afternoon."[13]

Lumley's Stand was an important intersection at the "junction of [the] Bradyville, [the] Manchester [to] Shelbyville, and [the] McMinnville roads." There, reported Col. Long, "three suspicious-appearing persons were here taken [prisoner.]" Additional patrols sent out "3 miles to the west" and toward "Pocahontas. . . six miles eastward" netted additional prisoners in the form of Confederate couriers. One of those "suspicious-appearing persons" turned out to be "a notorious character," though Colonel Long failed to further identify the man, who was presumably a local Confederate bushwhacker of some repute. Then, leaving the 2nd Kentucky Cavalry (U.S.) to picket the crossroads, Long fell back "2½ miles to camp. Wet weather all day," he noted, further complaining that "my train [was] not up in consequence of difficult traveling."[14]

"Difficult traveling" proved to be a considerable understatement. The total distance from Readyville to Manchester was just about 30 miles. On June 24, Palmer's van made 10 miles. On June 25, Turchin, with Long's brigade, took the lead and progressed to Lumley's Stand, another eight miles, meaning that Manchester now lay only 12 miles farther. But for most of the next 48 hours, Crittenden's entire column became so badly mired that forward progress halted completely.

In 1863, the best route from Bradyville to Manchester was via Gilley's (or Gillies) Hill Road, which followed the course of Brawley's Fork through Tolbert's Hollow until abruptly ascending Dickens Ridge at Gilley's Hill, six miles south of Bradyville. Two miles beyond that ascent, Hollow Springs sat atop the Highland Rim. Tolbert's Hollow, described by Sergeant Busbey as "a gorge-like valley," was between 740 and 760 feet above sea level, while, at its highest point, Dickens Ridge rose to 1,295 feet. Where the road climbed the ridge, there was a steep elevation

---

13 Thomas Crofts, *History of the Service of the Third Ohio Veteran Volunteer Cavalry in the War for the Preservation of the Union from 1861-1865, Compiled from the Official Records and from Diaries of Members of the Regiment by Sergt. Thos. Crofts, Company C, Regimental Historian* (Toledo, OH: 1910), 103. Hawes Gap does not appear on existing maps. Crittenden's corps was moving toward Manchester through Tolbert's Hollow, ascending the Highland Rim at a place called Gillies Hill, five miles south of Bradyville. It is possible that "Hawes Gap" was a local name, or that the opening was a side passage.

14 *OR* 23, pt. 1, 567.

change of roughly 500 feet over a half mile's distance. "It was here manifest," Palmer reported, "that teams, even when moderately loaded and the roads dry, would ascend with great difficulty, and would find it nearly impassable as the road was then—softened and made slippery by the rain." Palmer's infantry marched up the ridge and slogged on to Hollow Spring, where there was sufficient water for the division. Palmer then sent men back to Gilley's Hill to begin the herculean task of hauling the trains up the Dickens Ridge.[15]

Shortly thereafter, Tom Wood came on the scene. "It has scarcely ever been my ill-fortune in eighteen years of active service (during which I have marched many thousands of miles) to have to pass over so bad a road," he wrote. "The geological formation of the broad plateau on which Manchester is situated is such as to make in wet weather the very worst roads conceivable. The soil is a mixture of clay and sand, which under the continued fall of rain became with the slightest travel an almost impassible quagmire." Facing this traffic nightmare, Wood knew his march was done for the day, so he ordered his men to make camp in Tolbert's Hollow, waiting for Palmer's trains to get past the bottleneck.[16]

That effort took far longer than anyone expected. "At 3:30 o'clock on the morning of the 26th, [Wood] dispatched a staff officer to see whether the road was clear. He returned, reporting it was not." Nor would it be any time soon, idling Wood's command for the entirety of June 26. Palmer's men were also halted, but they were hardly idle: where horsepower and mule-power failed, manpower took over. Lieutenant Ridgley C. Powers of the 125th Ohio, one of Hazen's officers, described the day's efforts. After the hill's slope "defied the combined strength of our disheartened mules," wrote Powers, "a regiment at first, and finally a whole brigade, was detailed to assist, but all would not do."[17]

On June 24, Rosecrans established his headquarters behind the XIV Corps at Mrs. James McGill's house on the Manchester Pike, about nine miles south of Murfreesboro on Big Springs Branch, which in turn was about 10 miles west of Bradyville. To facilitate communications with Crittenden, Rosecrans dispatched a company of the 15th Pennsylvania Cavalry to establish a courier line between

15 "Entry for June 25," Busbey Diary; OR 23, pt. 1, 529.

16 OR 23, pt. 1, 524.

17 Ibid.; Richard A. Baumgartner, ed., *Yankee Tigers II: Civil War Field Correspondence from the Tiger Regiment of Ohio* (Huntington, WV: 2004), 77. Lieutenant Powers was a soldier-correspondent for the *Western Reserve Chronicle* (Warren, OH), using the pen name CEYLON. This article was written on July 10 and was printed in the July 22, 1863, issue of the paper.

McGill's and Bradyville. As June 25 dawned, Rosecrans reported, "it was not yet certain whether the enemy would advance to test our strength on McCook's front, or mass on the flank of the Fourteenth Corps near Fairfield." He ordered Thomas, McCook, and Granger all to continue to threaten Bragg's positions at Wartrace and Shelbyville. He decided not to order the XXI Corps to move decisively toward Manchester until he knew whether Bragg would try to attack him at either Fairfield or Liberty Gap. Sufficient progress on June 25, however—especially on Thomas's front—convinced him to go ahead with the planned thrust.[18]

As late as the evening of June 25, Rosecrans remained unaware of the state of the roads on which Crittenden was floundering. Late on June 24, he told George Thomas that the XIV Corps trains might need to move via Bradyville, a suggestion that, fortunately for the Federal timetable, soon proved unnecessary. Crittenden reported Turchin's successful occupation of Lumley's Stand, but failed to make clear the lack of progress by the rest of his column. That night, unaware of Crittenden's circumstances, Rosecrans commanded the XXI Corps "to move on Manchester, by most direct route, early to-morrow morning [June 26], and, if possible occupy that place and commence the crossing of the Duck River to-morrow night." The Duck River flowed from northeast to southwest a mile or so east of Manchester, and by establishing a bridgehead across it, Crittenden would be able to either support Thomas or attack Bragg if the Confederates fell back on Tullahoma.[19]

Colonel John T. Wilder's startling success in forcing Hoover's Gap already had both Rosecrans and Thomas thinking aggressively. After some careful reconnoitering on the morning of June 25, Thomas determined that the Confederates had a brigade on each of the Fairfield and Manchester roads, but were "acting on the defensive." At 3:00 p.m. he sent Rosecrans a message. "I propose concentrating my corps [at Hoover's Gap] this p.m., and making an advance at daylight to morrow on Fairfield and Manchester pike; [Maj. Gen. Lovell H.] Rousseau [1st Division] on Manchester, [Maj. Gen. Joseph J.] Reynolds [4th Division] and [Brig. Gen. John M.] Brannan [3rd Division] on Fairfield, [Maj. Gen. James S.] Negley [2nd Division] in reserve, if you approve," wrote Thomas. At midnight, Rosecrans assented, with one modification: Thomas should "create the impression" that he intended to attack Fairfield, and "in the mean time push on your main column toward Manchester by way of Matt's Hollow." Wilder again

18 OR 23, pt. 1, 406; pt. 2, 449-450.

19 Ibid., pt. 2, 455.

would lead the march, with Rosecrans hoping to repeat the success of Hoover's Gap at this new "defile. Make as much of the distance to Manchester as possible to morrow."[20]

These instructions, coupled with Rosecrans's orders to Crittenden, were intended to concentrate at least two corps of the Army of the Cumberland at or near Manchester by the evening of June 26. Crittenden's mission was the most critical: He was to occupy Manchester and gain control of the Duck River crossings to the east of the town. Under normal circumstances, these objectives were not unreasonable. Manchester lay 16 miles from Hollow Springs and 12 from Lumley's Stand—a decent day's march for an infantry division. Seizing the river crossings added a mile or two. But circumstances were now far from normal. When he opened these orders on the morning of June 26, Crittenden must have read them with a mounting sense of dismay. "I at once informed the general commanding . . . that General Palmer's train was not yet up the hill, but that no time should be lost," he reported.[21]

All day long, with "50 men working at each wagon," Palmer's troops dragged vehicle after vehicle up the miry slope. At some point, with desperation mounting, Crittenden implemented a radical solution. "Orders came to burn the baggage, tents, mess boxes, blankets, trunks and cooking utensils, and they were hurled in one promiscuous mass into the flames. Even hand-trunks were destroyed, leaving many officers without a change of clothes. Ammunition and provisions were alone saved."[22]

Even this wholesale destruction did not improve Crittenden's timetable. At 4:10 p.m., he was forced to inform headquarters of the full extent of his circumstances, the horrendous road conditions, and the fact that he would not be anywhere near Manchester by nightfall. Fortunately for Crittenden, things were progressing well elsewhere, allowing Rosecrans room for magnanimity. At 5:15 p.m., Rosecrans replied from his newly established headquarters at Beech Grove that he "appreciates the obstacles you have to encounter; he does not, therefore, expect you to reach Manchester, but desires you to make as much of the distance as possible." Reading this, Crittenden admitted that he was "much relieved."[23]

20 Ibid., 458.

21 OR 23, pt. 1, 521.

22 Ibid.; Baumgartner, *Yankee Tigers II*, 77.

23 OR 23, pt. 1, 521; pt. 2, 460.

Brig. Gen. John B. Turchin, commander,
Second Division, Cavalry Corps,
Army of the Cumberland.

Chickamauga, 1888

Even for those Federals lucky enough not to be detailed to help with the near-Sisyphean task of hauling cannon, limbers, and army wagons up Gilley's Hill, two days' military limbo proved uncomfortable. Food was short. The men had been issued three days' rations to cook and carry with them on June 23. Even under normal circumstances, those supplies would be exhausted by the 26th; the pervasive rain, however, made matters worse. As William Curry of the 1st Ohio Cavalry observed, "during all this time our blankets were never dried out, and our rations in our old greasy haversacks were a conglomerated mass of coffee, sugar, salt, sow-belly, and hard-tack." The only available replacements for these ruined rations were in those same wagons back down in Torbert's Hollow—now seemingly a long way away.[24]

Reined in by Crittenden and Rosecrans, and with limited prospects for action, Turchin's cavalry hovered near Lumley's Stand on June 25 and 26. Colonel Long dispatched "nine companies of my command to assist in bringing forward the wagons," and on the afternoon of June 27, Turchin shifted Long's brigade to Pocahontas, presumably (though this was not specified in the reports) to cover Crittenden's right flank when he resumed his march toward Manchester. Here, a dry wit at brigade headquarters recorded the most interesting event of the day. "Someone stole General Turchin's coffee pot," he wrote. "It was of enough importance to send a staff officer in search of it, but he did not find it." As for the weather, "Rained."[25]

---

24 William L. Curry, *Four Years in the Saddle: History of the First Regiment Ohio Volunteer Cavalry, War of the Rebellion, 1861-1865* (Columbus, OH: 1898), 104.

25 Crofts, *Third Ohio Cavalry,* 103.

Turchin's and then Palmer's reduced trains finally cleared Gilley's Hill by 11:00 a.m. on June 27, after a grueling, nearly nonstop 48-hour effort. But Wood's division still had to climb the hill. Fortunately, Wood was better prepared and had the advantage of having observed Palmer's laborious efforts. His trains already had been stripped to the absolute minimum needed for field operations on June 23, and his men set to work with a will. The scene must have been nearly indescribable—the countryside littered with broken wagons, dead mules, and sputtering pyres of discarded equipment, all mired in a sea of sticky mud and washed by constant, steady, annoying rain. In his memoir, General Stanley described how these conditions rendered the roads nearly impassable. "Foot soldiers marching over the pale clay deployed like slow moving skirmishers," he recorded; "horsemen sought their own course; and as for artillery and supply wagons, they sunk in the mud to the axles and stayed there."[26]

Despite these obstacles, "at 2 p.m. on the 27th," Wood reported with evident pride, "the ascent . . . commenced, and by 1:00 a.m. on the 28th the whole . . . was at the summit. Exactly eleven hours were occupied in the ascent." Wood credited Brig. Gen. George D. Wagner for his direct supervision of this work, which "was rapidly, energetically, and skillfully done." Crittenden thought that for his foresight in stripping his divisional baggage before the march began, Wood was "entitled to the commendation of the general commanding."[27]

Meanwhile, as Crittenden struggled, Rosecrans set most of the rest of the army into motion. The next potential choke point facing the XIV Corps was Matt's Hollow, through which the Manchester Pike passed approximately six miles southeast of Beech Grove. Though not as sharply defined as Hoover's Gap, Matt's Hollow was another narrow defile; if properly defended, the Rebels could use it to greatly impede Thomas's advance. Given Wilder's rapid success on June 24, Rosecrans not surprisingly expected the Lightning Brigade to repeat that feat on June 26.

Wilder's men set out at 10:00 a.m. with the 123rd Illinois in the lead. To bypass the small Confederate force blocking the Manchester Pike, Wilder took a recommended detour, angling eastward until he struck McBride's Creek. From there a road paralleled the creek, running southwest and then returning to the pike a few miles below Beech Grove. This route completely outflanked the Rebels. The

26 David S. Stanley, *Personal Memoirs of Major-General D. S. Stanley, U.S.A.* (Cambridge, MA: 1917), 150-151.

27 OR 23, pt. 1, 521, 524.

stratagem worked so well that by the time Wilder's men returned to the pike, the Rebels had departed, and the other two brigades of Reynolds's division were already arriving. In order to secure the southern mouth of Matt's Hollow, Wilder repeated the flanking movement on a larger scale. "We then moved up McBride's Creek to the tableland, and marched rapidly around the head of Noah's Fork," he reported. From there, his column moved due south. Upon reaching the pike again, he discovered that the full length of Matt's Hollow was already in Union hands. Reynolds's "infantry column was passing," having met no resistance. That evening, the Lightning Brigade camped four miles north of Manchester. The total haul for the day "was a few prisoners," according to the 72nd Indiana's regimental history.[28]

Most of the Army of the Cumberland, meanwhile, converged on the Manchester Pike at Hoover's Gap. For Thomas, there was still the matter of Stewart's Confederates near Fairfield. Throughout June 25, Rebel batteries posted on the hills east of Hoover's Gap remained close enough to lob shells into the Union positions intermittently. At 6:00 p.m., Maj. Gen. Lovell Rousseau reported that Col. Benjamin F. Scribner's brigade of his division, on duty as pickets, "endured an artillery cross-fire from four different points. The fire was very heavy and very accurate, the balls ploughing up the ground all about [Scribner's] infantry and [the 1st Michigan] battery, all in full view of the enemy." Union artillery returned the fire and silenced the Confederate guns, but clearly Hoover's Gap had to be better secured before the rest of the army could begin to move south along the Manchester Pike. As a further worry, Thomas could not afford to let any Confederate force slip back into the gap between his moving columns, which at the very least would expose passing columns to unexpected attacks; such Rebel incursions also had the potential to isolate the advance elements of his corps, rendering them vulnerable to piecemeal destruction.[29]

Thus, while Reynolds thrust toward Manchester, Thomas deployed Rousseau's and Brig. Gen. John Brannan's divisions facing southwest, astride the Fairfield Road, with orders to drive the Rebels from Beech Grove toward Fairfield along the Garrison Fork. Rousseau commanded both divisions in this action. An early morning reconnaissance by the two generals revealed a scattered Rebel defense in the form of three brigades of A. P. Stewart's division. Brigadier General Henry D. Clayton's Alabamians were posted east of the Garrison Fork and the

---

28 Angle, *Three Years in the Army of the Cumberland*, 95; OR 23, part 1, 159; Magee, *History of the 72nd Indiana*, 133.

29 OR 23, pt. 1, 434.

Fairfield Road (which ran parallel there), while Brig. Gen. Bushrod Johnson's four Tennessee regiments stretched to cover a line of hills to the left. Johnson's 44th Tennessee held low ground on Clayton's left, on the west bank of Garrison Fork, followed in order by the 25th and 23rd Tennessee. The 17th Tennessee occupied the heights, with an open wheat field to its front. William Bate's brigade was widely dispersed, with the 9th Alabama Battalion blocking the Manchester Pike south of Jacob's Store on Clayton's right, the 20th Tennessee posted on yet another hill 800 yards to Johnson's left, and the remaining units posted to the rear. Captain Putnam Darden's Mississippi battery supported Johnson, while the Eufala Artillery of Bate's brigade was positioned with the 20th Tennessee. Presumably Capt. J. T. Humphreys's Arkansas battery bolstered Clayton's brigade, though none of the surviving Confederate accounts mention the battery's assignment.[30]

At 10:00 a.m., the Federals advanced. Rousseau led with his 3rd Brigade, consisting of five battalions of U.S. Army Regulars under Maj. Sydney Coolidge (Brig. Gen. John H. King, who normally commanded the Regulars, was still recovering from a wound received at Stones River). Coolidge's men advanced against the 23rd and 25th Tennessee, and were supported by Col. Henry A. Hambright's 2nd Brigade on their left, astride the Fairfield Road. Colonel Benjamin F. Scribner's 1st Brigade, having just come off picket duty at dawn, brought up the rear. Additionally, Rousseau ordered Brannan's men to advance on Coolidge's right, "with a view," as Brannan reported, "to turn the flank of the rebel position." Brannan led with his 1st Brigade, headed by Col. Moses Walker.[31]

Coolidge, "a great-grandson of Thomas Jefferson" who had been "educated at a [French] military school," was a veteran of the Franco-Austrian War (also known as the Second Italian War of Independence) in Italy in 1859, and was also a respected astronomer and explorer. When he reached the wheat field fronting the Rebel position, Coolidge opted for a rapid assault, forming his battalions into two columns behind a heavy skirmish line. The resultant charge impressed both the participants and observers. Four days later, Augustus B. Carpenter of the 19th U.S. Infantry described the moment in a letter home. "We started on the run making for them as fast as we could, giving cheer after cheer as we advanced," he wrote. "That was a nice little charge. I thought every minute would be my last. There we were running toward the hill with a battery firing at us and a line of musketry. . . . We

---

30 Mark W. Johnson, *That Body of Brave Men: The U.S. Regular Infantry and the Civil War in the West* (Cambridge, MA: 2003), 362-363.

31 OR 23, pt. 1, 435, 450.

thought we were sure to be hit, but nothing could stop us. As soon as we got to the hill the rebs seeing that their fire would not stop us, turned and run."[32]

Another member of the 19th U.S. observed this action, though from afar. Captain Alfred L. Hough had been detached from the regiment and was serving on General Negley's staff that day. Earlier, Negley had sent Hough to report to General Rousseau in case Negley's troops were needed. Some years later, Hough recalled witnessing the Regulars' charge. "Our advance was resisted by some artillery with infantry support," he wrote. "We brushed this away after a sharp fight, the 1st Division and principally the Regular Brigade did the work. . . . The Regular Brigade charged gallantly, and drove the enemy, suffering considerably."[33]

The rapidity of Coolidge's charge put the Regulars well in advance of the Federal formations on both flanks. Colonel Moses B. Walker's brigade deployed more conventionally, in two battle lines, with the 17th and 31st Ohio in front and the 38th Ohio and 82nd Indiana in support. Walker reported that he found "the 17th & 20th Tenn rebel Regts . . . strongly posted in the timber. A farm house, negro quarters & barn extending their left into the woods. Their position [was] covered by two rebel batteries. . . . The attack was gallantly made and with but little loss [and] the position was carried in five minutes or less time. . . . The rebel infantry did not stand the fight," enthused Walker, but he did admit that "the fire from their artillery was terrific."[34]

Private Frederick Marion of Company K, 31st Ohio, also took part in this charge, subsequently describing it to his sister in a letter. Contradicting Colonel Walker, Marion wrote that the 31st, on the brigade right, met stiff resistance from both the enemy artillery and infantry. "The rebles had cannons on a large hill," he wrote, "and we advance[d] on them and the rebles open on . . . us. Our brigade had to pass within three hundred yards of them and just as we was gowing double quick around them [to] outflank them there was four reble regiment[s] rose up by the side of their battery and give us volley after volley making dreadful destruction in our ranks. . . . [O]ur regiment lost some 30 men killed and wounded, and the 17th lost 40. . . ." Despite those casualties, Marion waxed enthusiastic about the result. "The

32 Johnson, *That Body of Brave Men*, 32; "Dear Parents," June 30, 1863, Augustus B. Carpenter Letters, Yale University, New Haven, CT.

33 Robert G. Athearn, ed., *Soldier in the West: The Civil War Letters of Alfred Lacey Hough* (Philadelphia, PA: 1957), 100.

34 Moses B. Walker, "A History of 1st Brig. 3rd Div. 14th A.C. during the Period in which W. S. Rosecrans Com'd Army of Cumberland," General Thomas Papers, RG 94, National Archives, Washington, DC.

rebles retreated in confusion," he continued. "They was scattered worst than sheep. The prisoners that we took said it was one of the bolder charge[s] of the war."[35]

Despite Federal claims, that retreat was by design, and, according to Bushrod Johnson, well conducted. Both divisional commander A. P. Stewart and Johnson, upon whose brigade of Confederates this blow primarily fell, understood that they were badly outnumbered. Early on, Stewart ordered Johnson to withdraw, falling back behind two of Bate's regiments posted to his rear. From his vantage point on one of the hills, Johnson estimated that he faced "perhaps 8,000 or 10,000 men," a guess that was not far from the actual number of Federals. As those swarms of Yankees closed on him, he disengaged. The Confederates fell back fighting, according to Johnson, using wooded ground (and at one point "a very heavy shower of rain") to conceal their movements from their foe.[36]

Out on the Rebel left, Col. Thomas B. Smith's 20th Tennessee and its shot-up new battle flag joined Johnson's retreat. Sergeant William J. McMurray, who later wrote the unit's regimental history, remembered that the 20th was already in considerable discomfort, since its men had been "in line and on picket all night . . . in a freshly plowed field of corn in mud about halfway to [our] knees." General Johnson reported that when the 17th and 23rd Tennessee retired under the intense enemy fire, the 20th Infantry and the Eufala Artillery also withdrew.[37]

Johnson's retreat forestalled more severe losses, but it doomed any remaining hope of Stewart's retaking Hoover's Gap or blocking the Union passage to Manchester. Throughout the three days' action, Stewart had no more than three brigades at hand, while George Thomas wielded Rosecrans's largest corps. During this time period, however, Braxton Bragg and William Hardee were more focused on the effort at Liberty Gap, where Hardee's other division, under Patrick Cleburne, was engaged. This was where Bragg still seemed to think the main Federal blow would land. In Bragg's and Hardee's eyes, Stewart's mission was to delay any Federal thrust towards Wartrace, not Manchester. At 8:30 p.m. on June 26, Hardee told Stewart as much, instructing him, "if the enemy shows any

35 "Dear Sister," June 28th, 1863, Frederick Marion Letters, Abraham Lincoln Presidential Library, Springfield, IL. Marion overestimated the damage; in their official reports, the 17th's officers recorded 22 casualties, and the 31st, 15 men. OR 23, pt. 1, 420.

36 OR 23, part 1, 606.

37 McMurray, *Twentieth Tennessee Regiment*, 261; OR 23, pt. 1, 606.

disposition to press, withdraw your forces to Wartrace for a march on Tullahoma."[38]

A month later, when "the excited state of the public mind" over the abandonment of Middle Tennessee produced "not a little speculation . . . in certain classes touching on the whys and wherefores of" Bragg's retreat, one Confederate correspondent vigorously defended Stewart's actions. "Some supposed that Hoover's Gap was the key—the only key—to General Bragg's position [and] that General Stewart was there to defend it, and had it been successfully defended there could have arisen no necessity for Gen. Bragg's change of base." The writer pointed out that other routes around Bragg's flank existed and, further, that when Stewart took command of the newly formed division on June 11, he did so at Fairfield and subsequently "received no order to place troops at the gap, or hold the position." Rosecrans's "countless hordes" could not have been stopped had Stewart's "division numbered three times as many as it did." Though waxing a bit hyperbolic, the author was basically correct: at the very least, Hardee's entire corps would have been needed to defend Hoover's Gap if Bragg intended to make a fight of it there.[39]

In connection with the fighting on June 26, the Federals reported 3 killed and 22 wounded among the Regulars, with 6 more dead and 41 wounded among Walker's regiments, for a total of 72 casualties. The Confederates suffered about half that number. Johnson's losses tallied 3 killed, 27 wounded, and 6 missing (presumed captured), for a total of 36. The 20th Tennessee's casualties were not reported, but a Union newspaper correspondent who interviewed three prisoners from the 20th wrote "that the loss in killed of the 20th Tennessee alone [was] 40 men." That figure certainly exaggerated the actual loss, which amounted to no more than a handful.[40]

Nor was the Confederate disengagement executed entirely without flaw. East of the Garrison Fork, Clayton's Alabamians were nearly left behind. As a soldier-correspondent for the Mobile Register noted, "Our brigade did not see the signal to retreat, and was nearly cut off, a large force of the enemy being abreast with us, before we retired." These Yankees were probably Coolidge's Regulars,

---

38 *OR* 23, pt. 2, 886.

39 "Hoover's Gap," *Chattanooga Daily Rebel*, July 26, 1863.

40 "The retreat of Bragg's Army," *The Daily Press* (Nashville, TN), June 30, 1863.

threatening Clayton's left flank, since Col. Hambright's troops, opposing Clayton's line astride the Fairfield Road, lagged behind Coolidge's rapid advance.[41]

George Thomas was again pleased with the day's results. The end of June 26 saw Wilder's men ready to descend on Manchester, while Reynolds's division secured Matt's Hollow. Rousseau and Brannan performed equally well, shoving the door to Manchester wide open when they drove Stewart's Rebels almost all the way back to Fairfield. Thomas wrote of their action, "The behavior of our troops was admirable—everything that could be desired."[42]

Rosecrans, meanwhile, had already decided to transfer the XX Corps to Manchester via Hoover's Gap. As early as 1:15 a.m. on June 26, he ordered McCook, after making "a sharp attack" at Liberty Gap, to "as soon as possible get your whole force across the Manchester pike, and follow in rear of General Thomas." McCook complied, reversing the order of his divisions. Sheridan's command now led the way, followed by Richard Johnson's and then by the division of Jef. Davis, whose men drew the task of serving as rear guard, holding Liberty Gap until the 27th.[43]

Though they did no fighting that day, Sheridan's troops, much like the men of the XXI Corps, regarded June 26 as one of the harder days of the whole campaign. The regimental history of the 36th Illinois recorded the day's miseries. "We were up at three o'clock, marched a little way, and then halted until eleven o'clock," noted the unit's historian. "Again it commenced to rain—if rain it might be called which came in such torrents that rubber was no protection—and the water varied from ankle to waist deep, with mud in proportion. The men pronounced it the hardest they had ever seen. We . . . camped at the entrance to Hoover's Gap, on the McMinnville [Manchester] pike, having marched only about four miles."[44]

Early on the morning of June 27, Wilder's Lightning Brigade swept into the town of Manchester. "Our regiment started in the advance and went into Manchester on a gallop," noted Maj. James Connolly of the 123rd Illinois Mounted

41 "The retreat of Bragg's Army," *The Daily Press* (Nashville, TN), August 13, 1863. This letter was written on July 7, printed in the Mobile Register, and then reprinted in *The Daily Press* a month later. Northern and Southern papers often scanned each others pages for content they could reprint.

42 *OR* 23, pt. 1, 420, 431, 610; "Manchester, Tennessee, June 27," *The Daily Press*, June 30, 1863.

43 *OR* 23, pt. 2, 450.

44 Lyman G. Bennett and William M. Haigh, *History of the Thirty-Sixth Regiment Illinois Volunteers, During the War of the Rebellion* (Aurora, IL: 1876), 437.

Infantry; "we swept by the deserted fortifications . . . on a full run, and while the citizens were at their breakfast tables we dashed into the public square, scattered out in small parties, and in five minutes every street and alley was occupied by Yankees . . . a rebel major and about 50 soldiers, left as a rear guard, were captured and marched to the courthouse." Colonel Wilder reported the captures as "about 40 prisoners, including 1 captain and 3 lieutenants." Benjamin Magee, historian of the 72nd Indiana, later wrote that "a lot of Commissary stores," as well as "300 prisoners," were captured.[45]

Thomas wasted no time in funneling the rest of his corps into Manchester. Reynolds and his remaining two brigades arrived next, around midmorning, while Wilder established extended picket lines around the town. The other three divisions of the XIV Corps closed up that evening, with Negley's troops arriving at 9:45 p.m., while Rousseau and Brannan, moving via Fairfield, got there between 1:00 and 3:00 a.m. on the 28th. By daylight, Thomas's entire XIV Corps was present and concentrated at Manchester, just 11 miles from Bragg's newly established headquarters at Tullahoma.[46]

McCook's men soon followed suit. Sheridan's division followed Rousseau and Brannan on the 27th, moving first to Beech Grove and then via Fairfield. Sheridan's 2nd Brigade, commanded by Col. Bernard Laiboldt, had a brief encounter with "a regiment of rebel infantry and one of cavalry" in Fairfield around 3:00 p.m. General Stewart's men were already on their way by then, not to Wartrace, but to Tullahoma. Stewart acted on a 4:00 a.m. order from Hardee "to put your command in motion at daylight this morning" for the latter location. Presumably these last two regiments were Stewart's rear guard, but if so, no surviving account documents either their identity or their orders. Any skirmishing that occurred during these movements was slight: Laiboldt's brigade reported only four men wounded for the entire campaign.[47]

The rest of McCook's corps was astride the Manchester Pike near Hoover's Gap by the end of June 27, while the last elements of Davis's division cleared Liberty Gap by late morning. These maneuvers put them all within easy striking distance of Manchester by early on June 28.

---

45 Angle, *Three Years in the Army of the Cumberland*, 94-95; OR 23, pt. 1, 459; Magee, *72nd Indiana*, 133.

46 OR 23, pt. 1, 435, 442; Walker, "A History of 1st Brig.," Thomas Papers.

47 OR 23, pt. 1, 423, 514-515; ibid., pt. 2, 888.

At long last, the XXI Corps was finally closing in on Manchester. At 6:00 a.m. on the 28th, having managed some rest after their titanic struggle with the thick, seemingly bottomless Tennessee mud, they set off for Manchester. Instead of leading the Federal advance into that place, however, Crittenden's men discovered that almost the entire Army of the Cumberland had preceded them.[48]

June 26 proved to be the critical day of the Tullahoma Campaign, at least thus far. Once Rosecrans discovered that Crittenden's men could not adhere to his timetable and reach Manchester that day, he could have opted to halt and consolidate his gains, reasoning that Bragg would have discovered the object of his movement. Such a decision also could have led to Rosecrans giving up the flanking attempt as a failed gambit. Instead, thanks to Wilder's success on June 24, the Federal commander simply switched his main effort, letting Thomas and the XIV Corps assume the lead.

William Rosecrans's campaign might have been slowed, but it certainly had not been stopped.

---

48 Ibid., pt. 1, 521.

Maj. Gen. Simon Bolivar Buckner, commander,
Department of Virginia and East Tennessee, tasked with
reinforcing Bragg's Army of Tennessee.

Library of Congress

The Confederate Response,
June 23 to 27, 1863

"*Publish* an article to this effect," ordered Francis M. Paul, the editor of the *Rebel* in Chattanooga, Tennessee:

"We are happy to see that re-enforcements continue to arrive for Bragg's army. Our trains to-day are loaded with troops," &c. Don't mention the names of the commanders.

So wrote Col. Alex McKinstry to Francis Paul on the evening of June 24 in yet another attempt to plant a bit of disinformation in Rosecrans's mind, which should have been easy enough since the *Daily Rebel* was widely read by both armies. In a follow-up the next day, McKinstry urged Paul specifically to mention Breckinridge's division as being returned from Mississippi. This was not true, of course, because Joseph Johnston needed every man he had to confront Grant.[1]

As for actual assistance, Bragg could count on very little. The recent departure of the IX Corps from Kentucky, where Maj. Gen. Ambrose Burnside had been poised to move into East Tennessee until tapped to help Grant, relieved pressure on Burnside's Confederate counterpart, Maj. Gen. Simon B. Buckner, in Knoxville. Since the end of the Kentucky Campaign the previous fall, both Bragg and President Jefferson Davis had regarded East Tennessee as a subsidiary of Bragg's department, from where Bragg could summon troops in times of need; concrete plans to do so were already in place. Buckner's overall force numbered

---

1 *OR* 23, pt. 2, 885.

only 16,000, however, with most of those troops scattered across the district in static garrisons. Nevertheless, Buckner had reorganized his command to free up a small division, and (to Richmond at least) he appeared ready to help, wiring Secretary of War Seddon on June 18 that he would "co-operate cheerfully with General Bragg."[2]

By the middle of June, President Davis was contending with numerous requests for reinforcements from across the entire Confederacy. Every day, the crisis in Mississippi grew increasingly desperate. Davis, who hailed from that state and whose own property had been despoiled by invading Federals, was bombarded with appeals for help from that quarter, both official and unofficial. On June 15 Johnston sent the Confederate war department a particularly distressing cable, which suggested that disaster was inevitable somewhere. "I cannot advise in regard to the points from which troops can best be taken," he warned, "nor is it for me to judge which it is best to hold—Mississippi or Tennessee; that is for the Government to determine." But, Johnston continued, "[w]ithout some great blunder of the enemy we cannot hold both." Gloomily, he concluded, "I consider saving Vicksburg hopeless." Writing privately on June 22, the president's brother Joseph beseeched, "Can the Army of Genl Bragg be sent to the relief of Vicksburg? The safety of the Confederacy is involved." On June 24, Joseph Davis wired again, pleading, "is it possible to reinforce [Joseph E.] Johnston or Vicksburg must fall." Davis could only reply, "[r]einforcements to the extent now asked [are] impossible without ruin to the confederacy."[3]

Simultaneously, in Virginia, Robert E. Lee was poised to cross the Potomac River and take the war into Union territory. Despite the fact that he already had been substantially reinforced in order to conduct his campaign in the north, Lee wrote to Davis on June 23, urging him to transfer Gen. P. G. T. Beauregard and a significant force from the Carolinas to Virginia, concentrate them at Culpeper Courthouse, and create at least the appearance of a new Confederate army poised to attack Washington while the Army of Northern Virginia moved into Pennsylvania. By doing so, Lee speculated, "we might even hope to compel the recall of some of the enemy's troops from the West."[4]

2 Ibid., 855, 876-877.

3 *OR* 24, pt. 1, 227; Lynda L. Crist, Mary S. Dix, and Kenneth H. Williams, eds., *The Papers of Jefferson Davis,* 14 vols. to date (Houston, TX: 1971-2015), 9: 235, 239.

4 Crist, *Papers of Jefferson Davis,* 9: 235.

Had it come sooner, or been discussed more fully, Lee's proposal might have had real merit. Given the burgeoning crisis in Mississippi, however, it came far too late to be implemented. Bragg faced a similar situation. Having already lost a quarter of his army to Johnston, he could not count on men returning to Tennessee, or on rapid reinforcements from any other region. With no real hope of regular Confederate troops coming to his aid (except perhaps a handful from Buckner, if summoned), Bragg resorted to a more extraordinary appeal: he wanted Tennessee Governor Isham G. Harris to call out the militia.

"On June 6, the Confederate government" asked the state of Tennessee to provide "six thousand men . . . for local defense and special service." They were to be mustered in on August 1, serving for six months. In response, "Harris issued a stirring proclamation on June 22" from the headquarters of the secessionist government at Winchester, south of the Elk River and 35 miles south of Shelbyville. A similar call, for another 8,000 men, came from Georgia Governor Joseph E. Brown the next day. Given the late timing, neither summons provided Bragg with immediate relief.[5]

That same Monday, June 22, Bragg outlined his appreciation of his circumstances, interlaced with a litany of complaints, in a lengthy letter to Johnston. He opened with news of his health—never good, but which at least had shown some improvement. "Since parting with you I have at no time been well enough until now to say that I am fit for duty, though I have not given up," Bragg wrote. For much of the previous month, however, he had suffered a "general breakdown." During that time, his opponents were busy shuffling troops. Though he correctly perceived that "the largest portion of Burnside's forces . . . have . . . gone to Grant," he doubted whether "Rosecrans is at all reduced." By "call[ing] in all . . . outposts" and stripping Missouri and western Tennessee, he estimated that "some 30,000 men have been collected" by the Federals, destined for either Mississippi or for Nashville—more than enough troops to replace those lost by Burnside.

Then Bragg grumbled about recalcitrant subordinates. "Hearing of the evacuation of Kentucky [the IX Corps's departure], I ordered Morgan's division at once to move into that State, and asked [Simon B.] Buckner to let Pegram cooperate. Morgan, as usual, was not ready; wanted a week, but was refused and ordered off." And despite Buckner's reassurances to Richmond, Bragg found the

5 Sam Davis Elliott, *Isham G. Harris of Tennessee: Confederate Governor and United States Senator* (Baton Rouge, LA: 2010), 142; Crist, *Papers of Jefferson Davis*, 9: 236.

Knoxville commander neither cooperative nor cheerful. The two men squabbled over troop dispositions. Bragg was especially dissatisfied with "[Brig. Gen. John] Pegram's rapid retreat before an inferior force—a mere raid," and with the failure of either Buckner or Pegram to coordinate with Morgan in an attempt to capture those Federal raiders. "It seems [Buckner] has been to Richmond and arranged matters his own way," complained Bragg. He closed this missive with flattery, sympathizing with Johnston's own perceived woes in Mississippi. "I feel most acutely for you, general, in the position in which you find yourself," he concluded. "Great ends to be secured, high expectations formed, and most inadequate means furnished. . . . [W]hatever the result, general, I bear witness you are not responsible for the dangers brought upon us." Presumably, by extension, neither was Bragg himself.[6]

Despite the ominous gathering of Union hosts, neither Bragg nor his senior subordinates quickly awakened to the danger posed by Rosecrans's movements, which commenced the very next day. Stanley's and Granger's probes on June 23 triggered no unusual flurry of messages. Bragg did not even notify Richmond of the activity, almost certainly because these Federal efforts seemed like just another round of the small-scale thrust-and-parry that had characterized operations in Middle Tennessee for the past six months. Perhaps their only substantial effect on Confederate operations was in delaying Wheeler's proposed "dash" against the Union line of communications by a day. In a letter home, Lt. George Knox Miller of the 8th Confederate Cavalry explained that on the 23rd, his regiment "started towards Columbia. We had gone about eight miles when we were recalled to assist Gen. Wharton. . . . [A]fter a round or two night came on, and we proceeded on our course, Gen. Wheeler supposing that it was nothing more than a foraging part[y] of Yankees." Wheeler then took Miller's brigade to Spring Hill, which it reached sometime early on June 24.[7]

Someone at Bragg's headquarters should have thought to pay more attention to the army's existing cavalry screen, especially to the east, covering Hoover's Gap and the Manchester approaches. No one did. Bragg, not realizing how completely Morgan had exceeded his orders, thought his flanks were still adequately protected, and he assumed Wheeler had things well in hand on the Shelbyville front.

---

6 OR 52, pt. 2, 499-500.

7 Richard M. McMurry, ed., *An Uncompromising Secessionist: The Civil War of George Knox Miller, Eighth (Wade's) Confederate Cavalry* (Tuscaloosa, AL: 2007), 140-141. Had Wheeler not turned back to support Wharton, he would have been in Spring Hill on the 23rd and perhaps beyond effective recall by June 24.

Among the more unusual visitors to army headquarters on June 23 was the actress Pauline Cushman. Miss Cushman had fled south from Nashville some weeks earlier, ostensibly exiled from the Union lines due to her ardent and vocal expressions of Southern sympathy. By late June, the Confederates had reason to suspect that she was a Union spy. One correspondent of the *Savannah Republican* dubbed her "a crinoline scout," averring that she was discovered with "plans and drawings of [Confederate] fortifications" hidden on her person. Arrested by Forrest's cavalry, she was sent first to Columbia, and then to Shelbyville. Cushman's own highly dramatized account of her meeting with Bragg, reproduced as verbatim dialogue, reflects a general eager for news of his foe:

Bragg: Where is General Rosecrans's army located?

Pauline: I do not know. I only know that his head-quarters are at Murfreesboro.

Bragg: I should like to meet him. We have been waiting for some time, and when he comes, I shall give him a warm reception.

After that exchange, Bragg sent Cushman off under guard until a court-martial could be convened to consider her fate. She took ill at this time (possibly feigned), and was confined to a local hotel room.[8]

The next day's events also failed to produce any immediate action by Bragg, who was still attempting to make sense of the various reports now reaching headquarters. That night Hardee checked in, alerting both Bragg and his divisional commanders of the combats in each other's sector. "On the evening of June 24," noted Capt. Irving Buck of Maj. Gen. Patrick Cleburne's staff, "Hardee informed Cleburne that the enemy in force had advanced simultaneously on Liberty and Hoover's Gaps, and carried both positions." Cleburne already knew what had transpired at Liberty Gap, since Liddell's brigade of his own division had defended it, but word of the loss of Hoover's Gap was new, and potentially troubling. Hardee first learned of that fight when A. P. Stewart reported in at 3:45 p.m. Though that dispatch is lost, its contents can be inferred from Hardee's response, sent at 4:30 p.m. Hardee ordered Stewart to "collect the scattered regiments of cavalry

---

8 William J. Christen, *Pauline Cushman, Spy of the Cumberland: An Accounting and Memorandum of Her Life* (Roseville, MN: 2006), 126, 129-130. Though Cushman played up her role as a Union spy to great effect after the war and included many fanciful details in her writings and stage presentations, her presence at Shelbyville during the Tullahoma Campaign is well documented.

Maj. Gen. William J. Hardee, commander,
Hardee's Corps, Army of Tennessee.

Library of Congress

mentioned in your dispatch of 3:45 p.m., and, leaving enough to cover your front, send the remainder in pursuit of the enemy's force that has passed on in the direction of Manchester." Further, Hardee queried, "was there artillery with the enemy's cavalry?" If so, that would suggest a more substantial Federal move to follow. Hardee, however, was not willing to risk dividing his forces so greatly as to send infantry to Manchester, especially after he gleaned the details of the Liberty Gap fight. That news clearly triggered Hardee's 10:30 p.m. dispatch to Stewart, mentioned earlier, ordering the latter to "fall back gradually toward Wartrace."[9]

The most alarming news in Stewart's 3:45 p.m. report was the mention of a Union cavalry force headed for Manchester. Although no substantial Union force was yet approaching Manchester on June 24, and none moving via Hoover's Gap, Stewart relayed information obtained from brigade commander William Bate, who had reported some unknown force of Union cavalry working around to his rear. In addition to ordering Stewart to send whatever force of Rebel cavalry he could collect after those Federals, Hardee relayed this news to Bragg. At 6:15 p.m. Bragg informed Leonidas Polk that he was sending John Wharton and two cavalry regiments to Manchester, instructing Polk to replace them with "a regiment of infantry on the Murfreesborough pike, to support [the Rebel] outpost[s]." Additionally, either late on June 24 or early on the 25th, Bragg alerted Simon B. Buckner in Knoxville that the Federals were on the move, and requested immediate reinforcements. Beyond that limited response, however, Bragg continued to await developments.[10]

Underlying this apparent lack of concern about a larger threat to Manchester was a fundamental uncertainty among the army's senior commanders concerning Bragg's strategy, never resolved in spite of the Army of Tennessee's six months of relative inactivity in Middle Tennessee. Everyone—from Johnston and Bragg on down to the privates in the ranks—expected Rosecrans to move eventually. What the Confederate response should be when that day came, however, never crystalized into a concrete plan of action, be it attack, defend, or conduct a wholesale retreat.

In his "sketch" of the beleaguered Army of Tennessee penned in the 1880s, A. P. Stewart observed, "some time before the Battle of Murfreesboro General Bragg . . . remarked that he would never again 'use the spade'; that in the beginning of the war he had been compelled to resort to it, but he thought it did not suit the Genius of the Southern people, and he would not use it again. Subsequent events made clear his error." Given the scope of the earthworks constructed by Rebel troops at Shelbyville, Wartrace, Tullahoma, and at the various gaps, Stewart's remark seems

9 Buck, *Cleburne and His Command,* 130; OR 23, pt. 2, 883-884.

10 Elliott, *Soldier of Tennessee,* 91; Bragg's message to Buckner is lost, but the request can be inferred from Buckner's response on June 25. See OR 23, pt. 2, 885.

curious. Clearly Bragg relied on "the spade" extensively that summer. But Stewart did not necessarily intend for his comment to be taken literally; he meant it to demonstrate Bragg's strong preference for the offensive. Given the chance, Bragg attacked; he had done so at Shiloh, at Perryville, and at Murfreesboro. In Stewart's view, this was a mistake. He argued that if Bragg had dug in and let Rosecrans attack him, "possibly . . . [Bragg] might have held Murfreesboro through the winter, and until his army could be sufficiently reinforced to enable it to take the offensive."[11]

There was, of course, little chance of any reinforcement beyond whatever limited resources Buckner might provide, ruling out any prospect of a grand offensive. As noted, this left Bragg to contemplate a defensive-offensive strategy, withholding his strike until his opponent's movement was underway, then exploiting any opportunity that arose. It was the textbook solution for an outnumbered force. It also required highly effective intelligence gathering by Bragg's cavalry to distinguish the main attack from any feints and false alarms, and a clear understanding of the mission by all the army's subordinates, so they could perform their roles properly when the time came.

"Never," according to Army of Tennessee historian Thomas L. Connelly, "did either Bragg or Johnston fear a massive [Union] move via Columbia, but instead always considered that Rosecrans would feint in that direction." This was because, as previously noted, such a move would take the Union army away from Bragg's primary line of communications, not toward it. Instead, the area of greatest vulnerability always lay on the Rebel right, from as far as McMinnville (unlikely as a main objective but, as seen in Union planning, very likely to be a secondary goal) to Manchester, Wartrace, and Shelbyville. This expectation simplified matters, allowing the Confederates to concentrate both their cavalry and infantry assets with that threat uppermost. Additionally, Bragg's extensive spadework at Wartrace and Shelbyville lengthened the odds against Rosecrans making his main approach via either Liberty or Guy's Gaps, since doing so would lead to a frontal assault against heavily fortified Shelbyville. This left a move on Manchester, via Hoover's and

---

11 Alex. P. Stewart, "The Army of Tennessee. A sketch," in John Berrien Lindsley, ed., *The Military Annals of Tennessee, Confederate, First Series: Embracing a Review of Military Operations, with Regimental Histories and Memorial Rolls, Compiled from Original and Official Sources*, 2 vols. (Nashville, TN: 1886), 2: 79.

Gilley's Gaps, as the most likely threat—one foreshadowed by the Union thrust toward McMinnville in late April.[12]

Joseph E. Johnston's view, as articulated to Col. W. Preston Johnston back on March 24, was that Rosecrans would advance "through Manchester or . . . McMinnville. If he makes this move, and our forces fall back from Manchester to Tullahoma, he exposes his flank, and could gain nothing by it." Further, opined General Johnston, even "if he attained our rear without defeat from a flank attack, we could afford to exchange bases." On April 15, Preston Johnston wrote a much more detailed report, shedding some additional light on the Army of Tennessee's plans. "Tullahoma is regarded as the central point, but the greater part of the army is to the left [west] of it. It is not the intention or expectation of Generals Johnston and Bragg to await attack there, unless made in front, and this they do not expect. They believe that Rosecrans will attempt to pass our flank, most probably our right flank; in which case we would go out and attack him." At the time of this report, Hardee's corps was concentrated at Tullahoma, with a brigade each at Manchester and Wartrace, and Polk's corps was stationed around Shelbyville.[13]

Hardee dissented from his superiors' view. He disliked the army's reliance on Tullahoma as a base, and "preferred Decherd, as stronger and less easily turned." Here, Hardee followed 19th century military orthodoxy, which, as articulated by the Baron Antoine Henri de Jomini in 1838, asserted that "bases perpendicular to those of the enemy are more advantageous" than those "parallel to that of the enemy." A perpendicular line of communications directly to the rear was much harder to sever than one leading off to either flank. "The great art of properly directing lines of operation," Jomini concluded, "is so to establish them . . . to seize the communications of the enemy without imperiling one's own, and is the most important and most difficult problem in strategy."[14]

From Tullahoma, Bragg's line of communications ran through Decherd, 14 miles to the southeast and just across the Elk River. Decherd also lay 24 miles due south of Manchester, meaning that a Union force at Manchester could threaten the Confederate line of communications at Decherd directly, without first having to push through any Rebels massed at Tullahoma. Thus, Decherd was the theoretically stronger position, but at Decherd the Confederates would be

---

12 Connelly, *Autumn of Glory*, 116.

13 *OR* 23, pt. 2, 617-618, 724, 760.

14 Ibid., pt. 2, 760; Baron Antoine Henri de Jomini, *The Art of War* (London: 1992), 79, 120-121.

positioned too far south to be able to realistically defend the gaps in the Highland Rim. A retreat to Decherd would have effectively surrendered yet another large swath of Middle Tennessee, and its vital foodstuffs, to the Federals. Accordingly, Bragg settled on Tullahoma.

Further dispute occurred over the extent and quality of Tullahoma's fortifications. According to Colonel William Johnston, the works were "too weak to rely upon, and too strong to abandon to the enemy." Instead, he suggested that they should "be put in condition to be held by a small force against a larger one." This was also military orthodoxy. Bragg, however, did not want or expect to fight at Tullahoma. He intended to engage Rosecrans on the move. Colonel Johnston wrote (in a comment bolstering A. P. Stewart's postwar observation) that "General Bragg says heavy intrenchments demoralize our troops, and that he would go forward to meet the enemy, in which case that abatis would be an obstruction, to say the least."[15]

For the modern reader, all this inter-army discussion raises two very important questions. First, why did Joseph E. Johnston think Bragg's Army of Tennessee could afford to "exchange bases" with Rosecrans? Presumably, the Confederates understood how heavily fortified and well protected Rosecrans's Murfreesboro base really was, and that it would take a major large-scale effort, and perhaps a full siege, to capture it. In the meantime, would the Federals merely sit on their hands while the Confederates attempted it? Second, why did Bragg not want to put Tullahoma in a like condition? At the very least, a stout defense of Tullahoma by some portion of his army would buy him additional time to meet and defeat Rosecrans on a field of Bragg's choosing.

Unfortunately, the existing record is silent on both questions, suggesting that neither Bragg nor Johnston worked up any detailed plans to counter Rosecrans's advance. The extant comments of both men reflect only the haziest of musings, amounting to little more than the mouthing of military platitudes rather than a real plan of action. Speculatively, one hint to Bragg's thinking might be found in his desire to oversee the restoration of the Nashville & Decatur Railroad. A second functioning railroad would give Bragg an alternative line of communication and supply while operating against Rosecrans's flank or rear. It might even allow him to threaten Nashville, a possibility Rosecrans absolutely could not ignore. But as of late June, that railroad was still many weeks from operating and of no immediate

15 OR 23, pt. 2, 761.

Lt. Gen. Leonidas Polk, commander,
Polk's Corps, Army of Tennessee.

Library of Congress

use; nor did Bragg suggest its availability in any of his discussions of the upcoming campaign.[16]

16 Jeffrey L. Nash, *Destroyer of the Iron Horse: General Joseph E. Johnston and Confederate Rail Transport, 1861-1865* (Kent, OH: 1991), 57-66.

When Bragg ordered Hardee's corps to shift from Tullahoma to Wartrace in late April, he had advanced his army's center of gravity northward, moving closer both to the all-important gaps and to Polk's corps at Shelbyville. Hardee liked the position at Wartrace even less than he liked Tullahoma, but he dutifully established his headquarters at Beech Grove. John C. Breckinridge's division, with Brig. Gen. Benjamin H. Helm's brigade in the lead, was covering Hoover's Gap and the Manchester approaches. Six weeks later, Breckinridge departed. Stewart's newly constituted division took over that duty and left Hardee feeling so much reduced that on June 5 he informed Bragg, "my command is too much scattered for easy concentration." Presciently he added that "an enterprising enemy could force a passage through Liberty Gap and cut my command in two, dividing the force about Hoover's Gap from the force about Wartrace and Bell Buckle. It seems to me that Hoover's Gap is too far removed to be defended stubbornly unless with a large force, for it can be turned by Readyville and Bradyville." Most tellingly, Hardee noted, "the dispositions of my forces were made with the belief that we should fight at Tullahoma, and in that view the concentration would be easy. If it is your intention to fight elsewhere, other dispositions should be made." But no "other dispositions" were made, leaving Hardee to conclude that the army would indeed fight at Tullahoma. This explained Hardee's June 24 order instructing Stewart to fall back on Wartrace instead of blocking the way to Manchester.[17]

And what of Bishop Polk? Was his understanding of the situation any better than Hardee's? After all, if the main Union blow came against Hardee's lines, Polk's 16,500 men would become Bragg's *masse de décision*. Their attack would likely decide the campaign. But according to Thomas Connelly, Polk "seemed to have known practically nothing of Bragg's idea of a flank attack from Shelbyville." Further, "Bragg's notion of having Hardee make a stand at Tullahoma evidently was not even discussed with Polk before the crisis arose."[18]

The reality is that Bragg and Polk, though superficially cordial, had long since lost respect for each other's soldierly abilities. To Bragg, it seemed useless to give Polk orders at all. In a lengthy letter to President Davis on May 22, Bragg fumed that "with all his ability, energy, and zeal, General Polk, by education and habit, is unfitted for executing the orders of others. He will convince himself his own views are better, and will follow them without reflecting on the consequences." This

---

17 Nathaniel Cheairs Hughes, Jr., "William Joseph Hardee, C.S.A. 1861-1865," PhD thesis, University of North Carolina, 1959, 244; *OR* 23, pt. 2, 862.

18 Connelly, *Autumn of Glory,* 117.

shocking condemnation should have convinced Davis that either Bragg or Polk had to go, but in keeping with his previous lassitude toward the army's command problems, he took no action. Accordingly, while both men made their headquarters in Shelbyville, they spent no time discussing strategy. Astonishingly, they "continued to observe surface amenities—dining at one another's headquarters, sharing parade ground camaraderie, attending worship services together, exchanging civil correspondence." Polk even attended Bragg's baptism on June 2, though the fact that Polk's good friend, Bishop Stephen Elliott of Georgia, performed the ceremony may have influenced his decision.[19]

* * *

Bragg's inaction on June 24 can be explained away by uncertainty, as he chose to await further developments. The similar calm that prevailed at headquarters on June 25, however, is less explicable. Though the thrust of Gordon Granger's Union Reserve Corps and most of the Yankee cavalry toward Guy's Gap had dissipated (Granger's force was already turning eastward toward McCook and Thomas), the fighting at Liberty Gap intensified. The action became heavy late that afternoon, ending when the Federals drove Liddell's Arkansans completely out of the south end of the gap, a success which seemed to confirm Hardee's worry about his corps being cut in two. And though no immediate Federal lunge south from Hoover's Gap toward either Manchester or Wartrace took place that day, there was an observable concentration of Union infantry at the gap, as evidenced by the skirmishing and artillery fire between Stewart's men and troops of the XIV Corps.

Aside from two more efforts by Colonel McKinstry to plant false intelligence amidst the newsprint columns of the *Daily Rebel* (one each on the 24th and 25th), only two important messages crossed Bragg's desk on June 25. The first was sent by Mackall to Maj. Duff G. Reed, of Wheeler's Staff, who was still at McMinnville, directing Reed to "report the facts of the advance of the enemy to General Morgan. Order him to assemble his force, and fall on their rear if they pass him." Further, Reed was to "notify all commanders of the corps, and have them move *en masse* in the same direction." Mackall's closing reflected the degree of uncertainty then prevalent at army headquarters, due to the lack of information. "Report every half hour, and state the hour in your telegram."[20]

19 *OR* 52, pt. 2, 818.

20 Ibid., 885.

Brig. Gen. John Hunt Morgan, commander,
Morgan's Division, Cavalry Corps,
Army of Tennessee.

Library of Congress

Had Morgan started his great raid on the date he originally intended, June 20, Mackall's wire never would have reached him, for he would have been deep into Kentucky by the time it arrived in McMinnville. But since Morgan had been diverted by Bragg to chase a Union raid into East Tennessee (unsuccessfully, as it turned out), the men of Morgan's division were at that very moment resting and fattening their horses on the lush new summer grass along the south bank of the Cumberland River near Burkesville, Kentucky, just a few miles over the Tennessee line. Morgan himself was at or near McMinnville, arranging for some last-minute supplies. Though Burkesville was about 100 miles north of McMinnville, had Morgan been inclined to obey this order and press his command hard, his 2,500 horsemen could have moved against Rosecrans's supply lines perhaps as early as June 29. John Hunt Morgan, however, had no intention of once more allowing Bragg to thwart his great project—to cross the Ohio River. Instead of obeying Mackall's order, when Morgan returned to his division on July 1, he immediately issued orders of his own; his troopers would cross the Cumberland and head north the very next day.[21]

The second missive came from Knoxville. On June 25, Simon B. Buckner telegraphed a reply to an earlier message from Bragg (which has since been lost). "I have at last made out your dispatch," Buckner wrote. "Your wishes shall be complied with. I can send you two batteries and nearly 3,000 infantry. I will accompany them on your summons. I can move by —— tomorrow." This welcome news promised the arrival of what amounted to a small division, but even

21 Duke, *History of Morgan's Cavalry*, 454.

if Buckner began his move sometime on June 26, it would be at least the 28th before those men reached Bragg.[22]

There is no surviving correspondence of note between Bragg and either Hardee or Polk for this period. Since both Bragg and Polk were in Shelbyville, any discussion that passed between the two men likely occurred in person. In a letter Polk wrote to his daughter on the 25th, he dismissed the day's action as "a demonstration along all our front with cavalry, infantry and artillery." He did not yet regard it as significant. There is also no record of Bragg and Hardee meeting that day. Instead, the Army of Tennessee simply awaited Rosecrans's next moves.[23]

*   *   *

Like their commanders, the rank and file of Polk's corps had little to do but wait. During this time, Pvt. Simon Mayer of the 10th Mississippi merely recorded that "from the 24th to the 26th all remained quiet." Lieutenant Martin Van Buren Oldham of the 9th Tennessee Infantry, much like his Yankee counterparts, complained mostly about the rain. On June 24 he noted, "it has been raining the whole day. We went out to work but soon came back without doing much work. Who ever saw so much rain for this time of year[?]" The next day he wrote, "there was fighting on our right [Liberty Gap] yesterday and today." Continuing, Oldham complained, "it has been raining all day. It is rumored that Vicksburg has fallen." Then, on a personal note, he added, "I am going to a wedding in the country tonight as soon as the roll is called. Several will go with me. All without permission." Only on June 26 did Oldham reference the unfolding Union advance. "Rosy is advancing and we were ordered to keep two days' cooked rations in our packs," he wrote. "It seems our men were involved in the fight on our right yesterday and the day before." At least he managed a decent meal before the ball opened: "I went to the wedding last night and got my supper."[24]

---

22 *OR* 23, pt. 2, 885. Presumably, Buckner had trouble decoding Bragg's dispatch.

23 "My Dear Daughter," June 25, 1863, Leonidas Polk Papers, University of the South, Sewanee, TN.

24 "The Diary of Major Simon Mayer," June 24-26, 116, www.nps.gov/stri/learn/history culture/upload/SimonMayerDiary.pdf, accessed March, 23, 2019; entries for June 24-26, Martin Van Buren Oldham Diaries, University of Tennessee at Martin, www.utm.edu/ departments/special_collections/E579.5%20Oldham/text/vboldham_1863.php, last accessed March, 23, 2019.

So passed June 25 and the morning of June 26. Then, early in the afternoon of the 26th, Bragg "sent for General Polk . . . to hold a conference in regard to the situation of affairs." According to notes taken by Polk's aide-de-camp, Lt. William B. Richmond, Bragg now believed that Rosecrans's "right was in front of Liberty Gap and threatening that position, while his right [left] extended to the right [Union left] of Hoover's Gap." In response, Bragg "wished General Polk to move his corps out to Guy's Gap . . . that night, and by daylight next morning to move to the right and assail the enemy before Liberty Gap in flank and rear, it being understood that Hardee would press him from the east [south] side at the same time." Appalled, Polk believed the plan deeply flawed and "objected, considering the position he was about to be thrown in nothing short of a man-trap." Bragg, who probably expected some sort of objection on Polk's part, insisted on the move.[25]

Overtaken by events, the plan collapsed within hours. Shortly after this meeting, Bragg received a message from Hardee that upset everything. That missive, timed 2:00 p.m. on the 26th, informed Bragg that "the enemy, with a force supposed to be as large as Hardee's corps, was turning the left [flank] of General Stewart." That force was almost certainly Wilder's Lightning Brigade and Reynolds's division of the XIV Corps, pressing on to Manchester. Faced with an already-intransigent Polk and now armed with this new information, Bragg abandoned all thoughts of an offensive—in effect surrendering the initiative to Rosecrans for the remainder of the campaign.

In a 1998 essay, historian Steven Woodworth postulated that Polk served Bragg poorly here and that Bragg's offensive could have worked—likely forcing, if not the destruction of Rosecrans's army, a hasty retreat to Murfreesboro and an abrupt, ignominious end to the Union offensive. It is hard to see how such a victory could have played out. While Polk's 16,000 effectives certainly could have made their way through Confederate-held Guy's Gap easily enough on June 26, they would have had to contend with Gordon Granger's five brigades of Union cavalry and 7,000 blue-clad infantry at Christiana before turning east to seize the north end of Liberty Gap. Granger's orders for the 27th were to push back toward Guy's Gap, which he did. Woodworth asserts that this move would have been too late to stop Polk, who would have already been "at least four hours east of" Guy's Gap

<hr/>

25 *OR* 23, pt. 2, 618. Lieutenant William B. Richmond, a prewar friend of Polk, was once the treasurer of the Diocese of Tennessee as well as a former officer in the U.S. Navy. Polk regarded Richmond as a "man of coolness, nerve, and judgment . . . whose whole heart is in our cause." See Horn, *Leonidas Polk*, 242.

(assuming a rapid night march). Woodworth further argues that Polk would have captured Liberty Gap easily, establishing contact with Hardee and rendering his other line of retreat—Guy's Gap—unnecessary. Then, being closer to Murfreesboro (Rosecrans's base) than the bulk of Rosecrans's own army was, Polk's presence would have forced a precipitate Union retreat, much as Robert E. Lee had done to Joseph Hooker at Chancellorsville.[26]

Woodworth's thesis seems unlikely, not least because one it's underlying assumption is that Rosecrans, if confronted by a newly aggressive Army of Tennessee, would have imitated "Fighting Joe" Hooker and "turned turtle" while Bragg's plans unfolded. As has been seen, however, Rosecrans had reacted aggressively, not passively, when confronted with a setback—namely, in ordering Thomas to take Manchester in lieu of Crittenden's struggling force. Shifting Polk's corps north of the Highland Rim would have exposed it to complete disaster, much as Polk feared, for there were plenty of Federals in position to deal with Polk's 16,000 men.

A more intriguing theory comes from historian Christopher Kolakowski, presented in his 2011 work on the Stones River and Tullahoma Campaigns. Kolakowski has asserted that "a more fruitful use of Polk's troops would have been to march them the fourteen miles to Fairfield for a morning attack on June 27 toward Hoover's Gap and the Manchester Pike. Combined with Stewart's division, Polk's Confederates would have outnumbered Rousseau's and Brannan's Federals and pushed them back to Hoover's Gap. Choking off that road and pass would have cut Rosecrans's army in two." This suggestion is intriguing. If performed successfully, it would have left half of Thomas's XIV Corps isolated in Manchester, and Crittenden's men still struggling with the bad roads south of Bradyville, while McCook's, Granger's, and Stanley's cavalry all remained on the north side of the Highland Rim. "Such a development," argues Kolakowski, "would have short-circuited Rosecrans's operations."[27]

Perhaps; but it also would have positioned three of Bragg's four divisions directly in the middle of those three Union forces, leaving the Confederate cavalry and Cleburne's division to defend Liberty and Guy's gaps alone, holding off any threat to either Shelbyville or Polk's line of retreat. It also would have rendered

---

26 Steven E. Woodworth, "Braxton Bragg and the Tullahoma Campaign," *The Art of Command in the Civil War,* ed. Steven E. Woodworth (Lincoln, NE: 1998), 165.

27 Christopher L. Kolakowski, *The Stones River and Tullahoma Campaigns: This Army Does Not Retreat* (Charleston, SC: 2011), 123-124.

Tullahoma vulnerable to a Union assault from Manchester, if Thomas were inclined to continue his advance. But by seizing the initiative, Bragg at least would have been moving to disrupt Rosecrans's plan, and doing so while in a much better position than a thrust north of the rim would have left him.

But it was not to be. The Army of Tennessee was not the Army of Northern Virginia. Bragg was not Lee; Polk was not Jackson; and Hardee was not Longstreet. As Kolakowski observed, "there is no record that Bragg, Polk, or Hardee ever considered this option."[28]

Instead, at 4:00 p.m. on June 26, armed with this latest information, Bragg immediately informed Polk, "the movement proposed for to-morrow was abandoned." At 5:00 p.m., in yet another dispatch, Bragg "wishe[d Polk's] judgment as to whether it is possible to hold a line this side of Tullahoma, to strike the enemy successfully this side of Tullahoma, or is a retreat to Tullahoma a necessity?" Polk had little time to contemplate his answer, for as Lieutenant Richmond noted, arriving "at a later hour," Hardee's next dispatch imparted the even more alarming news that—just as Hardee had foreseen—"Stewart's right had also been turned." These Federals were Rousseau's and Brannan's divisions of Thomas's corps, spearheaded by Maj. Sydney Coolidge's regulars. Stewart, now doubly outflanked, was retreating to Wartrace. "At 11 p.m. the general [Polk] received orders to move his command at the earliest practicable hour next morning to Tullahoma. By 11:30 p.m. Polk had sent out the necessary orders to both his divisional commanders."[29]

A mere six hours later, at 5:30 a.m. on June 27, Bragg informed Polk that it was "of the utmost importance that your troops should be put in motion at once. If you think that the cavalry is not enough to protect your wagon train, leave a brigade of infantry." Bragg then closed with a stern warning that "the enemy is pushing to get ahead of us."[30]

Accordingly, Polk's corps lurched into action. Cheatham's large division left Shelbyville headed east. Cheatham intended to cross to the south bank of the Duck River at the Schoeffner Bridge, proceeding to Tullahoma via the Rowesville Road. Jones Withers's division was to move via the Flat Creek Road, parallel to Cheatham, but south of the Duck. The evacuation of the town, and especially its depot, became chaotic. Private John F. Roberts of the 7th Mississippi Infantry, one

28 Ibid., 124.

29 *OR* 23, pt. 1, 618.

30 Ibid., 619.

of Withers's men, recorded the morning's events. "We got orders this morning before day to be ready to march at daylight," he wrote. "It may be the opinion of most all, we are going on front, dident like this at all tho, I don't do as I like now tho." Roberts's regiment was manning part of the earthworks six miles north of town and had to pass through Shelbyville on its way south. Roberts himself soon fell out, footsore, and thus straggled into town after most of the troops had passed. "When I got to Shelbyville the whole army was gone," he wrote. "I saw sevrel piles of corn which we sold at $2 a sack. They either had to sell it or let the yankees get it. The town is in a stare [stir]. We knew the yanks wood soon be in for thar were nothing behind only Whealor's Cavalry. And as soon as we wood leave . . . , the yankees would make them scarce, for the yankees was a flanking us on our right so we had to get a way in a hurry or be cut off."[31]

Though Shelbyville had a considerable number of Unionist citizens who would doubtless welcome any Federals with open arms, there were still pro-Confederate civilians in town as well. Captain William W. Carnes, who commanded an artillery battery in Cheatham's division, recalled the plight of some of the latter. Carnes had been paying special attention to the Whiteside family, especially the two young daughters, Maggie and Ruth, as well as to a Mrs. Mitchell, whose husband served in Cleburne's division. Leaving his battery under the charge of his first lieutenant, Carnes rode into town that morning to find "Mrs. Mitchell and Miss Maggie . . . quite excited over the prospect of being left to meet the Yankee army. . . . Their distress," he recalled, "caused me to ask" some other officers (evidently gathered there for the same purpose—the girls' charms must have been rather considerable) "why [someone] did not devise some means to take them out of the city." Here Mrs. Mitchell cut in, stating, "I will ride behind any officer on his horse to get away from the Yankees." Carnes then put one of his battery wagons at the women's disposal (it was used for their luggage), and worked a deal with "Dr. Rice, Division Surgeon" to borrow an ambulance to carry the ladies away safely. Carnes next secured permission from "Genl. Cheatham . . . to leave the battery in charge of the First Lieut.," while Carnes personally escorted the ladies to Tullahoma.[32]

---

31 Ron Skellie, *Lest We Forget—The Immortal Seventh Mississippi,* 2 vols. (Birmingham, AL: 2012), 2: 522-523.

32 W. W. Carnes, "Flight from Shelbyville," *The Bedford County Historical Quarterly* (Shelbyville, TN), vol. 8, no. 3 (Fall 1982), 82.

Corporal William Mebane Pollard of the 1st Tennessee Infantry, also one of Cheatham's men, was detailed along with the rest of his company "at the depot to load trains." He recalled that the men worked at that duty "until the enemy began firing on out picket in the edge of town. We were then ordered to leave. The boys then at once began to break open boxes stored at the depot, and loaded themselves with clothing, and an abundance of good things, that had been sent to various ones from their homes." Though Bragg later dismissed the loss of army stores during this retreat as trivial, clearly some number of troops suffered considerable personal losses.[33]

Tullahoma lay some eighteen miles to the southeast, and most of Polk's troops began the day some distance north of Shelbyville—for Mississippian John Roberts, six miles—which meant they faced a march of 20 to 25 miles. That was a good day's marching, even in ideal conditions; but on this day, the conditions were far from ideal. Brigadier General Arthur Manigault, commanding one of Withers's brigades, merely recorded that "on the morning of the 27th of June, at daylight, the troops evacuated Shelbyville and moved towards Tullahoma, reaching it about dark on the same evening." That might have been true for the head of the column, but one of Manigault's officers, Lt. Joshua Callaway of the 28th Alabama, described a 24-hour ordeal. "We got to this place (Tullahoma) at day light Sunday morning after an awful march through the rain and mud."[34]

Lieutenant Martin Oldham's diary echoed Callaway's experience: "Instead of fighting as some expected," complained Oldham, "we are now retreating from Shelbyville. The reversal of Gen Stewart's Div [on] the right giving the enemy possession of important [roads] has made this move necessary. The roads are very muddy and we are limping only a few miles." On June 28th, Oldham added: "[We] reached [Tullahoma] today in the rain. We [had] no shelter our tents were burned before leaving Shelbyville. We have had a disagreeable time."[35]

The march was further slowed when both Cheatham's and Cleburne's divisions tried to use the same road. On the night of June 26, noted Capt. Irving

33 William Mebane Pollard diary and recollections, Confederate Collection, Tennessee State Library and Archives, Nashville.

34 R. Lockwood Tower, *A Carolinian Goes to War: The Civil War Narrative of Arthur Middleton Manigault, Brigadier General, C.S.A.* (Charleston, SC: 1982), 74; Hallock, *The Civil War Letters of Joshua K. Calloway*, 106.

35 Entries, June 27-28, Martin Van Buren Oldham Diaries, University of Tennessee at Martin, www.utm.edu/departments/special_collections/E579.5%20Oldham/text/vbold-ham_1863.php, accessed March 23, 2019.

Buck of Cleburne's staff, "orders were received to withdraw to Tullahoma, via Schoef[f]ner's bridge over [the] Duck River." Cleburne departed Wartrace at dawn. According to Lieutenant Richmond, Polk and his staff left Shelbyville at 8:00 a.m. on Saturday, behind Col. Otho F. Strahl's brigade, the last of Cheatham's formations to clear the town. At 1:00 p.m., Polk reached the bridge, where he "found Cleburne's division . . . had cut into the line." Polk ordered Cleburne to halt until Cheatham's men passed.[36]

Cleburne obeyed, but not without frustration. At 6:45 p.m., with his own division's rear still only "1½ miles south of Schoeffner's Bridge," he complained to Hardee that "some of General Polk's officers (Col. [D.M.] Donnell for one) stop his command . . . whenever a wagon breaks down. I ordered him to shove all the wagons which were broken down out of the road, and push on." Donnell refused, saying, "his orders from higher authority were to leave none of the wagons behind." Consequently, the entire column halted whenever a wagon had to be repaired. All the while, fumed Cleburne, "I can hear the enemy's artillery and small-arms on my flank and rear."

This complaint passed quickly up the chain of command, and, reflecting the new sense of urgency now gripping Bragg's headquarters, drew a swift rebuke from the commanding general. At 10:00 p.m. Bragg directed Chief of Staff Mackall to inform Polk that "General Bragg firmly and positively orders you to see that your baggage trains move on, and that those that break down be removed, instantly." As if to amplify the degree of difficulty of this march, Mackall's directive reached Polk at 1:45 a.m on June 28, while Polk was still "in the field, five miles from Tullahoma."

For his part, Polk insisted that Donnell's "conduct . . . is in the highest degree reprehensible, and entirely at variance with orders from these headquarters . . . , the impropriety shall be stopped, and the facts investigated." In his report of the campaign, Cleburne made no mention of the incident, but he did describe the march as exhausting; "the men had no changes of clothing, no tents, and could not even light fires to dry themselves. Many had no shoes, and others left their shoes buried in the deep mire of the roads."[37]

At 11:00 p.m., Bragg received even worse news, which further goaded Polk's and Hardee's struggling infantrymen. To the Bishop General, Bragg immediately

36 Buck, *Cleburne and His Command,* 131; OR 23, pt. 1, 587.

37 OR 23, pt. 1, 587, 619-620.

sent word to "push on your trains at once with the greatest dispatch. Martin's cavalry has been utterly defeated before Shelbyville."[38]

38 Ibid., 620.

Chapter Ten

Minty's Saber Brigade at Shelbyville,
June 27, 1863

*O*n June 23, 1863, the two divisions of Maj. Gen. David S. Stanley's Cavalry Corps—described by a New York newspaper man as the "corps of reliable gentlemen" and about 10,000 sabers strong—broke camp at Murfreesboro and rode toward Tullahoma in two columns. "The tents were scarcely struck in our old camp, when it began to rain in torrents," recalled Thomas B. Dornblaser of the 7th Pennsylvania Cavalry. "The mud was immense" and slowed the rate of march. The severe skirmishing that marked June 24 and 25 was all according to Rosecrans's plan; he wanted Bragg's attention fixed on Shelbyville. That changed on the evening of June 26 with Federals pouring through Hoover's Gap on the way to Manchester. That night, Bragg ordered the Army of Tennessee to abandon Shelbyville and head for Tullahoma. He left Maj. Gen. Joseph Wheeler's cavalry corps behind to hold Guy's Gap and cover the army's retreat.[1]

In the meantime, Col. Robert H. G. Minty's brigade, which had returned to the Shelbyville front by June 25, was now tasked with leading Stanley's advance. On the morning of the 26th, boasted the 7th Pennsylvania's adjutant, "One of the best equipped corps of cavalry in the Union army moved out of camp at daybreak." In

---

1 "Mr. E. D. Westfall's Despatches," *New York Herald*, July 8, 1863; Thomas F. Dornblaser, *Sabre Strokes of the Pennsylvania Dragoons, in the War of 1861-1865* (Philadelphia, PA: 1884), 117. Mitchell's division headed for Guy's Gap while Turchin moved east to link up with Crittenden. On June 25 Stanley recalled Robert H. G. Minty's brigade from Turchin to reinforce Mitchell.

addition, part of Maj. Gen. Gordon Granger's Reserve Corps continued with the cavalry, augmenting the Union strength to more than 13,000 men. This combined force headed for Shelbyville via the Shelbyville Pike, still intent on diverting the Rebels. The movement caught Wheeler by surprise. The Union cavalry drove in the Rebel pickets that day, pressing Wheeler's right and forcing him to draw reinforcements from his left. "The rebels showed a force about equal to ours, and evinced a desire to obstruct our further advance," reported a New York newspaper correspondent traveling with the cavalry. "They were driven slowly along the execrable road, through the village [old Fosterville], till they reached a dense woods beyond it, when they made a desperate stand, opening on our advance with two pieces of artillery. They held the woods and a ploughed field in front of it for an hour, shouting savagely and firing extremely wild."[2]

Divisional commander Brig. Gen. Robert B. Mitchell ordered the 2nd Michigan and 9th Pennsylvania Cavalry to dismount and charge across a field. The dismounted troopers struggled over soggy, plowed ground while drawing heavy fire, but they made it to within 30 yards of the Confederate line of battle, where they returned fire. Their severe volleys broke the enemy line—which proved to be Brig. Gen. William Martin's division of cavalry—and the men fled, leaving behind eight dead along with 60 wounded or dead horses, and carrying off their wounded and two pieces of artillery. By contrast, Mitchell suffered only two killed and six wounded. His men spent the night on the field.[3]

Rumors flew through the Union camps, including an alarming story that the Rebels had disastrously routed Brig. Gen. Philip H. Sheridan's division of McCook's XX Corps and that a vast enemy force was approaching the Reserve Corps on the Shelbyville road. General Granger was unable to obtain any positive information with respect to either of these exciting topics. "So isolated was the reserve that two days passed before we knew exactly where to find Rosecrans's headquarters," reported the correspondent. "During Thursday and Friday there was considerable skirmishing between pickets of the opposing parties, and our infantry were several times drawn up in line of battle, to await and repel an attack."[4]

Once Wilder's Lightning Brigade seized Hoover's Gap, the Confederates were left with no choice but to withdraw from Shelbyville. Rosecrans, realizing that the

---

2 George F. Steahlin, "Stanley's Cavalry. Colonel Minty's Sabre Brigade at Guy's Gap," *The National Tribune*, May 27, 1882; "Mr. E. D. Westfall's Despatches."

3 Ibid.

4 Ibid.

Brig. Gen. John A. Wharton, commander,
Wharton's Division, Cavalry Corps,
Army of Tennessee.

Library of Congress

enemy was now in retreat, ordered Granger's Reserve Corps, spearheaded by Stanley's cavalry, to renew its advance on Shelbyville, hoping to cut off Polk's corps of Confederate infantry as it withdrew toward Tullahoma. Wheeler set out to interpose his command between Stanley's large force and Polk's wagon train.[5]

Shelbyville was known as a town with strong Unionist sympathies and leanings. In the fall of 1862, *Harper's Weekly* described it as "the only Union town of Tennessee," and it had suffered while Bragg made his army's headquarters there. The Confederates referred to the town as a "Union hole," and they treated it as such. About 50 miles southeast of Nashville, Shelbyville sits atop a Highland Rim limestone bluff on the banks of the Duck River, which flows around the southern and eastern edges of the town. It was the seat of Bedford County, laid out in 1810 and incorporated in 1819. The Duck, normally a deep and rapidly flowing river, was even more of an obstacle given the recent heavy rain, and there were only two bridges across it at Shelbyville at that time. The town was also the terminus of a branch rail line to Wartrace on the Nashville & Chattanooga Railroad, making it the commercial center of the area. It had a population of about 1,500 in 1863.[6]

Colonel Abel Streight's April 21, 1863, Lightning Mule Raid had made Bragg nervous, and so, back on April 26, he had written to Wheeler, "There is a danger of the enemy by such movements as that made on the 21st prosecuted by a little more energy and determination." Consequently, he instructed his cavalry chief to

---

5 John Witherspoon Dubose, *General Joseph Wheeler and the Army of Tennessee* (New York: 1912), 175.

6 *Harper's Weekly*, October 18, 1862, 661; Fremantle, *Three Months in the Southern States*, 146; W. H. DePuy, ed., *The World-Wide Encyclopedia and Gazetteer*, 12 vols. (New York: 1908), 12: 2780-2781. This is an exaggeration, for East Tennessee was strongly Unionist. Perhaps it is more accurate to say that Shelbyville was the only Unionist town in Middle Tennessee.

Map 8. The Defenses of Shelbyville

Legend
Fieldworks
Railroad
Road
Stream
Woods
Slope

0   2000
Scale (yards)

establish a cordon of vidette posts along the entire front of the Army of Tennessee. Wheeler obeyed these orders, with John Hunt Morgan's cavalry division stationed to the right, picket posts covering nearly 150 miles through northern Tennessee and into Kentucky, and Wharton's and Martin's commands filling in the rest of the line as far as Shelbyville, where Forrest's cavalry took over. Wheeler himself remained active and vigilant, constantly looking for signs of enemy movement.[7]

In part because Bragg made his headquarters at Shelbyville, an extensive ring of defenses surrounded the town. These earthworks, strong and well designed, extended for miles on either side of the road to Murfreesboro. Lieutenant Colonel Fremantle visited Shelbyville less than a month prior to the beginning of the

7 OR 23, pt. 2, 794; Dubose, *General Joseph Wheeler and the Army of Tennessee*, 166.

Tullahoma Campaign. "The trench itself was a very mild affair, but the higher ground could be occupied by artillery in such a manner as to make the road impassable," he wrote of the town's defenses. "The thick woods were being cut down in front of the lines for a distance of eight hundred yards to give range." A New York newspaper correspondent left a similar description. "Those outer works consisted of a line of rifle pits with flanking batteries, extending from Duck river on the left to Hog Mountain on the right—a distance of eight miles," he wrote. "They had been built regardless of expense, and their completeness, location and finish showed them to be the work of a skillful engineer."[8]

When the Confederate infantry evacuated the town, however, Wheeler's cavalry, as the rear guard, could only occupy small sections of the defenses. Because Morgan and Forrest were not present, Wheeler had only Brig. Gen. William T. Martin's small division and part of Brig. Gen. John A. Wharton's division available to him. The Texans moved out early that morning, headed toward Shelbyville. Robert F. Bunting, serving as the chaplain of the 8th Texas Cavalry of Harrison's brigade, Wharton's division, recalled, "The deserted and burning camps of the infantry and their moving upon the pike awakened the unpleasant conviction that Shelbyville was to be evacuated," he observed. "The splendid fortifications are all deserted, and everything heads toward Dixie."[9]

On June 27, Wheeler's horse soldiers occupied the segment of the line to the north of the town and astride the turnpike. Further, and as General Stanley later noted, "The Confederate commander must have had full confidence in his ability to hold in line his troops, for they were formed with their backs to Duck River, at this time booming full with two bridges only, one back of the center of his line, and one a mile above this on his right flank, connecting with the left bank of the river, and these two bridges his only route of retreat." The events of that day demonstrated that neither Wheeler's cavalrymen nor his dispositions were well suited to a static defensive operation.[10]

Wheeler had only just recalled Martin's division from Spring Hill, from where he had intended to launch his own raid against Rosecrans's communications, until

8 Fremantle, *Three Months in the Southern States*, 146; "Mr. E. D. Westfall's Despatches."

9 Thomas W. Cutrer, ed., *Our Trust is in the God of Battles: The Civil War Letters of Robert Franklin Bunting, Chaplain, Terry's Texas Rangers, C.S.A.* (Knoxville: 2006), 167-168. Wharton's division was already short at least two regiments, which had been sent toward Manchester on June 24.

10 Samuel W. Fordyce, IV, ed., *An American General: The Memoirs of David Sloan Stanley* (Santa Barbara, CA: 2003), 145-146.

Brig. Gen. William T. Martin, commander,
Martin's Division, Cavalry Corps,
Army of Tennessee.

Library of Congress

the Union advance upended that plan. At least some of Martin's men were still en route, with Nathan Bedford Forrest's division following behind. Wheeler expected Forrest's command to reach Shelbyville by the night of June 26. Consequently, Wheeler sent elements of Wharton's division to guard his right flank at Wartrace and then ordered Forrest to hasten with all speed possible, as the enemy's cavalry corps rapidly bore down on Shelbyville. Martin's 1,000 troopers arrived about noon, amid a drenching rain, with every man in his beleaguered command soaked to the skin, and with nine out of 10 rifles unable to be fired due to wet powder. Martin's men took position alongside the rest of Wheeler's troopers, and all hoped that Forrest's command would arrive before Stanley's Federals did.[11]

Fortunately, the Union cavalry had an excellent and experienced commander leading the advance. Thirty-two-year-old Col. Robert Horatio George Minty would be personally engaged in 109 skirmishes and battles over the course of the war. He had five horses shot out from under him. Thirteen enemy bullets pierced his clothing. He was an extremely competent and aggressive cavalry commander, one of the most effective small-unit cavalry officers of the war.[12]

---

11 W. C. Dodson, *Campaigns of Wheeler and His Cavalry 1862-1865* (Atlanta, GA: 1899), 86; Dubose, *General Joseph Wheeler and the Army of Tennessee*, 175.

12 "Military Record of Robert H. G. Minty, in the United States Volunteer Army of the Civil War, 1861-1865," included in the Proposed Volunteer Retired List, *Senate Documents*, vol. 8, 59th Congress, 1st Session (Washington, DC: 1906), 80-81. Minty was born in Westport, County Mayo, Ireland, on December 4, 1831. His father was Irish-born, and his mother was Scots by birth. His father, a respected officer in the British Army, had served in the 1st West India Regiment of Foot, a colored regiment with white officers. After his father died of a tropical fever in 1848, the 17-year-old Minty entered the British army as an ensign and served

Col. Robert H. G. Minty, commander
of the Sabre Brigade, Second Division, Cavalry
Corps, Army of the Cumberland.

Judith Minty

Minty led the 1st Brigade, 2nd Cavalry
Division, Army of the Cumberland, an
excellent, veteran brigade of horse
soldiers. His command included his own
4th Michigan Cavalry, the 4th U.S.
Cavalry (one of the six U.S. regular cavalry
regiments), the 7th Pennsylvania Cavalry,
and a battalion of the 3rd Indiana Cavalry.
Minty's regiments were known for their
proficiency with the saber and were
famous for their thunderous mounted
charges. The men also carried revolvers and a mix of Sharps, Smith, and Burnside

---

contracting a severe attack of inflammation of the liver while serving in Sierra Leone, Minty
sold his commission and emigrated to the United States. Settling in Canada, Minty took up
railroading. He worked for the Great Western Railroad Company, which ran trains between
Niagara Falls on the American side and Sarnia and Windsor, Ontario, on the Canadian side. On
November 11, 1857, he married Grace Ann Abbott of London, Ontario, at St. Paul's Cathedral
in Port Sarnica, Ontario. The newlyweds were described as "a brilliant match . . . , a handsome
couple, well to-do, socially prominent, traveled, proud, and secure." Their first child, Nan R. G.
Minty, was born on September 29, 1858. After Nan's birth, the family moved to Michigan so
that Robert could accept employment with the Detroit and Milwaukee Railway. He was still
working there when the storm clouds of war began gathering in the spring of 1861. Minty was
commissioned a major in the 2nd Michigan Cavalry in 1861, lieutenant colonel of the 3rd
Michigan Cavalry a few days afterward, and colonel of the 4th Michigan Cavalry on July 31,
1862. He commanded the brigade that included the 4th Michigan for most of its service in the
field. The diminutive officer had wild blonde hair and a thick beard. He stood 5'7" and had
hazel eyes. According to the "Military Record of Robert H. G. Minty, in the United States
Volunteer Army of the Civil War, 1861-1865," 80-81, he also had a "clear and ringing voice."
Minty was "natty, fair-haired, and debonair," a devout Episcopalian, a teetotaler who did not
use profanity. He loved music. He had a reputation as "an educated soldier of great intelligence
and enterprise . . . a dandy cavalryman . . . an excellent disciplinarian, and as good a leader as
[Napoleonic marshal Joachim] Murat himself." He was also reputed to be headstrong and
bumptious by nature. A Confederate officer once said, "Colonel Minty is one of the most
gallant and dashing officers in the Federal army, and those who 'scare him up' may count on
having to fight."

carbines—single-shot, breech-loading weapons that could lay down rapid and effective firepower. They were about to prove their mettle at Shelbyville.[13]

The 4th U.S. Cavalry was originally known as the 1st U.S. Cavalry. Organized on March 26, 1855, at Jefferson Barracks in St. Louis, Missouri, it saw its first action in "Bleeding Kansas" the following year. Its early officers included Col. Edwin V. Sumner, Lt. Col. Joseph E. Johnston, and Lt. Col. Robert E. Lee, and its antebellum ranks included Lt. J.E.B. (Jeb) Stuart and Capt. George B. McClellan. With the coming of war in 1861, the U.S. Army's five mounted regiments were all reorganized and redesignated in order of seniority, with the 1st U.S. Cavalry becoming the 4th U. S. Cavalry. Two companies of the 4th briefly served in the war's Eastern Theater as headquarters escort companies with the Army of the Potomac; they rejoined the regiment after the September 17, 1862, Battle of Antietam. In the war's early phases, the 4th's remaining companies saw action in Missouri, Mississippi, and Kentucky and participated in the Forts Henry and Donelson Campaign of 1862. On December 31, 1862, two companies of regulars had charged and routed an entire Confederate cavalry brigade during the Battle of Stones River.[14]

The 7th Pennsylvania Cavalry was raised mainly in Schuylkill County, Pennsylvania, and many of its men came from Pottsville. Colonel George C. Wynkoop, a veteran of the Mexican-American War, was selected as the regiment's first commander when the unit mustered in the fall of 1861, but Wynkoop left the regiment before long, leaving Lt. Col. William B. Sipes to lead it in the field. The new regiment was sent to Nashville, Tennessee, where incessant drilling quickly established its proficiency with the saber. It became so skilled with the blade that it soon earned the moniker "the Saber Regiment of the Army of the Cumberland" at the specific order of Maj. Gen. William S. Rosecrans. The 7th Pennsylvania was a proven, reliable regiment.[15]

---

13 Sipes, *The Saber Regiment*, 46; Vale, *Minty and the Cavalry*, 9.

14 Vale, *Minty and the Cavalry*, 7-29. The other prewar regular army mounted units were the 1st Dragoons, the 2nd Dragoons, the Regiment of Mounted Rifles, and the 2nd U.S. Cavalry. The 1st Dragoons, the oldest mounted unit, became the 1st U.S. Cavalry. The 2nd Dragoons, as next oldest, became the 2nd U.S. Cavalry. The Regiment of Mounted Rifles was redesignated the 3rd U.S. Cavalry. The 1st U.S. became the 4th, and the 2nd became the 5th. A new regiment of regulars, the 6th U.S. Cavalry, was also recruited. These six regular army mounted units never served together as a single brigade or division during the Civil War.

15 OR 23, pt. 1, 30-48, 135-136. Wynkoop was discharged on June 25, 1863, after a long absence due to disability. Sipes was promoted to colonel a month later.

The 4th Michigan Cavalry, Minty's own, was organized in Detroit on August 28, 1862. It departed for duty in Louisville, Kentucky, at the end of September, serving with the Army of the Ohio until November 1862, when the army was renamed upon Rosecrans's arrival. About that time, Minty became brigade commander, so command of the regiment fell to Lt. Col. Josiah B. Park. The 4th Michigan had earned a solid reputation as a reliable, hard-fighting regiment that also was known for its proficiency with the saber.

The remaining formation under Minty's command was a part of the 3rd Indiana Cavalry. Unusually, the 3rd Indiana was divided into an East Wing and a West Wing. The East Wing—Companies A, B, C, D, E, and F—served in the Army of the Potomac's Cavalry Corps. The West Wing—Companies G, H, I, K, L, and M—was organized at Madison, Indiana, on October 1, 1861. Originally, only four companies (G, H, I, and K) were sent west. Two additional companies—L and M—were raised and then assigned to the West Wing in 1862. Lt. Col. Robert Klein commanded the West Wing of the 3rd Indiana Cavalry, having been promoted through the ranks from captain. His battalion joined Minty's cavalry on June 3, 1863, and became an integral part of the brigade.[16]

Minty, the brigade's senior officer, had stepped up to head the brigade in December 1862 when its assigned commander, Col. Edward M. McCook, who had led the brigade at Perryville, fell ill and had to go on sick leave. Minty led the brigade for most of the rest of the war.[17]

Minty had been in command only a few weeks when the Battle of Stones River commenced on December 31, 1862. After a fierce three-hour fight that day, his formation made a determined saber charge against Wheeler's cavalry on the Nashville Pike, which drove Wheeler's troopers from the field. Minty prevailed that day, even though the Confederates had two-and-a-half times as many cavalrymen.[18]

Minty and his Saber Brigade were especially well suited to the challenge that lay ahead of them at Shelbyville.

The bugles blew reveille in the Union cavalry camps at 3:00 a.m. on June 27. The men formed in columns of regiments in an open field in thick fog, preparing to advance on Shelbyville. By 7:00, the fog had burned off and the sun shone brightly. At 8 a.m., Stanley's entire Cavalry Corps was ordered to advance to Shelbyville via

---

16 William N. Pickerell, *History of the Third Indiana Cavalry* (Indianapolis, IN: 1906), 30-52.

17 Sipes, *The Saber Regiment*, 46.

18 Vale, *Minty and the Cavalry*, 117; Fitch, *Annals of the Army of the Cumberland*, 207.

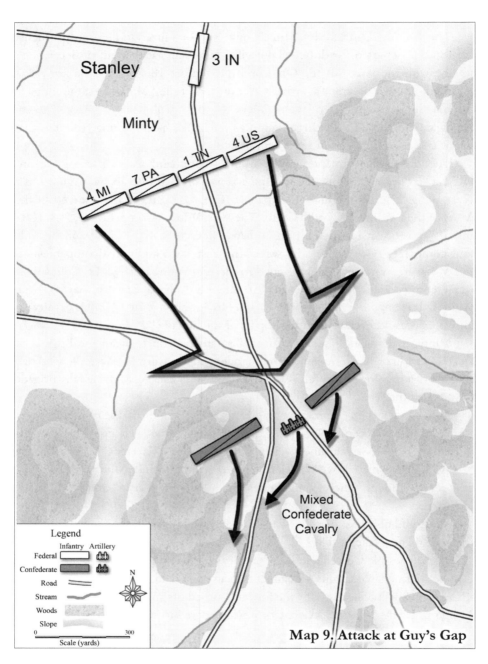

Map 9. Attack at Guy's Gap

Guy's Gap. Though Mitchell's 1st Division led the advance, as the column approached Guy's Gap, Stanley ordered Minty's brigade to the front, with the two additional regiments—the 5th Iowa Cavalry and the 1st Middle Tennessee Cavalry (U.S.)—temporarily assigned to him that morning. Stanley directed Minty to drive into town and head for the lower bridge across the Duck. In addition to his normal command, Mitchell ordered Col. Archibald P. Campbell's 1st Brigade of his division to cut through the fields and seize the upper bridge.[19]

Lieutenant Colonel Fremantle wrote that Guy's Gap was "very strong, and could be held by a small force. The range of hills extends as far as Wartrace, but I understand the position could be turned on the left." He noted that the extreme outposts of the Confederate videttes were two miles beyond Guy's Gap, placing them a full 16 miles beyond the Shelbyville defenses.[20]

Fremantle also described the dispositions of the gray-clad cavalrymen tasked with manning those vidette posts. "The Confederate videttes were at an interval of from 300 to 400 yards of each other," he explained. "Scouts are continually sent forward by both sides to collect information. Rival scouts and pickets invariably fire on one another whenever they meet." The woods on either side of the road and the houses in the area all showed evidence of the results of these daily confrontations. Since Guy's Gap was the only significant pass through the hills nearby, the Southerners knew that any Union thrust toward Shelbyville would have to come through it. The gap's defenders were ready, their mission made even more vital because Forrest, who was expected overnight at the latest, had yet to arrive. Still, on June 27 Wheeler "calculated that the force he had left to hold the Union cavalry in check at Guy's Gap would be able to maintain their position long enough to permit Forrest, who had the greater distance to travel, to effect the junction at the time agreed upon."[21]

Twenty regiments of Stanley's Cavalry Corps moved toward Shelbyville from Christiana, with Granger, Stanley, and Mitchell at the head of a column of fours that stretched along the pike for four miles. "It was a splendid show of strength, and calculated to terrify any force we expected to meet," recalled William R. Carter of the 1st Middle Tennessee. "It was an imposing [sight] to see 10,000 cavalry marching in perfect order, as if on parade, with bands playing and colors flying. As

---

19 Steahlin, "Stanley's Cavalry"; OR 23, pt. 1, 556; Fordyce, *An American General*, 146. Campbell's brigade consisted of three regiments: the 1st East Tennessee Cavalry, the 2nd Michigan Cavalry, and the 9th Pennsylvania Cavalry. The 5th Iowa Cavalry included Brackett's Battalion of Minnesota cavalry, and the 1st Middle Tennessee Cavalry. These were two hodgepodge commands.

20 Fremantle, *Three Months in the Southern States*, 160-161.

21 Ibid., 161; John A. Wyeth, "General Wheeler's Leap," *Harper's Weekly* (June 18, 1898), 601.

we moved forward in line of battle our horses trampled down and destroyed a field of wheat, that was ready for the sickle, but such is war."[22]

The Union cavalry spent a frustrating morning, impatiently waiting for the order to pitch into their foes. "The entire forenoon had passed in that most tiresome of all movements, advance a couple of hundred yards—halt—wait; dismount—wait," Minty recalled years later. One of his staff officers remembered that Minty "was raging like a chained lion at the little progress made." Finally, at about 11:20, one of Stanley's staff officers galloped up and said in a loud voice that could be heard by Minty's entire staff and escort, "Col. Minty, Gen. Stanley directs that you move to the front; that brigade in front is so damned slow he can do nothing with it." Responding, Minty cried out, "Mount—Forward, march—Trot, march," and his command was off. "The advance was sounded, when, for some cause," remembered Sgt. Harry Burns of the 7th Pennsylvania, "the men commenced cheering."[23]

The advancing Union cavalry presented an impressive sight. "A line of dismounted skirmishers nearly two miles in length covered the front; two thousand mounted men in columns of attack moved up the slope, on each side of the road, while on the pike, in serried ranks, pressed forward nearly three thousand more, forming a compact column over three miles in length." As Minty's troopers moved up to take the lead, an infantryman said, "Boys, there's going to be a fight. When them fellows are hurried to the front it means business."[24]

A strong force of Confederate skirmishers held the gap, using fences for shelter. They also had four pieces of artillery in support. A reinforcing column of what the Federals took to be Southern infantry came up, threatening Minty's right. Minty deployed the 4th U.S. to the front, while Stanley led the 7th Pennsylvania, 4th Michigan, and 3rd Indiana to the right. With Stanley personally leading their charge, these men drove the Confederates from their front. Stanley then ordered Minty to attack. The 4th U.S. advanced in line, while Minty and the 1st Middle Tennessee moved forward on the road. Minty then ordered the rest of his command to attack on the right. Lieutenant Colonel Robert Galbraith, commander

22 "Mr. E.D. Westfall's Despatches"; W. R. Carter, "A Story of the War," *Knoxville Journal*, December 10, 1893.

23 Vale, *Minty and the Cavalry*, 175; Robert H. G. Minty, "At Shelbyville, Tennessee. Gen. Minty Corrects the Comrades and Gives a True Account," *The National Tribune*, May 8, 1890; Franklin L. Burns, ed., "Sergeant Harry Burns and the 7th Pennsylvania Volunteer Cavalry," *Tredyffrin Easttown History Quarterly*, vol. 24, no. 1 (January, 1986), 12.

24 Vale, *Minty and the Cavalry*, 175; Sipes, *The Saber Regiment*, 63.

of the 1st Middle Tennessee and a resident of Shelbyville, led a dozen of his men forward to remove a barricade built across the road at the top of a hill. After removing the obstruction, Galbraith and his entire command dug their spurs into their horses' flanks, charged, and drove the Confederates, who fell back rapidly in the face of this ferocious attack. A member of Minty's staff witnessed the Rebels as they "fled in wild confusion, artillery, mounted and dismounted men, all mixed up together and down the road together." Minty, with the 1st Middle Tennessee and the 4th U.S., followed the "mounted [Confederate] force on a run," galloping for nearly three miles.[25]

Private John Wyeth of the 4th Alabama Cavalry, of Joe Wheeler's corps, watched the routed Confederates fleeing from Guy's Gap. "The incessant rains, together with the trampling of horses' hooves, had converted the road to beds of mortar, and these demoralized cavaliers were so bespattered with mud from head to foot that no one could have told what uniform they wore," he recalled. "Many of them were hatless, some had lost their guns, and fully one-half of them seemed to have lost heart and hope." Victorious Union troopers were hot on their heels. "So eager were our pursuers that we had scant time to jeer or 'guy' our unfortunate brothers." Wyeth spotted Joe Wheeler nearby. He and his comrades realized that if Wheeler himself was present to direct their activities, a fight was inevitable.[26]

Minty saw that Galbraith's command had scattered as a result of their successful charge and were gathering up prisoners. In response, Minty halted and formed his command in line of battle awaiting Galbraith's return. While they waited, some of the troopers of the 7th Pennsylvania produced a battered deck of cards and began playing poker to pass the time. Stanley spotted them, watched quizzically for a few moments, and then remarked to Lt. Col. William B. Sipes, the commander of the 7th Pennsylvania, "Did anybody ever see such cool impudence? Sitting down to gamble under fire of a battery of artillery?"[27]

About 20 minutes later, Galbraith sent word that the enemy had rallied and was resisting stoutly. Minty immediately pushed forward with the 7th Pennsylvania, 4th Michigan, and 3rd Indiana. They found the Confederates behind entrenchments about three miles north of Shelbyville, with an abatis of felled trees almost a quarter of a mile wide for the entire length of the entrenchments, and an open space about

25 Vale, *Minty and the Cavalry*, 175; OR 23, pt. 1, 556. Confederate cavalry often fought dismounted, using infantry drill, and were often mistaken for Rebel infantry.

26 Wyeth, "General Wheeler's Leap," 601.

27 OR 23, pt. 1, 556-557; Sipes, *The Saber Regiment*, 63.

a mile in width between the Union cavalry and the Confederate trenches. Minty established a command post at a house on a hill about a mile from the Confederate works. He understood that "he was fighting the whole of the rebel cavalry in the Department, except Forrest's division."[28]

Colonel James D. Webb, commander of Joe Wheeler's 51st Alabama Mounted Infantry, sent Maj. James T. Dye and seven men forward to reconnoiter. The Alabamian took up a position on a knoll with a commanding view of the Shelbyville Pike and soon reported that, "as far as the eye could reach, the broad white pike was filled with the mounted men and artillery of the foe, advancing steadily and confidently." Private Wyeth recalled seeing "a long array of Federal troopers, a deep blue fringe upon the border of the green forest beyond. There were so many of them it did not seem possible for us to stand up before them longer than it would take them to put spurs to their horses and ride over us." The Confederates braced themselves for the overwhelming force that was about to smash into their positions.[29]

Alarmed, and knowing that the tail of Polk's wagon train had only just departed Shelbyville and was completely unguarded, Wheeler sent two of his staff officers to find Forrest to apprise him of the critical state of affairs. They found Forrest's command at a halt, resting. Forrest assured them he would move rapidly toward the sound of the firing (which by then was loud) and would either join Wheeler on the Shelbyville Pike or attack the Union flank. "Tell General Wheeler to, at all hazards, hold the town until I arrive," Forrest added, "or I will be cut off, as the Shelbyville bridge is my only means of crossing Duck River." Forrest had already sent his wagons on a southerly route to Tullahoma, so there was nothing to impede his movements. One of Wheeler's troopers recalled, "while we were fighting this ponderous force of both infantry and cavalry, our brave little band were nerved with the conviction that each movement would bring to view the head of Forrest's column, which since early morning had been every minute expected."[30]

Minty ordered Maj. Charles C. Davis of the 7th Pennsylvania Cavalry to dismount his battalion, deploy as skirmishers, and engage the enemy, which

---

28 OR 23, pt. 1, 557; Vale, *Minty and the Cavalry*, 98, 178. An abatis is a field fortification consisting of an obstacle formed (in the Civil War era) of the branches of trees laid in a row, with the sharpened tops directed outward, toward the enemy. The trees are usually interlaced or tied with wire.

29 Dubose, *General Joseph Wheeler and the Army of Tennessee*, 175; Wyeth, "General Wheeler's Leap," 601.

30 Dodson, *Campaigns of Wheeler and His Cavalry*, 88.

Brig. Gen. Nathan Bedford Forrest, commander,
Forrest's Division, Army of Tennessee.

Library of Congress

promptly opened on the attacking Federals with artillery. Minty also ordered Maj. Frank W. Mix, commander of the 4th Michigan, to go to the right about three-quarters of a mile and push across the entrenchments to attack the Confederate right flank. He sent Lt. Col. Robert Klein and his 3rd Indiana to the left with the same instructions. He then sent for Capt. James B. McIntyre and his 4th U.S. Regulars to assault the center of the line. Finally, Minty next asked Robert B.

Mitchell to send up a couple of pieces of horse artillery, and then dispatched a galloper to update Stanley.[31]

Minty had told Klein he would send a guide to him, but no guide ever arrived. "We proceeded through thick woods, dense undergrowth, and tangled vines to the left, until we reached the enemy's abatis and rifle pits, where no horseman could go forward," reported Klein, "and, the firing having ceased, we knew not our exact position. "I sent for orders, and, on receiving them, turned to the right, to a point where I could cross the abatis and pits." They then followed minor roads through some dense woods until they hit the Murfreesboro Road. They followed that road into Shelbyville, entering the town near the railroad depot.[32]

Mix and his Michigan men followed a blind path for nearly two miles before stumbling onto a road leading across a creek and up to the main Confederate earthworks. They crossed the creek and captured two enemy pickets, scattering the rest. Mix and his regiment then pushed rapidly up the hill and entered the works, which proved to be unoccupied. He sent his 1st Battalion—commanded by Capt. Marcus Grant, reinforced with Company L under Capt. Benjamin D. Pritchard—forward as skirmishers. Pritchard and Capt. John C. Hathaway's company of Grant's battalion held the extreme right "and did good service with their companies, as they were obliged to move through an open field, exposed to the enemy's fire from the woods on both sides," reported Major Mix. Mix brought his entire regiment into line, forming the 2nd and 3rd Battalions to the left of the 1st. As soon as the Confederates opened fire, they pulled their artillery back into Shelbyville.[33]

After the artillery retired, the remaining Confederates attacked Mix's position, advancing in three distinct lines of 100-150 men each, while other parties tried to flank the Yankees on the left and right. Pritchard sent to Mix for reinforcements, but Mix had none to spare—he was heavily engaged in his own front. Mix immediately sent two orderlies to Minty to request reinforcements. The orderlies successfully made their way to Minty but were captured while returning.[34]

Mix then moved his entire command to the left, to escape enemy fire from the woods to his right. His force was surrounded on three sides—front, right, and

31 OR 23, pt. 1, 557.

32 Ibid., 559.

33 Ibid., 561.

34 Ibid.

rear—leaving him with no escape but to the earthworks on his left. He pushed his left forward in an effort to face his command to the right and clear his rear. As he did so, he could see the action developing on the pike to his front.[35]

"Colonel Minty now turns to the old 7th Pennsylvania, which he had held back, though fairly foaming with impatience, and orders a charge with drawn sabers," recalled Minty's brigade surgeon. The 7th moved out at a walk, passing over a bridge spanning a rain-swollen stream. It went up the hill at a trot until it reached the trenches. "Yelling like a thousand demons," the men forced their horses through the tangled abatis and then passed through the trenches at a gallop. The two leading battalions of the 7th Pennsylvania "dashed forward over the ditch and intrenchments and into the midst of the astonished enemy." The charging Union troopers "sabered such misguided beings as showed a belligerent disposition, and the line of rifle pits was ours." The 4th Michigan Cavalry came in line to its right, and the two regiments pressed on. "The enemy's line wavered, the men huddled like sheep, broke and went at full speed towards Shelbyville," exulted the 7th's adjutant. "The first battalion of the 7th Pennsylvania did not halt, but charged with impetuosity, cutting right and left, causing hundreds to fall."[36]

The intimidating sight of the advancing Federals impressed even the Confederates. "On either side of the highway, in column of fours, they advanced at a steady gallop, until they passed into the line of earth-works, through which the main road led, some two or three yards in our advance," recalled Alabama Pvt. John Wyeth. "As soon as they reached this point inside the works, still on the full run, they deployed from column of fours into line of battle, like the opening of a huge fan. This movement was made with as much precision as if it had been done in an open plain, on dress parade, or in some exhibition of discipline and drill."[37]

About the time that the regulars arrived, Minty heard the carbines of the Michiganders barking to the right as they attacked the earthworks; one officer and seven enlisted men were wounded in the process. In response, he ordered a charge, with the 7th Pennsylvania on the right of the road and the regulars on the left. Another Confederate described the scene within the earthworks. "Our orders were to stand until they approached within fifty yards, when we were to empty our rifles, draw our pistols, and then sauve qui peut," he wrote. "The Union troopers, with

35 Ibid.

36 Bitter, *Minty and His Cavalry*, 99; Vale, *Minty and the Cavalry*, 177; "Mr. E.D. Wesftall's Despatches"; Steahlin, "Stanley's Cavalry."

37 Wyeth, "General Wheeler's Leap," 602.

sabres high in the air, made no sound whatever beyond the rumbling tattoo which their horses' hoofs played upon the ground." The Confederates leveled their rifles at the onrushing Yankees and fired their final volley, with the enemy now on top of them. "In an incredibly short space of time," the Confederate continued, "the writer found himself on the ground and well in rear of the charging line." Wheeler's 4th Alabama Cavalry fought bravely but had its line broken. The 51st Alabama, which had been badly mauled three days earlier at Liberty Gap, now broke and ran nearly three miles. The 51st's Major James T. Dye, numerous other officers, and many men were captured. The entire Confederate line now fell back in confusion.[38]

"Not 50 guns would fire, & our stand was ineffectual and our retreat now became a rout, and for two miles we were pushed at headlong speed thro' cedar roughs & over fences by a cloud of Yankee cavalry & mounted infantry," recalled Capt. George Knox Miller of the 8th Confederate Cavalry. "My company having stood after most of the line was broken, suffered severely in men & horses. The wildest confusion now prevailed. A party of the enemy got between me and town, & as I rode up to them they fired several times not ten feet from me. I attempted to fire at one fellow, but my pistol snapped. I however scared him a little and taking advantage of the moment dashed thro' them unharmed & made my way to Shelbyville where I rallied the few remaining men of my company and again formed line of battle." The only remaining question was whether Wheeler could hang on long enough for Forrest to arrive—but Forrest had already turned to the rear, looking for another way across the Duck River. As a last ditch, Wheeler formed about 600 men of his command on the courthouse square in the heart of Shelbyville.[39]

In the meantime, Major Davis and his battalion of the 7th Pennsylvania pushed forward. Lieutenant Heber S. Thompson and few of his troopers re-laid the planks that had been torn off a small bridge on the road in their front. Seeing that the enemy was giving way, Minty brought the Pennsylvanians into the road in column of fours and ordered them to charge in that formation, supported by the regulars.

---

38 OR 23, pt. 1, 577; Wyeth, "General Wheeler's Leap," 602. Dye was held as a prisoner of war at the dreaded prison camp for Confederate officers at Johnson's Island, in Lake Erie in Ohio. According to Dye's service records, he was a captive there until March 1864, when he was exchanged and returned to duty with his regiment. James T. Dye compiled service records, RG 109, M311, roll 445, NARA.

39 McMurry, *An Uncompromising Secessionist*, 141; Dubose, *General Joseph Wheeler and the Army of Tennessee*, 176.

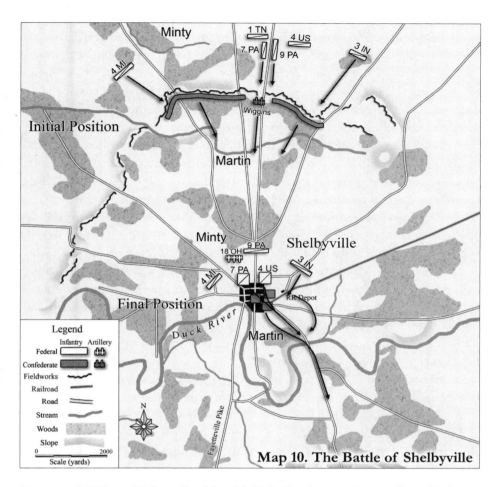

Map 10. The Battle of Shelbyville

Lieutenant William O'Connell of the 4th U.S. Cavalry was thrown from his horse and his shoulder was broken during the charge.[40]

Captain Alfred Abeel commanded Company H of the 4th Michigan Cavalry. His company, part of Mix's 3rd Battalion, formed on the left, facing the Shelbyville Pike. "We skirmished and charged through the woods, shooting and found them thick on the pike," recalled trooper John C. McLain of the 4th Michigan. The Wolverines charged the enemy, which was in considerable force in their front and to their right. That charge routed the Confederates on Abeel's front, driving them across an open field, but they formed again on the edge of some woods. The nature of the ground traversed by the charge so broke up Abeel's line that he had to pause

40 *OR* 23, pt. 1, 557-558.

to reform his line behind some old buildings, taking fire the whole time. As soon as the Wolverines formed, they charged again, driving the enemy across the Shelbyville Pike. Some of the Confederates retreated toward the town, while the rest crossed the pike, heading east. Abeel and his troopers followed for some distance. Abeel soon found himself "separated from the other companies of the battalion, and with but a portion of my own command, the horses of the rest having given out." Abeel halted his men, reformed them, and gathered up some nearby stragglers until he had accumulated a force of about 60. He then put spurs to his horse and his little command surged forward in pursuit of the fleeing Rebels, cutting them off by a side road, and helping to steer them toward a trap.[41]

Seeing the charge unfold in their front, the other two battalions of the 4th Michigan put spurs to their horses and charged. Mix reported, "before I could check them they were mixed up with the 7th Pennsylvania, charging down the pike at a furious gallop." Hathaway's company charged down a parallel road, merging with the main column at an intersection just in time to cut the enemy columns in two, and turning the rear of the left column. The routed Confederates made for an opening into a large garden with the 4th Michigan and 7th Pennsylvania in close pursuit. The garden had a stout fence that penned up the Confederates, and the Federals captured nearly 250 of them.[42]

Amazingly, the 7th Pennsylvania lost only one man, Pvt. Felix Herb of Company A, killed in the garden. Two Confederates threw up their hands in surrender to Herb, but when they realized he was alone, they changed their minds and shot him. Sgt. James A. Wilson of Company F saw it happen and immediately shot and killed the two Confederates. Just as he dispatched the second man, Adjutant George Steahlin of the 7th Pennsylvania rode up. "Adjutant!" Wilson snarled. "The devils shot Felix Herb after they had surrendered, so I made short work of them."[43]

Minty's victorious troopers now pursued the fleeing Confederates with abandon. "What a thrilling scene!" remembered a trooper of the 1st Middle Tennessee Cavalry years after the war. "What a roar and clash as the cavalry and artillery went thundering along the turnpike toward Shelbyville, intermingled with the sharp crack of our carbines and the roar of the loud-mouthed cannon." "The

---

41 Entry for June 27, 1863, John C. McLain diaries 1862-1865, Special Collections, Main Library, Michigan State University, East Lansing, Michigan; OR 23, pt. 1, 563.

42 OR 23, pt. 1, 561.

43 Steahlin, "Stanley's Cavalry."

chase for the last four miles was of the most exciting character," noted another observer. He continued:

> Houses along the road were filled with Union people, who came to the roadside fences, shouted, clapped their hands, hooted at the pale and panting rebels, and cheered the pursuers on. Here and there a jaded rebel horse would drop, with the blood gushing from its mouth and pouring from its wounded sides; the next instant ferocious blue jackets would be upon its terrified rebel rider, with keen sabre in hand, demanding unconditional surrender or swift death. Rebel canteens, haversacks, broken muskets, clothing and corn meal were strewn along the pike throughout the whole distance, from the earthworks to the town, and dead bodies were numerous.[44]

Captain Joseph Hofmaster, commander of the 4th Michigan's Company L, dashed into town, selected a position the fleeing enemy would have to ride past, drew his saber, and hacked away until wounds disabled his left arm and right hand. Some of his fingers and the grip of his saber were nearly severed. A ball hit his hat, cutting it open on the top. Private Mason Brown of Company I found a carbine and tried to fire it at the enemy, but when it misfired, he turned it around to use it as a club and "did good service among the rebels with whom he was in close contact."[45]

Wheeler had posted four pieces of horse artillery in the town square of Shelbyville. When Minty's audacious charge came within a quarter mile of the town, these guns began barking. Minty sent back to Mitchell for artillery support, but soon realized that the Confederate artillerists were getting the range on his troopers. The first charge had run its course and, as Minty concluded he could not wait for artillery support to arrive, he ordered yet another saber charge. As his men formed, a battery of horse artillery—18th Ohio Battery—arrived. Minty ordered two guns placed on either side of a pond less than a quarter of a mile from the Confederate artillery. He rode over to the battery commander and said, "Captain, all I want is a little smoke; place one gun on each side of the street and fire one shell from each gun; give all the room you can for my column to [move] between your guns." The artillerist did as instructed. A heavy cloud of smoke settled over the guns.[46]

44 Carter, "A Scene of the War"; "Mr. E. D. Westfall's Despatches."

45 OR 23, pt. 1, 562.

46 Ibid. 558; Minty, "At Shelbyville, Tennessee." The specific battery has not been identified. Minty called the battery commander Captain Ayreshire in this article and indicated that he

Maj. Charles C. Davis,
7th Pennsylvania Cavalry, who received
the Medal of Honor for valor in the
Battle of Shelbyville.

Kenneth C. Turner

With the smoke obscuring his command, Minty promptly ordered the 7th Pennsylvania to charge the artillery. Here the 7th's commander, Lt. Col. William B. Sipes, rode up. Adjutant George F. Steahlin repeated Minty's order. Sipes replied, "My regiment is back with the prisoners. I cannot make another charge."

Minty overheard this remark and replied, "Your third battalion is in good order—horses comparatively fresh. All the other horses of the brigade have been run down." Sipes understood and responded, "If I must make the charge, I'll take the artillery and drive them into [the] Duck River." These 274 Pennsylvanians faced a daunting task. They were to charge down a straight street that gradually ascended to the position of the enemy artillery at the courthouse, which was supported by a brigade of cavalry. "To look upon these preparations, it seemed that utter destruction was inevitable to all those who dared advance," wrote an admiring Lieutenant Colonel Sipes, "and yet, with sabers drawn, and with shouts of defiance, the men rushed onward, never faltering for an instant, and, to all appearance, utterly destitute of any apprehension of danger." Years later, Sipes would describe this attack as "a forlorn hope." The intrepid Maj. Charles C. Davis led the charge, with Sipes riding along under his command. The Union horsemen "dashed forward with an impetuosity never before surpassed on any field," noted Lt. Joseph Vale. The Confederate gunners loaded and fired their guns "with all the rapidity and precision possible, hurling

commanded an Ohio battery, but no other details have been identified. This was probably Capt. Charles C. Aleshire, commanding the 18th Ohio Battery, attached to the Reserve Corps.

canister in double-shotted charges at and through the dense ranks of onrushing cavalry."[47]

The bugles blared, and "through the smoke, down the hill went the little band, yelling like mad," remembered Adjutant Steahlin. "We were on the dead run. Half the distance between the mile post and the Confederate battery was passed in safety. Two shots screamed over our heads, but the third shot hit Company G, killing three men and a horse, but onward we ran." They reached a ravine a few hundred feet from the battery that sheltered them from the guns, which continued belching at them. "As we reached the slight rise going into Shelbyville we saw the Confederate cavalry waver and break. The artillery limbered up and joined the fleeing cavalry." Davis's Pennsylvanians pushed onward. "Yelling like demons and spurring their horses to the wildest speed," the Northerners "reached the square, leaping their horses over the guns, and sabering the gunners alongside their pieces." Major Davis wrote that "although the gunners stuck to their pieces to the last the mighty rush of the Seventh could not be stayed."[48]

"The last piece of artillery turned the corner of a street as the two hundred began to sabre the cannoniers," Davis continued. "Then the riders were cut off the horses. One piece was ours in a twinkling. The second piece was also ours in two minutes." Major Davis himself captured the second gun by compelling the battery commander to surrender. The Pennsylvanians thundered on toward the railroad depot. "Like a field of grain bending before the wind," marveled Sipes, "the Confederates bent in the retreating race toward Duck river."[49]

Like Union Lieutenant Colonel Galbraith, many of his troopers of the 1st Middle Tennessee Cavalry were Shelbyville residents. "In the midst of the fierce charge upon the battery, and the hot, desperate fight from the square to the railroad depot," wrote Joseph Vale, "the loyal people recognized their men and the standard of the First Middle Tennessee, and in a wild burst of patriotic enthusiasm, dozens of ladies rushed from their houses, and, standing on the steps, porches, door stoops, and many out on the curb of the pavement in the street, waved the stars and stripes, cheering and yelling to their friends, calling to them to 'Go on! Go

47 Steahlin, "Stanley's Cavalry"; *OR* 23, pt. 1, 565; Sipes, *The Saber Regiment*, 67; Vale, *Minty and the Cavalry*, 179.

48 Vale, *Minty and the Cavalry*, 179; "Major Davis' Own Story of the Shelbyville Charge," *The Harrisburg Telegraph*, January 22, 1909.

49 "Major Davis' Own Story of the Shelbyville Charge"; Steahlin, "Stanley's Cavalry"; Sipes, *The Saber Regiment*, 67.

on! You've got the rebels! They are running! They can't cross the river! God bless our boys in blue!'" While the locals cheered, "canister . . . , rifle and revolver balls, and Minnie slugs were hissing through the air, and all the wild pandemonium of battle was raging around them."[50]

Concluding at last that Forrest would not be coming to his relief, Wheeler decided to withdraw across the Duck River, extricating his command from a dangerous situation. One Rebel observed that "Wheeler rode about like a madman, trying to get his rebels in shape to make a fight." The withdrawal was well underway when a detachment of 10 men, consisting of staff officers and commissary details from Forrest's command, rode up to Wheeler and begged him to return to his position in Shelbyville, since Forrest was but a few hundred yards away and was coming to Wheeler's assistance. Wheeler called for volunteers and immediately returned and positioned his troops. He told them that they would, in all probability, be killed or captured, that he had selected them for this forlorn hope, and that he would stay with them and lead them personally. He was characteristically brave in ordering a suicidal charge that he intended to lead in person. "General Wheeler was everywhere, encouraging and animating the men to stand firm," recalled trooper John Wyeth. "His reputation for ubiquity, for dash, for 'bull-dog obstinacy' and for 'nerves of steel' was never so well earned as on that day."[51]

"This movement was observed by the enemy," noted one of Wheeler's troopers, "and appearances of activity on their part was unmistakable." Wheeler realized that the moment of truth had arrived. He rode to the head of his column and cried, "Charge!" The Confederate cavalry surged forward and "the impact was terrific," one of his men later recalled. The fighting was hand-to-hand, with clubbed pistols and carbines. Wheeler rode here and there, encouraging his men and crying, "Kill him!" and "Shoot him!" The Federals recognized him, calling out, "That's Wheeler!" The battlefield was a terrible sight; wounded horses neighed while unhorsed riders were ridden down on every side.[52]

Another column of cavalry was spotted moving on the road on which Forrest was expected to arrive. As it drew near, the Confederates realized it was more Union troopers, not friends. Three other heavy columns were driving Wheeler's

---

50 Vale, *Minty and the Cavalry*, 185.

51 "Mr. E. D. Westfall's Despatches"; Dodson, *Campaigns of Wheeler and His Cavalry*, 89; Wyeth, "General Wheeler's Leap," 602.

52 Dodson, *Campaigns of Wheeler and His Cavalry*, 89; Dubose, *General Joseph Wheeler and the Army of Tennessee*, 176.

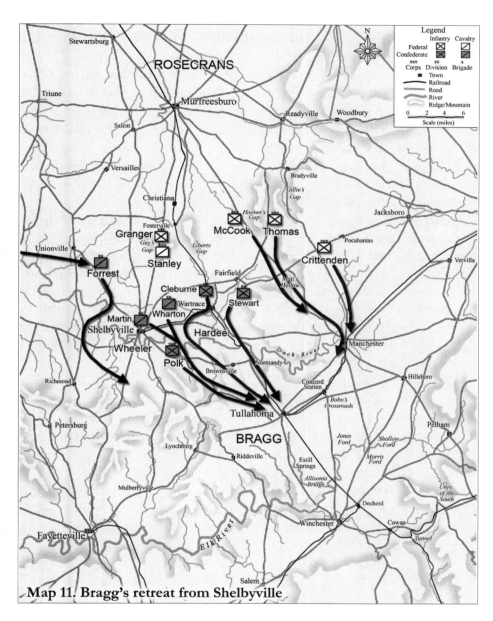

Map 11. Bragg's retreat from Shelbyville

men, and the general, who stubbornly remained with his soldiers, soon found himself completely surrounded. Wheeler charged through a column of enemy cavalry that blocked his line of retreat. He might have escaped, but realized that a portion of his command had been cut off, and that the enemy held the bridge over the Duck River, which would enable the Union cavalry to pursue and overtake Polk's wagon train. Wheeler quickly gathered about 60 men and led a charge on the enemy flank, driving the Federals back into the center of town in confusion, and opening the road for a withdrawal.[53]

The Federals again pursued. A platoon of the 4th U.S. commanded by Lt. Neil J. McCafferty led the way, followed by all of Galbraith's 1st Middle Tennessee, the rest of the 4th U.S., and then the Pennsylvanians. The Confederate horse artillery got off a single volley into the face of the charging troopers, but did little damage, killing one man and two horses. When the Union column reached the railroad depot in town, a detachment of Confederates troopers poured carbine fire into the head of the 7th Pennsylvania's column, killing Lt. Amos B. Rhoads, Sgt. Francis W. Reed, and two privates.

Reed had been riding alongside his friend Henry Snyder during the charge. Snyder did not see Reed fall, or he would have stopped. "I did not know that he was dead until the battery was taken and the battle over," Snyder wrote to Reed's mother. "I was so struck when I heard it, that I almost fell off my horse." Snyder found Reed, laid him out straight, and washed the blood and dirt from his face. He stayed with his friend's body all night. Reed was then buried in Shelbyville with the other casualties from the 7th Pennsylvania Cavalry. Snyder concluded his letter with, "I know that I have lost in him a good and true friend and deeply mourn his loss."[54]

The 1st Confederate Cavalry tried to rally on the hill behind the railroad depot, but in so doing lost its commander, Col. Henry C. King, its lieutenant colonel, and a number of other officers captured. During this melee, Minty's adjutant, Robert Burns, watched as "one poor fellow was pitched headlong from his horse into a mud puddle a few inches deep, and as I passed him, his eyes were setting and his mouth gasping, being half filled with mud and water."[55]

An officer brought Colonel King to Minty, who declared, "My devotion to my General, sir, caused my capture." Minty replied, "Colonel, you made a gallant charge to check us, and the loss to your General of such a regiment, with such a commander, must be irreparable, and our gain in capturing you and your gallant

53 Dodson, *Campaigns of Wheeler and His Cavalry*, 89-90, 93.

54 Henry H. Snyder to Frances Reed, July 1863, Frances Reed Papers, *Civil War Times Illustrated* Collection, Archives, U.S. Army Heritage and Education Center, Carlisle, PA.

55 *OR* 23, pt. 1, 558; Bitter, *Minty and His Cavalry*, 99.

regiment is proportionately great." Nearly the entire 1st Confederate Cavalry was captured intact. [56]

After ordering the Pennsylvanians to charge, Minty also sent Lt. George W. Lawton of the 4th Michigan to Captain McIntrye with orders to take his regulars through the woods to the left and turn the Confederate right flank, which would cut off Wheeler's line of retreat by Newsom's (or Skull Camp) Bridge over the Duck River, approximately a mile from the courthouse square. At the moment of Lawton's arrival, however, General Mitchell also appeared and checked McIntyre, stating instead that he would send a fresh regiment from his division. Unfortunately, the regiment Mitchell ordered on this mission lacked a guide and made a wrong turn, arriving about a minute too late.[57]

Confederate Capt. N. D. Johnson realized that Martin and Wheeler were in imminent danger of being captured, so he gathered up "a considerable number of men" and checked the pursuers. Sergeant Phil Duncan of Capt. George Knox Miller's company of the 8th Confederate Cavalry personally saved Martin's life by knocking a pursuing Yankee from his horse. Miller himself did not fare as well. "The mass of men and horses all rushed for the bridge, & nine were trampled under foot & killed," he reported. "I came very near being killed myself having an ankle badly sprained & [my] horse being at one time lifted entirely off the ground by the throng." McIntyre later lamented, "had it not been for this delay of four or five minutes, I feel confident I could have captured all the rebel cavalry, who retreated to the left of the town, and perhaps the two generals reported to have been there."[58]

Wheeler spotted another enemy column and was preparing to charge it when a staff officer grabbed his arm and pointed to his rear, where the Union cavalry had again surrounded him. Wheeler called out, "Every man for himself!" The bearer of Wheeler's personal battle flag dropped his standard at the entrance to the bridge,

56 Minty, "At Shelbyville, Tennessee." There is some confusion over who was captured here. Minty identified Colonel King, and King's service record shows him "captured at Shelbyville, June 27, 1863," but according to Col. John T. Cox's service record, Cox was appointed colonel of the 1st on June 6, 1863, and is sometimes, in other sources, identified as the man taken prisoner that day. It seems most likely that King was in command, and was captured. Cox, whose service record does not record any capture, led the regiment from then on. See RG 109, M258, roll 1 for Cox and roll 3 for King.

57 Minty, "At Shelbyville, Tennessee."

58 McMurry, *An Uncompromising Secessionist*, 142; OR 23, pt. 1, 557-558, 566.

and the pursuing Federals rode over it, leaving it behind. Private William Sommers of Company A of the 4th U.S. Cavalry got credit for its capture.[59]

"Let's show them the way!" cried Wheeler. Reversing course and heading straight for the Duck River, he charged through the pursuing Federals. He reached it at a spot where the bank loomed about 15 feet above the water. Digging his spurs into his horse's flank, man and beast leapt into the current below. Unseated in the descent, Wheeler grabbed his mount's neck, guiding the swimming animal across the river to safety. Martin found an easier incline and swam his horse across. On reaching the steep bank on the other side, the horse was unable to ascend, forcing Martin to swim further downstream in search of a better spot. Captain Johnson's horse was washed downstream to the bridge abutment. Union troopers standing on the bridge captured Johnson, and he spent nearly two years as a prisoner of war. In the meantime, Captain Miller and other officers gathered some of the men who had crossed safely, formed them on the opposite bank, and opened fire on the pursuing Federals, blunting their zeal.[60]

"The scene at the bridge beggars description," declared the New York newspaper correspondent. "Men and horses crowded upon it inextricable confusion, the stream filled with rebels struggling to gain the opposite bank, our exasperated soldiers firing at them in the water; Wheeler frantically calling for volunteers to stay the Union torrent long enough for his escape."[61]

When the Union horsemen arrived at Skull Camp Bridge, the 3rd Indiana, which had kept well to the left after crossing the earthworks, swept down on the railroad depot. "My men coming up rather scattered, the enemy commenced firing and advancing, until my men got somewhat formed, when, firing a volley, we drew saber and charged into their ranks," recounted Lieutenant Colonel Klein. "They fled in disorder near a half mile toward the mill, where, the commons narrowing into a lane, they must fight or be run down." Klein noted that the Confederates fought desperately, hand-to-hand, for nearly 300 yards, swinging sabers and using muskets and pistols as clubs. The Federals swept down the south bank of the Duck River and drove a crowd of fugitives before them. With the bridge completely blocked by a disabled wagon, they drove many of these Confederate fugitives

59 Sipes, *The Saber Regiment*, 68; OR 23, pt. 1, 566.

60 Calvin L. Collier, *The War Child's Children: The Story of the Third Regiment, Arkansas Cavalry, Confederate States Army* (Little Rock, AR: 1965), 60; Dodson, *Campaigns of Wheeler and His Cavalry*, 90; Dubose, *General Joseph Wheeler and the Army of Tennessee*, 176-177.

61 "Mr. E. D. Westfall's Despatches."

headlong into the river, and captured the badly wounded adjutants of both the 51st Alabama and 8th Confederate regiments. The river was filled with men and horses struggling against the swift current. Many drowned, while others struggled to make it up the steep bank on the other side. Still others, dismounted, stood shivering in their drenched clothing. As Major Davis colorfully described it, "A multitude, the number never was nor ever will be known, were drowned, and the finest cavalry of the rebellion there found a grave in the mud and slime of Duck River."[62]

Nathan Bedford Forrest's long-awaited arrival never materialized. On June 24 his command was centered around Spring Hill, nearly 40 miles west of Shelbyville, picketing the Confederate left flank. That day William R. Dyer, a member of Forrest's personal escort, recorded that Forrest traveled to Shelbyville to confer with Bragg directly. The next day Forrest returned, according to his earliest biographers, with orders "to break up the outposts at Spring Hill and repair without delay with his division to Shelbyville. Accordingly, on the night of June 25, the march began via Rigg's Crossroads," 17 miles due east of Spring Hill and 10 miles south of Triune. Some of Forrest's men may have started towards Rigg's Crossroads on the 25th, but Forrest himself did not. Private Dyer again provided the timeline, noting on June 26 that the escort was "ordered to prepare rations and be ready to move at 3 PM. We started and went towards Riggs Crossroads." According to his biographer, Col. James W. Starnes, commanding Forrest's old brigade, "camped at College Grove [about five miles north of Rigg's Crossroads] the night of June 26th. All scouts were ordered to report in before midnight. To coordinate his march with that of Gen. Forrest and Armstrong's brigade, [Starnes] moved out at 1 AM" on June 27.[63]

Forrest's strength and constitution were legendary, but even he had his limits. On June 13 at Columbia, Tennessee, one of his own officers, Lt. Andrew Wills Gould, confronted him. Gould commanded a section of artillery that had been overrun and captured at Sand Mountain on April 30, during the pursuit of Abel Streight. Even though Forrest eventually retook the guns when Streight

---

62 OR 23, pt. 1, 559; Steahlin, "Stanley's Cavalry"; "Major Davis' Own Story of the Shelbyville Charge." An 1887 history of the state of Tennessee claimed that the fleeing Confederates "threw a large brass field-piece from the bridge into the river." To this day, that cannon lies in the mud at the bottom of the river. *History of Tennessee Illustrated* (Nashville: 1887), online version, http://homepages.rootsweb.com/~khopkins/GdspdBedford.html.

63 Wayne Bradshaw, ed., *The Civil War Diary of William R. Dyer, a Member of Forrest's Escort* (2009), 71; Jordan and Pryor, *Campaigns of General Forrest*, 290; H. Gerald Starnes, *Forrest's Forgotten Horse Brigadier* (Laurel, MD: 1995), 84.

surrendered, he decided Gould had lost his nerve and tried to transfer him out of his command. Gould demanded an explanation, but Forrest would hear none of it. The argument escalated. Forrest rushed Gould with a pen knife, opening it with his teeth as he lunged forward. Gould fumbled with a pistol in his pocket, which discharged, striking Forrest above the left hip. Forrest plunged his knife into Gould's side, between the ribs. Gould fled into the street. Forrest, enraged, exclaimed, "No damned man shall kill me and live!" Snatching up a pistol, he pursued Gould, who died shortly thereafter, of either sepsis or pneumonia. Forrest's wound was not fatal, but he was bedridden for several days. How much this wound still affected him by the beginning of the Tullahoma Campaign is unknown, but he made a nearly 80-mile round trip to Shelbyville and back on June 24 and 25.[64]

Despite Wheeler's expectations, Forrest's command spent the night of June 26 somewhere near Rigg's Crossroads, with Starnes camped just a few miles to the north at College Grove. Sometime late on June 26 or early on June 27, Forrest received an updated order from Wheeler, a message that had been "detained by high water [by] some twelve hours." The Federals were not the only ones troubled by the unending rains. Wheeler directed Forrest to join him "on the turnpike from Murfreesboro to Shelbyville." Private Dyer recorded in his diary only that on June 27 he and the rest of Forrest's column "continued our march," adding that they "went to Unionville and Shelbyville" before they "turned around and crossed the Duck River below."[65]

General Forrest came no closer to Shelbyville than the earthworks outside of the town. "When within ten miles of Shelbyville . . . the sounds of a considerable skirmish were audible," inducing Forrest to send Frank Armstrong and his brigade "to push on rapidly for the scene." There, reported Forrest's biographers, "Armstrong found the Federal cavalry engaged with and driving Wheeler's force along a dirt road half a mile from . . . the turnpike." Armstrong also observed Joe Wheeler's troopers retreating "so fast" that "Forrest found it impossible to effect the junction." Wheeler's most ardent campaign chronicler asserted that once he reached the now-abandoned earthworks, Forrest called a halt and sent a scout to reconnoiter. When he heard the firing by Martin's men, Forrest then determined that "he could be of no service," so he turned back and crossed the Duck River

64 Wills, *A Battle from the Start*, 122-127.

65 Jordan and Pryor, *Campaigns of General Forrest*, 290; Bradshaw, *Diary of William R. Dyer*, 71.

Brig. Gen. Frank Armstrong, commander, Armstrong's Brigade, Forrest's Division, Army of Tennessee.

Tennessee State Library and Archives

several miles west of town, where he caught up to Polk's floundering wagon train.[66]

Back in Shelbyville, evening was closing in, and darkness began to fall; the conditions were not favorable for the Federal cavalry to continue chasing the beaten Confederates. "After the pursuit was over we led our panting, steaming horses out into an open field where the mud was less than ankle deep and dismounted," recalled Henry M. Hempstead of the 2nd Michigan Cavalry. "In doing so my mare, who had cut her leg in the chase twitched up her smarting leg with a rapid forward movement and gave me a severe blow on my right leg which caused me much pain."[67]

In the meantime, Polk's vulnerable wagon train was no more than five miles away, moving slowly. Had Stanley known this, he could have bagged the train intact. Major General Granger begged him to pursue the train that night, but beyond posting a guard on the east end of the bridge, Stanley did nothing, and the prize slipped from his fingers. That evening, an admiring Stanley sent an aide to the camp of the 7th Pennsylvania Cavalry with orders for the troopers to remain saddled and ready to march. Colonel Sipes replied, "Please give my compliments to General Stanley, and say that the horses of the Seventh are greatly fatigued, and we would like permission to rest them as much as possible."[68]

66 Jordan and Pryor, *Campaigns of General Forrest*, 290-291; Dodson, *Campaigns of Wheeler and His Cavalry*, 90. Though Jordan and Pryor's work usually covered Forrest's exploits very closely, providing details often found nowhere else, the movements of June 25 to June 28 are covered in a single paragraph.

67 Henry Mortimer Hempstead diary, entry for June 27, 1863, Manuscripts Collection, Bentley Historical Library, University of Michigan, Ann Arbor.

68 Dubose, *General Joseph Wheeler and the Army of Tennessee*, 177.

The staff officer soon returned with a different message. "General Stanley presents his compliments, and says that the Seventh Pennsylvania can do exactly as it pleases."[69]

Minty's adjutant, Robert Burns, left an interesting account of the army politics at play:

> After the thing was over General Mitchell rode up, and about two hours after him in came General Granger, and the next day it is telegraphed all over the country that General Mitchell's Division of Cavalry had taken Shelbyville, and that General Granger had entered the place a conqueror, etc., etc. All sheer humbug, neither General Mitchell nor General Granger were within four miles of the town, while there was any fighting going on . . . not another soul had anything to do with it, excepting our First Brigade. We felt very sore when we saw the newspaper reports. All in the army here say it was the most brilliant cavalry dash of the war, and had it happened in the Potomac Army, would have been heralded far and wide.[70]

The Army of the Cumberland remained destined to labor in anonymity for the rest of the Tullahoma Campaign.

Minty reported that he captured three pieces of artillery and many prisoners. Mitchell came up to see the results for himself, and he and Minty rode forward a short distance. When Minty reassembled his brigade, he found that the losses were two officers and four enlisted men killed, as well as five officers and 21 enlisted men wounded. In addition to the three guns, the Federals captured 599 Confederates, including 30 commissioned officers. Major Frank Mix of the 4th Michigan Cavalry reported that his Wolverines captured officers and enlisted men from five different regiments and that, "to say the least, [Wheeler] must have had a force three or four time larger than my own, which we succeeded in driving nearly 2 miles." Minty also estimated that Wheeler had suffered about 300 men killed and wounded. Minty noted, however, that "[i]f Lieutenant Newell's section of artillery had still formed a part of the brigade, I could have entered Shelbyville two hours earlier than I did." Minty and his tired troopers bivouacked near the railroad station before returning to a position near Guy's Gap the next day.[71]

69 Sipes, *The Saber Regiment*, 69.

70 Bitter, *Minty and His Cavalry*, 100.

71 *OR* 23, pt. 1, 558, 559, 561. On July 4, 1863, the *Baltimore Sun* reported that Minty and his command had taken 60 or 70 officers and 700 enlisted men prisoners, adding that as many as

While Minty's troops secured Shelbyville and the lower bridge across the Duck, Campbell's brigade had to fight its way to the upper bridge and throw down several stout post-and-rail fences along the way. Campbell and his troopers arrived near the upper bridge in time to pour a few volleys into the escaping mob. General Stanley noted, "Had he been there five minutes sooner it would have made a difference of one thousand prisoners."[72]

"The remnant of the rebel force, who were so warlike in the morning, got off towards Tullahoma dispirited and dismayed," gloated an observer. That night, Wheeler struggled to rally the scattered and routed elements of his command. Bragg sent 500 Georgia and Tennessee cavalry that had not been engaged to reinforce what remained of Wheeler's corps. At dawn, a probe by the Union cavalry crossed the bridge, but the carbines of Wheeler's troopers turned them back. The Federals then retreated, allowing Wheeler's men and the rest of Bragg's army to escape largely unmolested.[73]

The victorious Yankees mingled with the loyal residents of Shelbyville that night. "It was cheering to meet so many loyal people as we met in Shelbyville," said the New York newspaper correspondent. "The town has not been belied. Old people and young people, young men and maidens, waving little copies of the Stars and Stripes, stained and dusty from a year's concealment in secret places, greeted us with 'Thank God, you've come at last!' The Union feeling is so universally evinced that I did not wonder longer why the rebels 'could not bear the town of New Boston.'"[74]

Minty's victory at Shelbyville freed Pauline Cushman. Although she was sick in bed, "the roar of artillery and small arms gave me great strength, and as the stars and stripes floated by my window," she rose from her sickbed and went out on the porch of the house where she was being held, wrapped in a blanket. Major Joseph S. Fullerton, an assistant adjutant general assigned to the Army of the Cumberland, dashed by, followed by Granger and Mitchell. Cushman called out to Fullerton, who responded, "I have no time; I will call when I return." When Cushman hailed Fullerton a second time, he stopped to see her, and she asked him to send Granger

---

100 more Confederates had drowned in the Duck. "From General Rosecrans' Army," *The Baltimore Sun*, July 4, 1863.

72 Fordyce, *An American General*, 146.

73 "Mr. E. D. Westfall's Despatches"; Dubose, *General Joseph Wheeler and the Army of Tennessee*, 177.

74 "Mr. E. D. Westfall's Despatches."

Pauline Cushman, actress and Union spy, in the uniform of a Union major.

Library of Congress

and Mitchell to visit her so that she could report on what she had learned. They returned at about 11 that night for a brief interview. Cushman was safe.[75]

What Minty's augmented brigade accomplished at Shelbyville was nothing short of remarkable. That night in his diary, 4th Michigander John McLain recorded, "It was a hard day's ride, but full of excitement." As Lt. Joseph Vale of Minty's staff noted, Shelbyville "was the first time in the history of the war, when strong lines of entrenchments, protected by an elaborate abatis, ditch and parapet, were stormed and taken by cavalry in a mounted saber charge." In short, a single brigade shattered and routed an entire corps of veteran Confederate cavalry and sent it flying into the cold, deep, rushing waters of the Duck River. "Colonel Minty, who commanded the advance on Shelbyville, for gallantry on that and many other occasions, merits . . . promotion" to brigadier general, declared Rosecrans in his report of the campaign. That promotion never came.[76]

---

75 Pauline Cushman, *An Inside View of the Army Police: The Thrilling Adventures of Pauline Cushman, American Actress, and Famous Federal Spy of the Department of the Cumberland* (Cincinnati, OH: 1864), 42-43.

76 McLain diary, entry for June 27, 1863; Vale, *Minty and the Cavalry*, 177; OR 23, 1:409; Bitter, *Minty and His Cavalry*, 102. Minty received brevets to brigadier general of volunteers and major general of volunteers in 1865, but he never received the promotion he so richly deserved. Blogger Craig Swain points to Minty's poor performance in pursuit of Wheeler's raiders on October 6, 1863, after which Minty was relieved of command of his brigade for failing to obey orders, as one possible reason. Undoubtedly, this episode badly damaged his chances for promotion. While Minty was restored to brigade command in 1864, he never achieved the rank

In particular, the repeated charges of the 7th Pennsylvania Cavalry were remarkable, especially the final assault against the Confederate battery on the courthouse square. "There can scarcely be instanced a finer display of gallantry than the charge made that day by the 7th Pennsylvania Cavalry backed by the United States Cavalry," observed Stanley. "I have read of nothing more admirable. To face a battery ready loading and waiting, supported on either flank by riflemen; to ride at the muzzles of the guns, and through them, is no baby's play, and this was done by the regiments I have mentioned, one composed by Pennsylvania blacksmiths, the other soldiers of the regular army. Their small loss in this charge only illustrates how a superior nerve force unnerves an enemy." Sergeant John Ennis of the 7th, who was an Englishman, claimed to have participated in the famed Charge of the Light Brigade at Balaklava during the Crimean War. Ennis remarked that the charge at Shelbyville "was not surpassed at Balaklava."[77]

In 1894, Stanley nominated Maj. Charles C. Davis of the 7th Pennsylvania for the Medal of Honor for his valor at Shelbyville, writing, "A more gallant charge was never made, and Major Davis rode well in front of the leading sabres, the beau ideal of a most magnificent trooper." The Medal of Honor subsequently was issued to the deserving Pennsylvanian.[78]

At the same time, Minty did not recognize the weakness of the Confederate earthworks. Private John Wyeth of the 4th Alabama Cavalry was one of the Southerners occupying those works when the attack came. "Wheeler's bold front had evidently impressed them with the idea that we were there in strength, and were probably trying to lead them into a trap," he wrote in 1898. "If they had ridden down upon us then our destruction would have been complete, for we had no avenue of escape except by one narrow bridge two miles in our rear. Instead of

---

or level of command his skills otherwise would have garnered for him. But for his bad day on October 6, 1863, it seems likely that he would have been promoted to brigadier general and ended up in command of a division of cavalry. See Craig Swain, "Minty's Bad Day," https://markerhunter.wordpress.com/tag/robert-minty/.

77 Fordyce, *An American General*, 146; Steahlin, "Stanley's Cavalry." The authors of this work have been unable to corroborate the claim that Ennis served in the British Light Brigade or that he made the charge at Balaklava. He was killed in a charge at Selma, Alabama, during the closing days of the war and did not leave behind any sort of an account of his own. The charge at Selma was remarkably similar to the one at Shelbyville.

78 David S. Stanley to Adjutant General, U. S. Army, February 20, 1894, Charles C. Davis Medal of Honor file, no. 383,346, RG 94, NARA. The citation on Davis's Medal of Honor reads, "The Congress to Maj. Charles C. Davis, 7th Pa. Cav. for gallantry at Shelbyville, Tenn., June 27, 1892."

smashing us then and there, as they could easily have done, and as they did after several hours of desultory fighting, they lost what they were fighting for," namely, Polk's wagon train.[79]

Still, Shelbyville was a crushing defeat for Wheeler's corps. "Our cavalry became entirely routed and dashed into Shelbyville," reported R. F. Bunting of the 8th Texas Cavalry, when he heard of the affair. "The rout was most disgraceful through the streets of the town. . . . The rout was complete, the panic was perfect, and no necessity for either." Bunting expressed the opinion that had his regiment been present, that rout would not have occurred. There is no reason to believe, however, that the presence of another regiment would have made any difference. Captain George Knox Miller of the 8th Confederate was similarly disparaging. "Altogether it was the greatest Cavalry disaster of the war, and I can attribute it to nothing but bad management," he wrote. "Gen. [Wheeler] was not himself at all. Had it been properly managed even with our wet guns & the limited amount of ammunition, we could have made a successful retreat from a place that it was impossible for us to hold." Miller had no way of knowing that Wheeler had returned to Shelbyville at the request of Forrest's staff officers in the hope of buying time for Forrest to reach him. Forrest's failure to do so sealed the defeat of Wheeler's cavalry that day.[80]

Wheeler's lack of manpower also was a severe hindrance. Without the 2,200 men of Morgan's division, and with Forrest's troopers nowhere to be seen, Wheeler had nothing like a sufficient force available to man the trenches, which were designed to hold two full divisions of infantry. Forrest's absence and Morgan's insubordination doomed Wheeler's corps to defeat. Later, Stanley boldly claimed that the "Confederate cavalry never recovered from the demoralizing effect which it experienced of being ridden down by the Union cavalry." While Stanley overstated the case—Wheeler's cavalry remained a spirited and formidable fighting force until the end of the war—the effect of the whipping certainly demonstrated that the Union and Confederate cavalry forces were now in parity with each other.[81]

Was Forrest negligent in failing to reach Shelbyville in time to join Wheeler? Possibly, though the terrible weather was a factor. Had he departed for Shelbyville

---

79 Wyeth, *General Wheeler's Leap*, 601.

80 Letter of R. F. Bunting of July 7, 1863 in *Tri-Weekly Telegraph*, August 19, 1863; Cutrer, *Our Trust Is in the God of Battles*, 168; McMurry, *An Uncompromising Secessionist*, 142.

81 Fordyce, *An American General*, 146.

on the afternoon of June 25, when he returned from Shelbyville with Bragg's orders in hand, he likely could have covered the 40 miles in the time allotted. But as Private Dyer noted, the division did not actually depart Spring Hill until 3 p.m. on June 26, nearly 24 hours later than has generally been assumed. Even a dawn departure on the 26th should have allowed Forrest to join Wheeler in the nick of time. Of course, less than a week previously, Forrest was bedridden with a gunshot wound and probably was not his usual aggressive, energetic self.

Additionally, poor communications played a role. Confederate telegraph lines continued to function between Columbia and Shelbyville up until at least the morning of June 27. And though there was considerable Union activity north of Shelbyville from June 23 onward, couriers could safely travel south of the Duck via Farmington to reach Shelbyville—Forrest himself rode to and from Shelbyville that way without incident on June 24 and 25. But there are no surviving dispatches between Forrest and Wheeler for this period. If Forrest had sent couriers to Wheeler at any time on June 26, when he departed Columbia, or overnight, when he made camp, Wheeler might have had some better idea of how soon Forrest could reach the scene. Sometime on June 27, Forrest sent Maj. Gilbert V. Rambaut, his commissary officer, to inform Wheeler of his arrival, but Rambaut only convinced Wheeler to try to hold the bridge open a few more minutes in the hectic afternoon hours of the fighting at Shelbyville.[82]

In the interim, John T. Wilder and his Lightning Brigade were about to go off on an expedition far behind enemy lines in the hope of interdicting Bragg's lines of supply and communications. If Wilder succeeded, Rosecrans might be able to entice Bragg to give battle on ground on the Ohioan's choosing.

---

82 Dodson, *Campaigns of Wheeler and His Cavalry*, 90.

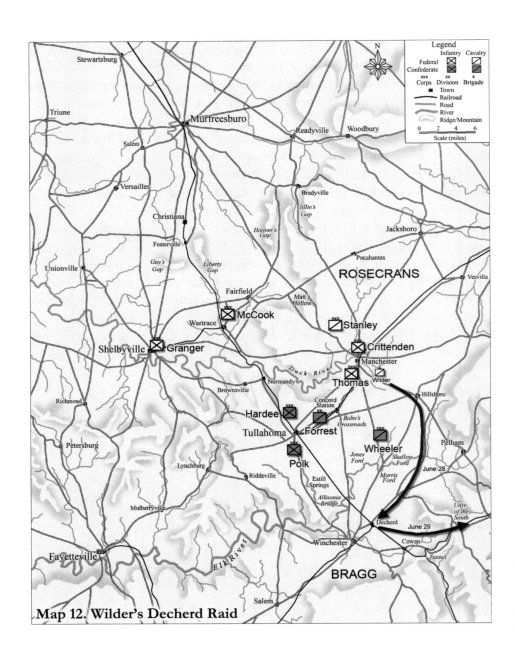

Legend

Infantry   Cavalry

Federal

Confederate

xxx   xx
Corps   Division   Brigade

Town
Railroad
Road
River
Ridge/Mountain

0   2   4   6
Scale (miles)

N

Stewartsburg

Triune

Murfreesburo

Salem

Readyville   Woodbury

Versailles

Bradyville

Christiana

Gillie's
Gap

Fosterville

Hoover's
Gap

Jacksboro

Guy's
Gap

Liberty
Gap

Pocahantas

ROSECRANS

Unionville

Fairfield

Vervilla

McCook

Matt's
Hollow

Wartrace

Stanley

Shelbyville   Granger

Crittenden

Manchester

Duck River

Thomas   Wilder

Richmond

Brownsville

Normandy

Concord
Station

Hillsboro

Hardee

Bobo's
Crossroads

Petersburg

Tullahoma   Forrest

Wheeler

Pelham

Lynchburg

Polk

Jones
Ford

Shallow
Ford

June 28

Riddeville

Estill
Springs

Morris
Ford

Mulberryville

Allisonia
Bridge

Univ
of the
South

Decherd   June 29

Fayetteville

Elk River

Winchester

Cowan

Tunnel

BRAGG

Salem

Map 12. Wilder's Decherd Raid

Chapter Eleven

Wilder's Raid Beyond the Elk River,
June 28 to 30, 1863

Having forced Braxton Bragg to abandon his base of operations at Shelbyville by threatening Tulla-homa, William S. Rosecrans determined, if possible, to repeat that success by cutting the railroad in Bragg's rear, severing his lines of supply even farther to the south. For this task, he once again turned to Col. John T. Wilder. On June 27, Rosecrans ordered Wilder's Lightning Brigade to burn the Elk River railroad bridge and destroy the tracks between Decherd and Cowan. Rosecrans urged Wilder "to strike quick and heavy blows."

The Lightning Brigade was to march at 6:00 a.m. on the 28th, "with none but serviceable horses, capable of enduring a very long and fatiguing march," recalled Maj. James A. Connolly of the 123rd Illinois. "As soon as that order came we knew it meant hard work for our brigade, so the Col. and myself sat down under a tree and wrote very brief letters to our respective wives, not knowing when they would ever hear from us again." Rosecrans also detailed Brig. Gen. John Beatty's XIV Corps infantry brigade and two mountain howitzers attached to Eli Lilly's battery to Hillsborough, where Beatty could cover and support Wilder's movements.[1]

---

1   OR 23, pt. 2, 474; Angle, *Three Years in the Army of the Cumberland*, 95; OR 23, pt. 1, 407, and pt. 2, 473; Rowell, *Yankee Artillerymen*, 85. Beatty's brigade was part of Gen. Negley's 2nd Division, XIV Corps. The distance from Shelbyville to Decherd is about 30 miles, and about seven from Decherd to Cowan. Hillsborough and Hillsboro were used interchangeably by both armies. We use the former spelling because it appears that way in the *OR* and *OR Atlas*.

Col. John Beatty, commander, First Brigade, Second Division, XIV Corps, Army of the Cumberland.

Generals in Blue

Wilder and the Lightning Brigade departed Manchester as ordered, heading southeast. They carried three days' rations in their haversacks and sheaves of wheat for the horses strapped behind their saddles. Since speed was essential, they traveled without supply wagons. Wilder expected to reach Decherd that evening. "Great hopes were entertained when [Wilder and the Lightning Brigade] left," noted a newspaper correspondent traveling with the Army of the Cumberland. The brigade moved rapidly to Hillsborough, eight miles from Manchester, leaving two companies of the 123rd Illinois there until Beatty's infantry brigade could come up to relieve them.[2]

While Wilder pushed south, Beatty occupied Hillsborough. On the night of June 28, the Confederates drove in Beatty's pickets on the Tullahoma Road, so Beatty formed his brigade to receive an attack. Although four regiments of Confederate cavalry were nearby, they did not advance. The next day, Beatty and his command left Hillsborough on the Manchester and Winchester Road and, after some heavy skirmishing, moved to the vicinity of Bobo's Crossroads. There Beatty unexpectedly encountered elements of Maj. Gen. Joseph Reynolds's division, who, Beatty noted, "had mistaken us for the enemy. Fortunately, no one had been injured" by the ensuing exchange of friendly fire.[3]

By then, the 123rd Illinois had rejoined Wilder's main body and the reunited command headed for the Elk River railroad bridge. "It still rained, and marching was slow and wearisome," noted a man in the 17th Indiana. Wilder intended to ford the Elk at Shallow or Morris fords, seven miles southwest of Hillsborough.

2 Wilson, "Wilder's Brigade of Mounted Infantry," 54; "Mr. F. G. Shanks' Despatches," *New York Herald*, July 8, 1863.

3 *OR* 23, pt. 1, 445-447.

However, near the mouth of Bradley's Fork, the Federals "found that the incessant rains had so swollen that stream that we could neither ford nor swim it, the current being so rapid that our horses were washed down stream." As one wag put it, when Wilder arrived at the river, "on trying to cross it, [we] found water enough to have discouraged old Noah, and too swift to swim."[4]

This forced a detour to Pelham, eight miles upstream to the east, where a bridge spanned the Elk. Approaching Pelham, Wilder learned that a force of Confederates guarded the bridge, intending to destroy it upon the approach of the Lightning Brigade. Wilder immediately ordered his lead regiment, Lt. Col. Edward Kitchell's 98th Illinois, reinforced with about 30 scouts from his various regiments, to go forward on the run and save the bridge from destruction. These men dashed up to and secured the bridge, taking two prisoners and capturing 78 mules. While at Pelham, Wilder burned a saddle factory and freed two Union sutlers that had been captured earlier. He just missed capturing a Confederate colonel who was out gathering in his men, who had been permitted to go home to harvest their wheat. Detailing a single company to drive the mules back to Hillsborough, Wilder led the rest of the Lightning Brigade across the Elk.[5]

Even with the bridge, the crossing proved strenuous. Wilder reported that he "found the river at Pelham nearly swimming around the bridge." Perhaps not trusting the span, he resorted to other means. "We soon reached the South Fork of Elk River, and found the water deep enough to swim our tallest horses. The stream, though rapid, could, by crossing diagonally, be swum; and, by tearing down an old mill, we made a raft that, by being towed with our picket ropes floated our two mountain howitzers over," he wrote. "The crossing occupied about three hours." The men laughed about their "gunboat," as they dubbed the raft that carried the mountain howitzers across the swollen river.[6]

Once across, Wilder detached Col. James Monroe and eight companies of the 123rd Illinois to march westward downstream along the south bank, "to destroy, if possible, the road and railroad bridges over [the] Elk River at Estill Springs, with orders, if successful, to come down the railroad and join me at Decherd, or below."

---

4 Wilson, "Wilder's Brigade of Mounted Infantry," 54; OR 23, pt. 1, 459; "Colonel Wilder's Expedition. *Indianapolis Journal* Narrative," included in Frank Moore, ed., *The Rebellion Record: A Diary of American Events, with Documents, Narratives, Illustrative Incidents, Poetry, Etc.*, 11 vols. (New York: 1861-1868), 7:204.

5 OR 23, pt. 2, 484.

6 Ibid.; "Colonel Wilder's Expedition," 7:204.

Wilder intended to cut the railroad between Tullahoma and Chattanooga at as many places as possible. Additionally, Monroe was to strike the railroad at Allisonia, the first station south of Tullahoma, destroy a bridge there, then follow the line and meet the rest of the brigade at Cowan, about 15 miles north of the Alabama border. Cowan, the last stop on the railroad before the Cumberland Plateau rises, was the location of the most vulnerable point on the Nashville and Chattanooga line, the 2,200-foot Cowan Tunnel through Cumberland Mountain. Wilder's men were to block that critical tunnel to prevent reinforcements moving via Chattanooga from reaching Bragg's army at Tullahoma, provided they could accomplish this without being captured. The Illinoisans faced a difficult march. As Major Connolly of the 123rd Illinois noted, "At five o'clock in the morning of the 28th I was in the saddle and wasn't out of it again until one o'clock in the morning of the 29th."[7]

While Monroe accomplished his tasks, the rest of the Lightning Brigade made straight for Decherd, about 15 miles southwest of Pelham, struggling across another swollen stream along the way. Reaching the railroad at about 8 p.m., Wilder immediately formed in line of battle and attacked a Confederate train guard of about 80 men, commanded by Capt. John W. House of the 2nd Tennessee Infantry, who were positioned behind a stockade and the railroad cut. House and his small detachment of Southerners, admitted Wilder, "made a pretty good resistance."[8]

"Captain House proved to be something of a strategist as well as a good fighter, and although at times completely flanked on both sides," recalled a Confederate, "after firing upon the front he would move quickly to the right and fire a volley over the railroad embankment which was a good fortification, and then he would move as rapidly to the left, protected to some extent by a high trestle-work (which it was his special business to defend) and then his whole command would turn loose upon the enemy, and thus by a rapid and strategic 'change of base,' he managed to make the enemy believe his antagonist was giving it to him in regular army style—fighting his centre and right and left wings all at the same time." In this fashion, House hung on for nearly an hour.[9]

---

7 Angle, *Three Years in the Army of the Cumberland*, 95-96.

8 Ibid.; "The Raid on Decherd," written by "One Who Has Investigated the Facts," *The Daily Rebel*, July 3, 1863.

9 "The Raid on Decherd."

Eventually the determined Federals pried the equally stubborn Confederates out of their defenses, but House was not ready to admit defeat. "We soon dislodged them, however, when they took a position in a deep ravine, with timber in it, completely protecting them, while our men had to approach over a bare hill to attack them, exposing themselves to sharp fire at 60 yards' range." Another sharp fight ensued.[10]

"Col. Wilder was down directing the movement when they began firing," recounted Pvt. Henry Tutewiler of the 17th Indiana. "The bullets flew all around us. I was very much alarmed for the Col.'s safety. [He] sent me to show the howitzers up onto a hill. Two rounds of grape scattered them." The Confederates fled, leaving Wilder and his men to their task of destroying the tracks of the Nashville and Chattanooga, using a device invented by Wilder's blacksmiths that prohibited the track from being straightened and used again. "We paid our respects to old Decherd . . . and captured twenty Rebs," declared Capt. William A. Owens of Company D, 17th Indiana.[11]

Captain Alexander A. Rice, the regimental adjutant of the 17th Indiana, had dismounted and was quietly leading his horse into Decherd to give instructions to the men destroying the water tank when the Confederates inside the stockade opened fire on him. The bullets rattled against a fence and spooked his horse. The frightened animal jerked loose from him, "leaving him in quite an unpleasant predicament, and his chances for Libby prison good," wrote Sgt. Benjamin Magee. But the horse did not run, and Rice caught its bridle. Just then, the Confederates loosed another volley, and their balls rattled the fence a second time; again Rice's horse broke away. "This was repeated, the Captain's hair standing on end, until the horse got out of range of the bullets, and then the Captain mounted and went out of there like a bird flying." Rice later admitted to having been scared.[12]

The Yankees also destroyed a trestle on a branch line to Winchester and burned the railroad depot, which contained telegraph instruments and was filled with commissary stores. "This [damage] could not be done very fast on account of the darkness," reported a newspaper correspondent traveling with Wilder's command. After tearing up about 300 yards of track, Wilder learned that a large force of the enemy was approaching from the north, so he ordered his troops to withdraw. They skirmished with the advance guard of the Confederates, capturing

10 *OR* 23, pt. 1, 484.

11 Baumgartner, *Blue Lightning*, 93.

12 Magee, *History of the Seventy-Second Regiment*, 133-134.

four or five prisoners, who informed Wilder that he faced six regiments of infantry, all about to attack. "Believing that I would have but little chance of success in a fight with them, on account of the darkness and our total ignorance of the ground, we moved off in the direction of Pelham," reported Wilder, "and, after going about 6 miles, went off the road into the woods at 2 o'clock and bivouacked without fires until daylight." It had been an exhausting ride. Even after crossing the Elk, the heavy rains made the going difficult, Wilder continued, and "we were compelled to ford streams that swam our smallest horses, and compelled us to carry our howitzers' ammunition on the men's shoulders across the streams."[13]

"We had now ridden fifty-eight miles since morning, all the way through a drenching rain and on the worst of roads, so we were glad to unsaddle and take a little rest," recalled Sgt. George Wilson of Company B of the 17th Indiana. "We were forbidden fires and our rations were soaked to a pulp and utterly unfit for use. Take it all together, we were a miserable set; but I got some sleep by spreading my saddle blanket on logs and covering it with a poncho. With all these discomforts, our perilous situation in the rear of and only a few miles from an enemy 40,000 strong was a matter of secondary consideration for us."[14]

"We had put in another hard day's work in the rain, and our beds were on the mountain side on the sharpest of rocks," wrote Sergeant Magee. "The mountain was so steep that we had to get our feet against the trees or rocks to keep from slipping down. And had not the surroundings been so desperate it would have been funny to see us try to sleep. You see a big, stout, long-legged soldier lay down flat of his back, his legs stiff and his feet braced against a tree; in two minutes he is asleep, his muscles being to relax, his knees fly up, and down he goes a-straddle of the tree." Magee recalled that he and the rest of the Hoosiers spent much of the night trying not to slide down the muddy hill, and not sleeping as the heavy rains poured down on them.[15]

---

13 "Colonel Wilder's Expedition," 7:204; *OR* 23, pt. 1, 460-461. The town of Decherd (pronounced "DECK-erd") owes its existence to the Nashville and Chattanooga Railroad. It was named for a local landowner named Peter S. Decherd, who gave the rights-of-way to the railroad company with a requirement that it establish a depot near his plantation. The railroad through the town was completed in 1851. Between Decherd and Cowan, the line passes through Cumberland Mountain via the strategically important Cowan Tunnel. Peter Decherd was the maternal uncle of Confederate divisional commander Alexander Peter Stewart, whose middle name was given in honor of his uncle. Stewart was a native of nearby Winchester. Elliott, *Soldier of Tennessee*, 6-7.

14 Wilson, "Wilder's Brigade of Mounted Infantry," 54.

15 Magee, *History of the Seventy-Second Regiment*, 134.

In the meantime, when Col. James Monroe and his 123rd Illinois arrived at the railroad on June 28, they found a large Rebel wagon train, as well as elements of Maj. Gen. Jones M. Withers's division of Polk's Corps guarding the bridges. The Federals could see that the road south was thronged with wagons, infantry, and batteries of artillery, all apparently marching rapidly toward Chattanooga. "Bragg's army was slipping away and we didn't have the strength to stop it," lamented Major Connolly. "How little did they think, as they were moving along, 12 miles in the rear of Tullahoma, that a regiment of Illinois Yankees was in the woods, within easy musket range of them, quietly watching their movements and noting their numbers." The Illinoisans chafed, wanting to pitch in as they watched regiment after regiment pass by, but "we did not dare attack them. To attack would have been madness, for there was a whole Division . . . with infantry, artillery, and cavalry, so we lay quiet for more than an hour while they were passing, then noiselessly countermarched, intending to return to where we left the brigade and follow its trail until we overtook it, but when we reached the point at which we had left it it was one o'clock in the morning, and we found that Gen. John Beatty's brigade had come there during the day and was encamped."[16]

Colonel Monroe noted that "the road was full of troops. I showed myself to draw attention from Wilder's movements." He also reported seeing "an immense wagon train, [and batteries] of artillery," and opined that the Confederates were moving everything across the Elk River. Obviously badly outnumbered, Monroe wisely fell back to Hillsborough, pursued by a force of rebel cavalry. He skirmished with the Confederate horsemen the whole way, holding them in check for several miles without taking any casualties.[17]

Monroe was mistaken when interpreting Bragg's intentions, but he was correct about the identity of the foe: two brigades of Withers's troops did indeed march south out of Tullahoma on June 28. William Bass of the 7th Mississippi Infantry of Patton Anderson's Brigade and Sgt. John H. Freeman of the 34th Mississippi in Edward C. Walthall's brigade both described wearying marches to Allisonia in their diaries. Bass noted that on "June 28 we got up early and moved on. We got up to our brigade that was camped. We staid here and rested a day." Freeman recorded that the Mississippians "marched from Tullahoma to Alsona 8 miles muddy and rainy roads. Our Regt. 34th marched. The balance of the brigade road on the cars. We then worked near all night on a fort." Freeman further noted "a false alarm in

16 Baumgartner, *Blue Lightning*, 96; *Cincinnati Commercial*, July 2, 1863.

17 OR 23, pt. 1, 445, 459; Angle, *Three Years in the Army of the Cumberland*, 96-97.

Brig. Gen. Edward C. Walthall, commander, Walthall's Brigade, Withers Division, Polk's Corps, Army of Tennessee.

Alabama Department of Archives and History

the night," likely due to Col. Monroe's martial display. The next day, had Monroe remained to observe, he likely would have seen those same brigades headed back north, for both Bass and Freeman recorded returning to Tullahoma on June 29. At this stage, Bragg still intended to make a fight of it.[18]

Nor was that all. More Rebels were headed to Tullahoma. By the 28th, Simon B. Buckner's promised contingent of reinforcements had begun to reach Bragg's army. Sergeant Robert Watson of the 7th Florida Infantry recorded that his command "left Chattanooga at 7½ a.m. with one engine in front one behind." It was a raucous trip, with "some of the boys pretty merry owing to the strength of whiskey and all in good spirits expecting to have a fight on our arrival at Tullahoma at which place we arrived at 5 p.m."[19]

Monroe can be forgiven for misreading Bragg's plans since he almost certainly observed the Army of Tennessee's wagons hauling as much extra equipment and supplies as they could farther south, away from what was now the front line at Tullahoma. Moreover, Rosecrans had plenty of other reports from his infantry commanders, which placed Bragg's army firmly at Tullahoma, apparently with every intention of giving battle.

Departing Hillsborough at about 3:00 a.m. on June 29, Monroe and his detachment "started up the Cumberland mountains in a terrible thunder storm. When we reached the summit of the mountains the elemental war was raging in its greatest fury," Major Connolly wrote. "[T]he reverberations of the thunder rolled

18 Skellie, *Lest We Forget*, 2:523; entry for June 28, 1863, John H. Freeman Diary, http://freepages.rootsweb.com/~mruddy/genealogy/freeman.htm, accessed May 18, 2019.

19 R. Thomas Campbell, ed., *Southern Service on Land and Sea: The Wartime Journal of Robert Watson CSA/CSN* (Knoxville, TN: 2002), 60.

through the valleys below us, and the lightning appeared to be flashing below our feet, all this, combined with the dangerous character of our expedition, was enough to try the nerves, but no one dared to fall out, for that would be certain capture at least." About noon, they struck the railroad again and found the track torn up, with rails bent and scattered around, a sure sign that the rest of the Lightning Brigade had passed through ahead of them. About 2 p.m., within about five miles of the Alabama state line, they overtook and joined the balance of the Lightning Brigade, resting in a deep wooded valley.[20]

Major General Joseph J. Reynolds commanded the Fourth Division of the XIV Corps, which included Wilder's Brigade. On the morning of June 29, he relayed Monroe's information up the chain of command, further noting that "our [Wilder's] movement surprises all citizens and soldiers." Even better, "citizens thought no force was on railroad where Wilder was going. They knew nothing of the brigade that Monroe met. Soldiers in squads returning to Tullahoma. The people did not know that we had possession of Shelbyville and thought the rebels would stand at Tullahoma."[21]

Also on June 29th, Wilder and the rest of his command started up the Cumberland Plateau on the Brakefield Point Road. Wilder decided to break the Nashville and Chattanooga below Cowan if possible. For Wilder's men, the going became, if anything, even harder. "The want of rest and sleep was telling on us, and we were constantly falling asleep and reeling in our saddles like drunken men," remembered Magee. "The route was almost impracticable, and the howitzers had to be pulled up by hand. When we got to the top of the mountain we could see reinforcements pouring into Decherd. The rebels had been struck suddenly there and were fearfully scared, not knowing whence the Yankees came, or whither they went."[22]

Wilder then advanced to the University of the South's campus at University Place, Tennessee. The Lightning Brigade paused for a light breakfast—a cup of coffee while enjoying the spectacular view from the top of the mountain. The men then destroyed the railroad spur that passed through the town, which was used to carry coal from mines around Tracy City to Cowan, where the coal fueled Nashville and Chattanooga trains. Here, Wilder ordered Col. John J. Funkhouser and 450 men of the 98th Illinois to venture another eight miles south to destroy the railroad

---

20 OR 23, pt. 1, 445, 459; Angle, *Three Years in the Army of the Cumberland*, 96-97.

21 OR 23, pt. 2, 484.

22 Ibid., pt. 1, 461; Magee, *History of the Seventy-Second Regiment*, 134.

at Tantallon. Wilder headed with the rest of his brigade to Anderson, a small depot on the Tennessee-Alabama state line, about 17 miles south of University Place, where he intended to inflict yet more damage to the railroad.[23]

Funkhouser soon sent word that three railroad trains filled with troops were at Tantallon, and Wilder's scouts reported two more trains at Anderson. Since both places, deep in mountainous terrain and accessible only by bridle paths, were difficult to approach, Wilder determined it would be impossible to accomplish anything more. Before long, Confederate cavalry, elements of Nathan Bedford Forrest's division, drove in the Union pickets guarding Wilder's rear at the university, preceding a force of infantry that arrived via the railroad. In light of this new threat, Wilder decided the wiser course of action was to withdraw. Deep behind enemy lines, pursued by heavy bodies of Rebel cavalry, and with the rails humming with Confederate troop movements, Wilder reported, "I collected my force, and determined to extricate them."[24]

"The whole of the Rebel cavalry and Buckner's division of infantry were after [Wilder], and his men had been in the saddles and their horses under them for seven days," noted one Union participant. "His men were out of rations, and his horses starved, and the mountains without farms or inhabitants, and to leave them [in the mountains] was certain capture." Leaving a rear guard to skirmish with the Confederate cavalry and draw them down the mountain, Wilder started the Lightning Brigade on the road through Sweeden's Cove toward Chattanooga, from where he could double back northward.[25]

Given the swollen state of the Elk River, Wilder's only hope of escape was the bridge at Pelham. Lieutenant Robert A. Vance of Company I of the 17th Indiana led a small detail to the bridge, arriving just in time to repel a Confederate force sent to seize it. The Hoosiers tore up the floor of the bridge, carried the boards to their

23 *OR* 23, pt. 1, 461; Wilson, "Wilder's Brigade of Mounted Infantry," 55. The University of the South was founded in 1857 by a group of delegates from 10 Episcopal dioceses, led by Bishop Leonidas Polk—who, in 1863, was Lt. Gen. Leonidas Polk, commander of one of Bragg's infantry corps—for the purpose of establishing a Southern university without Northern influence. Given the connection with Polk, it is not surprising that Union soldiers would destroy the campus buildings after the Tullahoma Campaign. After the war, the school began using the name "Sewanee" and today refers to itself as Sewanee: The University of the South.

24 *OR* 23, pt. 1, 461. These carloads of Rebels could have been troops from Bragg's army, sent from Tullahoma, or the last elements of Buckner's East Tennessee contingent. The lack of Confederate reports leaves the question unanswered.

25 "Colonel Wilder's Expedition," 7:204; *OR* 23, pt. 1, 461.

side of the river, built breastworks with them, and held their position until morning, ensuring that the Lightning Brigade would be able to use the important bridge to get across the Elk.[26]

Though the rain continued to pelt down, making the withdrawal ever more difficult, it obliterated any trail or sign of the Lightning Brigade's march. About eight miles out from the university, Wilder moved his entire command off the road and about two miles eastward into the woods, while the pursuing Confederate cavalry continued along the road, headed off in the wrong direction. Wilder left a rear guard to drive the pursuers down the mountain. "Of course it is the policy of a raiding party to avoid an engagement unless a special object is to be gained by fighting; so, under the circumstances, Wilder successfully adopted Indian tactics to baffle pursuit," remembered Sgt. George Wilson of the 17th Indiana. "As we moved on towards Chattanooga, the command began to scatter to the left in detachments of regiments, all moving in the same general direction, to concentrate at a point where a road leads down the mountain, not far from the Elk River Bridge, by which we hoped to cross the next day." The dense stands of timber, thinly populated and largely unbroken by farms or fields, provided cover for the marching column as it made its way across the countryside. The rear guard then escaped and joined the main body, although some of them did not arrive until morning.[27]

"As soon as the rebel column had passed us, we struck through the mountains, without guides, in the direction of Pelham, and came out at the place we intended to strike, and reached the foot of the mountain, at Gilham's Cove, over a very rocky and steep road," reported Wilder. The men passed single file along a narrow bridle path. "We bivouacked at 10 p.m., and next morning at daylight started for Manchester, just getting ahead of Forrest, who, with nine regiments of cavalry and two pieces of artillery, aimed to intercept us at Pelham," Wilder continued. That night, forage and supplies were distributed. According to Sergeant Wilson, "for the first time on the trip, horses and men had a fair feed."[28]

---

26 Magee, *History of the Seventy-Second Regiment*, 135.

27 Wilson, "Wilder's Brigade of Mounted Infantry," 55.

28 Angle, *Three Years in the Army of the Cumberland*, 97; OR 23, pt. 1, 461; Wilson, "Wilder's Brigade of Mounted Infantry," 56. University Place is about 14 miles away from Pelham. The mention of Forrest's men refers specifically to Col. George G. Dibrell's brigade, which was originally Forrest's own brigade of Tennessee cavalry.

Wilder's weary column trudged into Manchester about noon on the last day of June, "having been in the saddle or fighting about twenty hours out of each twenty-four for eleven days, and all the time drenched with rain, our men half starved and our horses almost entirely without forage, yet our officers and men seemed willing and cheerful, and are now only anxious for another expedition, if by such they can accomplish any good." One they arrived at Manchester, the weary men of the Lightning Brigade learned General Rosecrans had shifted his base of operations to Tullahoma based on Wilder's reports of the movements of Bragg's army.[29]

About two hours earlier, Major General Stanley, commander of the Army of the Cumberland's Cavalry Corps, had been chatting with Rosecrans. He gloomily opined that the Lightning Brigade would never get back, that it would almost certainly be surrounded and captured. Rosecrans and Stanley were still discussing this possibility when Wilder, covered with mud and completely soaked, dismounted from his jaded horse at the entrance to Rosecrans's headquarters tent and walked in to report to the astonished generals. "All right, [Wilder], I know you now," declared Rosecrans. "Take your brigade any place you can find forage and rest yourselves until you are again needed. I want you to furnish me a body guard of 300 of your men."[30]

Wilder's soldiers managed to make the expedition without the loss of a single man, "having marched one hundred and twenty-six miles in two days and a half, swam four streams, tore up three railroads, and got back safely—the tiredest set of mortals you ever saw," one of the men proudly declared.[31]

The Lightning Brigade bivouacked at Manchester on the night of June 30. The next morning, the men moved "into a beautiful valley where food and water were abundant, and turning our horses loose let them eat all day while we slept," recalled Major Connolly. It was the first day since they departed Murfreesboro on June 24 that it did not rain, meaning that "we lived in the rain, slept in the mud and rain and were as wet as fish in the river all that time, but it has not caused me a moment's sickness, and I feel first rate after it all."[32]

29 *OR* 23, pt. 1, 461.

30 Angle, *Three Years in the Army of the Cumberland*, 98.

31 "Colonel Wilder's Expedition," 7:204.

32 Angle, *Three Years in the Army of the Cumberland*, 99.

Wilder proudly reported that he achieved all he did without losing a single man during the mission. "If our course had not been impeded by the streams flooded beyond all precedent, we must have captured one or two railroad trains, one of them having General Buckner and staff on board," he wrote; "we should have had ample time to have thoroughly torn up the railroad in daylight at several points, whilst on account of the darkness we were compelled to follow the main roads and the time lost in going via Pelham enabled the rebels to throw a large force in pursuit of us."[33]

Sergeant George Wilson, a mounted infantryman with the 17th Indiana, Wilder's brigade, took a more jaundiced view. "In the three days we had ridden 110 miles in drenching rains, by miserable roads and through mountainous country, and had swum three of four streams," he explained. "Horses and men subsisted on next to nothing, and both were well nigh worn out. As to the results of the raid I can say but little. In my opinion," Wilson continued,

> spasmodic [efforts] of this kind directed against an enemy's communications generally miscarry. Something is apt to happen to prevent a full realization of expected results. In this instance, the bad condition of the roads and swollen streams caused delays which prevented our getting at the road in but one place, and then with time to destroy 300 to 500 yards of track. The material damage to the enemy was slight, and I doubt if the moral effect was commensurate with the risks and costs of the expedition.[34]

One member of the 72nd Indiana reported, "Upon the 28th, 29th, and 30th of June the rains were the most constant and heavy we had ever witnessed—would have done credit to the days of that old flatboatman Noah. We were allowed no fires at night to warm by—didn't need any for cooking purposes, as our rations did not average more than a cracker per day, and hot coffee or meat were out of the question. It may be very naturally supposed we had a wet time of it, and so we had, and a cold one, too, for drowning mother earth was our bed, and the Yankee uniform in which we marched was our only bed-clothing at night. But like true Hoosiers we 'worried it through.' Our horses were nearly all broken down with fatigue."[35]

---

33 OR 23, pt. 1, 461.

34 Wilson, "Wilder's Brigade of Mounted Infantry," 56-57.

35 "Tippecanoe" to editor, dated July 5, 1863, *The Lafayette Daily Courier* (Lafayette, IN), July 16, 1863.

Major Connolly observed, "from the time we left Manchester until our return there our horses had nothing to eat except what leaves and grass they could nip as we went along, and they got so that they would eat blankets, saddle skirts and anything else they could get into their mouths. I have frequently read of such privations but never believed it to be true, but I know such things to be true now." Connolly claimed that the expedition to Decherd and beyond "used up 500 horses." The men of the Lightning Brigade did not get a chance to rest until July 1, remaining almost constantly on the move the entire time. The nonstop movement, lack of fodder, heavy rains, thick mud, and mountainous terrain took a heavy toll on Wilder's mounts.[36]

"In actual damage to the enemy this expedition was a failure, but in unifying the brigade and giving each man confidence in himself and his officers, it was a grand success," was how Sgt. Benjamin Magee of the 17th Indiana candidly described the exhausting mission. "The rebels had hitherto had it all their own way in raiding railroads; this expedition demonstrated that we were just as competent to raid rebel railroads as rebels were to raid Union railroads. This raid had a very demoralizing effect on General Bragg, and he began to evacuate Tullahoma in two hours after he heard the report of our guns at Decherd, thinking he had been flanked by the whole army."[37]

Predictably, Wilder's foes dismissed the raid as a mere nuisance. "The only damage done to the railroad was fully repaired in three hours," boasted one Confederate on June 29, "and today the trains are running over the road." He continued, "I forgot to mention that the abolitionists burst a water tank, but on the whole, the damage amounts to nothing, and it is certain that the enemy lost several men killed and wounded." Aside from the casualties, this was an accurate assessment. The effort to cripple the railroad had failed, even though Wilder's men successfully pulled off their long march across the Army of Tennessee's vulnerable rear.[38]

As many of the participants observed, other than the destruction of a few hundred yards of the Nashville & Chattanooga Railroad at Decherd, the expedition inflicted little actual damage. However, it definitely had a significant impact on the

---

36 Angle, *Three Years in the Army of the Cumberland*, 99; Samuel E. Munford to his sister, July 4, 1863, Samuel E. Munford Letters, Smith Memorial Library, Indiana Historical Society, Indianapolis.

37 Magee, *History of the Seventy-Second Regiment*, 135.

38 "The Raid on Decherd."

campaign: the presence of a large force of mounted Union troops operating in his rear drew Bragg's attention and drew away resources, which enabled Rosecrans to sidle around the Army of Tennessee's flank and contributed to Bragg's June 30 decision to retreat from Tullahoma.

In the greater scheme of things, Wilder's expedition furthered Rosecrans's audacious plan to maneuver Bragg's army out of Middle Tennessee, and hastened Bragg's decision to retreat again, to Chattanooga.

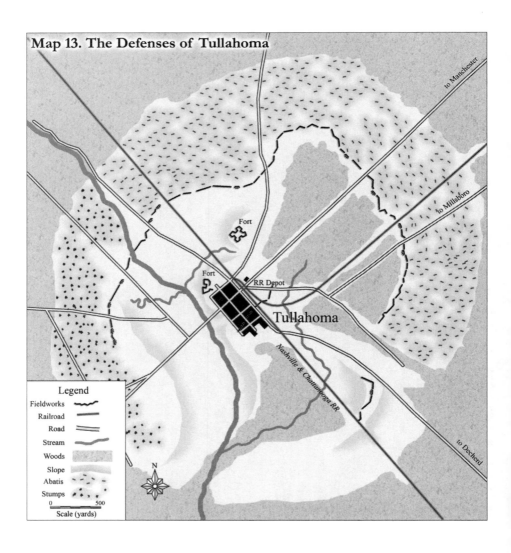

Map 13. The Defenses of Tullahoma

to Manchester

to Millsboro

to Dechard

Fort

Fort

RR Depot

Tullahoma

Nashville & Chattanooga RR

Legend

Fieldworks
Railroad
Road
Stream
Woods
Slope
Abatis
Stumps

0   500
Scale (yards)

N

Chapter Twelve

The Battle that Wasn't: Tullahoma,
June 28 to 29, 1863

While John Wilder set out as ordered on his expedition across the Elk, William Rosecrans contemplated his next moves. He now believed he had the Army of Tennessee just where he wanted it. His bold maneuvers had pried the Confederates loose from their defenses along the rim and driven them back to Tullahoma.

Rosecrans advanced his headquarters to Manchester on June 27, where he took stock of his army and its dispositions. Since Crittenden's XXI Corps, which was supposed to deliver the decisive blows, had bogged down in thick mud near a rural crossroads called Pocahontas, Thomas's column quickly assumed the role as the Union army's primary strike force, supported by McCook's XX Corps. Wilder's brigade would soon be menacing Bragg's rear. Elements of Granger's Reserve Corps were coming up behind McCook or at Shelbyville, but other substantial elements of Granger's force were tied down garrisoning Nashville and Murfreesboro, in no position to help. Though Rosecrans hoped Wilder might accomplish some good, he knew he would have to rely on Thomas, McCook, and—as soon as the XXI Corps could come up—Crittenden for the main blow. All would have to move quickly if Rosecrans could have a chance to spring his trap against Bragg's army. However, the unprecedented heavy June rains made the sort of rapid movement required impossible.[1]

---

1 Bradley, *Tullahoma*, 81-82.

On June 28, Rosecrans reported his circumstances to Halleck. "Heavy roads, made nearly impassable by constant rain, detained General Crittenden's column, en route from Bradyville to this place, and it has not yet all arrived. Bragg put his whole army in retreat upon Tullahoma yesterday morning. General Gordon Granger and General Stanley advanced from Christiana yesterday morning, and entered Shelbyville at 6:00 p.m., capturing three pieces of artillery and 300 prisoners." Continuing, he wrote, "The bridge across Duck River was saved. At 9:00 p.m. last evening Granger started in pursuit of Bragg's train, not then more than 9 miles beyond Shelbyville. He has not yet been heard from. A cavalry force was sent from here last night, to cut the railroad toward the Tennessee. Nothing but heavy and continued rain has prevented this army from reaching Tullahoma in advance of Bragg." Now Rosecrans resolved to try to strike at Tullahoma before Bragg finished concentrating his force there.[2]

Rosecrans ordered at least one brigade of Granger's Reserve Corps to advance to Manchester, and instructed Granger to bring up the rest of the corps as soon as possible. One priority was to protect the 1st Michigan Engineers, who had already begun repairing the railroad toward Wartrace. He instructed Stanley to send the cavalry assigned to his left wing to lead the advance in the hope of running down Wheeler's beaten command. Desperate for accurate intelligence, Rosecrans recognized that with his entire army spread out across the countryside of Middle Tennessee, he remained exposed to cavalry raids and, potentially, a significant counterattack.[3]

The rest of the XIV Corps lumbered into Manchester on the morning of June 28. "Fell into battle line and continued all day," a soldier of the 79th Pennsylvania of Negley's division recounted in his diary. "Caught a colonel and sergeant on the bank of the creek, not ten feet from our line of battle." There would be no respite for the Federals, however. Rosecrans instructed George Thomas to push two divisions of the XIV Corps toward Tullahoma. He wanted the lead division to advance to a defensible position located five or six miles out, and then to send scouts ahead to try to find the enemy.[4]

To increase their speed, once again the men were ordered to travel light: no supply wagons would accompany them, and they were to carry three days' rations

2 OR 23, pt. 1, 402.

3 Ibid., pt. 2, 477.

4 Adam S. Johnston, *The Soldier Boy's Diary Book; or, Memorandums of the Alphabetical First Lessons of Military Tactics* (Pittsburgh, PA: 1866), 43; OR 23, pt. 2, 477.

in their haversacks. Rosecrans, frustrated at what he regarded as disobedience to these instructions on previous marches, circulated a new order throughout the army:

> The general commanding has noticed with great regret the criminal neglect to obey department orders in reference to the reduction of baggage. If this army fails in the great object of the present movement, it will be mainly due to the fact that our wagons have been loaded down with unauthorized baggage. Officers and soldiers who are ready to die in the field do not hesitate to disgrace themselves and imperil the army by luxuries unworthy of a soldier. . . . Any quartermaster whose train shall be found carrying chairs and such other needless weight, usually the fruit of thieving, will at once be arrested, and the officer claiming it be severely punished.[5]

At 8:00 a.m. on June 28, Granger reported from Shelbyville, "I was much disappointed last night in not being able to continue our pursuit of the enemy. After a long and hard march and constant fighting yesterday afternoon, our men and horses were too exhausted to move. Forrest pressed around our rear last night, moving eastward. Had I known he was so doing, I could have thrown my force between the retreating rebel army and his forces, but even then our men and horses were too badly used up to insure any prospect of success."[6]

At 12:30 a.m. on June 29, Rosecrans sent another courier galloping off to find Granger, inquiring whether Granger's supplies had come up yet and informing him that the telegraph line was complete as far as Christiana and was rapidly being constructed to Shelbyville. He instructed Granger to order reinforcements up from

---

5 OR 23, pt. 2, 478-479. As was his practice, Rosecrans included meticulous instructions on how to strip down all excess encumbrances. His order included the following details: "The general commanding directs that all baggage trains be reduced to the minimum. To effect this, all tents, except shelter tents and one wall tent to each regiment, will be dispensed with. The ammunition now carried in the company wagons will be turned over to the division ordnance officers, who will be furnished with a sufficient number of additional wagons to transport it. This will enable the transportation of each regiment to be reduced to 7 wagons, which reduction will be at once made. All wagons in excess of this allowance will be turned over to the division quartermaster, who will, under the direction of the chief quartermaster of each corps, organize them into a supply train for the division. Surplus baggage will be sent to Murfreesborough by the returning trains for storage. The wagons will carry five days' rations of short forage, one tent to a regiment, and medical supplies. All commissioned officers will hereafter carry one ration on their person. Third. All knapsacks will be sent to the rear, and nothing will be carried by the men except shelter tents, blankets, 1 shirt, 1 pair of socks, and 1 pair of drawers. Fourth. Corps and division commanders will be held responsible for the throwing out of every unauthorized article of baggage."

6 Ibid., pt. 1, 534.

Nashville and to report back to him by messenger. Reflecting the state of uncertainty prevailing at army headquarters, Rosecrans concluded, "It is doubtful whether Bragg will make a stand at Tullahoma or fall back on Chattanooga. What do you think?"[7]

Granger replied at 1:45 a.m., although his answer did not reach Rosecrans until 9:25 that night. He advised Rosecrans that Baird's division had taken position at Shelbyville and that he had ordered nearly all the troops left behind at Nashville to come up and join him. "From the best information I can obtain, Bragg's army, in mass—horse, foot, and dragoons—are falling back as rapidly as possible upon Bridgeport," he wrote. "I feel confident that the rebel cavalry has abandoned the line of Franklin and Duck River, and are pushing on to join the main column, in the direction of Chattanooga. I have only retained three regiments of cavalry, just barely sufficient to keep the pike open between Murfreesborough and Shelbyville, to protect supplies sent to Baird's command, and also to protect the working parties on the railroad." He concluded, "I shall be in Murfreesborough to-night, to put things in shape, and get everything fairly and properly started. I may go to Shelbyville to-morrow, but that will depend upon how much I have to do at Murfreesborough, and how long I will be detained there. I will push through the railroad and telegraph without delay." To free himself for the main task, Rosecrans placed Granger in charge of all the military posts above the Duck River. Additionally, Granger was to gather as much intelligence as possible and cover the army's right flank. Baird's division would remain in Shelbyville.[8]

Rosecrans also sent Stanley's troopers to Wartrace, asking the cavalryman to provide information on the whereabouts of Forrest's command. At 7:45 that morning, Rosecrans wrote to Thomas, "it would be better position to withdraw Negley to Sutton's [farm], behind Crumpton's Creek, holding the advanced brigade at Bobo's Cross-Roads, and Reynolds to Taylor's or Anderson's [houses], holding an advanced force at Concord Church, and leaving Brannan where he is. The inclemency of the weather and the state of the roads, however, leave but little probability of his assuming the offensive." After Thomas responded, Rosecrans next ordered him to advance the XIV Corps toward Tullahoma as far as Bobo's Crossroads, thereby commanding the Hillsborough, Lynchburg, and Pelham roads. Rosecrans also advised Thomas that Philip Sheridan's XX Corps division would move out on the Manchester and Lynchburg Road to fall in on Thomas's

7 Ibid., pt. 2, 479.

8 Ibid., 479-480.

right. He concluded with, "Find out by careful reconnaissance what the intentions of the enemy are."[9]

At Bobo's Crossroads, one road from Tullahoma to Hillsborough intersected with a second road running from Manchester to Winchester, making it a vital strategic point. If Thomas could mass sufficient manpower here, he could send troops due south toward Estill Springs and Allisonia, which would definitively cut the railroad and turn Bragg's flank, prying Bragg's forces out from behind the Tullahoma defenses and giving the Army of the Cumberland a renewed opportunity to destroy the Army of Tennessee in open battle. Thus, Reynolds's 4th Division spent the night of June 28 camped at Concord Church on Crumpton's Creek, while Negley's 2nd Division occupied the crossroads.[10]

Pursuant to Rosecrans's orders, Reynolds's division moved out on the Tullahoma Road, "or under it," as Henry Campbell of Lilly's battery quipped, "as the mud is hub deep some places the wheels would sink until the gun would drag on the ground." He noted that the wretched road was covered with water and that "[a]ll day long we passed wagon after wagon, mired down and upset teamsters swearing mules pulling their utmost and everybody mad. By constant prying lifting and doubling teams, we managed to get the Battery 9 miles before dark. Don't think the transportation wagons will ever get through."[11]

That day, more intelligence filtered into the Army of the Cumberland's headquarters. Brigadier General John M. Brannan, who commanded Thomas's 3rd Division, led the advance along the Manchester-Tullahoma Road. "It has been the impression that Bragg would fight at Tullahoma," he reported. "Rebel Army of the Tennessee is supposed to be from 35,000 to 50,000. Some reported as high as 55,000; generally supposed to be 50,000. Some time ago he had heard that the rebels had sent 15,000 men to Vicksburg. All of Breckinridge's forces, except [J. C.] Brown's brigade, had gone there. Brown's brigade was ordered to Knoxville, but stopped at Loudoun. It was reported that this force was coming back from Vicksburg, but this is not so. Fortifications on this side of Tullahoma are on this side of town. Water is on the other side. There is no running stream [after] leaving Crumpton's Creek until arriving at Tullahoma."[12]

9 Ibid., 481-482.

10 Bradley, *Tullahoma*, 84-85.

11 Campbell journal, entry for June 29, 1863.

12 *OR* 23, pt. 2, 482.

About 9:15 that morning, Brannan added the update, "I am pressing the enemy in front and right with more than a brigade." A member of the 10th Indiana Infantry recalled that this move triggered a considerable engagement. "It was a veritable hornets' nest and General [James B.] Steedman watching the fight, expected to see every man killed," he wrote. After considerable resistance, Brannan eventually reached a position about two miles out along the Tullahoma Road. "I did not advance farther," Brannan reported, "as General Sheridan's being the only division of the Twentieth Corps so far advanced, he was unable to support me on the right." Brannan threw out two regiments about a mile to the front on the Winchester Road, but withdrew them that night once Brig. Gen. Joseph Reynolds's 4th Division of the XIV Corps arrived at Bobo's Crossroads.[13]

Rosecrans reacted quickly after receiving Brannan's extremely accurate intelligence, ordering Thomas "to make a prudent and sharp reconnaissance, driving those regiments of the enemy which General Brannan reports in his front, and find out what they are about . . . , also report your direction and position with reference to some point we know—say, Bobo's; also the character of the ground for moving troops." Thomas responded, "From what I can learn, the country is not very accessible; chiefly timbered, with here and there an opening. As you near Tullahoma it becomes more open. The roads are exceedingly bad." Thomas directed Brannan to press the enemy as hard as he could, and then ordered Brig. Gen. James S. Negley to have his division ready to march on a moment's notice.[14]

When Thomas reported his progress to army headquarters, he indicated that the headquarters of the 2nd and 4th divisions had been established at a temporary defensive position along at Crumpton's Creek, with the 4th Division camping at Concord Church, at the point where the road to Tullahoma diverges from the Manchester and Winchester Road. The 2nd Division was camped at Bobo's Crossroads. A brigade of the 3rd Division had advanced along the Tullahoma Road, where it engaged the enemy's outposts and cavalry videttes, driving them toward Tullahoma. The fighting was brisk. "At times when we had forced back the enemy's line more rapidly than they approved, they opened on us with artillery to check our advance," recalled Lt. Col. Judson Bishop of the 2nd Minnesota Infantry. "The surgeon of the regiment on our right, who was riding behind the advancing line, was very suddenly let down by a shell from the enemy's battery,

---

13 OR 23, pt. 1, 452-453; James Birney Shaw, *History of the Tenth Regiment Indiana Volunteer Infantry: Three Months and Three Years Organizations* (Lafayette, IN: 1912), 203.

14 *OR* 23, pt. 2, 483.

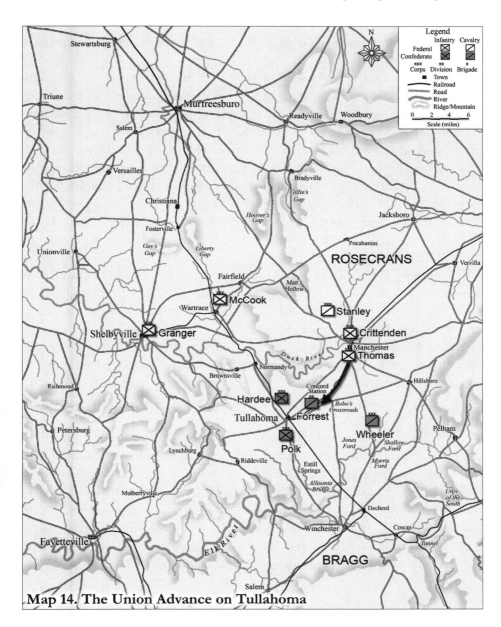

Map 14. The Union Advance on Tullahoma

which entered the breast and exploded in the body of the horse without hurting the doctor. The boys unmercifully guyed him as he gathered up his saddle and went to the rear." The Federals believed they killed or injured a good many of the enemy at a loss of two men slightly wounded. All the while, concluded Bishop, in yet another reference to the incessant precipitation, "the road from Manchester to this point was rendered nearly impassable by one of the strongest and steadiest rains ever experienced."[15]

Lieutenant Colonel Charles Lamborn led six companies of the 15th Pennsylvania Cavalry on a scouting expedition toward Tullahoma that morning. After marching about eight miles, the advance guard, consisting of Adjutant William F. Colton and five men of Company F, encountered the enemy's cavalry picket. Colton ordered his little detachment to charge, driving the pickets back upon their reserve of about 50 men, who were drawn up in line of battle along the bank of a stream. The men of Company F drew sabers and charged, scattering the Confederates. They captured 13 troopers of Col. W. N. Estes's 3rd Confederate Cavalry and two men from Bragg's personal escort, commanded by Louisiana Capt. Guy Dreux. The victorious Pennsylvanians then thundered on to within two miles of Tullahoma.[16]

Companies E and G came up to reinforce Company F, and the three units dismounted to form line of battle at the edge of a clearing that extended to the main Confederate works. "We waited for the attack we knew would come," recounted Charles H. Kirk of the 15th Pennsylvania. "The 'long roll' sounded in the enemy's camps, and soon after, a long line of rebel infantry, with one or two guns, came over the breastworks toward us." A detachment of cavalry supported the Southern infantry, so Lamborn wisely ordered his little command to retreat after only a few shots were exchanged. The soggy Pennsylvanians made their way back to Manchester in a heavy rain.[17]

John Beatty's brigade of James Negley's XIV Corps division endured an ordeal of its own that day. After escorting Wilder's Lightning Brigade to Hillsborough for part of the expedition (as detailed previously), Beatty's brigade was ordered to join the rest of the division at Bobo's Crossroads, an 11-mile march from its June 28 campsite. As Beatty's weary infantrymen slogged along, elements of Nathan Bedford Forrest's cavalry division attacked them about four miles into the march. Beatty deployed the brigade in line of battle, with a battery of artillery in the middle, advancing until they met no resistance. The Federals repulsed Forrest's probe but

15 Judson W. Bishop, *The Story of a Regiment; Being a Narrative of the Service of the Second Regiment, Minnesota Veteran Volunteer Infantry, in the Civil War of 1861-1865* (St. Paul, MN: 1890), 89; OR 23, pt. 1, 426. Confederate losses here are unknown.

16 Charles H. Kirk, ed., *History of the Fifteenth Pennsylvania Volunteer Cavalry which was Recruited and Known as the Anderson Cavalry in the Rebellion of 1861-1865* (Philadelphia, PA: 1906), 192-193; OR 23, pt. 1, 577-578.

17 Kirk, *History of the Fifteenth Pennsylvania Cavalry*, 193.

took some losses, including a lieutenant of the 104th Illinois Volunteer Infantry. Continuing a terrible march through thick mud in heavy rain, Beatty's men eventually reached their destination at Bobo's Crossroads. There, as previously noted, they had a brief and fortunately bloodless exchange of fire with Reynolds's command, after which they finally made a miserable camp. "No fires were built," recalled John Beatty, "and the darkness was impenetrable."[18]

A few hours later, Thomas reported some more extremely useful intelligence to Rosecrans's headquarters. "Have just captured a dispatch from Wheeler to [Brig. Gen. Thomas] Harrison, commanding cavalry brigade, dated 4 miles in advance of Tullahoma, on Manchester road. He directs Colonel Harrison to send a company to an intermediate position between his and Harrison's, so as to better observe the movements of the enemy (us), and to fall back as he falls back. I take it from this dispatch that they mean to draw us upon Tullahoma, so as to fight us behind their fortifications. Will make the proper disposition to drive them back as soon as General Reynolds gets into position. Our skirmishers are 2½ miles from General Brannan's headquarters." Most of Thomas's corps covered about six sodden miles that difficult day before establishing what one waterlogged Pennsylvanian of Negley's division called "Camp Swamp." Adjutant Angus Waddle of the 33rd Ohio recalled his regiment's rudimentary accommodations. "The ceremony of going into camp was dispensed with," he wrote, "and a halt in the road, with the collection of a few fence rails and the spreading of a rubber blanket was our bivouac." The exhausted men spent a long, wet night trying to get some sleep amid yet more heavy rain.[19]

Sheridan's division was the only XX Corps division to participate in the actions of June 29, coming within a few miles of Tullahoma. His men also had an extremely difficult time of it, thanks to the weather. "Mules would go down the full length of their (hind) legs in the mud, and wagons to the axle," recalled a member of the 73rd Illinois. "Eight, and sometimes ten, mules were required to pull the wagons out of the mire." He noted that the road conditions were so bad that the men often preferred to march in the fields alongside, as the way was a bit easier. "I saw cannon wheels sink in the clay to the hub on the highest hills," recalled a member of the 27th Illinois, also in Sheridan's division. "I think that would be called mud-bound

18 William Wirt Calkins, *The History of the One Hundred and Fourth Regiment of Illinois Volunteer Infantry* (Chicago: 1905), 93-94; John Beatty, *The Citizen-Soldier, or Memoirs of a Volunteer* (Cincinnati, OH: 1879), 287.

19 OR 23, pt. 1, 426; Johnston, *The Soldier Boy's Diary Book*, 43; Angus L. Waddle, *Three Years with the Armies of the Ohio, and the Cumberland* (Chillicothe, OH: 1889), 49.

in the East; but even under such difficulties we sometimes move in Tennessee." Sheridan's column finally reached a position about six miles from Tullahoma before making camp. The men could plainly hear Brannan's skirmishing as they tried to dry out.[20]

Due to the incessant rain and terrible road conditions, the other two divisions of the XX Corps did not reach Manchester until very early on the morning of June 29, when they went into camp per Rosecrans's orders. Most of the XXI Corps did not arrive at Manchester until midday, meaning there were now two corps stacked up behind Thomas's troops at Manchester. The XXI Corps bivouacked upon its arrival, at a site described by Brig. Gen. William B. Hazen, who commanded the 2nd Brigade, 2nd Division, XXI Corps, as "the foulest grounds it ever rested upon." When Stanley and the Cavalry Corps reached Manchester on the afternoon of the 29th, the Army of the Cumberland was finally concentrated and ready for the final movement against Bragg's position at Tullahoma, though more than 24 hours later than Rosecrans's plan had stipulated.[21]

Upon reaching Manchester, the Federals now fully entered that geographic region of Tennessee known as "the Barrens," which, in the eyes of the soldiers, fully lived up to its reputation. Henry Campbell of Lilly's battery described it as "an elevated plateau of waste land bordering the Cumberland mountains, about 50 miles in width, and extending all along the range of mountains. This plateau, or shelf of the mountains is almost as level and flat as a floor, [with] sandy unproductive soil, producing nothing but 'Jack Oaks,' very thinly settled and then only in spots where an oasis occurs . . . , where the inhabitants are of the lowest order of whites, and eak out a miserable existence from sandy, barren soil upon which they live."[22]

"Between the lines the treacherous soil was filled with quicksand, which only needed the soaking of the week's rain to render it impassable," recalled a Union officer. "To advance against the Confederate works over this ground, through a dense abatis of tangled tree-tops, in the face of a storm of grape-shot and minie-balls, would have been to doom one-half the army to destruction." While this was a

20 OR 23, pt. 1, 515; *A History of the Seventy-Third Regiment of Illinois Volunteers, Published by Authority of the Regimental Reunion Association of Survivors of the 73d Illinois Infantry Volunteers,* (Springfield, IL: 1890), 181; Gene Kelly, comp., *Collection of Civil War Letters Written by Mercer County Soldiers* (Mercer County, IL: 1900), 91.

21 OR 23, pt. 1, 467, 531.

22 Campbell journal, entry for June 27, 1863.

bit of an exaggeration, the terrible weather and worse road conditions ultimately spoiled Rosecrans's plan to bring Bragg to a decisive battle outside Tullahoma's defenses.[23]

Colonel William Innes, who commanded the 1st Michigan Engineers, faced a stern task on June 29. Innes had his headquarters at Bell Buckle, on the railroad. His men were trying to repair a 2.5-mile gap in the line between Bell Buckle and Wartrace, destroyed by the retreating Confederates, who had removed the rails and shipped them south to repair other damaged railroads in the Deep South. Innes also faced the daunting task of rebuilding a 350-foot bridge across the Duck River as well as a 150-foot trestle at Normandy. Innes told Rosecrans that he would work as quickly as he could to restore the critical line—the army needed supplies in order to continue its advance. In the meantime, Rosecrans was forced to rely on his over-stressed wagons for transport. Granger, who was now at the army's base of supplies at Murfreesboro, telegraphed Rosecrans that a large supply train was departing Murfreesboro for Manchester, but, he warned, "Heaven knows when it may reach you owing to the bad state of the roads."[24]

James Garfield, Rosecrans's chief of staff, found a few minutes to pen another letter to his wife Lucretia. "We are now preparing for an immediate advance on Tullahoma," he told her. "If the rebels stand we shall give them the biggest fight we are able. We somewhat expect they will retreat beyond the Tennessee River, but hope not. If they stand," Garfield continued, "I think we shall be able to damage them materially. Our operations thus far have been successful beyond the expectations of everyone outside headquarters. I have studied all of these movements carefully beforehand, and I am delighted to see how fully my judgment has been vindicated."[25]

That night, the weary Northerners heard train whistles echoing from behind the Rebel lines in Tullahoma. Those whistles meant one of two things: Bragg was receiving reinforcements or he was evacuating. Either way, "they seemed very busy all night," mused Hoosier Henry Campbell. Which was it?[26]

---

23 Gilbert C. Kniffin, "Maneuvering Bragg Out of Tennessee," included in Robert U. Johnson and Clarence C. Buel, eds., *Battles and Leaders of the Civil War*, 4 vols. (New York: 1884-1887), 3: 637.

24 *OR* 23, pt. 1, 583; Bradley, *Tullahoma*, 85.

25 Williams, *The Wild Life of the Army*, 285-286.

26 Campbell journal, entry for June 29, 1863.

The truth was that even Bragg, uncertain as to what Rosecrans intended, didn't know. He remained confused and ill-prepared to respond. Should he stand and fight, or fall back to relative safety below the Elk River?

* * *

Tullahoma, where Bragg made his headquarters, originally had been laid out as a lovely summer resort for wealthy Nashville residents. In late June 1863, however, nobody would mistake it for a resort. The place was filthy and, with an entire army's worth of men and animals in the area, it stank. As one Southern correspondent put it, Tullahoma "is nondescript. A hell of a place the soldiers say." The town was strongly entrenched with a redan line of rifle pits and a bastioned fort. It was further protected by the steep defiles of the Duck River, which was narrow, swift, and deep at Tullahoma, as well as by a line of hills. The Cumberland Mountains towered in the distance. Responding to a question about the derivation of the name "Tullahoma," a witty officer on Hardee's staff quipped that it came from two Greek words, "tulla," which meant "mud," and "homa," which meant "more mud." As early as January 1863, Hardee had warned Bragg that Tullahoma left a lot to be desired as a position from which to make a stand. He noted then, "it can be turned, not only by the direct road leading from Manchester to Decherd and Winchester, but from the nature of the country, our flanks can be turned at this point. I see no advantage in this position which can compensate for superiority of numbers." In his view, Tullahoma was the ideal place for Rosecrans to either bring the Army of Tennessee to battle or to flank it out of Middle Tennessee altogether.[27]

As if to cast yet more gloom over the Confederate army, news of the Shelbyville debacle soon filtered back to headquarters. Alarmed, at 3:00 a.m. on June 28, Leonidas Polk wrote to Brig. Gen. John A. Wharton, one of Wheeler's two divisional commanders, to state, "I have been informed that General Martin has been badly defeated at Shelbyville, from which I take it for granted that the rear of the column on the Rowesville and Tullahoma road is uncovered by cavalry." Polk ordered Wharton to reverse course and move to guard that road so it remained available for use by Polk's and Hardee's retreating corps, which were now exposed

---

27 Emily E. Molineaux, *Lifetime Recollections: An Interesting Narrative of Life in the Southern States before and during the Civil War, with Incidents of the Bombardment of Atlanta, the Author Then Being a Resident of that City* (San Francisco, CA: 1902), 23; J. Cutler Andrews, *The South Reports the Civil War* (Princeton, NJ: 1970), 339; Buck, *Cleburne and His Command*, 108; OR 23, pt. 1, 477.

to Federal thrusts. Meanwhile, as the infantry slowly filed into Tullahoma, the men were deployed into line to face the Federals at Manchester.[28]

Worst of all, neither Wheeler's corps nor Forrest's division was in position to defend the Army of Tennessee's vulnerable lines of communication and supply. Initially this was due to Wheeler's unfortunate decision to concentrate his forces at Spring Hill in anticipation of launching his own raid against Rosecrans's communications. Then came the need to screen the approaches to Shelbyville, as well as Bragg's hasty effort to dispatch at least some mounted force (drawn from Wharton) back to cover the Manchester approaches. Taken together, these dispositions left Bragg's rail lifeline almost completely unguarded. Next came the lopsided Union victory at Shelbyville. Wheeler, Martin, and Forrest spent June 28 falling back to Tullahoma, while Polk hurriedly attempted to shift Wharton back westward to protect the suddenly vulnerable army trains that were still toiling toward Tullahoma. Bragg's cavalry arm, now badly disorganized, was out of position to screen the main body of the army against the Federal threat looming from Manchester, let alone worry about the Nashville and Chattanooga line south of the Elk. "Our infantry left Shelbyville that morning for Tullahoma, which place we reached on the 28th, just in good time to cover the retreat of our army from there," noted a disgusted Capt. George Knox Miller of the 8th Confederate Cavalry. Wilder's Lightning Brigade, meanwhile, had already overrun the pickets holding the Elk River Bridge at Pelham and secured it for future use before heading on to Decherd, the next important rail and supply center on the Nashville & Chattanooga Railroad, some 12 miles south of Tullahoma.[29]

By daylight on June 28, the entire Army of Tennessee was in motion. The country to the south of the Duck River, "being made up of a peculiarly spongy soil, which when softened by the heavy rains then falling became almost impassable for trains, and in places difficult even for horses, the condition of the roads throughout the campaign was therefore a constant obstacle," observed General Polk's son and biographer. The conditions slowed the army's pace to a crawl as it fell back from Shelbyville. Polk's corps began leaving from there early on the 27th, but the army's rear guard and wagon trains did not arrive at Tullahoma, a mere 20 miles away, until 4:00 p.m. on June 28. Slogging through the thick mud wore out men, horses, and mules, leaving them exhausted when they finally reached their destination. "From the 24th to the 28th, when we reached Tullahoma, we were in rain and mud,"

28 OR 23, pt. 1, 620.

29 McMurry, *An Uncompromising Secessionist*, 142.

reported Brig. Gen. St. John Liddell, commanding one of Cleburne's brigades. "I had 300 men without shoes."[30]

The rank and file of the Army of Tennessee expected to stand and fight at Tullahoma. "A great battle will be fought no doubt—in a few days," predicted Capt. Daniel Coleman of the 15th Mississippi Battalion Sharpshooters, of Cleburne's division, in his diary on June 28. "Oh God be with our army & give us the victory." It remained to be seen whether Captain Coleman's prediction would come to pass.[31]

In spite of its delays, Rosecrans's masterful strike had thoroughly befuddled Bragg. Though Bragg now knew that his army was in grave danger, he responded to this threat in his customary fashion: slowly and tentatively. By June 27, he was fully aware of the Army of the Cumberland's presence in Manchester, only about 12 miles from his headquarters at Tullahoma. If Rosecrans crossed the Elk River and struck southward, the Federals could not only destroy the line that supplied Bragg's army from Chattanooga; they could also block Bragg's primary route of retreat through Decherd. Alternatively, Rosecrans could move eight miles or so to Hillsborough and from there move on to seize the main Chattanooga Road at University Place, or he could march 22 miles to Cowan, which lay beneath the northern face of the Cumberland Mountains astride both the Chattanooga Road and the railroad. The Union army could easily block the railroad a couple of miles south of Cowan at the nearly half-mile-long Cowan Tunnel through the mountain, which had been built by slaves between 1849 and 1853. Finally, Rosecrans could leave Manchester and move along the southern bank of the Elk River to seize and hold the river crossings between Tullahoma and Decherd, completely cutting off Bragg's line of march and forcing him to fight on ground of Rosecrans's choosing. Each of these options was perilous to the Army of Tennessee, and any miscalculation on Bragg's part could prove disastrous.[32]

On the 28th, with barely any rest, the leading elements of Bragg's cavalry attacked Rosecrans's column near Manchester, checking its progress. When Forrest reached Tullahoma, Bragg ordered his division "to picket and scout . . . the approaches from the northward." Accordingly, Forrest sent Col. George Dibrell

---

30 William M. Polk, *Leonidas Polk: Bishop and General*, 2 vols. (New York: 1915), 2: 220; OR 23, pt. 1, 583, 591.

31 Daniel Coleman diary, entry for June 28, 1863, Southern Historical Collection, Wilson Library, University of North Carolina, Chapel Hill, NC.

32 OR 23, pt. 1, 620.

and "a detachment from the Eighth Tennessee, 200 strong. . . , towards Hillsboro," which Dibrell soon reported was in Federal hands, with "a large force" headed to Decherd. The remainder of Forrest's old brigade under Col. James W. Starnes, supported by William Bate's brigade of infantry, threw out a heavy skirmish line along the Manchester Pike. Fighting broke out at Bobo's Crossroads, about five miles northeast of Tullahoma. The 1st and 3rd Divisions of Thomas's XIV Corps were advancing on Tullahoma when they encountered Starnes's dismounted troopers, spread across the road. The Union infantry's superior numbers began driving the Confederate pickets, so Starnes rode out to encourage his men to hold their positions. As the Federals began overlapping the Confederate left, some of his troopers asked Starnes to go back and out of danger, but he refused. A few minutes later, a Union sharpshooter mortally wounded Starnes, who died 36 hours later. Starnes was apparently carrying a dispatch for Wheeler at the time, as he was seen tearing something up after he was wounded. "His death created quite a gloom," lamented a trooper of Starnes's own regiment, the 4th Tennessee Cavalry, "and had he lived, he would certainly have achieved higher rank."[33]

Despite the constant rains and nearly impassable roads, Rosecrans continued to push the advance and, by the morning of June 29, threatened to turn Bragg's flank and cut off the Army of Tennessee between the south bank of the Elk River and Chattanooga. The Army of the Cumberland advanced in line of battle along three different roads, creeping within five miles of Tullahoma, and prompting Bragg to order Polk to deploy his men to receive an attack. In a nod to securing his rear, at 6:00 a.m. on June 29 Bragg also ordered Polk to detail 500 men to hold Fort Rains, at the confluence of the Tennessee River and Battle Creek, near South Pittsburg. This fort represented precisely the sort of bastion that had to be secured if the Army of Tennessee would be able to keep its retreat route open.[34]

---

33 Jordan and Pryor, *Campaigns of General Forrest's Cavalry*, 291; Dodson, *Campaigns of Wheeler and His Cavalry*, 94; Starnes, *Forrest's Forgotten Horse Brigadier*, 86-88; Bishop, *The Story of a Regiment*, 89; Guild, *Fourth Tennessee Cavalry Regiment*, 20. The Federals claimed that they found the torn-up message after the Confederates withdrew and were able to piece it back together.

34 *OR* 23, pt. 1, 621. Fort Rains was about 50 miles southeast of Tullahoma, and roughly two-thirds of the way to Chattanooga. The fort, which was the site of a pontoon bridge across the Tennessee, was probably named for Col. James E. Rains of the 11th Tennessee Infantry. After it fell into Union hands, it was renamed for Maj. Gen. Alexander M. McCook, commander of the Army of the Cumberland's XX Corps. A small engagement had taken place there in 1862. John D. Bennett, *Placenames of the Civil War: Cities, Towns, Villages, Railroad Stations, Forts, Camps, Islands, Rivers, Creeks, Fords and Ferries* (Jefferson, NC: 2012), 80.

About 9:00 a.m., Polk called on Bragg for further orders. Bragg informed him that the enemy had destroyed the railroad at Decherd, thereby interrupting his communications with Chattanooga. He also notified Polk that Rosecrans's mounted forces were so superior as to render it impossible for Bragg to prevent them from wreaking havoc, but that he was determined to give battle at Tullahoma even though a significant Union force was in his rear. Bragg next told Polk to recall Brig. Gen. Edward C. Walthall's brigade of Mississippians from Allisonia, where they were guarding the bridge over the Elk. Polk was alarmed, but only remarked that if Bragg was determined to fight at Tullahoma, recalling Walthall was the right thing to do. Polk next rode along his lines to determine whether his position was good, and called on Hardee to advise his fellow corps commander of Bragg's determination to stand and fight at Tullahoma. Then, somewhat at odds with his apparent agreement with Bragg about making a stand, Polk commented to Hardee that he thought the decision to fight at Tullahoma was injudicious.[35]

About 3:00 that afternoon, Polk and Hardee rode to Bragg's headquarters for a council of war. In addition to Bragg and the two infantry corps commanders, Bragg's chief of staff, Brig. Gen. William W. Mackall, and Lt. Col. David Urquhart, acting as Bragg's private secretary, attended the conference. Bragg still wanted to stand and fight. Perhaps expecting agreement, he asked for Polk's opinion. Polk reminded Bragg that his line of communications had been severed and suggested Bragg's first responsibility was to restore those communications. Bragg indicated that this had been accomplished since he and Polk had last spoken about it that morning. "How do you propose to maintain them?" asked Polk. Bragg replied, "by posting [Wheeler's] cavalry along the line." Polk then opined that Bragg lacked sufficient cavalry to cover both his line of communications and other critical points—a point Bragg himself had conceded that morning—and predicted that the enemy would drive off the Confederate cavalry and seize control of the line in less than 36 hours. If Rosecrans did so, Polk insisted, he would do it with enough force to completely cut Bragg off from Chattanooga and leave the Army of Tennessee besieged, much like Lt. Gen. John C. Pemberton's command at Vicksburg.[36]

Polk outlined a worst-case scenario, laced with dire warnings. He argued that Rosecrans, rather than strike a blow and fight a bloody battle, would either reduce the Army of Tennessee by starvation and eventually force its capitulation, or force it to retreat through Fayetteville and Huntsville and across the Tennessee River

35 *OR* 23, pt. 1, 621-622.

36 Ibid.

near Decatur. Polk reminded Bragg that under those circumstances, animals and men would be exhausted for want of food, leaving them unfit for duty, and that Bragg's entire wagon train, including ordnance and artillery, would likely be captured due to the lack of serviceable animals. Worse yet, such a retreat would leave the Army of Tennessee stranded in the hills of northern Alabama without food, leaving Bragg again to face the choice between surrendering or dispersing his army to fight as guerrillas. Meanwhile, Rosecrans and the Army of the Cumberland would cross over the Cumberland Mountains, seize Chattanooga, and march through Georgia and the Carolinas without resistance, eviscerating the Confederacy. Polk told Bragg that to avoid all of this, he should fall back in the direction of Chattanooga, covering his line of communications at all times.[37]

"That is all very well," Bragg responded, "but what do you distinctly propose to have done?" Polk replied that Bragg should fall back immediately, as he did not think there was a moment to spare. "Then," said Bragg, "you propose that we shall retreat." Polk said, "I do, and that is my counsel."[38]

While Polk spoke, word arrived from Decherd that the damage to the railroad was not as bad as originally reported; only a couple hundred yards of track had been damaged, and it could be repaired in a few hours. Bragg asked Hardee for his opinion. Polk's opinion carried great weight with him, he replied, but he was not prepared to advise a retreat because of the news from Decherd, and thought it best to have some infantry sent along the line to support the cavalry and wait for further developments. While Polk agreed that the news from Decherd made a difference, he remained convinced that the Army of Tennessee should retreat beyond the Elk River. The generals all agreed on retreat, and that the infantry should be ordered back along the line of the railroad; with this, the council of war ended.[39]

In the meantime, though the Army of Tennessee suffered from the constant rain, the men prepared for battle. Captain Coleman of the 15th Mississippi Battalion Sharpshooters spent the day worrying about hearth and home. "A battle supposed to be imminent," he noted in his diary on June 29. "Thoughts much occupied about home and the suffering it will bring there if we have to give up this

---

37 Ibid.

38 Ibid.

39 Ibid. Fortunately, Lt. W. B. Richmond, who served on Polk's staff, carefully recorded these events for posterity. Colonel Urquhart also prepared a record of the subject of the discussions that afternoon, and his memorandum adds detail to the Richmond account. See Statement of Lt. Col. David Urquhart, June 29, 1863, included in the Bragg Papers.

place." He noted that reports filtered in that the Army of the Cumberland was moving on the Confederate right flank. Something had to happen soon, and the stress grew more difficult to bear while the Southerners waited for Rosecrans to launch his attack.[40]

Reports also reached Bragg's headquarters that because of the constant heavy rains, the Elk could no longer be forded, which made holding the bridges critical. If they were lost, the Army of Tennessee would be pinned against the flooded river and left with no choice but to give battle or be surrounded and forced to surrender. There were only four viable bridges, and the one at Pelham, upstream on the Elk, was already in Union hands. The other three were a few miles south of Tullahoma. One was the road bridge at Bethpage near Estill Springs, and the others were the railroad and pike bridges at Allisonia on the south bank of the Elk opposite Estill Springs. If these bridges fell, then Bragg would be completely cut off.[41]

Polk ordered his two division commanders, Maj. Gen. Benjamin F. Cheatham and Maj. Gen. Jones Withers, to erect breastworks along several sparse portions of their lines and to prepare to receive an attack. Hardee's men did the same. "We hastened on to Tullahoma and offered battle there," reported a member of A. P. Stewart's division, "but the enemy declined it." The Army of Tennessee remained in line of battle for the entire day and night on June 29, digging earthworks and suffering in the heavy rains. "We occasionally heard a bullet pass," recounted a Confederate cavalryman. "It seemed they were advancing, but slow and cautious."[42]

Bragg received intelligence that Union infantry was moving along the north bank of the Elk River from Manchester to seize the bridges at Bethpage and Estill Springs. Unsure where Rosecrans's left lay, about 4:00 p.m., Bragg told Wheeler, "It is of the very first importance that we should have positive information of the movement and extension of the enemy on our right." He urged Wheeler to find the Army of the Cumberland's left flank, ascertain what forces were operating on that flank, and to observe it during the night so that it could not make a flanking movement without being detected. Wheeler was told to report any enemy movement immediately, and his troopers soon fanned out as ordered. They soon

---

40 Coleman diary, entry for June 29, 1863.

41 *OR* 23, pt. 1, 583.

42 "The Retreat of Bragg's Army," *Nashville Daily Union*, August 13, 1863; *OR* 23, pt. 1, 622; Julia Morgan, *How It Was: Four Years among the Rebels* (Nashville, TN: 1892), 183.

Maj. Gen. Benjamin F. "Frank" Cheatham, commander,
Cheatham's Division, Polk's Corps, Army of the Tennessee.

Library of Congress

uncovered the advance of the XIV Corps on Tullahoma and struck at Thomas's column, forcing the Northern infantrymen to halt and deploy for battle.[43]

43 *OR* 23, pt. 2, 891-892; Dodson, *Campaigns of Wheeler and His Cavalry*, 95.

Maj. Gen. Jones M. Withers, commander,
Withers' Division, Polk's Corps,
Army of the Tennessee.

Library of Congress

Late that night Bragg learned that both Union infantry and cavalry were operating in his rear. Another strong mounted force had disrupted his lines of communication near University Place before Forrest drove them back toward Manchester. As Bragg told Joseph E. Johnston a few days later, "The enemy established himself in strong position on the defensive, and moved another heavy column against our bridges over Elk River, now swollen by heavy rains."[44]

Nervous and worried, Bragg paced up and down the piazza of his headquarters, tugging his beard as he fretted. "I could see that matters were critical," noted a Confederate signalman who watched this drama play out, "and his indecision was finally determined by the advice given by Gen. Polk to the effect that expedience required our retiring to Chattanooga, as to remain where we were would be to place us in the position of a rat in a barrel with the bunghole closed, the bung in this case being the tunnels in our rear, through which our subsistence must necessarily be transported. With this condition confronting him, no prudent general like Rosecrans would attack when he could flank us and destroy the line of communication in our rear."[45]

Bragg remained keenly aware of the danger posed by Rosecrans's flanking move and was desperate for accurate intelligence. He had also now realized that his army was in extreme jeopardy. Tullahoma was not the place to stand and fight, since his command could be trapped there and destroyed.

What would Bragg do?

44 Buck, *Cleburne and His Command*, 109.

45 W. N. Mercer Otey, "Operations of the Signal Corps," *Confederate Veteran*, vol. 8, no. 3 (March 1900), 129.

Chapter Thirteen

A Miserable Affair,
June 30 to July 6, 1863

Just as June 26 had proved to be the pivotal day of the Tullahoma Campaign for William Rosecrans, June 30 became the most consequential day of the campaign for Braxton Bragg. While his decision to abandon any thought of a counterattack on June 27 effectively surrendered the initiative to Rosecrans, Bragg still hoped, even at that late stage, to retain Middle Tennessee via a defensive stand at Tullahoma.

John T. Wilder's foray south of the Elk River altered the Rebel commander's calculations. Despite the lack of extensive damage, the Lightning Brigade's Decherd raid had sent chills up and down Bragg's spine. In previous campaigns, Confederate cavalry generally had savaged Union lines of communications, not vice versa. But if the Federals could seize and hold Cowan, blocking the railroad tunnel through Cumberland Mountain, they would completely sever the Army of Tennessee's line of retreat and resupply. Such a move would force Bragg to choose between fighting it out where he was, risking a potentially disastrous withdrawal toward Alabama, or surrendering. With Rebel cavalrymen Wheeler and Martin both out of position due to their crushing defeat at Shelbyville, and after Wilder's raid demonstrated the vulnerability of this line, Bragg had every reason to be worried. Even if Rosecrans's men were not able to seize Cowan, Rosecrans could still send a strong infantry force across the Elk River and then sweep west along the south bank, capturing the crossings between Tullahoma and Decherd, producing almost the same result.

Thus, late on the afternoon of June 29, Brig. Gen. William Mackall sent Wheeler an urgent dispatch. "The important question to us now is what progress the enemy is making to pass our right and interrupt our communications," he wrote. "The general [Bragg] does not so much feel anxiety about the [Federal] troops marching on Hillsborough Road to this place [Tullahoma], as on the Hillsborough Road to Estill Springs." Information was the critical commodity, stressed Mackall, who closed with the admonition to "try and get it soon and accurate."[1]

At about 11 a.m. on the 30th, word filtered into Bragg's command tent that the Army of the Cumberland was again on the move. Advancing from Manchester, the Federals were pushing up against the Army of Tennessee's defensive positions along the Manchester and Hillsborough roads. But was this Rosecrans's main effort or was it, as Bragg now feared, a covering movement for a strike south of the Elk?[2]

Bragg's well entrenched army held a strong position at Tullahoma. "We have constructed temporary breastworks and are yet awaiting the enemy, who has not made his appearance out to skirmish with our cavalry," Pvt. Van Buren Oldham of the 9th Tennessee noted in his diary. "Every available man is now out ready to fight. We want the enemy to come and let us try him behind our works." A newspaper correspondent using the pseudonym "Shadow" further boasted that "if Rosecrans fights this time, his chances for disastrous defeat are better than they were at Murfreesboro in December or any time before."[3]

Captain Daniel Coleman of the 15th Mississippi Sharpshooters certainly expected a fight. "Our Brig[ade] sent out to engage the enemy to hold him in check," he noted. "Every indication of a battle. My company with another is sent out as skirmishers. We can hear the Cavalry videttes in front cracking away. We look every minute to engage them ourselves. We move forward short distances and halt but no enemy appears."[4]

But while the rank and file of the Army of Tennessee expected—and perhaps even welcomed—a chance to stand and fight, their commanding general did not. Bragg had already issued orders for retreat; the army would head south across the Elk to Decherd and Cowan. The news flummoxed Captain Coleman. "Order

---

1 *OR* 23, pt. 2, 892.

2 Ibid., pt. 1, 622-623.

3 Oldham diary, entry for June 30, 1863; "Letter from Chattanooga," under the byline "Shadow," *Memphis Appeal*, July 1, 1863.

4 Norman M. Shapiro, ed., "Daniel Coleman Diary January 1863-August 1864," *The Huntsville Historical Review*, vol. 26, no. 2 (Summer-Fall 1999), 24.

comes—assemble skirmishers & move toward Tullahoma. . . ," he wrote. "The retreat has begun. Oh God—and must we leave our homes and our loved ones to the mercy of the ruthless foe again and that too without an effort to prevent it."[5]

The decision to retreat was triggered by alarming intelligence that reached Bragg sometime on the afternoon of June 30, though that information did not come from Wheeler. Instead the source was a Confederate politician, Arthur St. Clair Colyar, currently with the Tennessee provisional state government in Winchester, his hometown. Colyar relayed "positive information" that as many as 10,000 additional Union soldiers had reached a position within three miles of the Bethpage Bridge over the Elk, uncomfortably close to the vital Estill Springs and Allisonia bridges. Colyar's informant was a local man, an unnamed spy "who left Manchester today [June 30], and came all along the road. He is reliable and had a pass, the enemy believing he was a friend." Ten thousand men was the better part of a Union corps, and if they took the bridges, it would not be that easy to drive them back.[6]

Faced with this confirmation of his most pressing concern, Braxton Bragg had no real choice but to abandon Tullahoma. Remaining in place was simply too dangerous. He had to fall back at least across the Elk, eight miles to his rear. The Confederate retreat began late in the day on the 30th and continued through the night.

Because of the nonstop heavy rains, however, the mud was knee-deep, and the roads were nearly impassable. Consequently, it took the Army of Tennessee nearly 24 hours to cover those eight miles. The Rebel infantry finally finished crossing the Elk at noon on July 1. That evening, Bragg relayed crushing news to Richmond, casting it in the best light he could. "Finding my communications seriously endangered by movements of the enemy," he reported, "I last night took up a more defensible position this side of Elk River (which now, by reason of heavy rains, is impassable except at the bridges), losing nothing of importance."[7]

As Captain Coleman had suggested, the order to retreat surprised the rank and file. "Rosy instead of moving to attack moved to our right causing us to evacuate at 11 o'clock at night," noted Oldham in his diary that night. "We burned all our tents

5 Ibid.

6 OR 23, pt. 1, 622-623, and pt. 2, 891-893; Clyde L. Ball, "The Public Career of Col. A. S. Colyar, 1870-1877," *Tennessee Historical Quarterly*, vol. 12, no. 1, (March 1953), 24-27.

7 OR 23, pt. 1, 583.

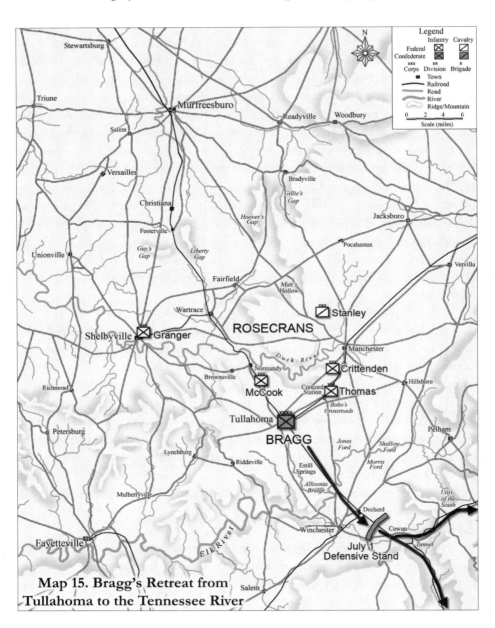

Map 15. Bragg's Retreat from Tullahoma to the Tennessee River

and unnecessary baggage. We are now bivouacked near Allisonia Station on the road."[8]

8   Oldham diary, entry for July 1, 1863.

Brig. Gen. St. John R. Liddell, commander, Liddell's Brigade, Cleburne's Division, Hardee's Corps, Army of Tennessee.

Library of Congress

The shock of the abrupt withdrawal was not confined to the men in the ranks. Brigadier General St. John Liddell, one of Cleburne's brigade commanders, was equally stunned at the news. Reading the account Liddell penned three years later, one can clearly sense his lingering sense of consternation. Liddell reached Tullahoma on June 28, paying a visit to his old West Point classmate Bragg on the way through town. "Although unwell and suffering from chronic diarrhea," recalled Liddell, "he told me that he had determined to fight at Tullahoma." Like Leonidas Polk, Liddell believed this was the wrong decision. "The country was so open . . . no natural advantages were offered for a weak force to contend with a strong one." Liddell argued that it would be much better for the Army of Tennessee to "fall back to the base of the mountains in the rear, where all these chances would favor us. But no, [Bragg] was positive and fixed in his determination that we should fight at Tullahoma."[9]

Returning to his command, Liddell relayed this news to one of his subordinates, Col. Daniel C. Govan, commanding the 2nd Arkansas Infantry, who proved to be far more prescient. "No, General, he will not fight here," Liddell recalled Govan saying.

"But, Colonel, I have General Bragg's word for it," Liddell replied.

"No matter."

"But Bragg would not so positively assert to me such a thing."

"No matter, General, I don't believe it, and I will go an oyster supper on it."

9 Hughes, *Liddell's Record*, 128-129.

"Very well, the first time we shall be in New Orleans after the war." Liddell concluded, "I owe the Colonel . . . for the lost wager yet (August 24th, 1866), but we have not met since the war ended."[10]

As Hardee had predicted (and contrary to Bragg's assertion that they had lost "nothing of importance") the speed of the withdrawal, along with the lack of sufficient transport to haul all of the baggage of Hardee's Corps, meant that a great deal of gear had to be destroyed. A soldier in Brig. Gen. William Churchill's brigade of Cleburne's division, Pvt. William J. Oliphant of the 6th Texas Infantry (now consolidated with the 10th and 15th Texas Cavalry, both dismounted), remembered that after arriving at Tullahoma in May, "we were furnished with new gray uniforms and a full supply of fine tents. All of the new tents furnished our regiment bore the inscription '33rd Indiana,' and the train of new wagons furnished had also been captured from the enemy." These, the spoils of Thompson's Station, were now a liability. "All our tents [were] burnt at Tullahoma," mourned Oliphant.[11]

The men in the ranks suffered anew. "Hour after hour we marched through the mud, so tired we can scarcely put one foot before the other," complained Oliphant's comrade, Sgt. William Heartsill of the 6th/10th/15th Texas; "every hundred yards may be seen one, two or half a dozen men by the road side sick or too tired to go further without rest."[12]

The Confederate cavalry covered the army's retreat, fighting rearguard actions against Rosecrans's advance. Trooper John Wyeth of the 4th Alabama Cavalry recalled the withdrawal. "Nothing so depresses an army as a retreat," he wrote; "no duty is so harrowing and demoralizing as that of fighting rear guard actions every day." Bragg's dogged horsemen had their hands full with the aggressive Union

---

10 Ibid.

11 James M. McCaffrey, ed., *Only a Private: A Texan Remembers the Civil War—The Memoirs of William J. Oliphant* (Houston, TX: 2004), 41-42.

12 Bell Irvin Wiley, ed., *Fourteen Hundred and Ninety-One Days in the Confederate Army: A Journal Kept by W. W. Heartsill for Four Years, One Month and One Day; Or Camp Life; Day by Day of the W. P. Lane Rangers from April 19, 1861, to May 20, 1865* (Jackson, TN: 1953), 134. Heartsill's presence with the Army of Tennessee began in a particularly convoluted fashion. Churchill's brigade was captured at Arkansas Post in January 1863, exchanged in Virginia that April, then transferred to Bragg's army that same month. Heartsill's regiment, the 2nd Texas Cavalry, was not present at Arkansas Post; Heartsill was in one of the four cavalry companies that had been on detached duty there. When the brigade was exchanged, the four companies were consolidated into a single command and arbitrarily attached to the 6th/10th/15th Texas. Eventually Heartsill deserted this ad hoc command to return to his parent formation, the 2nd Texas Cavalry, and continued to serve in the Trans-Mississippi Theater.

cavalry; only they stood between the pursuing Federals and catastrophe for the Army of Tennessee.[13]

The nearly nonstop rains that had made it extremely difficult for the Federals to pursue Braxton Bragg's Army of Tennessee from Wartrace and Shelbyville, and that now tortured Rebel soldiers trudging southward, similarly dogged Rosecrans's advance toward Tullahoma. "The troops, by dint of labor and perseverance, had dragged their artillery and themselves through the mud into position," Rosecrans later reported. The soft and spongy nature of the ground in the Barrens meant that the heavy wagon and iron-sheathed wheels cut deeply into it as if it were a swamp, while horses bogged down in the muck. At the close of the campaign, Rosecrans reported that it took Thomas Crittenden's XXI Corps four days to cover the 21 miles across the Barrens to Manchester at the start of the offensive. From there, things only seemed to deteriorate further. "The dreadful condition of the roads embargoes the troops, and rains have greatly retarded the forward movement," observed a correspondent from the *Cincinnati Commercial*. Private Benjamin Baker of the 25th Illinois, Jefferson C. Davis's division, told his mother, "We are fighting for every step we gain. The fighting is only skirmishing, but it makes slow marching."[14]

Just as Bragg feared, the Federals were indeed striving to outflank him. George Thomas hoped to turn Bragg's position and cut the railroad, forcing the Confederates to stand and fight. Accordingly, to fix the Army of Tennessee in place, Thomas sent out multiple probes that Tuesday. Brigadier General James B. Steedman's brigade of Brannan's division, two regiments of Reynolds's division, and two regiments from Negley's division were dispatched to reconnoiter on separate roads. Additionally, Phil Sheridan sent Col. Luther P. Bradley's 3rd Brigade of his division forward on yet another road to do the same. These moves encountered only cavalry in their front, but despite this, each detachment reported that Bragg's army was still present in force and that they expected Bragg to stand and fight at Tullahoma.[15]

---

13 John Allan Wyeth, *With Saber and Scalpel: The Autobiography of a Soldier and Surgeon* (New York: 1914), 223.

14 *OR* 23, pt. 1, 407; "Telegraphic Correspondence Daily Commercial from Manchester, Tennessee," *Cincinnati Commercial*, July 2, 1863; Benson Bobrick, ed., *Testament: A Soldier's Story of the Civil War* (New York: 2003), 137-138.

15 *OR* 23, pt. 1, 407.

"We were ready to move early this morning," Sgt. William B. Miller of the 75th Indiana, George Thomas's XIV Corps, recorded in his diary on the 30th. "There was heavy skirmishing soon after leaving camp," he continued, "and we expected a hard battle today but only moved a short distance. We still expect warm times tomorrow from the movements today. We have plenty of mud and our trains can hardly move at all." Sergeant Miller concluded his entry by speculating about the reason for the slow pace: "I presume the cause of the delay is repairing the railroad so as to supply us. The Rebels destroy all the bridges as they retreat and our engineers have to repair as they advance."[16]

Echoing Sergeant Miller's account of "heavy skirmishing," Thomas M. Small of the 10th Indiana, Steedman's brigade, took the time to record the day's sharp action in his diary. Two companies drawn from his regiment, along with two more companies from the 4th Kentucky Infantry, "ran into [the] 2nd Georgia Cavalry reg. [and] had a hot engagement lasting an hour." The fighting, which produced 15 wounded on the Union side, ended when the "rebel [cavalry] skiped out." A larger battle the next day now seemed certain.[17]

In preparation for the expected combat, Thomas personally reconnoitered the ground in his front. Sometime on the afternoon of June 30 he relayed his observations to Rosecrans. "I . . . think [our] present position is a strong one and cannot be easily flanked on the left by the enemy unless he makes a march of from 10 to 12 miles, which he cannot do without encountering my pickets and outposts," he concluded. In short, Rosecrans held the advantage and had the Army of Tennessee largely cornered. That analysis, as it turned out, was mistaken.[18]

In the meantime, the rest of the XIV Corps established its camps. The men had few rations, and there was not much fodder for horses and mules. Now more than 30 miles from the railhead at Murfreesboro, and with the roads in bad shape, the Army of the Cumberland was running short of provisions. What few rations that were brought forward were typically supplemented by boiling ripe wheat from nearby fields and slaughtering wild hogs found in the woods. The heavy rains only made these activities even more unpleasant for the Union soldiers.[19]

16 William B. Miller Diary, entry for June 30, 1863, Smith Memorial Library, Indiana Historical Society, Indianapolis.

17 OR 23, pt. 1, 407; Thomas M. Small diary, entry for June 30, 1863, Smith Memorial Library, Indiana Historical Society.

18 OR 23, pt. 1, 427.

19 Calkins, *The History of the One Hundred and Fourth Regiment*, 94.

That same morning, Rosecrans took time to consider the larger strategic picture. It was possible, he reasoned, that Bragg might switch his base of operations to northern Alabama, which would foil Rosecrans's attempt to keep Bragg from falling back toward Chattanooga and could potentially threaten General Grant's ongoing siege of Vicksburg. To forestall this possibility, Rosecrans called on the U.S. Navy for help. "The enemy is driven back of the Duck River upon Tullahoma," he wrote to Capt. A. M. Pennock, commander of a small flotilla of gunboats based at Cairo, Illinois. "Can't you come up the Tennessee and head off any attempt they may make to cross at Florence or Decatur? Do so, if possible." The gunboats did not answer Rosecrans's call, but fortunately for the Federals, Bragg was not contemplating a retreat into northern Alabama.[20]

July 1 dawned hot and steamy and brought surprising news. A civilian advised Thomas that the Army of Tennessee had evacuated Tullahoma. James Steedman's XIV Corps brigade cautiously advanced at daylight on July 1, hoping to confirm that intelligence. About 8:15, Steedman reported that he was within half a mile of the Confederate lines, that he was ready to move whenever ordered, and that he could hear trains coming and going from Tullahoma every hour, suggesting that troops were either arriving or departing. It soon became clear that they were leaving. After questioning a handful of captured Rebels, Steedman occupied Tullahoma about 11:30 that morning. "Prisoners captured state that the enemy were 35,000 (infantry) strong, with all their cavalry and artillery—Wheeler, Wharton and Forrest," reported Steedman's division commander, John Brannan. "The last of the infantry left between midnight and daylight, and their cavalry since. I believe that their rear is totally disorganized." Again, Thomas Small of the 10th Indiana recorded the day's events. "We entered the Rebel Breast works at 1 pm," he wrote. "4 Ky first to place stars and stripes in Tullahoma. Bragg in full retreat for Chattanooga. He commenced to evacuate at Noon yesterday."[21]

The Yankees had spent two days nerving themselves for a bloody job ahead. "We started for Tullahoma and we were all expecting a fight sure as it was promised to us ever since we left Murfreesboro and they are reported to be concentrated," reported Sergeant Miller of the 75th Indiana. "We left our camp determined to do our duty and stand up to work as long as there is enough left to make a fight." He wrote of the advance on the Confederate works at Tullahoma. "Who can describe

---

20 OR 23, pt. 2, 486. Rosecrans greatly overestimated the state of Bragg's logistics, which effectively precluded such a retreat.

21 Ibid., pt. 1, 452, and pt. 2, 498; Small diary, entry for July 1, 1863.

their feelings advancing on a line where he expects every step will bring death and destruction all around," he wrote, "but we crawled on and under and over the timber and the large guns frowning on us from the works, but we reach the works and find that the enemy is gone and with a shout we mount and turn and look back."[22]

For Crittenden's XXI Corps, July 1 was also a difficult day, but not because of Confederate opposition. Prior to discovering the evacuation of Tullahoma, Rosecrans ordered Thomas Crittenden to move his corps south toward Hill's Chapel, six miles south of Manchester and roughly three miles east of Bobo's Crossroads, "to form on the left of Thomas." The march replicated the men's agonizing experience of the previous week. Major General John M. Palmer's division moved out first, with Hazen's brigade in the lead. The troops slogged along a miserable road that "seemed almost lost as we marched through woods and with almost bottomless mud." Despite starting at 10:00 a.m., Palmer's column did not reach the chapel until 4 p.m., averaging one mile per hour, by which time, Palmer noted, "[I] was overtaken by orders to march to Hillsboro." Once Rosecrans learned of Bragg's departure, he redirected Crittenden to move via Hillsborough to Pelham, from whence his XXI Corps could march toward Decherd, University Place, or Cowan, as needed. Crittenden now reversed the order of the march, sending Brig. Gen. Thomas Wood's division directly to Hillsborough from Manchester, where Wood encamped at 9:00 p.m. Palmer's exhausted men rested at Hill's Chapel.[23]

Rosecrans wasted no time in informing Washington of these developments. "[We] found that the enemy had fled in haste last night, much demoralized," he crowed. The Federals captured some heavy artillery and occupied Bragg's lines. Brannan later reported that the "rebel works were considerable, and well constructed, effectually covering the road by which I advanced. They had evidently been abandoned in great haste, as I found three large guns and considerable subsistence stores on entering the town. The guns, carriages, and a great portion of the subsistence had been set on fire by the rebels, and were still burning when I arrived. No ammunition was found." Musician Charles B. Stiles of the 36th Illinois, Sheridan's division, wrote in his diary, "So great was their hurry that they left their tents staked to the ground and ripped them to pieces with their knives." Despite

22 Miller diary, entry for July 1, 1863.

23 William B. Hazen ledger book, entry for July 1, 1863, William B. Hazen Papers, U.S. Army Heritage and Education Center, Carlisle, PA; *OR* 23, pt. 1, 521-522, 529-530.

Bragg's claims to the contrary, the Confederates had clearly abandoned considerable quantities of equipment.[24]

In addition to the issues associated with the pursuit, Rosecrans also had to address his army's increasingly frayed logistics. His supply base was still in Murfreesboro, and as he pursued Bragg, that line of supply grew increasingly attenuated. On the morning of July 1, Rosecrans pushed Granger to send up supplies from Murfreesboro, to repair the railroad, and to take steps to repair the telegraph in order to speed communications. Then Rosecrans immediately rode forward to establish his headquarters at Tullahoma.[25]

The Army of Tennessee had stolen a march on the Federals, and by the evening of July 1 it was mostly south of the Elk River. Rosecrans's men had no choice but to follow along roads already cut to pieces by the Rebel movements. To help compensate for those delays, Rosecrans now pushed south toward the river on multiple axes. With the Elk running dangerously high from the week's rain, control of the limited crossing sites, and most especially the all-important bridges, became paramount.

The most important of those crossings were the rail and wagon bridges at Allisonia, and the Winchester Pike bridge (the direct road from Tullahoma), approximately 2.5 miles downstream from the rail bridge; Polk's Corps crossed at the latter location. Captain A. T. Fielder of the 12th Tennessee Infantry, which was now combined with the 47th Tennessee, belonged to Preston Smith's brigade of Frank Cheatham's division, Polk's command. The morning of July 1 "found us marching along slowly through mud and water, hungry and sleepy, not having slept any last night," Fielder noted. "The morning was exceedingly warm—We reached [Allisonia] at 9½ oclk. We were ordered to stack arms and rest." Fielder's men ate and managed to grab "some two or three hours" of sleep. "We lay about all the evening[,] troops passing nearly all the time—Our men burned the R. R. Bridge across the Elk River at this place today." Designated as rear guard, Fielder and his men managed a full night's sleep and a chance at breakfast on July 2, before being "called into line at 6½ oclk and marched off on the road to Winchester." The destruction of the rail bridge made it clear they would not be returning any time soon.[26]

---

24 John Stiles Castle, ed., *Grandfather was a Drummer Boy: A Civil War Diary and Letters of Charles B. Stiles* (Solon, OH: 1986), 80; *OR* 23, pt. 1, 402, 438, 446.

25 *OR* 23, pt. 2, 495.

26 Cathey, *Fielder's Civil War Diary*, 236.

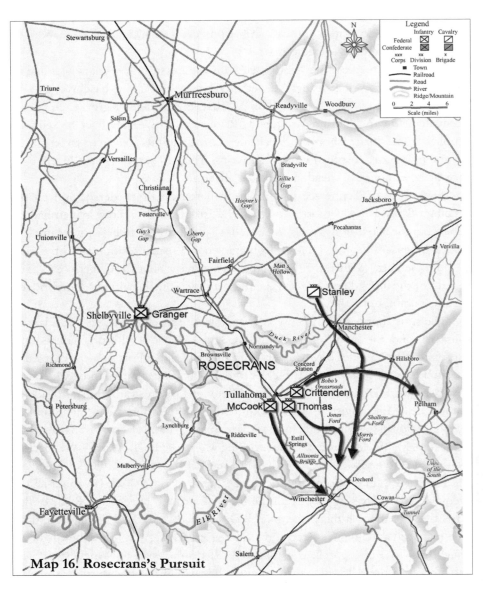

Map 16. Rosecrans's Pursuit

Hardee's Corps crossed at Bethpage Bridge, which lay a mile upstream (northeast) of the Allisonia Bridge, where a side road turned east off the road running from Bobo's Crossroads to Winchester. That movement commenced in the dead of night on June 30, when Hardee's troops began filing out of Tullahoma's trenches. "We were ordered to move further on the wright some 2 miles and thar we were in line of battle and thought the fight would come off thar the next day but alas that was the orders," recounted Ben Seaton of the dismounted 10th Texas

Cavalry, Churchill's brigade, Cleburne's division. "I heard attension battalion in a vary low tone voice—it almost sounded like a death bell everything was very still and in the distin[ce] the bugal softly blows—won could hardley hear the sound of a voice along the hole line but alas as they were already off we started—I new not wher—but soon found out that we wer on a heavy march for the night. We went to Elk River that night some 12 or 15 miles."[27]

Lieutenant Robert M. Collins of the 15th Texas Dismounted Cavalry, another of Churchill's soldiers, recalled that "about day light we crossed Elk river and went into camps footsore, weary, and out of humor generally, then commenced the figuring by all the boys as to what was the matter that the great army of Tennessee should be retreating. The conclusion was pretty generally reached that old Rosencrans was flanking us, but this did not satisfy, for the boys insisted that if he flanked us why in the Hades couldn't we flank him[?]"[28]

Not everyone blamed the army commander for the disappointing movement. Adjutant C. Irvine Walker of the 10th South Carolina, also in Polk's Corps, defended Bragg by arguing the retreat was militarily sound. In a letter home he opined, "we could easily have defeated the enemy had he dared attack us [at Tullahoma]. But such was not his intention, he kept on moving on our right and threatening our communications. We were not in sufficient force to attack him, and he would not attack us, but threatened to destroy our line of communications— hence arose the necessity of a further retreat. We, in a night march over the most execrable road fell back across Elk River and occupied Allisonia." This left only Confederate cavalry north of the river to contest the Union advance.[29]

In addition to the bridges, several important fords offered the Federals passage over the Elk, especially once the river levels dropped—which, as the rain started to ease up, would not be far off. Jones Ford, Morris Ford, and Shallow Ford all lay upstream from (and east of, thanks to a bend in the river) Bethpage Bridge. Additionally, Rock Creek Ford lay just about a half mile downstream from Allisonia. Their presence and growing utility further complicated Bragg's position at Decherd.

27 Harold B. Simpson, ed., *The Bugle Softly Blows: The Confederate Diary of Benjamin M. Seaton* (Waco, TX: 1965), 35.

28 Robert M. Collins, *Chapters from the Unwritten History of the War Between the States; or, The Incidents in the Life of a Confederate Soldier in Camp, on the March, in the Great Battles, and in Prison* (St. Louis, MO: 1893), 136.

29 William L. White and Charles Denny Runion, eds., *Great Things Are Expected of Us: The Letters of Colonel C. Irvine Walker, 10th South Carolina Infantry, C.S.A.* (Knoxville, TN: 2009), 59-60.

The first Federals to reach the Elk (aside from Wilder's expedition) belonged to Brig. Gen. John Beatty's brigade of Negley's division, which was stationed at Bobo's Crossroads on the morning of July 1. Beatty reported that at "10 o'clock in the morning," after learning from "a citizen" that the Rebels had evacuated Tullahoma, his brigade was "ordered forward to reconnoiter in the direction of Winchester." A battalion of the 2nd Kentucky Cavalry (U.S.) preceded Beatty's men and the rest of Negley's command followed in support. Bobo's Crossroads was seven miles north of the Bethpage Bridge, which in turn was about halfway to Winchester. Beatty reported that the cavalry soon ran into the enemy, including artillery, which forced him to deploy the 15th Kentucky (U.S.) and 104th Illinois regiments in support and bring up his own battery. A short artillery duel followed. Then, wrote Beatty, "I pushed forward the column, my skirmishers exchanging shots continually with the enemy, who retired slowly, halting and planting his battery at six different points on the road. . . . [W]e drove him from every position, and finally halted for the night . . . 1½ miles north of [the] Elk River."[30]

Beatty's halt did not end the hostilities. Negley ordered Col. William L. Stoughton, commanding the 2nd Brigade, to move up on Beatty's right and press on toward the river. Part of the 1st Ohio joined the 2nd Kentucky Cavalry (U.S.) there, and the combined force pressed ahead. "The enemy seemed to be in considerable force," Stoughton reported, "and a heavy skirmish ensued."[31]

This fight drew Churchill's Confederates back across the river to support their own cavalrymen—fellow Texans from the 8th and 11th Cavalry regiments of Colonel Harrison's brigade, Wharton's division, accompanied by Captain White's Tennessee battery. Chaplain Robert F. Bunting, the careful chronicler of the 8th Texas's experiences, noted a sharp fight and some loss. "White's battery opens upon the enemy, and he replies with great accuracy," Bunting wrote. "Several horses are killed, and one man is slightly wounded. Later in the afternoon the enemy presses heavily, and Cleburne's division . . . came up to Wharton's relief." Bunting also noted, admiringly, that "the 11th Texas sat on their horses in line of battle and fought most gallantly and desperately. They lost several men and a large number of horses. There are no better fighters in the army than the gallant 11th."[32]

Robert Collins of the 15th Texas also recollected that afternoon's events. "About 3 o'clock . . . we were ordered to recross the river, and move back toward

30 *OR* 23, part 1, 445-446.

31 Ibid., 448.

32 Cutrer, *Our Trust is in the God of Battles*, 169.

the enemy," he wrote. "This suited us, for we were red hot for a fight." Captain James P. Douglas's Texas battery, which served as Churchill's brigade artillery, also deployed to defend the crossing, unlimbering while supported by the 8th, 11th, and 6th/10th/15th Texas regiments. There, Col. Roger Q. Mills, the commander of the combined 6th/10th/15th, "made us a speech. . . . Texas cavalry on the right; Texas cavalry on the left; a Texas battery in center, all supported by Texas Infantry and who dare come against us!" No one dared, apparently, for no attack came, and that evening, the rear guard slipped across the Elk to continue on its way south.[33]

Though Beatty's troops suffered only a handful of actual battle casualties, the active pace of the skirmishing in the hot weather did indeed take a toll. Beatty reported the loss of one man killed and four wounded, "one mortally, one seriously," and two "slightly." Moreover, "the day was oppressively hot, and nearly 50 of my men had fallen down in the woods and by the roadside, utterly exhausted; quite a number of them were carried [away] from [the] effects of the extreme heat."[34]

At 9:00 p.m. on July 1, Thomas informed Rosecrans of the day's events. "Negley . . . march[ed] to Heffner's Mill" (about a mile north of Bethpage Bridge), where "he then went into camp for the night." Rousseau's division followed Negley. Thomas added that he had instructed Reynolds's and Brannan's divisions "to rejoin the corps at Heffner's Mill to-morrow morning. . . . The enemy made quite a stubborn resistance, wounding a good number of our men, but they were steadily driven until we encamped for the night."[35]

Having learned that Bragg was now across the Elk, Rosecrans gave Thomas marching orders early on July 2. "Our rule is now to push with all vigor," he declared. "Remind all officers leading the advance that whenever a vigorous attack is made, the enemy naturally supposes that our whole army is upon them." He concluded, "It is of the greatest importance that no time is lost. Please advise me frequently."[36]

Rosecrans told Crittenden to occupy Pelham on July 2, and Wood's men were ordered to seize the bridge over the Elk there as soon as they could. Palmer was instructed to move to Hart's Tanyard, about four miles north of Pelham, and then

33 Collins, *Chapters from the Unwritten History*, 136.

34 OR 23, pt. 1, 446.

35 Ibid., 428.

36 Ibid., pt. 2, 504.

turn south "to examine the Elk River" at a place called "Stamper's Ferry, and ascertain the facilities for crossing there."[37]

Meanwhile, elements of Alexander McCook's XX Corps and Thomas's XIV Corps took possession of Tullahoma on the afternoon of July 1. Rosecrans intended for McCook to pursue Polk's column early the next day, and at midnight he ordered McCook to start Phil Sheridan's 3rd Division at 3 a.m. "on the Winchester Road in pursuit of the enemy, directing him to push forward with the utmost vigor, and, if possible, assault the enemy's rear and inflict a heavy punishment on him." Sheridan marched at the appointed hour, his force led by a mixed battalion of four companies of the 39th Indiana Mounted Infantry and four companies of the 2nd Kentucky Cavalry.[38]

Any trained military man understood that the pursuit of a beaten or retreating foe required well-handled cavalry, and Rosecrans fully intended to use Stanley's cavalry corps in that capacity. The army commander's first orders to Stanley, however, duplicated Tom Crittenden's mission, for he instructed the cavalryman "to proceed with all your available force . . . to Pelham, by way of Hillsborough, and from there push forward [one] reconnoitering party by way of Gillem's Cove, over the mountain, to discover the route of the enemy's retreat and to send another such effort to Decherd." In other words the Federal commander was trying to push Stanley's more nimble mounted force beyond the Rebel flank to perhaps once again threaten Bragg's exposed rear. When his most recent intelligence came in, however, Rosecrans modified the orders. The enemy, he learned, "are retreating in great confusion, with their whole force, upon Winchester." This was somewhat farther west than Rosecrans perhaps had anticipated when he issued his first order to Stanley. Rather than have his cavalry veer too far east and miss a shot at Bragg's column, Rosecrans now instructed Stanley to "move with your whole command by the most direct route to Decherd." Rosecrans closed with what had become his standard refrain to his commanders: "Push your march to the utmost."[39]

From his headquarters at Decherd, Bragg's new position now seemed to him as perilous as the one he had occupied at Tullahoma. Despite the earlier rains, the Elk was now beginning to fall quickly, and Rosecrans's men soon would be able to ford it at several locations. Lacking the manpower to defend every potential crossing site, Bragg could not hold the line of the south bank of the Elk indefinitely.

37 Ibid., pt. 1, 529.

38 Ibid., pt. 1, 457, and pt. 2, 496.

39 Ibid., pt. 2, 497.

Maj. Gen. Philip H. Sheridan, commander,
Third Division, XX Corps,
Army of the Cumberland.

Library of Congress

Rosecrans would shortly be able to outflank him from just beyond Hardee's right all the way to the Union bridgehead at Pelham, which was only 14 miles north of the Army of Tennessee's depot at Decherd. The unusual curve of the Elk River between Allisonia and Pelham, combined with the slant of the Cumberland Mountains to Bragg's rear, offered Rosecrans ample choices for maneuver; all the roads converged at Decherd, and from there, Cowan was not far. Given the relative positions of the two armies, Bragg felt he had little choice but to continue to fall back.[40]

Still, thanks to the weather and Bragg's successful evasion, Rosecrans's pursuit was by necessity slow, and his crossing options still—for the moment—limited. Perhaps aggressive action on Bragg's part might have crushed the leading elements of the Army of the Cumberland in detail as they tried to force their way across the river, but since abandoning Tullahoma, Bragg appeared indecisive and unsure of his next course. This indecision triggered a new crisis within the Army of Tennessee's high command.

No longer trusting Bragg's judgment, Polk and Hardee acted largely on their own initiative, moving in stops and starts as they saw fit. Early on the evening of July 1, Bragg, in a dispatch reflecting his indecision, queried Polk: "The enemy have reached your front; close up. The question to be decided instantly, Shall we fight on the Elk, or take post at the foot of the mountains at Cowan? Answer." Polk responded promptly, "I reply, take post at foot of mountain at Cowan. In that case I think that as much of our wagon train as possible should be thrown over the

40 OR 23, pt. 1, 583, and pt. 2, 894-895; Howard M. Hannah, *Confederate Action in Franklin County, Tennessee* (Sewanee, TN: 1963), 25-34.

Maj. Gen. James Negley, commander,
Second Division, XIV Corps,
Army of the Cumberland.

Library of Congress

mountain, and supplies of grain ordered up by railroad for animals which we must retain on this side."[41]

By now greatly alarmed, Hardee dashed off a letter to Polk at 8:30 on the night of July 1. "I have been thinking seriously of the condition of affairs with this army," he wrote. "I deeply regret to see General Bragg in his present enfeebled state of health. If we have a fight, he is evidently unable either to examine and determine his line of battle or to take command on the field. What shall we do? What is best to be done to save this army and its honor? I think we ought to counsel together. Where is Buckner? The enemy evidently believes we are retreating, and will press us vigorously to-morrow. When can we meet? I would like Buckner to be present."[42]

Later that evening Hardee followed this missive with a second note. After telling Polk that he thought the army should take up a position at Cowan, he penned, "this decision will render unnecessary the meeting which I sought to-night; we can talk about the matter tomorrow." He then told Polk that he did not want anyone but the bishop and Buckner to know of his discomfort, and that the decision to stand at Cowan eased his mind somewhat. Nevertheless, the Army of Tennessee's senior subordinates remained ill at ease with their army commander's tremulous decision-making, and for good reason. Bragg reversed himself frequently and repeatedly, abruptly issuing contradictory orders to his corps commanders. However, Hardee's and Polk's connivance, hinting that Bragg might have to be replaced, bordered on mutiny.[43]

41 OR 23, pt. 1, 623.

42 Ibid.

43 Ibid., 624.

Hearing the same answer from both Hardee and Polk convinced Bragg that falling back to Cowan and preparing to give battle there was the correct course of action. He ordered Polk to send his engineers to repair the road over the mountain as far as University Place for use by the army. Polk and his staff rode to Bragg's headquarters at Allisonia to see him that afternoon, returning about 5:00 p.m.[44]

On the night of July 1, while Polk and Hardee schemed, Bragg ordered his quartermaster and commissary generals to establish the army's base of operations at Cowan. He also instructed Polk to send a brigade and his corps wagon train to Cowan, while Hardee was ordered to park his wagon train at Decherd. Polk, in turn, ordered Cheatham to send one of his brigades to Cowan to hold the place until the rest of the army arrived. Cheatham again turned to Smith's brigade to lead the march, with Captain Fielder of the 12th Tennessee noting that he and his men trudged into Cowan at "about 4½ oclk." Bragg then ordered Polk and Hardee to fall back to Cowan. About dawn on July 2, he reversed himself again and ordered the army to halt at Decherd. Shortly thereafter, Bragg countermanded this new order and instead directed the army to continue the march to Cowan. In doing so, Bragg abandoned any hope of holding the south bank of the Elk River.[45]

For his part, Rosecrans was eager to come to grips with the enemy as quickly as possible. Thomas's, McCook's, Crittenden's, and Stanley's marching orders for July 2 all called for the troops to move out well before dawn, and all four commanders set out in accordance with their latest instructions. The question remained: Did Bragg have too great of a head start?

The first fighting on July 2 occurred at Bethpage Bridge. Negley's orders were to capture the ford near the bridge, since the Federals assumed the Rebels had burned the bridge the night before. Negley's and Rousseau's XIV Corps divisions caught up to the Confederate rear guard there, with John Beatty again in the lead. Beatty found a strong force of the enemy's cavalry and infantry present, "in position on the bluffs on the opposite side of the . . . river, with his artillery planted so as to sweep the road." Surprisingly, the bridge was still intact. Beatty halted and sent for his artillery. Negley brought up two batteries and opened on the Southerners, "who replied, but with no effect. [The Confederate] guns were soon silenced by dismounting one and driving the gunners from their posts," Negley reported, "compelling the whole force, with the exception of a few sharpshooters, to fall back from their position." A deserter from Wheeler's Corps later confirmed

44 Ibid.

45 Ibid., pt. 2, 895, and pt. 1, 624; Cathey, *Fielder's Civil War Diary*, 237.

that the Union artillery had indeed punished the Rebel battery, dismounting one of its guns, damaging a caisson, wounding several of its men, and compelling the Confederates to withdraw after trying to set the bridge on fire.[46]

The 104th Illinois played a dramatic role in this action. One of the regiments captured by Morgan at Hartsville, Tennessee, the previous December, the 104th now saw a chance for some payback. "Near the bridge . . . was a small log stockade occupied by rebel sharpshooters, who annoyed our advance skirmishers. . . . General Beatty call[ed] upon the One Hundred and Fourth to furnish a detail of ten men to capture the stockade. Colonel Moore selected Sergeant George Marsh to lead the party. The Sergeant called for volunteers, who promptly responded." Moving forward in what the regimental historian described as "a forlorn hope . . . the little band deploying as skirmishers, and covered by the fire of our batteries, double-quicked across the plain, the rebel sharpshooters firing at them, and gained the river without a casualty, then rallying on the left, they rushed for the stockade. The dozen rebels inside, seized with a panic at the bold action, left in confusion, swimming the Elk, took to the woods, from which they sent back a few shots. The [assault] party was soon after ordered back and received the personal thanks of the General. Captain [George W.] Howe, with Company B, was then sent down with a detail to put out the fire at the bridge." Howe and his men extinguished the fire and saved the bridge, which was used to cross the infantry. In 1897, Sergeant Marsh received the Medal of Honor for his courageous action on July 2.[47]

Negley reported that about 3,000 men of Buckner's Corps, some of Cheatham's men, and other Confederate infantry had been in the area that morning. After the previous night's scrap, Hardee's troops apparently had moved farther south and thus were not close enough at hand to resist the crossing. Confederate reports and recollections of the fighting along the Elk are all but nonexistent, making an accurate determination of Negley's opposition here nearly impossible. However, one clue to the identity of these Confederate troops can be found in the consolidated service records of one of Buckner's regiments, the 54th Virginia Infantry. According to a modern historian of that regiment, "one man was wounded, and four others were captured on [July] 1st, while five more were taken prisoner over the next three days" in fighting around the Elk River crossings.[48]

46 Beatty, *Citizen-Soldier,* 291; OR 23, pt. 1, 443, 447.

47 Calkins, *The History of the One Hundred and Fourth Regiment,* 96; OR 23, pt. 1, 447.

48 Jeffrey C. Weaver, *54th Virginia Infantry* (Lynchburg, VA: 1993), 71.

Writing years after the assault, Sgt. William J. McMurray of the 20th Tennessee, from Bate's brigade of Stewart's division, claimed that his regiment had been called back to the river. "We had gone three miles beyond the bridge on the side of the mountain, when a courier came dashing up to Colonel [Thomas B.] Smith and said the Yankees were driving our cavalry from the bridge . . . , so we were double-quicked back and found that Martin's cavalry had been driven away by the enemy's artillery. . . . The Twentieth Regiment, on their arrival deployed as skirmishers and drove the enemy back and burned the bridge." Here McMurray's recollections, penned in 1904, failed him, for contemporary Federal reports clearly indicate that the bridge was not destroyed.[49]

Meanwhile, Rousseau's division detoured to Jones Ford on the Elk upstream from Bethpage Bridge, where Col. Henry A. Hambright's 2nd Brigade forced its way across the river with considerable effort, the men using ropes stretched across the stream as handholds as they struggled through the fast-flowing, shoulder-deep water. "The ford being very deep," reported Thomas, "it was with great difficulty that the brigade effected a passage, damaging much of their ammunition by the water getting into their cartridge boxes." Hambright next sent a squad of the 1st Wisconsin Infantry ahead almost a mile and a half to reconnoiter. Its commander reported encountering only a small force of cavalry and that the enemy had left the area around the ford. He also noted that prisoners told him Bragg had retreated by way of Cowan and Pelham (this was an error—no Confederates except perhaps a few cavalry had moved through Pelham) and then across the Cumberland Mountains. The rest of the Rousseau's division camped on the north bank of the Elk; one Federal noted that the stream reeked of dead horses and men.[50]

Thomas then notified army headquarters of his status. "I have arrived too late for the bridge over Elk River," he reported. "Rebels are across, and the bridge burned. They have left a strong force on the opposite side of the river. Their army has retreated via Decherd." Thomas said he intended to cross the Elk upriver—a reference to Rousseau's movement to Jones Ford—and would try to flank the enemy out of its position on the south bank. Once across the river, he intended to strike. "If we can cross today," he continued, "it is probable the General Stanley and myself can destroy their trains, if not them. Rest assured that I will press them closely. Please see that we have rations before [July 6], as all we have will then be out. If you can keep us supplied, we will drive them out of Tennessee before we

49 McMurray, *Twentieth Tennessee*, 262.

50 *OR* 23, pt. 1, 422-423, 435.

stop." This last passage of Thomas's dispatch highlighted the increasing importance of getting supplies to the Army of the Cumberland as it pursued Bragg, over an ever-more-tenuous supply line.[51]

In a 3:30 p.m. dispatch, Negley described his fight to Thomas: "I have sent scouting parties to Allisona, who report three guns in position, supported by one regiment of infantry in view and some cavalry; and some wagons and tents." Further, "although we have scouted a distance of 4 or 5 miles along the railroads, meeting with stragglers from Sheridan's and Johnson's divisions [of the XX Corps], we have failed to open communications with either of these generals."[52]

That same day, McCook's XX Corps pursued the Confederates along the railroad. Sheridan's division led the way, spending much of the morning searching for fordable crossing sites. When Sheridan arrived at Rock Creek Ford, he found the river still too swollen for anything but cavalry to cross, and encountered opposition in the form of some of Wheeler's troopers holding the south bank of the Elk. However, Sheridan's mounted force greatly outnumbered the Southern horsemen and drove them away, securing the ford. "A cable was then stretched across, by which means the weak men of the division were crossed," reported Sheridan. "The rest of the men, placing their cartridge boxes on their shoulders, went in with a cheer, en masse, supporting each other, and the entire command was crossed without any loss, although the stream was deep and rapid." Sheridan then deployed two regiments of infantry and a detachment of the 39th Indiana Mounted Infantry to drive the Confederate sharpshooters from his front, clearing them from some hastily constructed earthworks. At 4:30 that afternoon, he informed McCook, "one of my brigades is already over, and I will cross my whole division in a short time." Echoing Negley's information, Sheridan added, "I find the enemy still hold their position at Allisona; they can be plainly seen . . . some distance on my left. I have captured some 60 or 70 prisoners."[53]

The day's other significant action occurred at Morris Ford, upstream from Bethpage Bridge and Jones Ford. Rosecrans, having recognized that speed and mobility increased the effectiveness of his pursuit, had earlier ordered Stanley and the cavalry to take the lead in pursuing the Army of Tennessee. He further

51 Ibid., pt. 2, 504-505. As noted above, Thomas's report was only partially correct concerning the Bethpage Bridge. It was damaged, not destroyed.

52 Ibid., 505. Reports on both sides frequently referred to Allisonia as Allisona. The spellings were used interchangeably.

53 Ibid., pt. 1, 408, 513, 515.

instructed Stanley to send scouts over the Cumberland Mountains by way of Decherd to identify and try to cut off Bragg's lines of supply, communication, and retreat. Anxious for detailed intelligence, Rosecrans told his cavalry chief, "It will be of the utmost importance for us to know promptly all the developments of your expedition. Report frequently and fully." Follow-up instructions informed Stanley to cross the Elk at Morris Ford.[54]

That morning, Stanley and the Cavalry Corps marched to Manchester. Brigadier General Robert B. Mitchell's 1st Cavalry Division led the way, with Minty's detached brigade bringing up the rear. John Turchin, the Russian-born former Tsarist officer commanding the Army of the Cumberland's 2nd Cavalry Division, led about 400 troopers of Col. Eli Long's cavalry brigade and a section of horse artillery forward from Hillsborough along the Decherd Road. Turchin found more of Wheeler's troopers guarding the Elk River crossings near Morris Ferry, and promptly engaged them until the arrival of Mitchell's division gave the Union cavalry a sufficient numerical advantage to drive Wheeler. Colonel James D. Webb of the 51st Alabama Partisan Rangers was killed during this skirmish. The Union cavalry then forced its way across the river before darkness halted the pursuit.[55]

William Martin's Rebel cavalry division defended Morris Ford. The brigadier deployed his dismounted troopers along the southern bank of the Elk, where they skirmished with Stanley's men while the blue cavalry and artillery sheltered in the thick woods along the northern bank. Bushrod Johnson, also present, brought up Capt. Israel P. Darden's Mississippi guns to support the cavalry. One of Darden's sections opened on the enemy in the wood line at a range of 250 to 300 yards. Taking their cue from Martin, the Mississippi gunners raked the woods. "The enemy commenced falling back at the first shot," Johnson reported, "and by the time the sixth shot was fired their cavalry had gained the lane bordered by wide fields beyond the woods, along which they moved in column, presenting an admirable mark for our artillery, and one upon which every shell seemed to take effect. They were thrown into great confusion," he added, "and many loose horses were seen running away without their riders" as the Union guns withdrew.[56]

Johnson reported that he could see a lengthy Federal wagon train extending into the woods beyond, but could not tell whether it was ambulances or a pontoon

54 Ibid., pt. 2, 497; John Bachelor diary, entry for July 1, 1863, Special Collections, Abraham Lincoln Presidential Library and Museum, Springfield, IL.

55 *OR* 23, pt. 1, 408, 540, 545. Long was colonel of the 4th Ohio Cavalry.

56 Ibid., 609.

train. The wagon drivers tried to turn away once Darden's guns opened on them, but when a couple of shells dropped among them and exploded, mass confusion reigned. The teams became badly tangled up with the fleeing Union cavalry, creating chaos. Eventually, nearly all the Federals escaped. Johnson estimated that "the loss of the enemy here is supposed to have been quite large, and recent reports, through Northern papers, confirm this impression. Captain Darden here fired 48 rounds of shell."[57]

Once Mitchell's Federals added their weight to the fight, Martin's troopers and Johnson's infantry retreated to an intersection south of Bethpage Bridge, from where they could continue to screen the approaches to both Decherd and Winchester. When Johnson arrived, he found that Martin's troopers had been driven to that point, so he formed a line of battle about a mile to the rear with a section of Darden's battery in support. They held this position for about an hour until Brig. Gen. John A. Wharton came up from Cowan with substantial reinforcements. Just as Johnson received orders to withdraw, Wheeler arrived, so Johnson left the cavalryman to handle the rearguard duties and pulled back to the base of the Cumberland Mountains to rest for the night.[58]

The fight for the crossings consumed all of July 2, buying much-needed time for Bragg's main body to put distance between itself and the pursuit. The stubborn Confederate resistance frustrated the Federals. "It was readily understood that this was for the purpose of delaying our river crossing as long as possible, in order to enable the infantry and trains to get to the mountains," reported a newspaper correspondent traveling with Thomas's command. "To aid them in this, very heavy rains came up, and the river rose very high. Natives say that they never saw the river as high as at present." David Stanley, still frustrated by the time he wrote his memoir, dismissed the whole affair as nothing more than "a senseless cannonade across the deep and swollen Elk River."[59]

The delay also meant a respite for some Federals, including Francis A. Kiene of the 49th Ohio Volunteer Infantry, which was part of August Willich's brigade of Richard Johnson's 2nd Division, XX Corps, that had been assigned to garrison Tullahoma. "We were glad when we heard that we would not march and could rest," Kiene exulted in his diary. More ominously he added, "we are ordered on half

57 Ibid., 608-609.

58 Ibid., 610.

59 "From Rosecrans' Army," *Canton Register*, (Canton, OH), July 13, 1863; Stanley, *Personal Memoirs*, 149.

rations." In response to that directive, Kiene and a few others went out to forage and came back with a quarter of beef and a hog. He and his hungry messmates ate well that day.[60]

Fortunately for Union arms, a pause in the rain meant that the Elk was now falling rapidly, and before long, all its fords would be available for use by the Army of the Cumberland. Rosecrans advised Henry Halleck on the afternoon of July 2 that those conditions "will enable them to strike [Bragg's] retreating columns, already forced from the Pelham route across the mountains to the interior and more distant one by Decherd."[61]

The Confederate army was in motion for Cowan on July 2. Polk's corps had obeyed Bragg's dawn orders and marched to the town, where it formed in line of battle to protect its own immense wagon trains and those of Wheeler's cavalry. Polk had chosen a good position. The Cumberland Mountains protected both of his flanks, and the best road up to the top of the plateau lay directly to his rear.

The Federals, however, wasted no time in pressing the Rebel rear guard. At 8 a.m. on July 2 Wheeler reported that "the enemy have come up the mountain and driven in our outposts. A prisoner taken states that the force of the enemy is three regiments of cavalry and four regiments of infantry. They are now fighting our advance line, and our whole line will be engaged in a few minutes." A bit later, Wheeler told Polk, "The enemy are engaging us very warmly at this point. Our men are maintaining their ground bravely. The enemy have infantry and cavalry, and are evidently reinforcing." Then, at 3:40 that afternoon, Wheeler advised Bragg that at least one regiment of the enemy had gotten across the Elk at the ford near Hatton's Mill and that a small number had also crossed at Bethpage Road.[62]

Because of this aggressive Federal pursuit, at 4:00 p.m. Bragg ordered Polk to begin sending his trains up Cumberland Mountain "at once," escorted by two brigades of Cheatham's division. Though Polk had suggested such a move earlier, Bragg's urgent dispatch was yet another signal that he was not going to attempt a stand at Cowan. He had either reversed himself again or he never intended to offer battle at Cowan in the first place, even though both Polk and Hardee had believed

---

60 Ralph E. Kiene, Jr., ed., *A Civil War Diary: The Journal of Francis A. Kiene 1861-1864—A Family History* (privately published, 1974), 159.

61 *OR* 23, pt. 1, 428, 402-403. Rosecrans was still under the impression that some of Bragg's men had retreated via Pelham.

62 Ibid., 615. The first two messages here are dated July 1, presumably by Wheeler's headquarters, but their content, the locations given, and the context of other messages all dated July 2 clearly indicate that the July 1 date is incorrect.

that Bragg intended to fight there. With this decision, Bragg abandoned Middle Tennessee to Rosecrans and the Army of the Cumberland.[63]

Bragg would later justify this last retreat as one of necessity. Although Bragg had his back to the mountains at Cowan and his flanks protected, his army was dangerously low on rations and he did not believe he could force Rosecrans to attack him in a position of his own choosing. These justifications do not seem entirely valid. The Army of the Cumberland was advancing toward Cowan, but the chances that Rosecrans would get ahead of the retreating Rebels diminished by the hour. By mid-afternoon on July 2 Bragg knew the Federals had driven Wheeler away from the Elk River crossings near Allisonia, and that they had crossed the Elk at Rock Creek Ford (Sheridan), Bethpage Bridge (Negley), and Jones Ford (Rousseau). Other Union elements were attempting to cross the river at Morris Ford and Shallow Ford (Stanley's cavalry), but each of these routes converged at Decherd, northeast of Cowan, and offered no easy access to Bragg's line of retreat atop the mountains. Cowan was a solid defensive position. Further, should the Army of Tennessee need to withdraw, two good routes of retreat were available to it: southeast across the mountain to University Place, or directly south through the Crow Creek Valley (the route of the railroad) and then on to Bridgeport or Jasper. Rosecrans could not easily bypass the Confederates without getting badly bogged down in the extremely rough country on either flank. Plus, Bragg had a direct rail connection with Chattanooga, which gave him a more secure supply line than Rosecrans possessed. In spite of these important advantages, Bragg elected not to make a fight of it.[64]

Ascending the Cumberland Plateau required yet another long and brutal march. Exhausted Confederate soldiers fell out by the score all along the muddy road. "Never in my life . . . was I as completely worn out," Sergeant Heartsill wrote in his diary on July 3; "my feet are almost one solid blister and my shoulders are worn out." In his diary, Captain Fielder noted that on July 3 his Tennesseans ascended the mountain amidst a "very hard" rain. "The road was rough up a steap mountain and very slipry but up we went tho slowly. . . . We were the rear guard . . . and found the roads awfully torn up and in many places a perfect mire. We . . . marched about 10 miles which all things considered was one of the hardest days

---

63 Ibid., 625.

64 Ibid., 584, 615; Connelly, *Autumn of Glory*, 133.

march we have ever done." But there was no rest for the weary—the stakes remained too high.[65]

About 2:00 a.m. on July 3, Polk arrived at University Place, the site of the college he helped found, and where for a short time he had made his home just before the war. By then, the wagons and troops had all passed by on their way to Chattanooga. Only Wheeler's horsemen remained to defend the passes and dispute the Army of the Cumberland's advance. Confederate Signal Corps officer Mercer Otey was the son of James Hervey Otey, Polk's fellow bishop, close friend, and fellow cofounder of the university. Young Mercer observed General Polk here on July 3. Sometime that morning, Otey recollected, "Gen. Polk . . . called his body servant, Altamont, to fetch his cane chair . . . and had it placed at a point that had been cleared of surrounding trees, called 'inspiration point,' I think, commanding a full view of the great valley stretched at our feet." Refreshed with buttermilk from the university caretaker's kitchen, "here we rested for an hour or more on historic ground, and together talked of the hopes and plans that he and my father entertained for the building of the great university."[66]

There was only so much time for extended, leisurely reminiscences, however, and Polk enjoyed only a brief visit at the site of his greatest accomplishment before departing with his staff about 4:00 that afternoon. He rode another six miles or so and camped with Cheatham's division.[67]

There was little rest to be had among the Union ranks either. Rosecrans intended to thrust his corps forward on all available roads. At 1:30 a.m. on July 3, Garfield had advised Crittenden that the Elk probably would be fordable by morning. "Whether this will meet opposition or not, remains yet to be seen," he wrote. "General Thomas thinks this is evidence that a portion of Bragg's army will endeavor to escape, by way of Pelham, across the mountains." Accordingly, Garfield ordered Crittenden to send Thomas J. Wood's division to Pelham that day and intercept Bragg's army if possible. "It can only be a fragment that will attempt to escape by that route," cautioned Garfield. "The enemy's force are greatly demoralized, and are deserting hourly."[68]

65 Wiley, *Fourteen Hundred and Ninety-One Days*, 136-137; Cathey, *Fielder's Civil War Diary*, 237-238.

66 *OR* 23, pt. 1, 625; Otey, "Operations of the Signal Corps," 129.

67 *OR* 23, pt. 1, 625.

68 Ibid., pt. 2, 508.

Brig. Gen. Jefferson C. Davis, commander,
First Division, XX Corps,
Army of the Cumberland.

Library of Congress

On Thomas's front, James Negley's division pushed south from Bethpage Bridge. By 2:00 p.m. his men reached the farm of a man named Pennington, where Negley met some talkative locals including a knowledgeable African-American man. Here, Negley learned several fragments of news, including that Bragg had left Decherd on July 1 and that a large wagon train had passed through Decherd that same day. "The troops who were in my front yesterday retreated via a road leading to the left from this place, and passing through about 2½ miles above Decherd; 7 miles from here to Winchester; 5 miles from here to Decherd; good roads, 2½ miles from Winchester to Decherd." He also apprised Thomas of the Federal cavalry's clash with Wheeler's men the prior evening, noting that Wharton had retreated during the night, and that the Yankees were pursuing him toward Winchester. "I hear some firing on my left, toward Decherd," he concluded. "In consequence of the heavy rains this a.m., the road over which I came to this place is getting very badly cut up, and will need repairs." Private Randall Packard of Battery C, 1st Ohio Light Artillery, which served with Brannan's division, concurred about the state of the roadways. Packard recorded that the artillery "found the worst roads we have had yet" that day. Similarly, Maj. Gen. Joseph J. Reynolds's Third Division of the XIV Corps crossed the Elk River at Morris Ford but covered only two and a half miles "over a road that had to be worked nearly all the way."[69]

On McCook's XX Corps front, Sheridan's division, supported by Brig. Gen. Jefferson C. Davis's 1st Division, crossed the Elk River near Allisonia and entered Winchester. Just north of town, the 39th Indiana Mounted Infantry scattered a force of about 300 Southern horsemen, almost certainly from Wharton's

---

69 Ibid., pt. 1, 408, 447, and pt. 2, 510; Randall Packard Diary, Battery C, 1st Ohio Light Artillery, entry for July 3, 1863, Bentley Historical Library, University of Michigan, Ann Arbor.

command. After Davis's division came up, Sheridan continued toward Decherd. He found no opposition there, just elements of Stanley's Cavalry Corps, and so moved through the town without pause toward Cowan.[70]

After expected enemy contact at any moment for most of the preceding week, the Federals were on edge—especially since not every enemy wore a uniform. Sheridan's advance dealt with possible bushwhackers, which sometimes resulted in deadly mistakes. "A sharpshooter from our brigade saw something on the opposite hill," drummer Charlie Stiles of the 36th Illinois wrote in his diary. "He supposing it to be a rebel fired and it fell. Then he saw someone rush out and thinking it a comrad coming out to carry the other one dropped him too. Then another came out and our man was about to fire when our Brigadier [General William H.] Lytle stopped him. He could see with his glass that the man was unarmed. Upon crossing and going to the house it was found that, first a dog and then a little boy some 14 years of age were killed and the father had a narrow escape." Stiles also observed that Confederate deserters filled the woods, just waiting to be captured.[71]

Another short but sharp fight occurred along a stream known as the Boiling Fork, where, Sheridan noted, the Rebels made a stand, "wounding 4 of Colonel Harrison's" men of the 39th Indiana. Sheridan turned to Lytle's infantry for support. "As we approached [Cowan] we saw from a height plainly visible to the naked eye, the enemy's line of mounted skirmishers," General Lytle told his wife in a letter. "Our cavalry (new troops) hesitated a little about going in and Sheridan ordered me to throw forward my skirmishers and drive the enemy out. The cavalry was finally brought to the scratch & charged driving the rebels from the town."[72]

Once in Cowan Sheridan learned that the Army of Tennessee had fled across the Cumberland Mountains near University Place via Sweeden's Cove, leaving only Wheeler's and Forrest's cavalry on the north side of the mountains as Bragg's rear guard. "My command is in fine spirits, but I must have my haversacks filled before going farther," declared Sheridan. Optimistically he added that "I will, perhaps, be able to collect some forage in this section." Sheridan also asked whether his troops should fire an Independence Day salute the next day.[73]

70 OR 23, pt. 1, 515-516.

71 Stiles, *Grandfather Was a Drummer Boy*, 81.

72 OR 23, pt. 1, 516; Ruth C. Carter, ed., *For Honor, Glory, and Union: The Mexican and Civil War Letters of Brig. Gen. William Haines Lytle* (Lexington, KY: 1999), 177-178.

73 OR 23, pt. 1, 441, 514-516.

Wheeler continued to throw up opposition. On the afternoon of July 3, he updated Bragg concerning his efforts. "We commenced ascending the mountain at about 2 p.m., cutting down trees to obstruct the road behind us. . . . At about 3 o'clock the enemy appeared with infantry and cavalry. We are still obstructing the road." In a postscript, he added, "Since writing the above, the work of obstructing the road has ceased, the enemy having appeared in such large force that the men were not able to continue the work."[74]

The final clash of the Tullahoma Campaign came the next day on July 4. Rebel cavalry had halted at University Place on the 3rd, and on the morning of the 4th John Wharton's troopers detected the presence of a regiment of Union horse soldiers, supported by infantry, deployed in line of battle about three and one-half miles away. Wheeler placed two regiments of cavalry at the road junction near University Place to protect against any potential advance by those Union forces.[75]

Sheridan, who was at Cowan, decided to find out whether reports that the enemy had taken up a position at the university were true. He ordered Col. Louis D. Watkins to take his command—the 5th and 6th Kentucky Cavalry (U.S.) plus six companies of the 3rd Indiana Cavalry—"to feel the enemy, and drive him until he was satisfied [the enemy] was there in force." Watkins led with three companies of the 5th Kentucky under Maj. John Q. Owsley and ordered them to advance toward the university campus. Owsley soon engaged Wheeler's pickets and drove them back to the main enemy line, which was hidden in thickets, behind trees, and in heavy undergrowth. Suddenly, Watkins had a fight on his hands. "I have the honor to inform you we are in a considerable engagement," Watkins told Sheridan.[76]

These Rebels were the 8th and 11th Texas Cavalry regiments of Brig. Gen. Thomas Harrison's brigade, Wharton's division—hard fighters all. Chaplain Robert F. Bunting of the 8th Texas (also known as "Terry's Texas Rangers") recorded the progress of the fight. First, he noted, the Federal cavalry charged, cutting the Rebels in two and driving them back onto their reserves. The Union troopers got within five paces of the gray line before being driven back almost 400 yards, with Capt. Ferguson Kyle's Company D of Terry's Rangers in close pursuit. Watkins ordered Major Owsley to fall back to the Union main body, which he did,

---

74 Ibid., 615.

75 Ibid., 616-617.

76 Ibid., 418, 516, 550. Watkins's force was an ad hoc brigade, nominally part of Col. Archibald Campbell's 1st Brigade, Mitchell's 1st Division, of Stanley's cavalry. On July 8, the 4th, 5th, and 6th Kentucky Cavalry were organized into a new 3rd Brigade under Watkins's command.

and the Texans also retired to their original position, where they reformed to charge again. A hand-to-hand fight erupted and the Texans retreated a second time; but they staged a ferocious counterattack that repulsed the Northerners.[77]

Watkins now changed tactics and tried to outflank the Texans with a large dismounted attack along a railroad cut, supported by a renewed assault against the center of the Confederate line by the 5th Kentucky. This determined onslaught forced the Rebels to fall back again, onto their reserve, the 4th Tennessee Cavalry. They withdrew slowly behind a screen of Tennesseans, who took up the rear guard. "It is thought that this was the most brilliant fight which the Rangers have ever had," declared Chaplain Bunting in a letter subsequently published in a Houston newspaper. "The officers and men all acted so gallantly that it would seem invidious to particularize." According to Bunting, "[a]lthough the ground was rough and covered with thick undergrowth, yet it seemed not to check the course of our boys when the foe was to be met." After the battle, the Texans retreated, leaving the university campus to the tender mercies of the Federal cavalry.[78]

The fighting was severe enough to alarm Wheeler. About 10 a.m. Polk received a courier from Wheeler who brought news of the fight at University Place. "The enemy are engaging me very warmly at this point," Wheeler wrote, adding that "our men are maintaining their ground bravely. The enemy have infantry and cavalry, and are evidently reinforcing." Ninety minutes later, Wheeler sent a second dispatch. "I would respectfully suggest that infantry be left to block up some of the roads, as the cavalry can retire by one road and can block up the road behind them as they go down, if axes can be left by the infantry to accomplish the work," he urged. "These precautions may prove unnecessary, but, if the enemy press us very warmly, may be of some advantage." Polk agreed and ordered that all available axes—perhaps a dozen—be sent to Wheeler.[79]

Wheeler's 4:00 p.m. report was more upbeat, signaling a victory. "I have just retired one brigade, leaving one brigade upon the mountain. Fighting this morning quite heavy for a short time, the enemy being repulsed; their loss considerable, including a colonel and lieutenant colonel. They show no disposition to follow any farther." Colonel Watkins, for his part, reported that his command had sustained one lieutenant and two privates killed, one lieutenant and 13 enlisted men wounded, and 26 horses killed or wounded. He also claimed a measure of success,

77 Cutrer, *Our Trust is in the God of Battles*, 171-172.

78 Ibid.

79 *OR* 23, pt. 1, 615-617.

stating that he captured 22 prisoners during the fierce 45-minute fight and that he believed the enemy's losses greatly exceeded his own.[80]

Sheridan correctly assessed that Wheeler's cavalry was there only to guard the wagon train as it headed down the mountain, so he did not expect them to remain much longer. The next day he ordered Watkins to sortie again to determine whether the enemy's position near the university was temporary or permanent. He also sent part of the 3rd Indiana Cavalry to scout off to the right toward Mountain Top, and another part down the road into Crow Creek Valley toward Bridgeport and Stevenson. "Colonel Watkins found that the enemy had fled," reported Sheridan. "[Lt. Col. Robert] Klein, Third Indiana Cavalry, found that a small portion of the enemy had crossed on that road. He captured 41 head of beef-cattle from the enemy's rear guard and brought them into camp." There was some light fighting near University Place on July 5, but no more attempts were made to ascend the mountains. Rosecrans's pursuit of the Army of Tennessee was at an end.[81]

After the action at University Place, the Tullahoma Campaign quickly reached its denouement. On July 3, Bragg, exhausted by ill health and the strain of the campaign, left his struggling command to toil through the mountains while he rode ahead to the sleepy depot town of Bridgeport, Alabama. Once there, he updated both the Confederate government in Richmond and Gen. Joseph E. Johnston of his army's movements. His message to Jefferson Davis was succinct. "Unable to obtain a general engagement without sacrificing my communications, I have, after a series of skirmishes, withdrawn the army to this [the Tennessee] river," he wrote. "It is now coming down the mountains. I hear of no formidable pursuit."

To Johnston, Bragg was more forthcoming. After describing the opening maneuvers of the campaign and his decision to retire to Tullahoma, he told Johnston (who at that moment had his own hands full commanding the Confederate "Army of Relief" that was trying to lift the siege of Vicksburg) that Rosecrans had moved strongly against the Elk River crossings. "By making a rapid march and using the railroad successfully, we saved all our supplies, and crossed the Elk just before a heavy column appeared at the upper bridge. We were now back against the mountains, in a country affording us nothing, with a long line of railroad to protect, and half a dozen passes on the right and left by which our rear could be gained." Faced with such an undesirable situation, and threatened with the possible destruction of his army without a battle, Bragg "reluctantly yielded to the necessity

---

80 Ibid., 617, 551-552.

81 Ibid., pt. 2, 513, and pt. 1, 516.

imposed by my position and inferior strength, and put the army in motion for the Tennessee River," where he intended to take up a new defensive position.[82]

By daylight on July 4 the entire command behind him was in motion once again. The gray infantry descended the plateau toward the Tennessee River Valley. "We came down the mountain this morning and after marching about 15 miles crossed the Tenn River at the mouth of Battle Creek on pontoon bridges," noted Private Oldham of the 9th Tennessee of Maney's Brigade, Cheatham's division. "Will rest near the crossing until morning. We have suffered for rations."[83]

At Battle Creek, the Rebel cavalry, its wagon train, and Buckner's infantry were directed to march west along the north bank of the Tennessee and cross the river at Bridgeport. Polk's entire corps crossed the Tennessee into Alabama on a pontoon bridge about a mile above the mouth of Battle Creek. Withers's division established its camp at Shellmound Depot, while Cheatham's division camped closer to the river. By 5 a.m. on July 5, Polk's and Buckner's forces were all established on the south bank of the Tennessee, soon to be headed for Chattanooga.[84]

The supply depot at Shellmound had been largely depleted, and Polk made it known that his corps desperately needed rations and ammunition. Army headquarters reported that supplies would be sent to Shellmound for Polk's use, but Polk remained unhappy. His command still had 20 miles or so to cover before reaching Chattanooga. By 5:00 a.m. on July 6, Polk resumed his movement. By dark, Withers's division reached its designated campsite near Chattanooga, but Cheatham's division would not arrive until late on July 7. At this point, many of Polk's men were shoeless and footsore, so they welcomed the opportunity to rest. As Bushrod Johnson's brigade established its camp at Wauhatchie Station, on the Nashville & Chattanooga Railroad at the foot of Lookout Mountain, Johnson, thoroughly disgusted, declared, "Here the movement, which will probably be known as the Evacuation of Middle Tennessee, terminated."[85]

The campaign had been brutal. "The Army of Tennessee, Gen. Braxton Bragg commanding, has arrived thus far on its retreat from the advancing army of Rosecrans," reported an unidentified Alabamian of Clayton's brigade, A.P. Stewart's division, writing from high above Chattanooga on Lookout Mountain, in

82 Ibid., 584.

83 Oldham diary, entry for July 4, 1863.

84 OR 23, pt. 1, 626.

85 Ibid., 627, 610; Oldham diary, entries for July 5 and 6, 1863.

a letter published in the *Mobile Register* "After thirteen days of unparalleled sufferings, consisting of forced marches, hard work, sleepless nights, drenching rains, barefoot walking over stoney roads, hunger, famine, heat by day and cold by night, we have succeeded in escaping from the terrible Yankees, and put, as a peace-maker between them and us, the surging current of the deep, wide, majestic Tennessee. Here we rest our broken down bodies for a brief season, and hope to recuperate our exhausted strength, and repair, in some degree, our heavy losses in articles of clothing and camp equipage." He continued, "Our sufferings have been awful beyond description. For seven consecutive days and nights, we had wet feet and wet shoes, which were not once dry during the entire week. Our clothes, too, were wet all the time. The roads were horrible. Without sleep, without adequate food, often without water, we marched, worked, stood in line of battle, in mud and water, stood guard all the night, and suffered for thirteen days all that humanity can suffer in the flesh. It is ended now, but it will require weeks to restore us to our former morale, for we are greatly exasperated and demoralized." He concluded by reporting that the men had lost everything, including all their clothing, and had nothing but what was on their backs.[86]

"The whole army has crossed the Tennessee," Bragg advised the Confederate war department on July 7. "The pursuit of the enemy was checked and driven back at University Place, on the Cumberland Mountains. Our movement was attended with trifling loss of men and materials." While that was a mostly true statement, it completely downplayed the loss of Middle Tennessee to the Army of the Cumberland, almost without a fight.[87]

In official and semiofficial announcements, various Confederates went to great lengths to portray the withdrawal in a positive light. "During the retreat not a gun was lost by the corps; not a pound of ordnance or quartermaster's stores, and not $2,000 worth of commissary stores, and these last were distributed to the families of soldiers at Shelbyville," claimed Polk staffer William B. Richmond proudly. "Though there was some straggling, there were not 1,000 men absent from the corps that started with it from Shelbyville; and, owing to recruits that met it on its arrival in Chattanooga and en route, it was absolutely stronger on its arrival than when it began the retrograde movement."[88]

---

86 "The Retreat of Bragg's Army," *Nashville Daily Press*, August 13, 1863. The Nashville paper reprinted a letter gleaned from the *Mobile Register*, a common practice during the war.

87 *OR* 23, pt. 1, 584. Bragg's official combat losses were few; but desertions spiked.

88 Ibid.

"By a masterly strategic retrograde movement, Gen. Bragg has outwitted Rosecrans, forcing him to follow our army across the mountains and leaving his base of supplies over 75 miles in the rear, greatly exposed to our cavalry," the anonymous correspondent "290" audaciously declared in a letter to a Georgia paper. "Our retreat for the last two days has been conducted with great skill, the enemy following us up, and skirmishing having been continuous." Even more outrageous was his statement insisting that "every confidence is felt in Gen. Bragg, his present position giving him great advantages over the enemy."[89]

This bombast did not reflect the true state of affairs. While the Army of Tennessee remained numerically strong, its repeated retreats wrecked morale. Despite contrary claims, large quantities of supplies were left at Wartrace, Shelbyville, and Tullahoma. Worst of all, Bragg's defeatist attitude and unpredictable conduct exacerbated the ongoing command crisis within his army. His senior subordinates no longer trusted his decision-making. More trouble was brewing, and the only question was when that discord would come to a head.

Like the Rebels, the Federals also finally had a chance to rest. Sheridan's July 4 assessment that the enemy's stand at University Place was only temporary was borne out. Though the balance of the Army of the Cumberland came up and took positions along the northern foot of the Cumberland Plateau, it made little additional progress. Nearly without rations and faced with roads churned to thick mud and made impassable by the relentless rains and Bragg's passage, Rosecrans had no choice but to halt until supplies could be forwarded from Murfreesboro.[90]

As a result, July 4 had passed agreeably for most of Rosecrans's army. "This has been a quiet day," Williamson Ward of the 39th Indiana Mounted Infantry noted in his diary. "No sound of mirth or revelry as is our usual custom on this, our Independence Day. Even the cannons, which are wont to open their mouths and thunder forth their rejoicing to the cause of freedom, are all hushed to silence. Nothing to remind us of our National Holiday but the memory of the past." A fellow Hoosier of the XIV Corps recalled, "our boys feel good over the news of Lee's defeat at Gettysburgh, PA," but, he complained, "we drew two days rations, and it consisted of four crackers, one fourth lb. meat, and a spoonful of coffee. This is small for a man who feels like he could devour a government mule, but we go on

---

89 "Army Correspondence," bylined "290," *Macon Journal and Messenger* (Macon, GA), July 15, 1863.

90 *OR* 23, pt. 1, 408, and pt. 2, 513. As one example, Maj. Gen. Jefferson C. Davis's XX Corps division occupied Winchester after Sheridan's troopers left there to advance on Cowan.

principle to live while we can and eat it all up and then starve until we draw more. A man can eat all we drew to the man at one meal doing such duty as we do."[91]

"We are very pleasantly camped here and would not object to remaining for some time," wrote C. D. Bailey of the 9th Kentucky Infantry to his wife that day. After griping about the salt pork that served as a staple of the Civil War soldier's diet, Bailey proclaimed, "I would give anything for one of your good dinners."[92]

Still, a giddy air of triumph permeated the army, especially at Rosecrans's headquarters, which was awash with rumors of Rebel disaster. "General Cheatham's division is said to have dissolved, and the fleeing fragments are making their way through the mountains to the federal lines," boasted a correspondent from the *Cincinnati Commercial*, who was traveling with army headquarters. "Over sixty deserters have come in to Tullahoma today, and taken the oath of allegiance." The same writer bemoaned, "there is not anything savoring of the offensive that will transpire until our supply trains reach us. The horses are jaded and hungry, and the men, with scant rations, look anxiously for the coming of the train."[93]

"This forenoon the whole force advanced to the foot of [the mountain] at Cowan to find the enemy," noted an Illinois newspaper correspondent. "We have lost not over 1,000 by casualties. All kinds of troops suffered much from heat and rain. The sun is now shining brightly. We have 1,500 to 2,000 prisoners, many of them deserters." Further, the correspondent bragged that "the enemy is entirely out of Tennessee, and our communications intact. The railroad will be running to [Tullahoma] tomorrow." A Chicago correspondent sounded a similar note. "Bragg's army is terribly demoralized," he reported. "Deserters are coming in by scores, who say the mountains are full of men afraid to show themselves to the Federals, not knowing what will befall them, yet resolved to fight no more."[94]

Such tantalizing tales only frustrated the Union soldiers who, smelling victory, wanted to finish off Bragg once and for all. "Our forces have swept Tennessee as far as Tullahoma," proudly declared Thomas Prickett of the 9th Indiana of Crittenden's XXI Corps. "General Rosecrans's headquarters is at that place now."

91 Williamson D. Ward diary, entry for July 4, 1863, Smith Memorial Library, Indiana Historical Society; Miller diary, entry for July 4, 1863.

92 C. D. Bailey to his wife, July 4, 1863, C. D. Bailey Letters, Smith Memorial Library, Indiana Historical Society.

93 "Telegraphic Correspondence Daily Commercial from Manchester, Tennessee," *Cincinnati Commercial*, July 4, 1863. See also *Nashville Daily Press*, July 4, 1863.

94 "From Rosecrans' Army," and "From Tullahoma: Everything Going on Well with Rosecrans," *Chicago Tribune*, July 6, 1863.

He noted the march to Manchester, which should have taken two days took five due to the wretched road conditions. "I don't think we will have any hard fighting until we reach Chattanooga," he added, and "I think if the weather had been favorable for us we would have taken a great many prisoners and their camp equipage, baggage, etc." Lieutenant Albion Tourgée of the 105th Ohio noted in his diary, "A few more successes and the Rebellion will be a forgotten thing."[95]

In Washington, the Lincoln administration sensed great things in the offing. News of George Meade's victory at Gettysburg had already been circulating across the country, and the latest word to reach the capital from Vicksburg, dated approximately July 1, also hinted at triumph. Early on the morning of July 4, Secretary of War Edwin M. Stanton had telegraphed Rosecrans with some critical news. He reported Meade's triumph, and that a letter from Jefferson Davis to Gen. Robert E. Lee dated June 28 had fallen into Union hands. The letter advised Lee that reinforcements could not be sent to his Army of Northern Virginia from Richmond because "General Bragg has been weakened by withdrawing his troops and sending them to Joe Johnston; that he is threatened with attack; has fallen back to his intrenched position at Tullahoma, and called on Buckner for aid." This dispatch seemed to confirm the reports of Bragg's decreasing strength, which only whetted Stanton's appetite for big news out of Tennessee.[96]

In reply, Rosecrans cabled Stanton the details of his successful campaign in Middle Tennessee. "Our movement commenced on 24th of June," he wrote. "Have driven Bragg from his intrenched positions at Shelbyville and Tullahoma. Either of them is stronger than Corinth. Have pursued him through the mountains. Incessant rains and the impassable state of the roads alone prevented us from forcing him to a general battle." He advised Stanton that the Army of Tennessee had completely abandoned Middle Tennessee and had retreated toward Bridgeport and Chattanooga. "Every effort is being made to bring forward supplies and threaten the enemy sufficiently to hold him," he continued. "The loss of the enemy may be safely put at 1,000 killed and wounded, 1,000 prisoners, 7 pieces of artillery, 500 or 600 tents. The country is filled with deserters from the Tennessee troops, and it is generally thought a very large portion of these troops will never leave their native state. Nothing but the most stringent coercion can detain them." Rosecrans

---

95 Thomas Prickett to his wife, July 5, 1863, Thomas Prickett Letters, Smith Memorial Library, Indiana Historical Society; Dean H. Keller, "A Civil War Diary of Albion W. Tourgée," *Ohio History,* vol. 74 (Spring, 1965), 111.

96 *OR* 23, pt. 2, 511-512.

ended by lamenting the unseasonable rainfall. "It is impossible to convey to you an idea of the continuous rains we have had since commencement of these operations or the state of the roads. I pray God that every available soldier may be sent to me, and that our arms may be successful against Lee. He should be destroyed."[97]

In particular, the Union cavalry needed rest. "The incessant rain and consequent condition of the roads rendered the operations of the cavalry difficult and exceedingly trying to men and horses," noted Stanley in his after-action report on the campaign. "The impossibility of bringing up forage in wagons, and the absence of feed in the 'Barrens' of the Cumberland Mountains, the constant rain depriving our poor beasts of their rest, has reduced the cavalry considerably." He concluded, "They now require some little rest and refitting."[98]

After nine days of intense marching in some of the worst conditions imaginable, with heavy fighting at Hoover's and Liberty gaps and the great cavalry clash at Shelbyville, Rosecrans's bold campaign of maneuver was over. With losses of only 85 killed, 462 wounded, and 13 missing, the Army of the Cumberland drove Bragg's army out of Middle Tennessee and all the way back to Chattanooga without a general engagement, all during relentless rains that turned unpaved roads into bottomless seas of impenetrable muck. "These results," Rosecrans proudly reported, "were far more successful than was anticipated, and could only have been obtained by a surprise as to the direction and force of our movement."[99]

97 OR 23, pt. 1, 403. Rosecrans was referring to the heavy earthworks faced by General Halleck during the latter's 1862 advance on Corinth, Mississippi.

98 Ibid., 541.

99 Ibid., 408.

Chapter Fourteen

Aftermath: July 1863

Middle Tennessee fell into Federal hands for an extraordinarily low cost: fewer than 600 men killed, wounded, captured, or missing. The officially reported total loss amounted to 11 officers and 73 enlisted men killed or mortally wounded, 31 officers and 442 enlisted men wounded, and one officer and 12 enlisted men captured or missing—570 casualties in all. Impressively, this final tally only exceeded the preliminary number Rosecrans included in his July 24 report (given in the preceding chapter) by 10 men. Contrasted with the staggering Federal butcher's bills for the other two campaigns that culminated that first week of July—Vicksburg and Gettysburg—the cost was trifling. Meade's total casualties at Gettysburg alone were 23,049; adding in all the other actions of the campaign from June 3 to August 1, Meade reported aggregate losses of 32,043 men. Grant's losses at Vicksburg were less carefully tabulated and were not reported as a single total for the campaign, but they still amounted to over 9,000.[1]

Tallying Confederate losses is considerably more difficult. Rosecrans thought they would number several thousand, mostly prisoners and deserters. The Army of the Cumberland's provost marshal, Maj. William M. Wiles of the 44th Indiana, recorded receiving 1,634 prisoners during the campaign, of which "616 claimed to have delivered themselves to our forces voluntarily." Ninety-six of those immediately enlisted in the Union ranks. Though Bragg characterized the Army of Tennessee's loss as "trifling," a comparison of the Confederate returns for June 20

---

1 OR 23, pt. 1, 424, and OR 27, pt. 1, 187, 194.

at Shelbyville and July 10 at Chattanooga tells a different story. On June 20, Bragg reported 47,249 officers and men present for duty, with an aggregate present of 55,070. By July 10, he had only 42,417 troops in the first category and 49,876 in the second—suggesting a loss of about 5,000 officers and men. These figures do not include any of General Buckner's losses, which went unrecorded.[2]

Rosecrans had inflicted losses that were up to nine times greater than those he had suffered, mostly in the form of desertions by demoralized Confederates. Bragg might not have wanted to admit those facts to President Davis, but he did confide in Dr. Charles T. Quintard, an Episcopal priest serving nominally as chaplain of the 1st Tennessee Infantry. Quintard, who often frequented Polk's and Bragg's headquarters, later recalled that, "on the morning of [July] 2nd, as I left the headquarters of General Bragg, I met my friend Governor Isham G. Harris. He looked very bright and cheerful and said to me: 'To-morrow morning you will be roused up by the thunder of our artillery.' But instead . . . I found myself in full retreat toward Winchester. Thence I rode to Cowan, where I found General Bragg and his staff, and General Polk with his staff. I rode up to them and said to General Bragg: 'My dear General, I am afraid you are thoroughly outdone.' 'Yes,' he said, 'I am utterly broken down.' And then leaning over his saddle he spoke of the loss of Middle Tennessee and whispered: 'This is a great disaster.'"[3]

It was a great disaster indeed. With Bragg's retreat to Chattanooga, more than two-thirds of the state of Tennessee—and by far the most productive two-thirds, both agriculturally and in terms of manufacturing—now lay irrevocably in Union hands. The only part of the state to remain under Confederate control was East Tennessee, where public sentiment leaned heavily pro-Union. In effect, the Tullahoma Campaign irretrievably cost the Confederate war effort the entire state of Tennessee.

Even the crossing of the Tennessee River, though unhindered by Federals, was not without blunder. Bragg reached Bridgeport, Alabama, on July 4, with peril not too far behind him. While Rosecrans reported to Washington that the Army of Tennessee was already across the river, this was only partially true; Polk's Corps was across, with the corps headquarters and Withers's division at Shellmound, and

---

2 OR 23, pt. 1, 425, 585-586. The strength of John Hunt Morgan's cavalry division continued to be included in Wheeler's figures for both the June 20 and July 10 returns, even though Morgan's command was detached and hadn't actually reported its real strength since early June; if Morgan's men are deducted, Bragg's effective loss would be even greater.

3 Arthur Howard Noll, ed., *Doctor Quintard, Chaplain C.S.A. and Second Bishop of Tennessee—Being His Story of the War (1861-1865)* (Sewanee, TN: 1905), 87.

Cheatham's division just over the pontoon bridge at Battle Creek. And although Bragg had ordered Polk to leave one of Cheatham's brigades on the west bank to guard that bridge, Polk failed to do so, later explaining, "Your order of yesterday (5 p.m.) did not reach me in time to leave a brigade on the other side of the river."[4]

Polk's Corps came very close to not crossing at all. When Cheatham's division reached the north bank of the Tennessee River about midday on July 3, it had discovered that "a freshet had broken the bridge about its center, and about half the boats were on either shore of the stream. The engineer officers seemed unable to get the bridge across again." Worse yet, Battle Creek, which flowed into the Tennessee from the north, was too swollen to cross. This meant that the route to Kelly's Ferry via the small settlement of Jaspar, Tennessee, was also temporarily cut off. With the army's engineers baffled, Cheatham turned to the navy, putting Capt. William W. Carnes in charge of fixing the bridge. An artillery commander who "had resigned from the US Naval Academy in the spring of 1861, his senior year," and who had last been seen organizing the personal evacuation of some of Shelbyville's comelier residents, Captain Carnes, by dint of an improvised mast, managed to have the wayward pontoons sailed back into position. Then Cheatham's "troops began crossing over late in the day, after a most vexatious delay, with the enemy in rear and a broken bridge and swollen stream in front."[5]

On July 5, Withers's and Cheatham's gunners were safely across the Tennessee, and they began dismounting their artillery and ammunition chests from their respective carriages, intending to ship them the rest of the way via the rails. This posed a new problem, since Buckner's men were still at Bridgeport, about to board cars for the return trip to East Tennessee, and there was not sufficient rolling stock to accommodate all those needs. Furthermore, Buckner's departure would leave only Wheeler's cavalry to oversee the last stages of the retreat at Bridgeport.[6]

Hardee's Corps was still on the north bank, marching toward a second pontoon bridge thrown up at Kelly's Ferry. His troops had forded Battle Creek higher upstream, thus avoiding the flooding faced by Polk's command, but this left him one narrow road to use along the north bank of the Tennessee. His corps trains and one brigade of Cleburne's command crossed that afternoon, but the remaining

4 OR 23, pt. 2, 899.

5 Lindsley, *Military Annals of Tennessee*, 2: 819; George G. Kundahl, *Confederate Engineer: Training and Campaigning with John Morris Wampler* (Knoxville, TN: 2000), 227-228.

6 OR 23, pt. 2, 899; William G. Robertson, *River of Death: The Chickamauga Campaign—Volume One: The Fall of Chattanooga* (Chapel Hill, NC: 2018), 83.

seven brigades of his corps stretched back from Kelly's Ferry nearly 18 miles to Jasper; the men camped along the road that night, wherever they halted. Forrest's cavalry screened Hardee's rear during this effort. Hardee's command resumed crossing on the 6th, amid yet more rain. Robert Collins of the 15th Texas described a bizarre incident at the bridge that seemingly epitomized all the bumbling and frustration of the campaign. Under orders, the Confederate provost guards held all the stragglers and unorganized men (of which Collins was one) on the north bank of the river until their respective commands came up, so they could rejoin their units. "They were having some difficulty in holding [us]," Collins admitted. "We all wanted to get the river between us and the Yankees, just as quick as possible. . . . Our corps commander, Gen. Hardee, was there; a long, keen Texas soldier said he was going over anyhow; when he started Gen. Hardee drew his sword and made a dive at him. The fellow jumped into the river and the General plunged in after him on horseback. This created some excitement and no little amusement." The fracas also gave Collins and many of his comrades the chance to slip over the bridge while the guards and Hardee's staff struggled to sort out the ensuing confusion.[7]

That night, in the words of historian William Glenn Robertson, "wet, weary, and depressed, Hardee relinquished command to Cleburne and departed for Chattanooga with his staff." Disillusioned with Bragg and with the army's failure to fight for Tennessee, Hardee would leave the Army of Tennessee entirely in little more than a week, transferring to Mississippi to help Joe Johnston salvage what he could of the Vicksburg disaster. If he hoped for better times, he was disappointed. In Mississippi, Hardee found a situation no less demoralizing than the one he had just left behind. On July 27, writing from his new post in Mississippi, Hardee gloomily informed Polk that Johnston's force was "much reduced in numbers by desertion and somewhat demoralized. . . . I fear I will not be able to do as much good as you anticipated. I know I wish I were back at Chattanooga with my corps."[8]

With the Confederate army now safely on the south bank of the Tennessee, the Rebels took up the pontoon bridges; Polk, however, very nearly had the bridge at Battle Creek destroyed instead, so great was his fear that the Federals might capture it. That bit of carelessness averted, the pontoon bateaux were eventually towed upstream to Chattanooga, with the last of them being removed on July 12.[9]

---

7   Robertson, *River of Death*, 85-86; Collins, *Unwritten Chapters of the War*, 140.

8   Robertson, *River of Death*, 87; *OR* 23, pt. 2, 902, 908; Hughes, "William Joseph Hardee," 251.

9   Kundahl, *Confederate Engineer*, 228.

This left just one critical structure spanning the Tennessee River: the newly rebuilt Nashville & Chattanooga Bridge at Bridgeport. It had been destroyed once before in the summer of 1862, when Union troops under General Don Carlos Buell were threatening Chattanooga. It was rebuilt at great cost and considerable effort the following September, since it was needed to sustain Bragg's army in Middle Tennessee. During this latest retreat, temporary wooden planks were laid on it to allow wagons and men to march over the river more easily, but after Wheeler's last few horsemen crossed to the south bank, it had to come down again.

The men charged with this destructive task were members of Brig. Gen. John K. Jackson's brigade of Cheatham's division. Doctor Nathaniel Alexander Morgan, an assistant surgeon in Jackson's brigade, described the last few days of the retreat to his wife Fanny. Writing on July 9, he had inquired, "What sort of a 4th of July did you have? A pleasant one I hope. I will never forget it. We passed the day + night in the trenches expecting to be attacked every minute by the Enemy, but were not. The great battle of the war will not be fought at Tullahoma. . . . Everything is in confusion in our present camp. We expect to be moved to Chattanooga soon. Braggs army is there now but is said to be moving to different points . . . [but] it is folly to speculate on army movements." In a subsequent missive penned on July 20, Morgan described the ensuing destruction. "I shall never forget the evening we left Bridgeport. Our Brigade was the rear guard + was charged with burning everything. We crossed just at dark with the town in a blaze + then set fire to the magnificent Railroad bridge. It reminded me of the night we left Corinth. I did hate to see the fine bridge burnt. It was new + had cost so much labor + money. . . . [I]t looks like our authorities have made some great blunders. Every body is abusing Bragg now for falling back without a fight, + very unjustly I think. I am not one of his admirers, but I would like to see him have a fair chance one time."[10]

Although the bridge's destruction hindered and complicated Rosecrans's subsequent operations in the fall of 1863, its absence did not derail his next offensive movement. Instead, Rosecrans planned for the bridge's loss and compensated in other ways. Had the Confederates displayed the foresight to try to damage the 2,200-foot railroad tunnel at Cowan, Rosecrans would have faced a much more difficult logistical problem, since for the next phase of the Union campaign against Chattanooga, he transferred his forward supply base from

10 Letters of July 9 and 20, 1863, Dr. Nathaniel Alexander Morgan to Wife Fanny, Baylor University, Waco, TX, online at https://blogs.baylor.edu/believemeyourown/, accessed June 8, 2019.

Fortress Rosecrans at Murfreesboro to new bases at Bridgeport and Stevenson. The only means of accomplishing this transfer was via the railroad, and passing through the Cowan Tunnel in the process.

Of course, destroying that tunnel was no easy matter in an era before dynamite or other forms of ready-to-use high explosives. But that did not mean, however, that it could not be done. In August 1862, John Hunt Morgan severely damaged the "Big South" Tunnel at Gallatin, Tennessee, a feat that shut the rail line down for 98 days. He did so by ramming a burning train into a timber barricade that had been placed inside the tunnel. The Cowan Tunnel had been bored through much harder granite and thus was not as vulnerable to efforts like Morgan's. With some forethought, however, the Confederates could have interdicted it by drilling and removing the interior shoring. At the very least, having abandoned the line of the Elk on July 2, the Army of Tennessee's engineers could have repeated Morgan's stunt. Damaging or destroying that tunnel should have been Bragg's top priority. Leaving it intact was a gift to the Federal army, one that Rosecrans used to full advantage.[11]

The destruction of Morgan's cavalry division in Ohio was another disaster that depleted the Confederate ranks, but though it might well be added to the Army of Tennessee's campaign losses, blame for it can hardly be laid at Bragg's feet. On July 19, a large force of Union cavalry overwhelmed Morgan at Buffington Island in Meigs County, inflicting heavy casualties and fracturing Morgan's command. Prevented from re-crossing the Ohio River into West Virginia there, Morgan and about 800 survivors (roughly a third of his initial strength) turned north and east to escape yet more converging Union columns. As related by historian David L. Mowery, after a further week of skirmishes, "a total of 364 men and officers surrendered at the Burbick farm on July 26, 1863, only twelve miles short of the Pennsylvania border." Morgan and many of his officers, including his brother-in-law, Col. Basil W. Duke, ended up as prisoners at the Ohio Penitentiary in Columbus, taken completely out of the war for many months. Morgan's decision to flagrantly ignore Bragg's orders resulted in the destruction of his entire command, reducing the Army of Tennessee's cavalry force by 2,500 officers and

---

11 Destroying the tunnel also posed a political problem, however, for it would have effectively signaled the permanent abandonment of Tennessee to the Federals. While Union resources would have been strained in repairing it, the Confederacy likely would have found the damage impossible to fix, and no Confederate army could permanently return to Middle Tennessee without a secure rail connection.

men. Only a handful of his troopers escaped capture, reuniting in southwest Virginia a month later.[12]

Perhaps unsurprisingly, Bragg's health again crumbled under the strain of this campaign. Once in Chattanooga, he informed Buckner that he had not been well since June 29. During the retreat his increasing feebleness was evident to both Hardee and Polk, which prompted their discussions about removing Bragg during those tense hours along the Elk River. In an indirect effort to influence Jefferson Davis, Bragg sent a private communication to Robert E. Lee on July 22 in which he aired his grievances concerning the state of affairs in the west and the Richmond government's seeming indifference to the plight of the Army of Tennessee, warning that the Federals might soon move against Confederate strategic resources at Atlanta and Augusta, Georgia. "If you think proper," wrote Bragg, "you may use [this] information in any way or suppress it." Then Bragg closed this remarkable letter with a personal complaint. "For two months my health has been anything but good," he noted. "Long continued and excessive labor of mind and body have produced its natural result on a frame not robust at best. Were it possible, I should seek repose, but at present I see no hope. Should affairs here allow it, I propose spending a part of my time at Ringgold, Ga., 20 miles off, on the Atlanta Railroad, where there is mineral water highly recommended for me."[13]

Broken and battered, defeated and discouraged, Bragg would spend much of August trying to recoup his mental and physical energies in those mineral waters at Catoosa Springs with his equally frail wife, Elise. His next challenge—Rosecrans's upcoming offensive against Chattanooga—was just a few short weeks away.

*   *   *

Rosecrans had officially ended his pursuit of Bragg on July 4. McCook's XX Corps and Thomas's XIV Corps halted at Winchester and Decherd, respectively. Crittenden occupied Manchester, with Wood's division stationed at Hillsborough and a brigade under Brig. Gen. George D. Wagner pushed forward to Pelham on the Elk River. Rosecrans transferred his headquarters first to Tullahoma and then to Winchester a few days later, though, as was his wont, he roamed freely among his

---

12 Mowery, *Morgan's Great Raid*, 128, 162. Morgan eventually escaped the prison and returned to active duty, but he was never able to reassemble his entire command. He was killed in action at Greenville, Tennessee, on September 4, 1864.

13 Bragg to Buckner, July 7, Bragg Papers, Western Reserve Historical Society, Cleveland, OH; *OR* 23, pt. 2, 924-925.

forward commanders. On July 5, he informed Gordon Granger, whose troops now secured the army's communication lines through Tullahoma and Shelbyville, that he "took Fourth of July dinner with McCook at Winchester."[14]

"Dinner" was an understatement. McCook threw a party for no less than 60 invited officers, ranging from Rosecrans and David Stanley of the Cavalry Corps down to brigade and even selected regimental commanders. In keeping with the theme of the recent campaign, heavy rain interrupted much of the planned festivities, forcing the guests to eat indoors instead of under "a temporary bower constructed of tree branches." But the party was still a smashing success.[15]

Parties notwithstanding, the Army of the Cumberland was now reduced to half rations. The Nashville & Chattanooga bridges spanning both the Duck and Elk rivers lay in ruins and had to be rebuilt before any sizeable Union force could venture across the Cumberland Plateau—a fact that seemed lost on the authorities in Washington. On July 7, Secretary of War Edwin Stanton telegraphed Rosecrans, then at Tullahoma. "We have just received official information that Vicksburg surrendered to Grant on the 4th of July," the message read. "Lee's army overthrown; Grant victorious. You and your noble army now have the chance to give the finishing blow to the rebellion. Will you neglect the chance?"[16]

Rosecrans was nonplussed. Just three days earlier, he had wired Stanton with the details of his advance, and the successes he achieved—all of which apparently fell upon deaf ears. Accordingly, Rosecrans tinged his quick reply with more than a hint of acid. "Just received your cheering dispatch announcing the fall of Vicksburg and confirming the defeat of Lee," he wrote. "You do not appear to observe the fact that this noble army has driven the rebels from Middle Tennessee, of which my dispatches advised you. I beg in [sic] behalf of this army that the War Department may not overlook so great an event because it is not written in letters of blood."[17]

While Rosecrans vigorously defended his army's accomplishments, he was not content to sit on his laurels. He continued applying pressure to restore the rail line, bombarding the army's military superintendent of railroads, Col. John B. Anderson, with telegraphic dispatches urging rapid action. On July 2, for example, Rosecrans had exhorted, "Push night and day. . . . Do not depend on your own

---

14 OR 23, pt. 2, 512, 515; see also U.S. Army Corps of Engineers, et al., *The Middle Tennessee Campaign of June and July, 1863*, map no. 3, (New York: 1891).

15 Robertson, *River of Death*, 7-8.

16 OR 23, pt. 2, 518.

17 Ibid.

resources alone. I will furnish you any amount of military help you may need. Speed is the only consideration. Answer." In a dispatch two days later, chief of staff Garfield threatened Anderson with removal if the pace of the repairs did not improve.[18]

The Allisonia Bridge over the Elk proved to be the key obstacle. It was a 550-foot-long wooden trestle built on stone piers. The Confederates burned the wooden trestle, but did not have time to damage the piers, leaving a gap of 500 feet. Brigadier General James St. Clair Morton's Pioneer Brigade began preliminary work on the bridge as early as July 3 (Rosecrans was inspecting these efforts when he received McCook's Fourth of July invitation), but Morton was pessimistic about the time needed: in another meeting with Rosecrans nine days later on July 12, Morton estimated that the job would take another four to six weeks, perhaps less if the 1st Michigan Regiment of Engineers and Mechanics were placed at his disposal.[19]

There was a considerable rivalry between Morton's pioneers—an all-purpose engineering command recruited from the army at large—and the 1st Michigan. Colonel William P. Innes's Wolverines were recruited specifically with engineering duties in mind, and the regiment contained a cadre of experienced railroaders. In that July 12th meeting, Innes and Lt. Col. Kinsman Hunton, who had already reached the scene at Allisonia with six companies of the 1st, were also present. Hunton and Innes informed the army commander that it would take the Michiganders only "eight to ten days" to repair the bridge, provided "Morton and his pioneers were ordered away." Rosecrans agreed, and the gamble paid off. To the strains of the regimental band, the first train would roll across the reconstructed bridge on the afternoon of July 18.[20]

On July 7, Rosecrans also took pains to secure his left flank. Brigadier General Horatio Van Cleve's division of the XXI Corps, which had remained at Fortress Rosecrans throughout the campaign, now departed for McMinnville, 40 miles east of Murfreesboro, in order to establish a permanent Union presence there. Marcus Woodcock of the 9th Kentucky Infantry, in Brig. Gen. Samuel Beatty's brigade, welcomed the change. Since June 28, the 9th had been toiling back and forth between Murfreesboro and Manchester, escorting supply wagons along the same

---

18 Ibid., 503; Robertson, *River of Death*, 8-9.

19 Mark Hoffman, "My Brave Mechanics": *The First Michigan Engineers and their Civil War* (Detroit, MI: 2007), 155.

20 Ibid., 156-157.

Brig. Gen. Horatio Van Cleve, commander, Third Division, XXI Corps, Army of the Cumberland.

Library of Congress

miry roads that so plagued the rest of the army. "We are very much pleased with the idea of a move," noted Woodcock, "for the country about Manchester is so efficiently stripped of everything fresh in the line of eatables that it is simply an impossibility to procure forage even to the amount of a mess of potatoes.... [A]s McMinnville lies rather out of the general field of operations we calculate that when we get there we will find plenty." The brigade reached its new quarters on July 10, and Woodcock appeared satisfied. "[We are] much pleased with the country ... as it promises great recompense to foragers, and as some citizens informed us that the people are largely secesh we will not be very scrupulous about taking what we actually need." Ever energetic, Rosecrans was not far behind. "Genls. Rosecrans and Crittenden, with their respective staffs, came to 'our town' ... and spent a short time in looking about."[21]

Barely three weeks previously, Morgan's cavalry division had headquartered at McMinnville, and Confederate troops, chiefly the 8th Tennessee Cavalry under Col. George Dibrell of Forrest's command, still occupied White County, 30 miles to the northeast. In August Colonel Minty's cavalry was dispatched to clear out those Rebels prior to Rosecrans's next major advance, but for the moment McMinnville marked the easternmost limit of Union control in Tennessee.

By July 10, Sheridan's division was camped at the foot of the Cumberland Mountains near Decherd, below the University of the South. The next day, several officers, including the regimental chaplain of the 27th Illinois, visited the campus. "We ascended with much difficulty the steep and rugged face of the mountain," recalled the churchman. "At almost every step we saw garments which members of

21 Kenneth W. Noe, ed., *A Southern Boy in Blue: The Memoir of Marcus Woodcock, 9th Kentucky Infantry (U.S.A.)* (Knoxville, TN: 1996), 175.

the retreating army had thrown away." They rode about six miles, passing only an empty blacksmith's shop and an abandoned Confederate campsite. "We went into the midst of the deserted camp and found several log cabins and two immense sheds. There was not a human being to be seen or heard. The doors and windows of this congeries of cabins were wide open; desolation reigned and silence that might be felt, but not described." The explorers soon learned that they were on the campus of the University of the South, that there was nobody around, and that they could not locate the cornerstone of the university building, which was still under construction.[22]

Another correspondent solved the mystery of the whereabouts of the missing cornerstone. "The cornerstone only is laid, or rather was laid, for some of the vandals of our Brigade, hearing that there was money in the stone, a few nights since, broke it open and rifled it of its contents," he reported. "It was a shameful, disgraceful deed, and Colonel Bradley has taken steps to ferret out the perpetrators of this sacrilege, and will bring them to punishment." An unidentified member of Company A of the 22nd Illinois provided additional details of its destruction. "The Corner Stone of the University has been distributed throughout the upper country by this Brigade. It was clandestinely removed from the foundation at night, and its documents fell into unknown hands. The boys immediately commenced breaking it up for trinkets, and it is now all used up."[23]

Any further advance by the Army of the Cumberland was now deemed useless, at least for the moment. Bragg was across the Tennessee, which the Federals could not cross without another period of extensive preparations. Rosecrans took the necessary time to rest, refit, and resupply his army before beginning his advance on Chattanooga. The remarkable Tullahoma Campaign was over.

*   *   *

The generalship exhibited at the highest levels of each army offers stark contrasts. William Starke Rosecrans planned and executed a meticulously coordinated campaign of deception and maneuver. Despite the horrendous

---

22 "Tennessee," *Church Journal of New York*, August 19, 1863.

23 *Chicago Evening Journal*, July 25, 1863; *Proceedings of the Board of Trustees of the University of the South at Their Session Held at University Place, Sewanee, Tennessee, July 12th-18th, 1871* (Rome, GA: 1871), 15-16. For a detailed discussion of these events, see Merritt R. Blakeslee, "How the Cornerstone Was Destroyed. Yes, It Was Union Soldiers. No, They Didn't Blow It Up," *Sewanee Magazine* (Summer 2011), 28-30.

weather, the Army of the Cumberland implemented its movements with precision and careful timing. Throughout the campaign, the various Federal formations, advancing on a broad front, generally avoided being ground to a halt by massive traffic jams—which was no easy feat given the limited road network and multiple chokepoints of mountain gaps and bridges. Rosecrans's forces repeatedly leveraged the Confederates out of extensive defensive works without resorting to the bloody frontal assaults that characterized so many other Civil War actions.[24]

By contrast, Braxton Bragg was the picture of indecision. He waited far too long to react to Rosecrans's advance, though arguably the fault for much of his initial delay must be attributed to Joseph Wheeler's failures. Still, the Confederate paralysis extended for a full 72 hours, from June 23 until noon on June 26, by which time the Federals had seized control of both Hoover's Gap and Liberty Gap and were already threatening Manchester. When Bragg did react, he ordered a hastily conceived counteroffensive with Polk's Corps through Guy's Gap to plug the north end of Liberty Gap, while Hardee held the south end. This attack never materialized; Hardee and Polk were very much opposed to the idea and felt it would bring on a Confederate disaster.

As discussed previously, historian Steven E. Woodworth thought that Bragg missed a real chance here, thrown away by Polk's temerity. Woodworth argued that Bragg's offensive could have worked, triggering at the least a hasty Federal retreat to Murfreesboro and an abrupt, ignominious end to the Union offensive. Rosecrans, like Hooker at Chancellorsville, would have had no choice but to retreat so as to defend his base.

Such an outcome presupposes several highly unlikely variables. The first is near-perfect Confederate intelligence, which had heretofore been completely lacking. The second is that after Polk's 16,000 effectives made it through Guy's Gap, they beat very long odds—Granger with nearly 8,000 cavalry and 7,000 infantry at Christiana, not to mention McCook's entire corps, plus Van Cleve's division at Murfreesboro. Even supposing Polk's willingness to push headlong into a potentially massive trap, he faced the XX Corps to his front and Granger's combined force of equal strength poised to cut off his retreat. Would even the rashest of Civil War commanders have ventured this move?

24 The significant exception, of course, was in Crittenden's corps as it marched through Torbert's Hollow and tried to climb Gilley's Hill from June 25 to 27, though that delay was mostly caused by the torrential rain.

A third variable was the sudden passivity or failure of nerve on the part of Rosecrans. A veteran Union infantry division ensconced behind extensive earthworks defended Murfreesboro. Even if Polk had assaulted the place, he could not have seized it easily. Rosecrans would have had plenty of time to react. Further, he had his entire army oriented along a good road in a straight axis from Manchester to Murfreesboro via Hoover's Gap, so there was no need to panic about supplies at the Army of the Cumberland's headquarters. With Hoover's Gap secure, Guy's and Liberty gaps became irrelevant. By June 28, Manchester was firmly in Union hands, and Tullahoma was sure to follow.

Historian Christopher Kolakowski's proposed scenario of sending Polk to retake Hoover's Gap and divide Rosecrans' army above and below the Highland Rim is a sounder proposition, though it is still very audacious and fraught with risk. Here Rosecrans's forces would indeed have been truly divided, and potentially subject to destruction in detail. Of course, Bragg would have been placing three quarters of his army into a three-sided box, surrounded by enemies, and would be counting on the disruption of Rosecrans's own plans to force a Union retreat. Kolakowski's proposal is an articulation of Napoleon's use of the interior (or central) position, thrusting oneself between two larger foes to defeat them in turn, one after the other. Sometimes that strategy worked. Other times, such as at Waterloo, the enemy refused to collapse and instead converged to crush the smaller force. Hence, the great risk to Confederate arms.

For success, these arguments for the offensive both rely heavily on a sudden burst of determination and enterprise on behalf of the Army of Tennessee, especially from its senior commanders, as well as competence from its cavalry. As has been shown, both enterprise and competence were woefully lacking. The first Federal troops had begun moving on June 23, and the whole of Rosecrans's army was in motion by the 24th. Hoover's Gap fell that day, with Liberty Gap firmly in Union hands by June 25. And yet, Bragg did not even contemplate taking action until midday on June 26, issuing orders to move only on the 27th, fully four days after the Union offensive began. How much would the command culture of the Army of Tennessee have had to change, literally overnight, for either of those proposed offensives to succeed?

Further, both scenarios fail to fully account for the disparity in relative tactical mobility between the two armies. As the campaign proved, Rosecrans's force could live for up to two weeks as far as 50 miles from its railhead. Bragg's army, conversely, had neither a secure forward base of stockpiled supplies to draw upon, nor the wagons necessary to support an extended movement. The Confederates were tightly leashed to their own railhead, and could not survive more than a day or two away from it without forgoing all rations or living off the country—and this country, as we have seen, had long since been foraged out.

That inequality in tactical mobility was a key factor in Rosecrans's success, for it meant he could turn a flank as needed, in ways that Bragg could not. This freedom of movement is why Rosecrans needed all those wagons and draft animals, despite Quartermaster General Meigs's very real warning that in the long term, too many draft animals would prove a logistical burden instead of a help. Rosecrans understood the long-term supply problem posed by their presence, but he also recognized the paradoxical freedom of movement they represented in the moment of action.

Bragg's vacillations at both Tullahoma and Cowan proved hugely damaging. In each case he seemed to show every intention of fighting, even going so far as to solicit agreements from both his corps commanders on the issue, and then abruptly changed his mind. Army morale was certainly affected, and Bragg lost a fair number of disgusted Tennesseans to desertion, but the real damage was to any lingering sense of trust his senior officers might retain concerning his fitness to command. Tullahoma was another stepping stone to disaster, laid alongside the retreats from Kentucky and from Murfreesboro. Lack of faith in Bragg led Polk and Hardee (and possibly Buckner) to contemplate an act of mutiny in front of Cowan at the beginning of July. Three months later, in early October, the issue came to a head outside of Chattanooga, despite the success of Chickamauga, and it forced President Jefferson Davis to rush to the army to try to restore order.

Throughout the Tullahoma Campaign, the performance of the various mounted forces assigned to the Army of the Cumberland was nothing short of spectacular. Wilder's Lightning Brigade achieved a stunning surprise at Hoover's Gap and then performed good service during the arduous Decherd Raid. The brigade not only proved the worth of mounted infantry, but also demonstrated how the firepower of their Spencer Rifles acted as a force multiplier. Its stand against Stewart's division on June 24 amply demonstrates how the intense firepower of the Spencer could compensate for fewer men. The Lightning Brigade would soon become the most famous Union command at the Battle of Chickamauga, and for good reason; seemingly everywhere, Wilder and his men left their mark all over that battlefield.

The units of the Army of the Cumberland's Cavalry Corps also shone during the Tullahoma Campaign, none more brightly than Robert H. G. Minty's Saber Brigade. Its saber charges at Shelbyville on June 27 were probably the most spectacular, most successful such charges of the war. With five regiments, the brigade launched two charges, shattering the better part of two divisions of Wheeler's cavalry and driving the Rebel horsemen headlong into the Duck River.

In the meantime, on June 9, 1863, the largest cavalry battle ever fought on the North American continent occurred among the hills and dales surrounding Brandy Station, an obscure stop on the Orange & Alexandria Railroad in Culpeper County, Virginia. During that 14-hour battle, nearly 21,000 Union and Confederate horse soldiers clashed. The Federal cavalry withdrew at day's end, leaving the battlefield in the hands of the Southern horsemen, but the fight proved to be a game-changer. From that day forward, no longer would the Confederate cavalry have the unchallenged advantage; Union and Confederate horsemen in the East were on equal terms until attrition ground down the Army of Northern Virginia's Cavalry Corps and permitted the Union cavalry to surpass it. Similarly, after Shelbyville, there could be little doubt that the Army of the Cumberland's Cavalry Corps, especially Minty's Saber Brigade, was a match for the Confederate cavalry in the Western Theatre. It was only a question of time before it eclipsed its Southern counterpart, just as the Army of the Potomac's mounted arm eventually eclipsed its rivals. June 1863 proved to be the turning point for the cavalry of both Union armies.[25]

By contrast, the Army of Tennessee's cavalry encapsulates the command and control issues that plagued the entire army's high command. Joseph Wheeler, while brave, simply was not competent to command a large corps of cavalry. His poor dispositions and bad decisions cost the Army of Tennessee dearly, both in the opening stages of the campaign and in an embarrassing debacle at Shelbyville. Forrest compounded that debacle by not coming to the sound of the guns. Perhaps the arrival of his command might have tipped the balance in favor of the Confederate cavalry; but Forrest never arrived, and Wheeler and his men were left to their fates.

Much to Bragg's discomfiture, the Rebel cavalry's failures were not confined to the tactical realm. Again, much of the fault lay with Wheeler. His decision to strip most of his cavalry from the Confederate right on June 22nd to launch a raid against Rosecrans's supply lines couldn't have come at a worse time. Moreover, Wheeler was merely duplicating Bragg's intentions for Morgan's raid, which was already underway and was supposed to accomplish the same thing. As a result,

---

25 Obviously, an in-depth discussion of the Battle of Brandy Station strays far beyond the scope of this chapter. For those interested in a detailed monograph on Brandy Station, see Eric J. Wittenberg, *The Battle of Brandy Station: North America's Largest Cavalry Battle* (Charleston, SC: 2010).

critical intelligence Bragg needed, especially information about Crittenden's movement toward Manchester and the Union thrust through Hoover's Gap, failed to reach him. Even though scattered elements of Confederate cavalry remained to screen against the advance of the XIV Corps, Wheeler's absence meant that the scattering of intelligence that filtered upward failed to reach Bragg in a timely fashion. With the first Federal activity beginning on June 23, and with the all-important left hook commencing at dawn on June 24, it wasn't until late in the afternoon of June 26 that Bragg realized he had to retreat toward Tullahoma.

In short, the Union cavalry proved superior to its Confederate counterpart during all phases of the Tullahoma Campaign. Worse yet for the Army of Tennessee, the Rebel cavalry's performance did not improve as the summer dragged on. Instead, in an echo of the Tullahoma fiasco, Wheeler's negligence in deployment and reconnaissance allowed the Army of the Cumberland to cross the Tennessee River at both Bridgeport and Stevenson, Alabama, at the end of August, effectively undetected. Civilians, not Rebel horsemen, brought the first word of those crossings to Bragg's headquarters in Chattanooga nearly a week later. Nor would the Confederate cavalry do better at Chickamauga.[26]

This reversal of fortune is even more remarkable because in the first half of 1863, Confederate cavalry had consistently dominated Union cavalry in battle. The aggressive, effective Rebel horsemen of Thompson's Station and Brentwood seemed to give way to a paler imitation of themselves. Of course, in May, Bragg lost both a cavalry division to Mississippi, and a highly effective cavalry commander, Earl Van Dorn. Van Dorn, who outranked Wheeler, likely would have emerged as the army's single cavalry corps commander, which might have made a real difference in that arm's subsequent performance. Instead, the Federals gained ascendency, and it cost the Confederacy first Middle Tennessee and then Chattanooga.

At the corps level, the Union leaders also outperformed their Confederate counterparts. Wheeler's failures have already been examined. Stanley and Granger, by contrast, staged a successful deceptive effort along Bragg's front, culminating in the storming of Shelbyville on June 27. Alexander McCook led the XX Corps competently, if not spectacularly. When Rosecrans decided to shift his main offensive thrust to Hoover's Gap thanks to Thomas's successful effort on June 24,

---

26 For a detailed discussion of the numerous failures of the Confederate cavalry during the Chickamauga Campaign, see David A. Powell, *Failure in the Saddle: Nathan Bedford Forrest, Joe Wheeler, and the Confederate Cavalry in the Chickamauga Campaign* (El Dorado Hills, CA: 2010).

McCook's columns moved effectively to comply. Thomas Crittenden, heading up the XXI Corps, struggled with the intended turning movement toward Manchester, but he also had by far the worst roads and most difficult terrain to overcome. If the constant rain crippled any formation's movements during the campaign, they were his.

Conversely, both Gens. Hardee and Polk lacked any faith in Bragg. Fearful of fighting under him, they often counseled retreat. Then, when they did advocate for a stand, Bragg either vacillated or simply elected to withdraw. Even in favorable terrain, backed up to the Cumberland Plateau and beyond the Elk River, Bragg's inconsistent decision-making and deteriorating health led an old Army Regular like Hardee to contemplate a mutiny. Effective, coordinated action was impossible in such circumstances.

No analysis of the Tullahoma Campaign can be considered complete without discussing the weather. At the beginning of the summer of 1863, much of the Western Theater was in drought. Water levels in the major river systems were low, hindering navigation; low water was mentioned often in Union telegraphic traffic. Illinois Lt. Chesley Mosman's diary recorded only one day of rain (May 6) and two more of showers (May 2 and 29) during the month prior to the campaign. In June it was wetter, raining for seven of the first 23 days of that month, but never more than four days running. Starting on June 24, however, of the ensuing 12 days prior to July 5, only two (June 29 and July 2) had "clear" weather. The days that did not see pouring rain were still recorded as "cloudy" and, often, "muddy."[27]

Rosecrans certainly understood the effect of all that rain, especially when coupled with the vagaries of the difficult local terrain. In his report dated July 24, 1863, he explained, "It is a singular characteristic of the soil on the 'Barrens' that it becomes so soft and spongy that wagons cut into it as if it were a swamp, and even horses cannot pass over it without similar results. The terrible effect of the rains on the passage of our troops may be inferred from the single fact that General Crittenden required four days of incessant labor to advance the distance of 21 miles."[28]

After a short rainy period at the beginning of June, there was a window of good weather between June 10 and 23 that would have been perfect for Rosecrans's intended campaign. The rest of July also resumed a more normal pattern, raining

27 Gates, *The Rough Side of War*, 53-63.

28 *OR* 23, pt. 1, 407.

five days of the remaining 26. Then in August, the drought returned, with only a single "shower" on August 5. Clearly, Rosecrans's timing was most inopportune.[29]

Few historians willingly speculate in alternative outcomes. We are prepared, however, to argue that Braxton Bragg was exceedingly fortunate. Rosecrans's advance coincided with an extended bout of very unseasonable weather, which severely crippled the Army of the Cumberland's movements, especially those of Crittenden's XXI Corps. Despite the weather, the Federals reached Manchester by the morning of June 28—the same day Bragg's army slogged into Tullahoma after an equally toilsome march from Wartrace and Shelbyville. Although the same rain and mud also hampered Bragg's retreat, uncertainty and poor intelligence were more responsible for Bragg's sluggishness. Absent the rain, would that uncertainty have been more of a factor? We think so.

Tullahoma was one of the more remarkable campaigns of the Civil War. It was a brilliantly conceived and executed piece of strategy in a conflict better known for command snafus and artless bloodbaths. A such, it deserves closer study. It was a masterpiece of organization, logistics, deception, and maneuver, and it will stand as William Rosecrans's most impressive military achievement.

---

29 Gates, *The Rough Side of War*, 67.

Order of Battle:
Tullahoma Campaign

UNION

Army of the Cumberland: Maj. Gen. William S. Rosecrans

General Headquarters:

1st Battalion Ohio Sharpshooters, 10th Ohio Infantry, 15th Pennsylvania Cavalry

Pioneer Brigade: Brig. Gen. James St. Clair Morton

1st Battalion, 2nd Battalion, 3rd Battalion, 4th Battalion, Bridges's Illinois Battery

XIV Corps:

Maj. Gen. George H. Thomas

Escort: Co. L, 1st Ohio Cavalry

Provost Guard: 9th Michigan Infantry

1st Division:

Maj. Gen. Lovell H. Rousseau

1st Brigade: Col. Benjamin F. Scribner

38th Indiana, 2nd Ohio, 33rd Ohio, 94th Ohio, 10th Wisconsin

2nd Brigade: Col. Henry A. Hambright

24th Illinois, 79th Pennsylvania, 1st Wisconsin, 21st Wisconsin

3rd Brigade: Brig. Gen. John H. King

1/15th U.S., 1/16th U.S., 1/18th U.S., 2/18th U.S., 1/19th U.S.

Artillery: Col. Cyrus O. Loomis

4th Indiana Battery, 1st Michigan Battery, H 5th U.S. Battery

2nd Division: Maj. Gen. James S. Negley

1st Brigade: Brig. Gen. John Beatty

104th Illinois, 42nd Indiana, 88th Indiana, 15th Kentucky, 3rd Ohio

2nd Brigade: Col. William L. Stoughton

19th Illinois, 11th Michigan,
18th Ohio, 69th Ohio

3rd Brigade: Col. William Sirwell

37th Indiana, 21st Ohio, 74th Ohio,
78th Pennsylvania

Artillery: Capt. Frederick Schultz

2nd Kentucky Battery, G 1st Ohio
Battery, M 1st Ohio Battery

3rd Division: Brig. Gen. John M. Brannan

1st Brigade: Col. Moses B. Walker

82nd Indiana, 17th Ohio,
31st Ohio, 38th Ohio

2nd Brigade: Brig. Gen. James B. Steedman

10th Indiana, 74th Indiana, 4th Kentucky,
10th Kentucky, 14th Ohio

3rd Brigade: Col. Ferdinand Van Derveer

87th Indiana, 2nd Minnesota,
9th Ohio, 35th Ohio

Artillery: (no commander listed)

4th Michigan Battery, C 1st Ohio
Battery, I 4th U.S. Battery

4th Division: Maj. Gen. Joseph J. Reynolds

1st Brigade: Col. John T. Wilder
(serving as mounted infantry)

98th Illinois, 123rd Illinois,
17th Indiana, 72nd Indiana

2nd Brigade: Col. Albert S. Hall

80th Illinois, 68th Indiana, 75th Indiana,
101st Indiana, 105th Ohio

3rd Brigade: Brig. Gen. George Crook

18th Kentucky, 11th Ohio, 36th Ohio,
89th Ohio, 92nd Ohio

Artillery: (no commander listed)

18th Indiana Battery, 19th Indiana
Battery, 21st Indiana Battery

XX Corps:
Maj. Gen. Alexander McDowell McCook

1st Division: Brig. Gen. Jefferson C. Davis

1st Brigade: Col. Sidney P. Post

59th Illinois, 74th Illinois,
75th Illinois, 22nd Indiana

2nd Brigade: Brig. Gen. William P. Carlin

21st Illinois, 38th Illinois,
81st Indiana, 101st Ohio

3rd Brigade: Col. Hans Heg

25th Illinois, 35th Illinois,
8th Kansas, 15th Wisconsin

Artillery: (no commander listed)

2nd Minnesota Battery, 5th Wisconsin
Battery, 8th Wisconsin Battery

2nd Division:
Brig. Gen. Richard W. Johnson

1st Brigade: Brig. Gen. August Willich

89th Illinois, 32nd Indiana,
39th Indiana (mounted, detached)
15th Ohio, 49th Ohio

2nd Brigade: Col. Joseph B. Dodge

34th Illinois, 79th Illinois, 29th Indiana,
30th Indiana, 77th Pennsylvania

3rd Brigade: Col. Philemon P. Baldwin

6th Indiana, 5th Kentucky,
1st Ohio, 93rd Ohio

Artillery: Capt. Peter Simonson

5th Indiana Battery, A 1st Ohio Battery,
20th Ohio Battery

3rd Division: Brig. Gen. Philip H. Sheridan

1st Brigade: Brig. Gen. William H. Lytle

36th Illinois, 88th Illinois,
21st Michigan, 24th Wisconsin

2nd Brigade: Col. Bernard Laiboldt

44th Illinois, 73rd Illinois,
2nd Missouri, 15th Missouri

3rd Brigade: Col. Luther P. Bradley

22nd Illinois, 27th Illinois,
42nd Illinois, 51st Illinois

Artillery: Capt. Henry Hescock

C 1st Illinois Battery, 11th Indiana
Battery, G 1st Missouri Battery

XXI Corps:
Maj. Gen. Thomas L. Crittenden

1st Division: Brig. Gen. Thomas J. Wood

1st Brigade: Col. George P. Buell

100th Illinois, 58th Indiana,
13th Michigan, 26th Ohio

2nd Brigade: Brig. Gen. George D. Wagner

15th Indiana, 40th Indiana,
57th Indiana, 97th Ohio

3rd Brigade: Col. Charles G. Harker

3rd Kentucky, 64th Ohio,
65th Ohio, 125th Ohio

Artillery: Capt. Cullen Bradley

8th Indiana Battery,
10th Indiana Battery, 6th Ohio Battery

2nd Division: Maj. Gen. John M. Palmer

Unassigned: 110th Illinois Battalion

1st Brigade: Brig. Gen. Charles Cruft

31st Indiana, 1st Kentucky,
2nd Kentucky, 90th Ohio

2nd Brigade: Brig. Gen. William B. Hazen

9th Indiana, 6th Kentucky,
41st Ohio, 124th Ohio

3rd Brigade: Col. William Grose

84th Illinois, 36th Indiana,
23rd Kentucky, 6th Ohio, 24th Ohio

Artillery: Capt. William E. Stannard

B 1st Ohio Battery, F 1st Ohio Battery, H
4th U.S. Battery, M 4th U.S. Battery

3rd Division:
Brig. Gen. Horatio Van Cleve

1st Brigade: Brig. Gen. Samuel Beatty

79th Indiana, 9th Kentucky,
17th Kentucky, 15th Ohio

2nd Brigade: Col. George F. Dick

44th Indiana, 86th Indiana,
13th Ohio, 59th Ohio

3rd Brigade: Col. Sidney M. Barnes

35th Indiana, 8th Kentucky,
21st Kentucky, 51st Ohio, 99th Ohio

Artillery: Capt. Lucius H. Drury

7th Indiana Battery, Independent
Pennsylvania Battery B,
3rd Wisconsin Battery

Reserve Corps: Maj. Gen. Gordon Granger

(includes only those troops
not assigned to garrisons)

Escort: F 1st Missouri Cavalry

1st Division: Brig. Gen. Absalom Baird

1st Brigade: Col. Smith D. Atkins

92nd Illinois, 96th Illinois, 115th Illinois,
84th Indiana, 40th Ohio

2nd Brigade: Col. William P. Reid

78th Illinois, 86th Illinois,
125th Illinois, 52nd Ohio

3rd Brigade: Col. William L. Utley

33rd Indiana, 85th Indiana,
19th Michigan, 22nd Wisconsin

Artillery: M 1st Illinois Battery, 9th Ohio
Battery, 18th Ohio Battery

2nd Division: At Nashville

3rd Division: At Fort Donelson,
Gallatin, and around Murfreesboro

Cavalry Corps: Maj. Gen. David S. Stanley

1st Cavalry Division:
Brig. Gen. Robert B. Mitchell

1st Brigade: Col. Archibald P. Campbell

2nd Michigan, 9th Pennsylvania,
1st Tennessee

2nd Brigade: Col. Edward M. McCook

2nd Indiana, 4th Indiana, 2nd Tennessee,
1st Wisconsin, D 1st Ohio Battery
(1 section)

3rd Brigade: Col. Louis D. Watkins
(formally organized July 8th, 1863)

4th Kentucky, 5th Kentucky,
6th Kentucky, 7th Kentucky

2nd Division: Brig. Gen. John B. Turchin

1st Brigade: Col. Robert H. G. Minty

3rd Indiana, 5th Iowa, 4th Michigan,
7th Pennsylvania, 5th Tennessee,
4th U.S., D
1st Ohio Battery (one section)

2nd Brigade: Col. Eli Long

2nd Kentucky, 1st Ohio, 3rd Ohio, 4th
Ohio, 10th Ohio, Stokes' Illinois Battery

CONFEDERATE

Army of Tennessee: Gen. Braxton Bragg

Escorts:

Dreux's Company Louisiana Cavalry,
Halloway's Company Alabama Cavalry

Unassigned:

Jackson's Brigade:
Brig. Gen. John K. Jackson

1st Confederate, 2nd Georgia
Sharpshooter Battalion, 5th Georgia,
5th Mississippi, 8th Mississippi,
Pritchard's Georgia Battery,
Scogin's Georgia Battery

Polk's Corps: Lieut. Gen. Leonidas Polk
Escort: Greenleaf's Company, Orleans
Light Horse Louisiana Cavalry

Cheatham's Division:
Maj. Gen. Benjamin F. Cheatham

Escort: G 2nd Georgia Cavalry

Maney's Brigade:
Brig. Gen. George E. Maney

1st and 27th Tennessee, 4th Tennessee,
6th and 9th Tennessee, 24th Tennessee
Battalion, Smith's Mississippi Battery

Smith's Brigade: Brig. Gen. Preston Smith

11th Tennessee, 12th and 47th
Tennessee, 13th and 154th Tennessee,
29th Tennessee,
Scott's Tennessee Battery

Strahl's Brigade: Col. Otho F. Strahl

4th and 5th Tennessee, 19th Tennessee,
24th Tennessee, 31st Tennessee,
33rd Tennessee,
Stanford's Mississippi Battery

Wright's Brigade:
Brig. Gen. Marcus J. Wright

8th Tennessee, 16th Tennessee,
28th Tennessee, 38th Tennessee,
51st Tennessee,
Carnes's Tennessee Battery

Withers's Division:
Maj. Gen. Jones M. Withers

Escort: Lenoir's Company
Alabama Cavalry

Anderson's Brigade:
Brig. Gen. J. Patton Anderson

7th Mississippi, 9th Mississippi,
10th Mississippi, 41st Mississippi,
44th Mississippi, 9th Mississippi
Sharpshooter Battalion,
Robertson's Alabama Battery

Deas's Brigade:
Brig. Gen. Zachariah C. Deas

19th Alabama, 22nd Alabama,
25th Alabama, 39th Alabama,
50th Alabama, 17th Alabama
Sharpshooter Battalion,
Garrity's Alabama Battery

Manigault's Brigade:
Brig. Gen. Arthur M. Manigault

24th Alabama, 28th Alabama,
34th Alabama, 10th and 19th South
Carolina, Waters's Alabama Battery

Walthall's Brigade:
Brig. Gen. Edward C. Walthall

24th Mississippi, 27th Mississippi,
29th Mississippi, 30th Mississippi,
34th Mississippi,
Fowler's Alabama Battery

Hardee's Corps:
Lieut. Gen. William J. Hardee

Escort: Raum's Company Mississippi
Cavalry (Warren Dragoons)

Breckinridge's Division:
Transferred to Mississippi

Cleburne's Division:
Maj. Gen. Patrick R. Cleburne

Escort: Sanders's Company
Tennessee Cavalry

Churchill's Brigade:
Brig. Gen. Thomas J. Churchill

19th and 24th Arkansas, 6th and 10th and
15th Texas, 17th and 18th and 24th and
25th Texas, Douglas's Texas Battery

Liddell's Brigade:
Brig. Gen. St. John R. Liddell

2nd Arkansas, 5th Arkansas, 6th and 7th
Arkansas, 8th Arkansas, 13th and 15th
Arkansas, Swett's Mississippi Battery

Polk's Brigade: Brig. Gen. Lucius E. Polk

1st Arkansas, 3rd and 5th Confederate,
2nd Tennessee, 35th Tennessee,
48th Tennessee,
Calvert's Arkansas Battery

Wood's Brigade: Brig. Gen. S. A. M. Wood

16th Alabama, 33rd Alabama, 45th
Alabama, 32nd and 45th Mississippi,
Hawkins's Battalion Sharpshooters,
Semple's Alabama Battery

Stewart's Division:
Maj. Gen. Alexander P. Stewart

Escort: Foules's Company
Mississippi Cavalry

Bate's Brigade: Brig. Gen. William B. Bate

9th Alabama Battalion, 37th Georgia,
4th Georgia Sharpshooter Battalion,
15th and 37th Tennessee,
20th Tennessee,
Eufaula Alabama Artillery

Brown's Brigade: Brig. Gen. John C. Brown
(transferred from Breckinridge)

18th Tennessee, 26th Tennessee,
32nd Tennessee, 45th Tennessee,
23rd Tennessee Battalion,
Dawson's Georgia Battery

Clayton's Brigade:
Brig. Gen. Henry D. Clayton

18th Alabama, 36th Alabama,
38th Alabama,
Humphreys's Arkansas Battery

Johnson's Brigade:
Brig. Gen. Bushrod R. Johnson

17th Tennessee, 23rd Tennessee,
25th Tennessee, 44th Tennessee,
Darden's Mississippi Battery

Cavalry:

Forrest's Cavalry Division:
Brig. Gen. Nathan B. Forrest

First Brigade:
Brig. Gen. Frank C. Armstrong

3rd Arkansas, 2nd Kentucky,
1st [6th] Tennessee,
McDonald's Tennessee Battalion

Second Brigade: Col. James W. Starnes,
Col. Nicholas N. Cox

4th Tennessee, 8th [13th] Tennessee, 9th
[19th] Tennessee, 10th Tennessee,
11th Tennessee

Artillery: Capt. John W. Morton

Freeman's Tennessee Battery,
Morton's Tennessee Battery

Wheeler's Cavalry Corps:
Maj. Gen. Joseph Wheeler

Morgan's Division: detached,
raiding into Kentucky and Ohio

Martin's Division:
Brig. Gen. William T. Martin

1st Brigade: Col. James Hagan

1st Alabama, 3rd Alabama,
51st Alabama, 8th Confederate

2nd Brigade: Col. Alfred A. Russell
4th Alabama, 1st Confederate
Artillery: Wiggins's Arkansas Battery

Wharton's Division:
Brig. Gen. John A. Wharton

Escort: Fulkerson's Company
Texas Cavalry

Scouts: Capt. M. L. Gordon's
Cavalry Company

1st Brigade: Col. Charles C. Crews

7th Alabama, 2nd Georgia,
3rd Georgia, 4th Georgia

2nd Brigade: Col. Thomas Harrison

3rd Confederate, 1st [3rd] Kentucky,
4th [8th] Tennessee, 8th Texas,
11th Texas

Artillery: White's Tennessee Battery

Army Artillery Reserve:
Col. James Deshler

1st Louisiana Regulars Infantry Regiment,
Lumsden's Alabama Battery,
Massenburg's Georgia Battery,
Havis's Georgia Battery,
Barret's Missouri Battery

**From the Department
of East Tennessee:**

Maj. Gen. Simon B. Buckner[1]

2nd Brigade: Col. Robert C. Trigg

1st Florida Cavalry (dismounted), 6th
Florida, 7th Florida, 65th Georgia, 54th
Virginia, McCants's Florida Battery

3rd Brigade: Brig. Gen. Archibald Gracie

43rd Alabama, 1st, 2nd, 3rd, and 4th
Battalions, Hilliard's Legion (Infantry),
63rd Tennessee,
Baxter's Tennessee Battery

1 Note: the list of troops brought by Buckner is somewhat speculative, based on primary source research and a July 31, 1863 organizational chart. There is no detailed list of the troops that moved to join Braxton Bragg from East Tennessee.

Bibliography

Primary Sources

NEWSPAPERS

Allegan Journal (Allegan, Michigan)

American Tribune (Indianapolis, Indiana)

Baltimore Sun

Canton Register (Canton, Illinois)

Chattanooga Daily Rebel

Chicago Evening Journal

Chicago Tribune

Church Journal of New York

Cincinnati Commercial

Cincinnati Gazette

Cleveland Plain Dealer

Columbus Ohio State Journal

The Daily Rebel (Chattanooga, Tennessee)

Harper's Weekly

Harrisburg Telegraph (Harrisburg, Pennsylvania)

Indianapolis Journal

Knoxville Daily Journal

Kokomo Tribune

Lafayette Daily Courier (Lafayette, Indiana)

Louisville Weekly Journal

Macon Journal and Messenger
Memphis Appeal
Memphis Bulletin
Murfreesboro Post
Nashville Daily Press
Nashville Dispatch
National Tribune (Washington, D.C.)
New York Daily Tribune
New York Herald
Northwestern Church (Chicago, Illinois)
Philadelphia Inquirer
Raftsman's Journal (Clearfield, Pennsylvania)
St. Louis Republican
Tiffin Weekly Tribune (Tiffin, Ohio)
Tri-Weekly Telegraph (Houston, Texas)
Weekly Wabash Express (Terre Haute, Indiana)

MANUSCRIPT SOURCES

Abraham Lincoln Presidential Library, Archives, Springfield, Illinois
    John Bachelor Diary
    Edward Kitchell Diary
    Frederick Marion Letters

Baylor University Libraries, Waco, Texas
Dr. Nathaniel Alexander Morgan Letters, https://blogs.baylor.edu/believemeyourown/, accessed June 8, 2019

Cincinnati Historical Society, Cincinnati, Ohio
    William E. Crane Journal

Duke University, Perkins Library, Durham, North Carolina
    Braxton Bragg Papers

Eli Lilly and Company, Archives, Indianapolis, Indiana
    Eli Lilly Papers

Historical Society of Pennsylvania, Philadelphia, Pennsylvania
    Thomas S. McCahan Journal

Indiana Historical Society, Smith Memorial Library, Indianapolis, Indiana
    C. D. Bailey Letters
    Orville Chamberlain Papers
    W. O. Crouse, "History of Eighteenth Indiana Battery"
    John Day Letters
    William B. Miller Diary
    Samuel E. Munford Letters
    Thomas Prickett Letters
    Joseph A. Scott Reminiscences
    Thomas M. Small Diary
    Williamson D. Ward Diary

Indiana State Library, Indianapolis, Indiana
    John T. Wilder Papers

Michigan State University, Special Collections, Main Library, East Lansing, Michigan
    John C. McLain Diary 1862-1865

National Archives and Records Administration, Washington, D.C.
    "Summary of Daily Intelligence Received," Army of the Cumberland, RG 94
    Compiled Confederate Service Records, RG 109
    Charles C. Davis Medal of Honor file, no. 383,346, RG 94
    Thomas Papers, RG 94
        Moses B. Walker, "A History of 1st Brig. 3rd Div. 14th A.C. during the
Period in which W. S. Rosecrans Com'd Army of Cumberland"
        "Compiled Service Records of Volunteer Union Soldiers Who Served in
Organizations from the State of Kentucky," M397, RG 94.

Stones River National Battlefield, Murfreesboro, Tennessee
    William H. Busbey Diary
    James B. Mitchell Letters

Tennessee State Library and Archives, Nashville, Tennessee
    William Mebane Pollard Diary and Recollections
    E. H. Rennolds Diary

Texas A&M University, Cushing Library, Archives, College Station, Texas
    W. W. Burns Papers

United States Army Heritage and Education Center, Archives, Carlisle, Pennsylvania:
    Civil War Times Illustrated Collection
        Frances W. Reed Papers
    William B. Hazen Papers
    William Stahl Diary and Letters

University of California–Los Angeles
    William S. Rosecrans Papers

University of Michigan, Bentley Historical Library, Manuscripts Collection, Ann Arbor, Michigan
    Henry Mortimer Hempstead Diary
    Randall Packard Diary

University of North Carolina, Wilson Library, Southern Historical Collection, Chapel Hill, North Carolina
    Daniel Coleman Diary

University of the South Library, Archives, Sewanee, Tennessee
    Leonidas Polk Papers

University of Tennessee at Martin, Martin, Tennessee
Martin Van Buren Oldham diaries, www.utm.edu/departments/special_collections/E579.5%20Oldham/text/vboldham_1863.php, accessed March 23, 2019

Wabash College, Lilly Library, Special Collections, Crawfordsville, Indiana
    Henry Campbell Journal

Western Reserve Historical Society, Cleveland, Ohio
    William B. Hazen to Benjamin H. Lossing, William P. Palmer Collection
    William A. Robinson Diary

Wisconsin Historical Society, Madison, Wisconsin
    Horatio Kirkland Foote Letters

Wright State University Libraries, Special Collections, Dayton Ohio
    Oliver Protsman Civil War Diary

Yale University, New Haven, Connecticut
    Augustus B. Carpenter Letters

INTERNET SOURCES

Diary of John H. Freeman, 34th Mississippi Infantry, http://freepages.rootsweb.com/
~mruddy/genealogy/freeman.htm, accessed May 18, 2019

Diary of Major Simon Mayer, www.nps.gov/stri/learn/historyculture/upload/SimonMayer
Diary.pdf, accessed March 23, 2019

Maps: The Middle Tennessee Campaign of June and July, 1863
    Map 1: www.loc.gov/resource/g3962tm.gcw0396000/?sp=2
    Map 2: www.loc.gov/resource/g3962tm.gcw0396000/?sp=3
    Map 3: www.loc.gov/resource/g3962tm.gcw0396000/?sp=4&r=0.359,0.29
5,0.506,0.311,0

GOVERNMENT PUBLICATIONS

United States War Department. War of the Rebellion: *A Compilation of the Official Records of the
Union and Confederate Armies*. 70 volumes in 128 parts. Washington, DC: Government Printing Office,
1880-1901.

THESES

Hughes, Nathaniel Cheairs, Jr. *William Joseph Hardee, C.S.A. 1861-1865*. PhD thesis, University
of North Carolina, 1959.

Morgan, George H. "Cavalry in the Eastern Theatre, 1862." Thesis, US Army War College,
1913-1914.

Ward, David Earl. *The Wrong Kind of General: The Resignation of Union Brigadier General William W.
Burns*. Master's thesis, Texas A&M University, 2005.

PUBLISHED SOURCES

"290." "Army Correspondence." *Macon Journal and Messenger*, July 15, 1863.

A History of the Seventy-Third Regiment of Illinois Volunteers. Springfield, IL: Regimental Reunion
Association of Survivors of the 73rd Illinois Infantry Volunteers, 1890.

Angle, Paul M., ed. *Three Years in the Army of the Cumberland: The Letters and Diary of Major James A.
Connolly*. Bloomington, IN: Indiana University Press, 1959.

Athearn, Robert G., ed. *Soldier in the West: The Civil War Letters of Alfred Lacey Hough*. Philadelphia:
University of Pennsylvania Press, 1957.

Barron, S. B. *Lone Star Defenders: A Chronicle of the Third Texas Cavalry, Ross' Brigade*. New York: Neale, 1908.

Baumgartner, Richard A., ed. *Yankee Tigers II: Civil War Field Correspondence from the Tiger Regiment of Ohio*. Huntington, WV: Blue Acorn Press, 2004.

————, and Larry M. Strayer, eds. *Ralsa C. Rice—Yankee Tigers: Through the Civil War with the 125th Ohio*. Huntington, WV: Blue Acorn Press, 1992.

Beach, John N. *History of the Fortieth Ohio Volunteer Infantry*. London, OH: Shepherd and Craig, 1884.

Beatty, John. *The Citizen-Soldier, or Memoirs of a Volunteer*. Cincinnati: Wilstach, Baldwin, 1879.

Benefiel, W. H. H. *History of Wilder's Lightning Brigade during the Civil War*. Pendleton, IN: Times Print, 1914.

Benham, Calhoun. *A System for Conducting Musketry Instruction, Prepared and Printed by Order of General Bragg for the Army of Tennessee*. Richmond, VA: *Richmond Enquirer* job office, 1863.

Bennett, Lyman G., and William M. Haigh. *History of the Thirty-Sixth Regiment Illinois Volunteers during the War of the Rebellion*. Aurora, IL: Knickerbocker and Hodder, 1876.

Bishop, Judson W. *The Story of a Regiment: Being a Narrative of the Service of the Second Regiment, Minnesota Veteran Volunteer Infantry, in the Civil War of 1861-1865*. St. Paul, MN: privately published, 1890.

Bobrick, Benson, ed. *Testament: A Union Soldier's Story of the Civil War*. New York: Simon and Schuster, 2003.

Bohrnstedt, Jennifer Cain, ed. *Soldiering with Sherman: The Civil War Letters of George F. Cram*. Dekalb, IL: Northern Illinois University Press, 2000.

Bradshaw, Wayne, ed. *The Civil War Diary of William R. Dyer, A Member of Forrest's Escort*. Wayne Bradshaw, 2009.

"Bragg's Army at Chattanooga." *Macon Journal and Messenger*, July 15, 1863.

Briant, C. C. *History of the Sixth Regiment Indiana Volunteer Infantry, of Both the Three Months' and Three Years' Services*. Indianapolis, IN: W. B. Burford, 1891.

Brown, Campbell H., ed. *The Reminiscences of Newton Cannon, First Sergeant, 11th Tennessee Cavalry, C.S.A., from Holograph Material Provided by his Grandson Samuel M. Fleming, Jr. (Late Lieutenant Commander, U.S.N.)*. Franklin, TN: Carter House Association, 1963.

Buck, Irving A. *Cleburne and His Command*. New York: Neale, 1908.

Burns, Franklin L., ed. "Sergeant Harry Burns and the 7th Pennsylvania Volunteer Cavalry." *Tredyffrin Easttown History Quarterly* 24, no. 1 (January 1986): 9-16.

Byrne, Frank L., ed. *The View from Headquarters: Civil War Letters of Harvey Reid*. Madison, WI: State Historical Society of Wisconsin, 1965.

Calkins, William Wirt. *The History of the One Hundred and Fourth Regiment of Illinois Volunteer Infantry*. Chicago, IL: Donohue and Henneberry, 1895.

Campbell, R. Thomas, ed. *Southern Service on Land and Sea: The Wartime Journal of Robert Watson, CSA/CSN*. Knoxville, TN: University of Tennessee Press, 2002.

Carnes, W. W. "Flight from Shelbyville." *Bedford County Historical Quarterly* 8, no. 3 (Fall 1982): 82-83.

Carter, Ruth C., ed. *For Honor, Glory, and Union: The Mexican and Civil War Letters of Brig. Gen. William Haines Lytle*. Lexington, KY: University of Kentucky Press, 1999.

Carter, W. R. "A Story of the War." *Knoxville Daily Journal*, December 10, 1893.

Castle, John Stiles, ed. *Grandfather Was a Drummer Boy: A Civil War Diary and Letters of Charles B. Stiles*. Solon, OH: Evans, 1986.

Cathey, M. Todd, ed. *Captain A. T. Fielder's Civil War Diary, Company B, 12th Tennessee Infantry, C.S.A., July 1861–June 1865*. Nashville, TN: A. Y. Franklin, 2012.

Collins, Robert M. *Chapters from the Unwritten History of the War Between the States; or, the Incidents in the Life of a Confederate Soldier in Camp, on the March, in the Great Battles, and in Prison*. St. Louis, MO: Nixon-Jones, 1893.

"Colonel Wilder's Expedition, *Indianapolis Journal* Narrative," in ed. Frank Moore, *The Rebellion Record: A Diary of American Events, with Documents, Narratives, Illustrative Incidents, Poetry, Etc.* 11 vols., 7: 203-205. New York, NY: G. P. Putnam, 1861-1868.

Cooper, James L. "Service with the Twentieth Tennessee Regiment." *Confederate Veteran* 33 (March 1925): 100-101.

Cope, Alexis. *The 15th Ohio Volunteers and Its Campaigns, War of 1861-5*. Columbus, OH: printed by the author, 1916.

Crist, Lynda L., with Mary S. Dix and Kenneth H. Williams, eds. *The Papers of Jefferson Davis*. 14 vols. to date. Houston, TX: Rice University Press, 1971-2015.

Crofts, Thomas. *History of the Service of the Third Ohio Veteran Volunteer Cavalry in the War for the Preservation of the Union from 1861-1865, Compiled from the Official Records and from Diaries of Members of the Regiment by Sergt. Thos. Crofts, Company C, Regimental Historian*. Toledo, OH: Stoneman Press, 1910.

Curry, William L. *Four Years in the Saddle: History of the First Regiment Ohio Volunteer Cavalry, War of the Rebellion—1861-1865*. Columbus, OH: Champlin, 1898.

Cutrer, Thomas W., ed. *Our Trust is in the God of Battles: The Civil War Letters of Robert Franklin Bunting, Chaplain, Terry's Texas Rangers*. Knoxville, TN: University of Tennessee Press, 2006.

Cushman, Pauline. *An Inside View of the Army Police: The Thrilling Adventures of Pauline Cushman, American Actress, and Famous Federal Spy of the Department of the Cumberland*. Cincinnati, OH: Rickey and Carroll, 1864.

Dedication of the Wilder Brigade Monument on Chickamauga Battlefield on the Thirty-Sixth Anniversary of the Battle, September 20, 1899. Marshall, IL: Herald Press, 1900.

Dennis, Frank Allen, ed. *Kemper County Rebel: The Civil War Diary of Robert Masten Holmes, C.S.A.* Jackson, MS: University and College Press of Mississippi, 1973.

Dillon, Edward. "General Van Dorn's Operations between Columbia and Nashville in 1863." *Southern Historical Society Papers*. 52 vols., 7: 144-146. Richmond, VA: Southern Historical Society, 1876-1959.

Dodd, Ephraim S. "The Diary of Ephraim Shelby Dodd," in Thomas W. Cutrer, *Terry Texas Ranger Trilogy*. Austin, TX: State House Press, 1996.

Dodge, William Sumner. *History of the Old Second Division, Army of the Cumberland: Commanders, McCook, Sill, and Johnson*. Chicago, IL: Church and Goodman, 1864.

Dodson, W. C. *Campaigns of Wheeler and His Cavalry 1862-1865*. Atlanta, GA: Hudgins, 1899.

Dornblaser, Thomas F. *Sabre Strokes of the Pennsylvania Dragoons in the War of 1861-1865*. Philadelphia, PA: Lutheran Publication Society, 1884.

Doyle, W. E. "Wilder's Brigade, Surrounded and Cutting Out." *American Tribune*, October 28, 1897.

Dubose, John Witherspoon. *General Joseph Wheeler and the Army of Tennessee*. New York, NY: Neale, 1912.

Duke, Basil W. *A History of Morgan's Cavalry*. Cincinnati, OH: Miami, 1867.

Fitch, John. *Annals of the Army of the Cumberland: Biographies, Descriptions of Departments, Accounts of Expeditions, Skirmishes, and Battles*. Philadelphia, PA: J. B. Lippincott, 1864.

Fitch, Michael Hendrick. *Echoes of the Civil War as I Hear Them*. New York, NY: R. F. Fenno, 1905.

Floyd, David B. *History of the Seventy-Fifth Regiment of Indiana Volunteers: Its Organization, Campaigns, and Battles (1862-1865)*. Philadelphia, PA: Lutheran Publication Society, 1893.

Fordyce, Samuel W., IV, ed. *An American General: The Memoirs of David Sloan Stanley*. Santa Barbara, CA: Narrative Press, 2003.

"The 49th at Liberty Gap." *Tiffin Weekly Tribune*, August 28, 1863.

Fremantle, Lt. Col. Sir Arthur. *Three Months in the Southern States, April-June 1863*. New York, NY: John Bradburn, 1864.

"From General Rosecrans' Army." *Baltimore Sun*, July 4, 1863.

"From Rosecrans' Army." *Canton Register*, July 13, 1863.

"From Tullahoma." *Columbus Daily Ohio State Journal*, August 8, 1863.

"From Tullahoma: Everything Going on Well with Rosecrans." *Chicago Tribune*, July 6, 1863.

Gates, Arnold, ed. *The Rough Side of War: The Civil War Journal of Chesley A. Mosman, 1st Lieutenant, Company D, 59th Illinois Volunteer Infantry Regiment*. Garden City, NY: Basin, 1987.

Gilmore, James R. *Personal Recollections of Abraham Lincoln and the Civil War*. Boston, MA: J. MacQueen, 1898.

Girardi, Robert I., and Nathaniel Cheairs Hughes, Jr., eds. *The Memoirs of Brigadier General William Passmore Carlin, U.S.A.* Lincoln, NE: University of Nebraska Press, 1999.

Grant, Ulysses S., with ed. John F. Marszalek. *The Personal Memoirs of Ulysses S. Grant: The Complete Annotated Edition*. Cambridge, MA: Harvard University Press, 2017.

Guild, George B. *A Brief Narrative of the Fourth Tennessee Cavalry Regiment, Wheeler's Corps, Army of Tennessee*. Nashville, TN: 1913.

Hallock, Judith Lee, ed. *The Civil War Letters of Joshua K. Callaway*. Athens, GA: University of Georgia Press, 1997.

"Harry." "Letter from the 17th Indiana Regiment." *Weekly Wabash Express*, July 22, 1863.

Hascall, Milo. "Personal Recollections and Experiences Concerning the Battle of Stones River." *Military Order of the Loyal Legion of the United States, Illinois*. 8 vols., 1887. Wilmington, NC: Broadfoot, 1991. Reprint of 1887 edition.

Henig, Dr. Gerald S., ed. "'Soldiering is One Hard Way of Serving the Lord': The Civil War Letters of Martin D. Hamilton." *Indiana Military History Journal* (October 1977).

Hill, Daniel Harvey. "Chickamauga—The Great Battle of the West," in eds. Robert U. Johnson and Clarence C. Buel, *Battles and Leaders of the Civil War*. 4 vols., 3: 638-662. New York, NY: Century, 1884-1887.

Hinman, Wilbur F. *The Story of the Sherman Brigade: The Camp, the March, the Bivouac, the Battle, and How "the Boys" Lived and Died during Four Years of Active Service*. Alliance, OH: Press of the Daily Review, 1897.

"Huntsville." "Hoover's Gap." *The Daily Rebel*, July 26, 1863.

J.T.G. "A Reliable Account of the Fight at Hoover's Gap." *Macon Journal and Messenger*, July 8, 1863.

Johnston, Adam S. *The Soldier Boy's Diary Book; or, Memorandums of the Alphabetical First Lessons of Military Tactics*. Pittsburgh, PA: privately published, 1866.

Johnston, Joseph E. *Narrative of Military Operations, Directed, during the Late War Between the States*. New York, NY: D. Appleton, 1874.

Jordan, Thomas, and J. P. Pryor. *The Campaigns of Lieut. Gen. N. B. Forrest, and of Forrest's Cavalry*. New Orleans, LA: Blelock, 1868.

Keller, Dean H. "A Civil War Diary of Albion W. Tourgée." *Ohio History* 74 (Spring 1965): 99-131.

Kelly, Gene, comp. *Collection of Civil War Letters Written by Mercer County Soldiers*. Mercer County, IL: 1900.

Kerr, Homer L., ed. *Fighting with Ross' Texas Cavalry Brigade C.S.A.: The Diary of George L. Grissom, Adjutant, 9th Texas Cavalry Regiment*. Hillsboro, TX: Hill College Press, 1976.

Kiene, Ralph E., Jr., ed. *A Civil War Diary: The Journal of Francis A. Kiene 1861-1864: A Family History*. Privately published, 1974.

Kimberly, Robert L., and Ephraim S. Holloway. *The Forty-First Ohio Veteran Volunteer Infantry in the War of the Rebellion, 1861-1865*. Cleveland, OH: W. R. Smellie, 1897.

Kirk, Charles H., ed. *History of the Fifteenth Pennsylvania Volunteer Cavalry, which was Recruited and Known as the Anderson Cavalry in the Rebellion of 1861-1865*. Philadelphia, PA: 1906.

Kniffin, Gilbert C. "Maneuvering Bragg Out of Tennessee," in eds. Robert U. Johnson and Clarence C. Buel, *Battles and Leaders of the Civil War*. 4 vols., 3: 635-637. New York, NY: Century, 1884-1887.

Larson, James. *Sergeant Larson 4th Cavalry*. San Antonio, TX: Southern Literary Institute, 1935.

Laws, Fannie May. "In Connection with Thompson's Station." *Confederate Veteran* 3, no. 6 (June 1900): 263.

"Shadow." "Letter from Chattanooga." *Memphis Appeal,* July 1, 1863.

"Lieutenant Colonel Bloodgood's Letter," in ed. Frank Moore, *The Rebellion Record: A Diary of American Events, with Documents, Narratives, Illustrative Incidents, Poetry, Etc.* 11 vols., 6: 442-443. New York, NY: G. P. Putnam, 1861-1868.

Longacre, Glenn V., and John E. Haas, eds. *To Battle for God and the Right: The Civil War Letterbooks of Emerson Opdycke.* Urbanna, IL: University of Illinois Press, 2003.

Lowe, Richard, ed. *A Texas Cavalry Officer's Civil War: the Diary and Letters of James C. Bates.* Baton Rouge, LA: Louisiana State University Press, 1999.

Magee, Benjamin F. *History of the 72d Indiana Volunteer Infantry of the Mounted Lightning Brigade.* LaFayette, IN: S. Vater, 1882.

———. "The 72d Indiana at Hoover's Gap and at Macon." *The American Tribune,* October 21, 1897.

"Manchester, Tennessee, June 27." *Nashville Daily Union,* June 30, 1863.

"Major Davis' Own Story of the Shelbyville Charge." *Harrisburg Telegraph,* January 22, 1909.

McBride, John R. *History of the Thirty-Third Indiana Veteran Volunteer Infantry during the Four Years of Civil War from Sept. 16, 1861, to July 21, 1865, and Incidentally of Col. John Colburn's Second Brigade, Third Division, Twentieth Army Corps, including Incidents of the Great Rebellion.* Indianapolis, IN: Wm. B. Burford, 1900.

McCaffrey, James M., ed. *Only a Private: A Texan Remembers the Civil War—The Memoirs of William J. Oliphant.* Houston, TX: Halcyon Press, 2004.

McDonald, E. "He Pulled the Lanyard at Hoover's Gap." *The National Tribune,* October 18, 1883.

McMurray, W. J. *History of the Twentieth Tennessee Regiment Volunteer Infantry, C.S.A.* Nashville: Publication Committee, 1904.

McMurry, Richard M., ed. *An Uncompromising Secessionist: The Civil War of George Knox Miller, Eighth (Wade's) Confederate Cavalry.* Tuscaloosa, AL: University of Alabama Press, 2007.

"Military Record of Robert H. G. Minty, in the United States Volunteer Army of the Civil War, 1861-1865," in the Proposed Volunteer Retired List, *Senate Documents,* vol. 8, 59th Congress, 1st Session, 78-81. Washington, DC: Government Printing Office, 1906.

Minty, Robert H. G. "At Shelbyville, Tennessee. Gen. Minty Corrects the Comrades and Gives a True Account." *The National Tribune,* May 8, 1890.

——— . "The Saber Brigade. An Expedition with the Gallant 'Little Phil' Sheridan." *The National Tribune,* December 15 and 22, 1892.

——— . "The Saber Brigade. Gen. Minty Tells of Its Part in the Shelbyville Battle." *The National Tribune,* August 3, 1893.

Molineaux, Emily E. *Lifetime Recollections: An Interesting Narrative of Life in the Southern States before and during the Civil War, with Incidents of the Bombardment of Atlanta, the Author Then Being a Resident of that City.* San Francisco, CA: C. W. Gordon, 1902.

Morgan, Julia. *How It Was: Four Years Among the Rebels.* Nashville, TN: Publishing House, Methodist Episcopal Church, 1892.

Morrison, James L., ed. *The Memoirs of Henry Heth.* Westport, CT: Greenwood Press, 1974.

Morton, John Watson. *The Artillery of Nathan Bedford Forrest's Cavalry.* Nashville, TN: House of the M.E. Church, South, 1909.

"Mr. E. D. Westfall's Despatches." *New York Herald,* July 8, 1863.

"Mr. F. G. Shanks' Despatches." *New York Herald,* July 8, 1863.

Noe, Kenneth W., ed. *A Southern Boy in Blue: The Memoir of Marcus Woodcock, 9th Kentucky Infantry (U.S.A.)* Knoxville, TN: University of Tennessee Press, 1996.

Noll, Arthur Howard, ed. *Doctor Quintard, Chaplain C.S.A. and Second Bishop of Tennessee: Being His Story of the War (1861-1865).* Suwanee, TN: University Press, 1905.

"One Who Has Investigated the Facts." "The Raid on Decherd." *Daily Rebel,* July 3, 1863.

Otey, W. N. Mercer. "Operations of the Signal Corps." *Confederate Veteran* 8 (1900): 129-130.

Patterson, William Elwood, with ed. Lowell Wayne Patterson. *Jasper County Yankee: Campaigns of the 38th Regiment, Illinois Volunteer Infantry, Company K.* Westminster, MD: Heritage Books, 2011.

Pickerell, William N. *History of the Third Indiana Cavalry.* Indianapolis, IN: Aetna, 1906.

Proceedings of the Board of Trustees of the University of the South at Their Session Held at University Place, Sewanee, Tennessee, July 12th-18th, 1871. Rome, GA.: J. W. Burke, 1871.

Prosser, W. F. "A Remarkable Episode of the Late War." *United Service* (December 1889): 621-623.

Records, W. H. "Hoover's Gap." *The National Tribune,* September 20, 1883.

———. "Wilder's Brigade at Hoover's Gap." *The National Tribune,* November 8, 1883.

"Rosecrans in Tullahoma." *Raftsman's Journal,* July 8, 1863.

Rosecrans, William S. "The Campaign for Chattanooga." *Century Illustrated Monthly Magazine* 34 (May-October 1887): 129-135.

Rugeley, H. J. H., ed. *Batchelor-Turner Letters, 1861-1864, Written by Two of Terry's Texas Rangers.* Austin, TX: Steck, 1961.

Saffield, James M. *A Geographical Reconnaissance of the State of Tennessee: Being the Author's First Biennial Report Presented to the Thirty-First General Assembly of the State of Tennessee, 1855.* Nashville, TN: G. C. Torbert, 1856.

Savage, John H. *The Life of John H. Savage.* Nashville, TN: 1903.

Scribner, Benjamin F. *How Soldiers Were Made; or the War as I Saw It under Buell, Rosecrans, Thomas, Grant and Sherman.* New Albany, IN: Donohue and Henneberry, 1887.

Shanks, William G. *Personal Recollections of Distinguished Generals.* New York: Harper and Brothers, 1866.

Shapiro, Norman M., ed. "Daniel Coleman Diary January 1863-August 1864." *Huntsville Historical Review* 26, No. 2 (Summer-Fall 1999): 1-46.

Shaw, James Birney. *History of the Tenth Regiment Indiana Volunteer Infantry: Three Months and Three Years Organizations.* Lafayette, IN: Burt-Haywood, 1912.

Shelton, Perry Wayne, ed. *Personal Letters of General Lawrence Sullivan Ross with Other Letters*. Austin, TX: Shelly and Richard Morrison, 1994.

Sheridan, Philip H. *Personal Memoirs of P. H. Sheridan. General, United States Army*. 2 vols. New York: Charles L. Webster, 1888.

Simmons, L. A. *The History of the 84th Regt. Ill. Vols*. Macomb, IL: Hampton Brothers, 1866.

Simpson, Harold B., ed. *The Bugle Softly Blows: The Confederate Diary of Benjamin M. Seaton*. Waco, TX: Texian Press, 1965.

Sipes, William B. *The Saber Regiment: History of the 7th Pennsylvania Veteran Volunteer Cavalry, 1861-1865*. Pottsville, PA: Pottsville Miner's Journal, 1905.

"Soldier in Gap." "The Capture of Hoover's Gap." *Memphis Appeal*, July 21, 1863.

Sparks, A. W. *The War Between the States as I Saw It: Reminiscences, Historical and Personal*. Tyler, TX: Lee and Burnett, 1901.

Stanley, David S. "The Tullahoma Campaign." *Sketches of War History 1861-1865*, Military Order of the Loyal Legion of the United States, Ohio Commandery. Vol. 3, 166-181. Cincinnati, OH: Robert Clarke, 1890.

———— . *Personal Memoirs of Major General David S. Stanley, U.S.A*. Cambridge, MA: Harvard University Press, 1917.

———— . "Rosecrans's Obituary," *Twenty-Eighth Annual Reunion of the Association of Graduates of the United States Military Academy, at West Point, New York, June 10th, 1897*. Saginaw, MI: 1897.

Steahlin, George H. "Stanley's Cavalry. Colonel Minty's Sabre Brigade at Guy's Gap." *National Tribune*, May 27, 1882.

Stewart, Alex. P. "The Army of Tennessee. A Sketch," in ed. John Barrien Lindsley, *The Military Annals of Tennessee, Confederate, First Series: Embracing a Review of Military Operations, with Regimental Histories and Memorial Rolls, Compiled from Original and Official Sources*. 2 vols. Nashville, TN: J. M. Lindsley, 1886.

Tatum, Margaret Black, ed. "'Please Send Stamps': The Civil War Letters of William Allen Clark, Part II", *Indiana Magazine of History* 91, no. 2 (June 1995): 197-225.

"Telegraphic Correspondence Daily Commercial from Manchester, Tennessee." *Cincinnati Commercial*, July 2, 1863.

"Telegraphic Correspondence Daily Commercial from Manchester, Tennessee." *Cincinnati Commercial*, July 4, 1863.

"Tennessee." *Church Journal of New York*, August 19, 1863.

"Tennessee Citizen." "Battle at Hoover's Gap." *Memphis Appeal*, July 29, 1863.

Thatcher, Marshall P. *A Hundred Battles in the West: St. Louis to Atlanta, 1861-65, the Second Michigan Cavalry*. Detroit, MI: privately published, 1884.

"The Retreat of Bragg's Army," *Nashville Daily Press*, August 13, 1863.

The War of the Rebellion: A Compilation of the Official Records of the Union and Confederate Armies. 128 volumes in 3 series. Washington, DC: United States Government Printing Office, 1889.

"Tippecanoe" to Editor, July 5, 1863, *Lafayette Daily Courier*, July 16, 1863.

Tomlinson, Helyn W., ed. *"Dear Friends": The Civil War Letters and Diary of Charles Edwin Cort.* 1962.

Tower, R. Lockwood, ed. *A Carolinian Goes to War: The Civil War Narrative of Arthur Middleton Manigault, Brigadier General, C.S.A.* Charleston, SC: University of South Carolina Press, 1982.

Vale, Joseph G. *Minty and His Cavalry: A History of Cavalry Campaigns in the Western Armies.* Harrisburg, PA: Edwin K. Meyers, 1886.

Van Horne, Thomas B. *History of the Army of the Cumberland: Its Organization, Campaigns and Battles.* 2 vols. Cincinnati, OH: Robert Clarke, 1875.

Vance, J. W., comp. *Report of the Adjutant General of the State of Illinois.* 9 vols. Springfield, IL: H. W. Boeker, 1886.

Villard, Henry. *Memoirs of Henry Villard, Journalist and Financier, 1835-1900, in Two Volumes.* Boston, MA: Houghton, Mifflin, 1904.

Waddle, Angus L. *Three Years with the Armies of the Ohio, and the Cumberland.* Chillicothe, OH: Scioto Gazette Book and Job Office, 1889.

White, William Lee, and Charles Denny Runion, eds. *Great Things Are Expected of Us: The Letters of Colonel C. Irvine Walker, 10th South Carolina Infantry, C.S.A.* Knoxville, TN: University of Tennessee Press, 2009.

Wilder, John T. "The Battle of Hoover's Gap," *Sketches of War History, 1861-1865.* Vol. 6, 166-173. Ohio Commandery, Military Order of the Loyal Legion of the United States. Cincinnati, OH: Monfort, 1908.

Wiley, Bell Irvin, ed. *Fourteen Hundred and Ninety-One Days in the Confederate Army: A Journal Kept by W. W. Heartsill for Four Years, One Month and One Day; or Camp Life, Day by Day of the W. P. Lane Rangers from April 19, 1861, to May 20, 1865.* Jackson, TN: McCowat-Mercer Press, 1953.

Williams, Frederick D. *Wild Life in the Army: Civil War Letters of James A. Garfield.* East Lansing, MI: Michigan State University Press, 1964.

Wilson, George S. "Wilder's Brigade of Mounted Infantry in the Tullahoma-Chickamauga Campaigns." *War Talks in Kansas*, Kansas Commandery, Loyal Legion of the United States, 45-76. Kansas City, MO: Franklin Hudson, 1906.

Wilson, James H. *Under the Old Flag: Recollections of Military Operations in the War for the Union, the Spanish War, the Boxer Rebellion, Etc.* 2 vols. New York: D. Appleton, 1912.

Winchester, George W. "The Battle for Hoover's Gap," *Daily Rebel*, July 3, 1863.

Wyeth, John A. "General Wheeler's Leap." *Harper's Weekly* (June 18, 1898): 601-602.

Younger, Edward. *Inside the Confederate Government: The Diary of Robert Garlick Hill Kean.* Baton Rouge, LA: Louisiana State University Press, 1957.

Secondary Sources

ARTICLES

Ball, Clyde L. "The Public Career of Col. A. S. Colyar, 1870-1877." *Tennessee Historical Quarterly*, vol. 12, no. 1 (March, 1953), pp. 24-27.

Blakeslee, Merritt R. "A Sharp Little Fight." *Sewanee Magazine* (Winter 2014): 24-29.

————. "How the Cornerstone Was Destroyed. Yes, It Was Union Soldiers. No, They Didn't Blow It Up." *Sewanee Magazine* (Summer 2011): 28-30.

Bradley, Michael R. "Varying results of Cavalry Fighting: Western Flank vs. Eastern Flank." *Blue and Gray* 27, no. 1 (2010): 21.

Davis, William C. "John Cabell Breckinridge," in eds. William C. Davis and Julie Hoffman, *The Confederate Generals*. 6 vols., 1: 126-127. New York, NY: National Historical Society, 1991.

Hewitt, Lawrence L. "William Brimage Bate," in eds. William C. Davis and Julie Hoffman, *The Confederate General*, 6 vols., 1:70-73. New York, NY: National Historical Society, 1991.

————. "Braxton Bragg," in eds. William C. Davis and Julie Hoffman, *The Confederate Generals*. 6 vols., 1:112-115. New York, NY: National Historical Society, 1991.

McMurry, Richard M. "William Joseph Hardee," in eds. William C. Davis and Julie Hoffman, *The Confederate Generals*. 6 vols., 3: 58-61. New York, NY: National Historical Society, 1991.

Pennington, Edgar Legare. "The Battle at Sewanee." *Tennessee Historical Quarterly* 9, No. 3 (September 1950): 217-243.

Woodworth, Steven E. "Leonidas Polk," in eds. William C. Davis and Julie Hoffman, *The Confederate Generals*. 6 vols., 5:44-47. New York, NY: National Historical Society, 1991.

————. "Braxton Bragg and the Tullahoma Campaign," in ed. Steven E. Woodworth, *The Art of Command in the Civil War,* 157-182. Lincoln, NE: University of Nebraska Press, 1998.

PUBLISHED SOURCES

Anderson, William M. *They Died to Make Men Free: A History of the 19th Michigan Infantry in the Civil War.* Dayton, OH: Morningside House, 1994.

Andrews, J. Cutler. *The South Reports the Civil War.* Princeton, NJ: Princeton University Press, 1970.

Bauman, Ken. *Arming the Suckers, 1861-1865: A Compilation of Illinois Civil War Weapons.* Dayton, OH: Morningside, 1989.

Baumgartner, Richard A. *Blue Lightning: Wilder's Mounted Infantry Brigade in the Battle of Chickamauga.* Huntington, WV: Blue Acorn Press, 2007.

Bearss, Edwin C. *The History of Fortress Rosecrans.* Washington, DC: National Park Service, 1960.

Belcher, Dennis W. *General David Stanley, USA: A Civil War Biography.* Jefferson, NC: McFarland, 2014.

———. *The Cavalry of the Army of the Cumberland.* Jefferson, NC: McFarland, 2016.

Bennett, John D. *Placenames of the Civil War: Cities, Towns, Villages, Railroad Stations, Forts, Camps, Islands, Rivers, Creeks, Fords and Ferries.* Jefferson, NC: McFarland, 2012.

Bilby, Joseph G. *A Revolution in Arms: A History of the First Repeating Rifles.* Yardley, PA: Westholme, 2005.

Bitter, Rand. *Minty and His Cavalry.* Privately published, 2006.

Bradley, Michael R. *Tullahoma: The 1863 Campaign for the Control of Middle Tennessee.* Shippensburg, PA: Burd Street Press, 2000.

Buford, Marcus Bainbridge. *A Genealogy of the Buford Family in America.* San Francisco, CA: privately published, 1904.

Burlingame, Michael. *Abraham Lincoln, A Life.* 2 vols. Baltimore: Johns Hopkins University Press, 2008.

Carter, Arthur B. *The Tarnished Cavalier: Major General Earl Van Dorn, C.S.A.* Knoxville, TN: University of Tennessee Press, 1999.

Christen, William J. *Pauline Cushman: Spy of the Cumberland.* Roseville, MN: Edinborough Press, 2006.

Collier, Calvin L. *The War Child's Children: A Story of the Third Regiment, Arkansas Cavalry, Confederate States Army.* Little Rock, AR: privately published, 1965.

Connelly, Thomas L. *Autumn of Glory: The Army of Tennessee, 1862-1865.* Baton Rouge: Louisiana State University Press, 1971.

Cooper, Edward S. *The Brave Men of Company A, The Forty-First Ohio Volunteer Infantry.* Madison, NJ: Fairleigh Dickenson University Press, 2015.

Daniel, Larry J. *Days of Glory: The Army of the Cumberland, 1861-1865.* Baton Rouge, LA: Louisiana State University Press, 2004.

———. *Battle of Stones River: The Forgotten Conflict between the Confederate Army of Tennessee and the Union Army of the Cumberland.* Baton Rouge, LA: Louisiana State University Press, 2012.

Davis, William C. *Breckinridge: Statesman, Soldier, Symbol.* Baton Rouge, LA: Louisiana State University Press, 1974.

DePuy, W. H., ed. *The World-Wide Encyclopedia and Gazetteer.* 12 vols. New York, NY: Christian Herald, 1908.

Dodson, W. C. *Campaigns of Wheeler and his Cavalry, 1862-1865, from Material Furnished by Gen. Joseph Wheeler to which is Added His Concise and Graphic Account of the Santiago Campaign of 1898.* Atlanta, GA: Hudgins, 1899.

Easton, Loyd D. *Hegel's First American Followers: John B. Stollo, Peter Keaufmann, Moncure Conway, and August Willich, with Key Writings.* Athens, OH: Ohio University Press, 1966.

Eicher, John H., and David J. Eicher. *Civil War High Commands.* Stanford, CA: Stanford University Press, 2001.

Eicher, David J. *The Longest Night: A Military History of the Civil War.* New York, NY: Simon and Schuster, 2001.

Elliott, Sam Davis. *John C. Brown of Tennessee: Rebel, Redeemer, and Railroader.* Knoxville, TN: University of Tennessee Press, 2017.

———. *Soldier of Tennessee: General Alexander P. Stewart and the Civil War in the West.* Baton Rouge, LA: Louisiana State University Press, 1999.

———. *Isham G. Harris of Tennessee: Confederate Governor and United States Senator.* Baton Rouge, LA: Louisiana State University Press, 2010.

Goff, Richard D. *Confederate Supply.* Durham, NC: Duke University Press, 1969.

Griffith, Paddy. *Battle Tactics of the Civil War.* New Haven, CT: Yale University Press, 1987.

Groves, Richard R. *Blooding the Regiment: An Account of the 22d Wisconsin's Long and Difficult Apprenticeship.* Lanham, MD: Scarecrow Press, 2005.

Hagerman, Edward. *The American Civil War and the Origins of Modern Warfare: Ideas, Organization, and Field Command.* Bloomington, IN: Indiana University Press, 1988.

Hale, Douglas. *The Third Texas Cavalry in the Civil War.* Norman, OK: University of Oklahoma Press, 1993.

Hannah, Howard M. *Confederate Action in Franklin County, Tennessee.* Suwanee, TN: Franklin County Civil War Centennial Committee, 1963.

Haughton, Andrew. *Training, Tactics, and Leadership in the Confederate Army of Tennessee.* London: Frank Cass, 2000.

Herberich, John L. *Masters of the Field: The Fourth United States Cavalry in the Civil War.* Atglen, PA: Schiffer, 2015.

Hess, Earl J. *Braxton Bragg: The Most Hated Man of the Confederacy.* Chapel Hill, NC: University of North Carolina Press, 2016.

———. *The Rifle Musket in Civil War Combat: Reality and Myth.* Lawrence, KS: University of Kansas Press, 2008.

Hill, Jeffery A. *The 26th Ohio Veteran Volunteer Infantry: The Groundhog Regiment, Second Edition.* Bloomington, IN: 2010.

Hoffman, Mark. *"My Brave Mechanics": The First Michigan Engineers and their Civil War.* Detroit, MI: Wayne State University Press, 2007.

History of Tennessee Illustrated. 2 vols. Nashville, TN: Goodspeed, 1887.

Horn, Huston. *Leonidas Polk: Warrior Bishop of the Confederacy.* Lawrence, KS: University Press of Kansas, 2019.

Hughes, Nathaniel Cheairs, Jr. *Liddell's Record: St. John Richardson Liddell, Brigadier General, CSA Staff Officer and Brigade Commander, Army of Tennessee.* Baton Rouge, LA: Louisiana State University Press, 1985.

———, and Thomas Clayton Ware. *Theodore O'Hara: Poet-Soldier of the Old South.* Knoxville, TN: University of Tennessee Press, 1998.

———, and Roy P. Stonesifer, Jr. *The Life & Wars of Gideon J. Pillow.* Chapel Hill, NC: University of North Carolina Press, 1993.

Johnson, Mark W. *That Body of Brave Men: The U.S. Regular Infantry and the Civil War in the West*. Cambridge, MA: De Capo Press, 2003.

Jomini, Baron Antoine Henri de Jomini. *The Art of War*. London, UK: Greenhill Books, 1992. Reprint of 1862 English translation.

Klement, Frank L. *The Limits of Dissent: Clement L. Vallandigham & the Civil War*. Lexington, KY: University of Kentucky Press, 1970.

Kolakowski, Christopher L. *The Stones River and Tullahoma Campaigns: This Army does not Retreat*. Charleston, SC: The History Press, 2011.

Kundahl, George G. *Confederate Engineer: Training and Campaigning with John Morris Wampler*. Knoxville, TN: University of Tennessee Press, 2000.

Lamers, William M. *The Edge of Glory: A Biography of General William S. Rosecrans, U.S.A*. Baton Rouge: Louisiana State University Press, 1999.

Longacre, Edward G. *Cavalry of the Heartland: The Mounted Forces of the Army of Tennessee*. Yardley, PA: Westholme Publishing, 2009.

Losson, Christopher. *Tennessee's Forgotten Warriors: Frank Cheatham and his Confederate Division*. Knoxville: University of Tennessee Press, 1989.

Martin, Samuel J. *General Braxton Bragg, C.S.A*. Jefferson, NC: McFarland, 2011.

Marvel, William. *Burnside*. Chapel Hill, NC: University of North Carolina Press, 1991.

McWhiney, Grady. *Braxton Bragg and Confederate Defeat, Volume 1*. Tuscaloosa, AL: University of Alabama Press, 1991.

Miller, Rex. *Wheeler's Favorites: 51st Alabama Cavalry*. Austin, TX: privately published, 1991.

Moore, David G. *William S. Rosecrans and the Union Victory: A Civil War Biography*. Jefferson, NC: McFarland, 2014.

Morris, Roy, Jr. "The Improbable, Praiseworthy Paper: The *Chattanooga Daily Rebel*." *Civil War Times Illustrated* 23, no. 7 (November 1984): 21-24.

Mowery, David L. *Morgan's Great Raid: The Remarkable Expedition from Kentucky to Ohio*. Charleston, SC: The History Press, 2013.

Muir, Rory. *Tactics and the Experience of Battle in the Age of Napoleon*. New Haven, CT: Yale University Press, 1998.

Nash, Jeffrey L. *Destroyer of the Iron Horse: General Joseph E. Johnston and Confederate Rail Transport, 1861-1865*. Kent, OH: Kent State University Press, 1991.

Noe, Kenneth W. *Perryville: This Grand Havoc of Battle*. Lexington, KY: University of Kentucky Press, 2001.

Nosworthy, Brent. *The Bloody Crucible of Courage*. New York, NY: Basic Books, 2008.

Purdue, Howell, and Elizabeth Purdue. *Pat Cleburne, Confederate General: A Definitive Biography*. Hillsboro, TX: Hill Junior College Press, 1973.

Parks, Joseph H. *General Leonidas Polk C.S.A.: The Fighting Bishop*. Baton Rouge, LA: Louisiana State University Press, 1992.

Polk, William M. *Leonidas Polk: Bishop and General.* 2 vols. New York, NY: Longmans, Green, 1915.

Poole, John Randolph. *Cracker Cavaliers: The 2nd Georgia Cavalry under Wheeler and Forrest.* Macon, GA: Mercer University Press, 2000.

Powell, David A. *The Chickamauga Campaign—A Mad Irregular Battle: From the Crossing of the Tennessee River through the Second Day, August 22-September 19, 1863.* El Dorado Hills, CA: Savas-Beatie, 2014.

————. *Failure in the Saddle: Nathan Bedford Forrest, Joe Wheeler, and the Confederate Cavalry in the Chickamauga Campaign.* El Dorado Hills, CA: Savas-Beatie, 2010.

Powell, David A., and David A. Friedrichs. *The Maps of Chickamauga: An Atlas of the Chickamauga Campaign, including the Tullahoma Operations, June 22-September 23, 1863.* El Dorado Hills, CA: Savas-Beatie, 2009.

Powell, David A., and Steven J. Wright. "Last Clash at Chickamauga," in *The Chickamauga Campaign—Barren Victory: The Retreat into Chattanooga, the Confederate Pursuit, and the Aftermath of the Battle, September 21 to October 20, 1863.* El Dorado Hills, CA: Savas-Beatie, 2016.

Ramage, James A. *Rebel Raider: The Life of General John Hunt Morgan.* Lexington, KY: University Press of Kentucky, 1986.

Reyburn, Philip J. *Clear the Track: A History of the Eighty-Ninth Illinois Volunteer Infantry, the Rail Road Regiment.* Bloomington, IN: Authorhouse, 2012.

Riddle, A. G. *The Life, Character and Public Services of Jas. A. Garfield.* Philadelphia: William Flint, 1880.

Robertson, William Glenn. *River of Death: The Chickamauga Campaign—Volume One: The Fall of Chattanooga.* Chapel Hill, NC: University of North Carolina Press, 2018.

Rowell, John W. *Yankee Artillerymen: Through the Civil War with Eli Lilly's Indiana Battery.* Knoxville, TN: University of Tennessee Press, 1975.

————. *Yankee Cavalrymen: Through the Civil War with the Ninth Pennsylvania Cavalry.* Knoxville, TN: University of Tennessee Press, 1971.

Sanders, Stuart W. "Maj. Gen. William Thompson Martin," in eds. Bruce Allardice and Lawrence Lee Hewitt, *Kentuckians in Gray: Confederate Generals and Field Officers from the Bluegrass State.* Lexington, KY: University of Kentucky Press, 2008.

Skellie, Ron. *Lest We Forget: The Immortal Seventh Mississippi.* 2 vols. Birmingham, AL: Banner, 2012.

Smith, Theodore Clarke. *The Life and Letters of James Abram Garfield.* 2 vols. New Haven, CT: Yale University Press, 1925.

Smith, Timothy B. *Corinth 1862: Siege, Battle, Occupation.* Lawrence, KS: University of Kansas Press, 2012.

————. *The Real Horse Soldiers: Benjamin Grierson's Epic 1863 Civil War Raid through Mississippi.* El Dorado Hills, CA: Savas-Beatie, 2018.

Smith, Tonia J. "Gentlemen, You Have Played This D——d Well," *North and South* 8, no. 3 (September 2005).

Starnes, H. Gerald. *Forrest's Forgotten Horse Brigadier.* Bowie, MD: Heritage Books, 1995.

Starr, Stephen Z. *The Union Cavalry in the Civil War. 3 vols.* Baton Rouge, LA: Louisiana State University Press, 1979-1985.

Sunderland, Glenn W. *Lightning at Hoover's Gap: Wilder's Brigade in the Civil War.* New York, NY: Thomas Yoseloff, 1969.

Symonds, Craig L. *Joseph E. Johnston: A Civil War Biography.* New York: W. W. Norton, 1992.

Thomas, Dean S. *Round Ball to Rimfire: A History of Civil War Small Arms Ammunition, Part Two: Federal Breechloading Carbines and Rifles.* Gettysburg, PA: Thomas Publications, 2002.

Warner, Ezra J. *Generals in Blue: Lives of the Union Commanders.* Baton Rouge, LA: Louisiana State University Press, 1964.

————. *Generals in Gray: Lives of the Confederate Commanders.* Baton Rouge, LA: Louisiana State University Press, 1959.

Weaver, Jeffrey C. *54th Virginia Infantry.* Lynchburg, VA: H. E. Howard, 1993.

Wheelan, Joseph A. *Libby Prison Breakout: The Daring Escape from the Notorious Civil War Prison.* New York, NY: Public Affairs, 2010.

Willett, Robert L. "We Rushed with a Yell," *Civil War Times Illustrated* 8, no. 10 (February 1970): 18-19.

————. *The Lightning Mule Brigade: Abel Streight's 1863 Raid into Alabama.* Carmel, IN: Guild Press, 1999.

Wills, Brian Steel. *A Battle from the Start: The Life of Nathan Bedford Forrest.* New York, NY: Harper Collins, 1992.

Wittenberg, Eric J. *The Battle of Brandy Station: North America's Largest Cavalry Battle.* Charleston, SC: The History Press, 2010.

Wyeth, John Allen. *That Devil Forrest: The Life of Nathan Bedford Forrest.* Baton Rouge, LA: Louisiana State University Press, 1989.

WEBSITES

Swain, Craig. "Minty's Bad Day." Https://markerhunter.wordpress.com/tag/robert-minty/.

Index

David A. Powell graduated from VMI (Class of 1983) with a BA in history. He is known for his tours of the battlefield of Chickamauga. He is married and lives and works in Chicago, Illinois.

In addition to articles and historical simulations, he is the author of many books, including the magisterial award-winning trilogy *The Chickamauga Campaign* (Savas Beatie, 2014-16). His groundbreaking cavalry command study *Failure in the Saddle: Nathan Bedford Forrest, Joseph Wheeler, and the Confederate Cavalry in the Chickamauga Campaign* (Savas Beatie, 2010) was awarded the Atlanta Civil War Round Table's 2010 Richard Barksdale Harwell Award, as was *Glory or the Grave* (his second book in the Chickamauga trilogy) in 2016, making him the first two-time recipient of this prestigious award.

Dave wrote (with David A. Friedrichs, cartographer) *The Maps of Chickamauga: An Atlas of the Chickamauga Campaign* (Savas Beatie, 2009), part of the Savas Beatie Military Atlas Series and has also authored a pair of books for the award-winning Emerging Civil War Series: *Battle Above the Clouds: Lifting the Siege of Chattanooga and the Battle of Lookout Mountain, October 16- November 24, 1863* (Savas Beatie, 2017), and *All Hell Can't Stop Them: The Battles for Chattanooga, Missionary Ridge, and Ringgold, November 24-27, 1863* (Savas Beatie, 2019). His most recent book is *Union Command Failure in the Valley: Major General Franz Sigel and the War in the Valley of Virginia, May 1864* (Savas Beatie, 2019).

Eric J. Wittenberg is an attorney and award-winning Civil War cavalry historian.

In addition to the articles he has written for a variety of different magazines, Eric is also the author, co-author, or editor of more than a dozen books on Civil War cavalry subjects, including *The Battle of Monroe's Crossroads: The Civil War's Final Campaign* (Savas Beatie, 2006), *Plenty of Blame to Go Around: Jeb Stuart's Controversial Ride to Gettysburg* (Savas Beatie, 2006), and *One Continuous Fight: The Retreat from Gettysburg and the Pursuit of Lee's Army of Northern Virginia, July 4-14, 1863* (Savas Beatie, 2008). His *Gettysburg's Forgotten Cavalry Actions: Farnsworth's Charge, South Cavalry Field, and the Battle of Fairfield, July 3, 1863* (Thomas, 1998; revised and expanded by Savas Beatie, 2011), was the recipient of the prestigious Bachelder-Coddington Literary Award. He has also written *Holding the Line on the River of Death: Union Mounted Forces at Chickamauga, September 18, 1863* (Savas Beatie, 2018) and *"The Devil's to Pay": John Buford at Gettysburg. A History and Walking Tour* (Savas Beatie, 2014), which won the Gettysburg CWRT's 2015 Book Award. He recently co-authored (with Edmund A. Sargus, Jr., and Penny Barrick) *Seceding from Secession: The Civil War, Politics, and the Creation of West Virginia* (Savas Beatie, 2020).

Eric, who regularly leads battlefield tours and speaks widely on the war, lives and works in Columbus, Ohio, with his wife Susan.